Strawberry Shortcake,
page 309

Roast Chicken with Rosemary, page 59; Buttery Cooked Carrots, page 60; and Garlic Mashed Potatoes, page 60

Kerry's Beany Salad,
page 215

3

Chocolate Turtle Cheesecake,
page 314

4

all recipes™
cookbook

Oxmoor House®

ISBN: 0-8487-2700-2
Printed in the United States of America
Second Printing 2003

To order additional publications, call 1-800-633-4910.

For more books to enrich your life, visit
oxmoorhouse.com

Cover: Apple Pie by Grandma Ople (page 317)

Allrecipes.com, Inc.
President: Bill Moore
Senior VP Development: Tim Hunt
Managing Editor: Esmée Williams
Senior Production Manager: Jill Charing
Senior Recipe Editor: Sydny Carter
Senior Food Editor: Jennifer Anderson
Recipe Editors: Emily Brune, Richard Kozel,
    Britt Swearingen
Creative Direction: Yann Oehl, Jeff Cummings

Allrecipes.com, Inc.
524 Dexter Avenue North
Seattle, WA 98109
(206) 292-3990
www.Allrecipes.com

Oxmoor House, Inc.
Editor-in-Chief: Nancy Fitzpatrick Wyatt
Executive Editor: Susan Carlisle Payne
Art Director: Cynthia R. Cooper
Copy Chief: Catherine Ritter Scholl

Allrecipes Cookbook
Editor: Allison Long Lowery
Copy Editor: Donna Baldone
Editorial Assistant: Diane Rose
Senior Photographer: Jim Bathie
Photographer: Brit Huckabay
Senior Photo Stylist: Kay E. Clarke
Photo Stylist: Ashley J. Wyatt
Contributing Photo Stylist: Lauren Carroll
Director, Test Kitchens: Elizabeth Tyler Luckett
Assistant Director, Test Kitchens: Julie Christopher
Recipe Editor: Gayle Hays Sadler
Test Kitchens Staff: Kristi Carter, Nicole Lee Faber,
    Jennifer A. Cofield, Ana Price Kelly,
    Kathleen Royal Phillips, Jan A. Smith
Publishing Systems Administrator: Rick Tucker
Director, Production and Distribution: Phillip Lee
Books Production Manager: Theresa L. Beste
Production Assistant: Faye Porter Bonner

Contributors:
Designer: Carol Damsky
Indexer: Mary Ann Laurens
Photo Stylist: Connie Formby

Table of Contents

Welcome from the Staff of Allrecipes!

Dear Friends:

For decades, talented home cooks have been making mealtimes more delicious by sharing their best recipes through family, friends, and community cookbooks. Today, **Allrecipes** has tapped into the power of the Internet to take this time-honored activity, once limited to back fences and church socials, to a global scale. The result is an enormous gathering of passionate home cooks who have collectively created a one-of-a-kind collection of beloved and dependable recipes to be enjoyed by anyone who appreciates great home cooking. Well over 2 million home cooks have visited **Allrecipes.com** to exchange recipes, preparation tips, and their personal experiences, making **Allrecipes.com** the world's largest community cookbook.

You now hold in your hands over 400 of the very best entrées, side dishes, and desserts from our vast collection of recipes—flip through the pages, peruse the tempting photographs, and find something delicious for dinner tonight.

Here are some of our favorite cookbook features:

- **Twenty menus for everyday meals and special occasions make quick work of building some of our most memorable recipes into show-stopping meals.**
- **Forty-eight pages of full-color, tantalizing photographs bring knockout recipes to life.**
- **Cooking tips and techniques from the expert cooks at *Allrecipes.com* are strategically placed throughout the book to answer your cooking and baking questions.**
- **Each recipe is accompanied with valuable information such as prep time and cook time, total number of ratings and reviews, and nutritional analysis to assist you in planning meals for you and your family.**
- **Reader reviews from the *Allrecipes.com* website accompany every recipe to provide preparation tips, serving suggestions, and substitution ideas.**

Whether you've been visiting **Allrecipes.com** from our inception over five years ago or you're just now tapping into an amazing new source for recipes, everything you need for dinner tonight can be found at your fingertips. Next time you're online, we encourage you to join our world-wide community of home cooks by visiting us at **www.Allrecipes.com** to share your family's favorite recipes and cooking experiences through recipe ratings and reviews—you'll be helping us fill the pages for next year's volume of top-rated recipes!

Happy Cooking,

The Staff of Allrecipes

What is Allrecipes.com?

Five years ago, we created a place for home cooks to share their favorite recipes via the Internet. As word spread, others joined in, and in no time, **Allrecipes.com** grew into the world's largest community of home cooks—over 2 million strong—and became the number-one source for online recipes. On the website, recipes are posted for everyday home cooks to put them to the test and then rate and review them online. It's an interactive recipe swap that's helping over 2 million people get dinner on the table with confidence.

About the recipes

Every recipe in this book includes a brief **comment from the contributor.** This may be a serving suggestion, where the recipe came from, or other valuable information about the dish. We always preserve the character of the contributed recipe, but we make slight changes where necessary to ensure consistency, accuracy, and completeness in the published version.

On **Allrecipes.com,** visitors post **recipe reviews,** and for this book, we've included the most helpful reviews alongside the recipes. Look for **"What other cooks have done"** in the box beside every recipe for these reviews that give serving suggestions or cooking tips.

Veterans of the website know to look not only to the **highest-rated, but also the most-rated recipes** when they're looking for winners. This means that lots of people have tried these recipes

at home and rated them online. For this book, we've included the number of ratings and reviews each recipe had received at the time of publication, and these numbers can only go up. Once you've made a few of these five-star recipes, go online and share what you think. Look on the next two pages for a list of the most rated and reviewed recipes from this book.

You may wonder why some of the recipe titles have **Roman numerals** attached to them, like Chicken Enchiladas II on page 22 or Beef Stew IV on page 284. Contributors submit multiple recipes with these titles, so we assign them a number to help keep up with all the variations. In this book, you'll find only one of the variations—the highest-rated, most-reviewed version—but you can find all the different takes on classic recipes online.

Prep and cook times are included as a basic guide with each recipe to help you plan meals. Remember that these times are approximate. How fast you chop, the accuracy of your oven's temperature, humidity, and other variations can affect your prep and cook time.

Need more information?

You'll find helpful tip boxes and charts throughout the book to help you with basic cooking and baking questions, and you can visit us online if you need more information. Check out the "Cooking Basics" section at **Allrecipes.com** where you can browse through articles and step-by-step cooking tutorials.

Recipe Hall of Fame

Check out the best of the best from this year's Allrecipes Cookbook. We've pulled together this all-star list of recipes with the most ratings and reviews from the website. The following recipes (in order of appearance in the book) received 200 or more ratings from the online community and come with the testimonies of home cooks everywhere who have made these their all-time favorites. Dig in and have fun!

▶ **Chicken Enchiladas II** (page 22)
410 Ratings • 292 Reviews
Creamy chicken, mild green chiles, and melted cheese mingle in a quick and easy Tex-Mex creation.

▶ **Garlic Green Beans** (page 29)
211 Ratings • 143 Reviews
Golden sautéed garlic and a sprinkling of Parmesan cheese elevate canned green beans to flavor perfection.

▶ **Chicken Marsala** (page 46)
239 Ratings • 154 Reviews
Lightly coated chicken breasts braised in Marsala wine and mushrooms serve as an elegant centerpiece to any Italian-inspired meal.

▶ **Jamie's Cranberry-Spinach Salad** (page 63)
302 Ratings • 245 Reviews
Tart cranberries, hearty spinach, and almonds lend varying textures, colors, and flavors for a sensory delight.

▶ **Awesome Carrot Cake with Cream Cheese Frosting** (page 64)
233 Ratings • 178 Reviews
Classic home-cooking reaches its pinnacle with this heart-warming cake that boasts truly "awesome" results.

▶ **Annie's Fruit Salsa and Cinnamon Chips** (page 85)
235 Ratings • 186 Reviews
Try something different at your next party with this fun take on regular chips and salsa. And even better—it's healthy!

▶ **Banana Crumb Muffins** (page 109)
294 Ratings • 201 Reviews
A buttery cinnamon-brown sugar topping crowns these muffins for an out-of-the-ordinary family favorite.

▶ **To-Die-For Blueberry Muffins** (page 110)
254 Ratings • 182 Reviews
Deli-style muffins abound with juicy, sweet blueberries, helping these muffins earn their "to-die-for" namesake.

▶ **Downeast Maine Pumpkin Bread** (page 111)
210 Ratings • 183 Reviews
Holiday fare doesn't get much better than this. Cinnamon and spices blend beautifully in moist pumpkin bread that makes an ideal gift for family and friends.

▶ **Banana Banana Bread** (page 112)
374 Ratings • 265 Reviews
You'll want a double dose of this bread that boasts big banana flavor. Try it toasted and slathered with butter.

▶ **Amish White Bread** (page 128)
260 Ratings • 205 Reviews
This old-fashioned, all-purpose yeast dough will fill your kitchen with the enticing aroma of freshly baked bread.

▶ **Jay's Signature Pizza Crust** (page 129)
270 Ratings • 204 Reviews
Take homemade pizza to a whole new level with a gourmet crust that's soft and chewy on the inside and crusty on the outside.

▶ **Awesome Slow-Cooker Pot Roast**
(page 138)
708 Ratings • 487 Reviews
Cooked-all-day flavor is just a few steps away with this simple roast that produces its own mouth-watering gravy.

▶ **Burrito Pie** (page 145)
403 Ratings • 272 Reviews
A spicy beef and bean mixture layered with cheese and tortillas makes a Mexican-style lasagna the kids will swoon over.

▶ **American Lasagna** (page 147)
342 Ratings • 238 Reviews
A homemade meat sauce brimming with tomatoes, oregano, basil, and garlic serves as the backdrop of this classic lasagna.

▶ **Baked Pork Chops** (page 160)
504 Ratings • 355 Reviews
Comfort food at its best, these pork chops bake in a succulent gravy made from simple pantry staples.

▶ **Cajun Chicken Pasta** (page 169)
258 Ratings • 174 Reviews
Feel free to kick up the ragin' cajun spices to your taste in this unforgettable one-dish meal.

▶ **Famous Butter Chicken** (page 170)
238 Ratings • 174 Reviews
Moist and tender crumb-coated chicken will find a place in your family's recipe hall of fame.

▶ **Salsa Chicken** (page 172)
217 Ratings • 157 Reviews
Basic baked chicken gets a face-lift with spicy taco seasoning, salsa, melted Cheddar cheese, and a dollop of cool sour cream.

▶ **Baked Dijon Salmon** (page 186)
278 Ratings • 190 Reviews
Serve this pecan-crusted salmon laced with a Dijon-honey sauce as an quick weeknight meal or as an elegant entrée.

▶ **Awesome and Easy Creamy Corn Casserole** (page 237)
255 Ratings • 182 Reviews
Delight in the rich texture of this simple side dish that's a cross between a sweet corn pudding and a light corn soufflé.

▶ **Easy Slow-Cooker French Dip** (page 259)
298 Ratings • 212 Reviews
A bottle of your favorite beer gives this classic sandwich a unique depth of flavor.

▶ **Baked Potato Soup** (page 274)
246 Ratings • 155 Reviews
On a chilly evening, nothing can warm the body and soul like a bowl of this piping hot, hearty soup.

▶ **Chocolate Lovers' Favorite Cake**
(page 296)
261 Ratings • 211 Reviews
Store-bought cake mix is transformed into pure chocolate bliss in this over-the-top, drop-dead decadent confection.

▶ **Apple Pie by Grandma Ople** (page 317)
240 Ratings • 187 Reviews
Simple ingredients—tart Granny Smiths, brown sugar, and butter—add up to simple goodness in this comforting dessert.

▶ **Award-Winning Peaches and Cream Pie**
(page 319)
224 Ratings • 178 Reviews
With a sweet, creamy filling and cinnamon-sugar topping, this crustless pie earned its blue ribbon.

▶ **Easy Key Lime Pie** (page 323)
210 Ratings • 146 Reviews
Refreshing Key limes add pizzazz to this easy-as-pie finale.

▶ **Caramel-Filled Chocolate Cookies**
(page 339)
258 Ratings • 195 Reviews
A hidden treasure of gooey candy awaits inside a moist chocolate cookie treat.

Recipe Highlights

Every single recipe in the Allrecipes Cookbook *has a banner to help you identify favorite features. Here's a guide to all the banners that are scattered throughout the book. Look for them in the index for more help in finding the perfect recipe for your needs.*

Around-the-World Cuisine ▼

Open your mind and your palate with these recipes that feature exotic flavors from around the globe.

Blue Ribbon Winner ▼

Contributors share some of their special prizewinning fare from around the country.

Classic Comfort Food ▼

Chicken and Dumplings, Meatloaf, Macaroni and Cheese, Bread Pudding . . . need we say more?

Company is Coming ▼

When you need a meal to impress your guests, look for this banner to fill your entertaining needs.

Covered-Dish Favorite ▼

Whether it's a church potluck or a family reunion, you'll have the right dish to carry along.

Crowd-Pleaser ▼

These recipes yield enough for a large party and are fit for all kinds of celebrations.

Family Favorite ▼

When it's reliable, family-pleasing recipes you're looking for, try these foolproof picks.

From the Grill ▼

Add a little spice to backyard barbecuing with these new approaches to grilling your favorite meals.

Healthy ▼

These guilt-free recipes are low in fat and calories and don't sacrifice flavor.

Holiday Fare ▼

We've made it easy to find the best recipes to celebrate the holidays with your family and friends.

Holiday Gift Giving ▼

Give a gift of the heart with these recipes for wonderful homemade gifts from your kitchen.

Hot & Spicy ▼

Hot and spicy fans can find their next indulgence here. Remember you can adjust the seasonings to taste.

Kid-Friendly ▼

Pull out these recipes for surefire hits with little ones and adults alike. Everyone will clean their plates.

Make-Ahead ▼

For parties or weeknight meals, plan ahead and make life easier with recipes that can be made ahead of time.

Meatless Main Dish ▼

Looking for a break from meat and potatoes? These vegetarian delights will please even die-hard meat-eaters.

One-Dish Meal ▼

Dinner can't get much easier than a whole meal in one dish. You'll enjoy all the flavor without all the fuss.

Out-of-the-Ordinary ▼

Shake up things at the dinner table with recipes that turn everyday meals into extraordinary feasts.

Party Food ▼

Put on your party hat and get cooking. You'll set the mood for your next gathering with style.

Quick & Easy ▼

These recipes save the day when you're on the run and there are hungry mouths to feed.

Restaurant Fare ▼

Make standout dishes from your favorite restaurant at home with these classic recipes.

Slow-Cooker Creation ▼

Delicious dinners will be waiting on you when you use these slow-cooker concoctions.

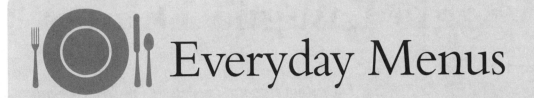

Everyday Menus

Looking for something new for dinner tonight? Try our everyday menus for family-pleasing meals that are perfect on any night of your busy week. From a vegetarian feast to a Tex-Mex spread, you'll have simple suppers with extraordinary flavor.

Very Veggie Lasagna Dinner

You can please vegetarians and carnivores alike with this hearty meal. Get the kids involved and prepare the Fruit Pizza ahead. They'll love creating a dessert masterpiece with their choice of fruit. While the lasagna cooks, assemble the stuffed mushrooms and pop them into the oven with the lasagna. Toss the salad while everything finishes in the oven.

Serves 6 to 8

Mouth-Watering Stuffed Mushrooms
Artichoke-Spinach Lasagna
Classic Tossed Salad
Fruit Pizza

Mouth-Watering Stuffed Mushrooms

Submitted by: **Angie Zayac**
"These delicious mushrooms taste just like restaurant-style stuffed mushrooms! They are my guy's absolute favorite!"

Party Food ▶

Prep Time: 25 minutes
Cook Time: 20 minutes
Average Rating: ★★★★☆
143 Ratings ▲ 106 Reviews

What other cooks have done:
"These mushrooms melt in your mouth! You'll have people asking for the recipe. To make the method easier, place the filling in a plastic bag, cut off a corner, then pipe it into the mushroom."

	Cooking spray
12	whole fresh mushrooms
1	tablespoon vegetable oil
1	tablespoon minced garlic
1	(8 ounce) package cream cheese, softened

¼	cup grated Parmesan cheese
¼	teaspoon ground black pepper
¼	teaspoon onion powder
¼	teaspoon ground cayenne pepper

1. Preheat oven to 350°F (175°C). Spray a baking sheet with cooking spray. Clean mushrooms with a damp paper towel. Carefully break off stems. Chop stems extremely fine, discarding tough end of stems.
2. Heat oil in a large skillet over medium heat. Add garlic and chopped mushroom stems to the skillet. Sauté until any moisture has disappeared, taking care not to burn garlic. Set aside to cool.
3. When garlic and mushroom mixture is no longer hot, stir in cream cheese, Parmesan cheese, black pepper, onion powder, and cayenne pepper. Mixture should be very thick. Using a little spoon, fill each mushroom cap with a generous amount of stuffing. Arrange the mushroom caps on prepared baking sheet.
4. Bake in the preheated oven for 20 minutes or until the mushrooms are piping hot and liquid starts to form under caps. **Yield:** 12 mushrooms.

Per serving: About 91 calories, 3g protein, 2g carbohydrate, 8g fat, 0g fiber, 22mg cholesterol, 95mg sodium

Artichoke-Spinach Lasagna

Submitted by: **David**

"This is a fabulous lasagna made with an artichoke and spinach mixture cooked with vegetable broth, onions, and garlic. The mixture is layered with lasagna noodles, pasta sauce, mozzarella cheese, and topped with crumbled feta."

	Cooking spray
9	uncooked lasagna noodles
1	onion, chopped
4	cloves garlic, chopped
1	cup vegetable broth
1	tablespoon chopped fresh rosemary
1	(12 ounce) can marinated artichoke hearts, drained and chopped
1	(10 ounce) package frozen chopped spinach, thawed, drained, and squeezed dry
1	(26 ounce) jar tomato pasta sauce
3	cups shredded mozzarella cheese, divided
1	(4 ounce) package herb and garlic feta, crumbled

1. Preheat oven to 350°F (175°C). Spray a 9x13 inch baking dish with cooking spray.

2. Bring a large pot of lightly salted water to a boil. Add noodles and cook for 8 to 10 minutes or until al dente; drain.

3. Spray a large skillet with cooking spray and heat on medium high. Sauté onion and garlic for 3 minutes or until onion is tender-crisp. Stir in broth and rosemary; bring to a boil. Stir in artichoke hearts and spinach; reduce heat, cover, and simmer 5 minutes. Stir in pasta sauce.

4. Spread ¼ of the artichoke mixture in the prepared baking dish; top with 3 cooked noodles. Sprinkle ¾ cup mozzarella cheese over noodles. Repeat layers 2 more times, ending with artichoke mixture and mozzarella cheese. Sprinkle crumbled feta on top.

5. Bake, covered, in the preheated oven for 40 minutes. Uncover and bake 15 minutes more or until hot and bubbly. Let stand 10 minutes before cutting. **Yield:** 6 to 8 servings.

Per serving: About 484 calories, 28g protein, 45g carbohydrate, 23g fat, 6g fiber, 66mg cholesterol, 2178mg sodium

◄ Meatless Main Dish

Prep Time: 20 minutes
Cook Time: 1 hour
Average Rating: ★★★★★
131 Ratings ▲ 91 Reviews
What other cooks have done:
"Try my modifications for this awesome lasagna: Substitute a 16 ounce jar of creamy alfredo for the tomato-based sauce; add a layer of sliced portobello mushrooms sautéed in olive oil; use tomato-and-basil feta cheese; and dissolve a veggie bouillon cube in 1 cup water for the broth."

Classic Tossed Salad

Submitted by: **Toni Bankson**
"This is a delicious salad that goes great with any meal, especially Italian!"

1	head romaine lettuce	2	tablespoons sesame seeds, toasted
1	head red leaf lettuce	6	cherry tomatoes, halved
6	ounces crumbled feta cheese	1	red onion, sliced
1	(6 ounce) can sliced black olives	6	fresh mushrooms, sliced
1	(4 ounce) package blanched slivered almonds, toasted	¼	cup grated Romano cheese
		1	(8 ounce) bottle Italian dressing

1. Chop, wash, and dry the romaine and red leaf lettuces.
2. In a large bowl, combine lettuces with feta cheese, olives, almonds, sesame seeds, tomatoes, onion, mushrooms, and Romano cheese. When ready to serve, add the Italian dressing and toss thoroughly.
Yield: 6 to 8 servings.

Per serving: About 391 calories, 11g protein, 13g carbohydrate, 34g fat, 4g fiber, 25mg cholesterol, 789mg sodium

Fruit Pizza

Submitted by: **Anne**
"A cookie dough crust, cream cheese filling, and fruit topping make a fun dessert pizza. For a quick crust, use one package of ready-made sugar cookie dough rolled out to fit a pizza pan. Use your favorite fresh fruit for the topping."

½	cup butter, softened	1	(8 ounce) package cream cheese, softened
¾	cup white sugar	½	cup white sugar
1	egg	2	teaspoons vanilla extract
1¼	cups all–purpose flour		Fruit for topping (peaches,
1	teaspoon cream of tartar		blueberries, kiwifruit,
½	teaspoon baking soda		pineapple, or strawberries)
¼	teaspoon salt		

1. Preheat oven to 350°F (175°C).
2. In a large bowl, beat together the butter and ¾ cup sugar until smooth. Mix in egg. Combine the flour, cream of tartar, baking soda, and salt; stir into the butter mixture until just blended. Press dough into an ungreased pizza pan.
3. Bake in the preheated oven for 8 to 10 minutes or until lightly browned. Cool.
4. In a large bowl, beat cream cheese with ½ cup sugar and vanilla until light. Spread on cooled crust.
5. Arrange desired fruit on top of filling and chill. **Yield:** 10 servings.

Per serving: About 324 calories, 4g protein, 38g carbohydrate, 18g fat, 0g fiber, 71mg cholesterol, 288mg sodium

Saucy Summer Cookout

Savor the summer months and enjoy a down-home cookout. Barbecue ribs and fresh corn make good use of the grill, and potato salad gets a face-lift with an oven-baked version that's topped with bacon and olives. Stop by the farmers market and pick up some fresh peaches for a classic peach cobbler. And don't forget the ice cream!

Serves 6

Barbecue Ribs
Baked Potato Salad
Miss Bettie's Zesty Grilled Corn
Peach Cobbler II

Barbecue Ribs

Submitted by: **Kristy**
"This recipe is easier than it sounds. I usually cook the ribs the day before, marinate them overnight, and grill them for a quick dinner the next night. FYI: The sauce is much better after it's cooked. It's not a dipping sauce. Try the marinade on chicken as well."

4	pounds pork spareribs	¼	cup rum
1	cup brown sugar	½	cup chili sauce
¼	cup ketchup	2	cloves garlic, crushed
¼	cup soy sauce	1	teaspoon dry mustard
¼	cup Worcestershire sauce		Dash ground black pepper

1. Preheat oven to 350°F (175°C).
2. Cut spareribs into serving sizes. Wrap ribs in double thickness of foil and bake for 1½ hours. Unwrap and drain drippings. Transfer ribs to a large roasting dish.
3. Combine brown sugar, ketchup, soy sauce, Worcestershire sauce, rum, chili sauce, garlic, mustard, and pepper in a bowl. Pour over ribs. Cover and marinate in refrigerator for 1 hour or overnight. Remove ribs from sauce. Bring sauce to a boil and reserve for basting.
4. Preheat grill to medium–high heat. Grill ribs, turning and basting with sauce, 30 minutes. Or bake ribs at 350° for 30 minutes, basting with sauce. **Yield:** 6 servings.

Per serving: About 504 calories, 30g protein, 23g carbohydrate, 30g fat, 0g fiber, 120mg cholesterol, 798mg sodium

◄ Make-Ahead

Prep Time: 15 minutes
Cook Time: 2 hours
Average Rating: ★★★★★
34 Ratings ▲ 28 Reviews
What other cooks have done:
"These were the most succulent ribs I have ever eaten. I did leave out the chile sauce and added some hoisin sauce and a touch of ginger. I also added some cloves of garlic during the initial baking. My three-year-old wouldn't stop eating these until they were gone! Definitely a keeper!"

Baked Potato Salad

Submitted by: **Tom**

"Is this a baked potato salad or a cheese and potato casserole? Try this recipe and decide for yourself."

8	potatoes	½	onion, chopped
½	pound bacon	1	cup mayonnaise
1	pound processed American cheese, sliced		Salt and pepper to taste
		¼	cup black olives, sliced

1. Preheat oven to 325°F (165°C). Butter a 9x13 inch baking dish.
2. Bring a large pot of salted water to a boil. Add potatoes and cook until tender but still firm, about 15 minutes. Drain, cool, and slice ¼ inch thick.
3. Place bacon in a large, deep skillet. Cook over medium–high heat until lightly brown. Drain, chop, and set aside.
4. Combine the potatoes, cheese, onion, mayonnaise, salt, and pepper. Mix well and pour into prepared baking dish.
5. Top with bacon and olives and bake in the preheated oven for 1 hour. **Yield:** 6 to 8 servings.

Per serving: About 687 calories, 18g protein, 24g carbohydrate, 58g fat, 2g fiber, 87mg cholesterol, 1235mg sodium

---

Covered-Dish Favorite ▶

Prep Time: 10 minutes

Cook Time: 90 minutes

Average Rating: ★★★★★

51 Ratings ▲ 39 Reviews

What other cooks have done:
"This is one of the best and easiest potato recipes I have found. I omitted the olives and used Cheddar cheese instead of American. I also added extra onions and used ½ cup mayo and ½ cup sour cream."

Miss Bettie's Zesty Grilled Corn

Submitted by: **Teresa Johnson**

"This is my mom's recipe for grilled corn. It's tangy and spicy, and the best corn recipe I have ever tasted!"

⅓	cup butter	1	teaspoon Worcestershire sauce
2	tablespoons prepared mustard	¼	teaspoon lemon pepper
2	teaspoons prepared horseradish	6	ears fresh corn

1. Preheat grill to medium heat.
2. In a small saucepan, melt butter. Stir in mustard, horseradish, Worcestershire sauce, and lemon pepper.
3. Remove and discard husks and silks from corn. Place each ear of corn on a 13x12 inch piece of heavy-duty aluminum foil. Drizzle with butter mixture. Wrap loosely, leaving space for the expansion of steam, and seal.
4. Grill for 15 to 20 minutes or until corn is tender. Small ears will take less time than larger ears. Carefully unwrap foil, and serve. **Yield:** 6 servings.

Per serving: About 173 calories, 3g protein, 18g carbohydrate, 11g fat, 3g fiber, 28mg cholesterol, 219mg sodium

---

From the Grill ▶

Prep Time: 20 minutes

Cook Time: 20 minutes

Average Rating: ★★★★☆

32 Ratings ▲ 21 Reviews

What other cooks have done:
"Very tasty—my husband loved this. I wasn't able to grill it, but it worked great broiled in the oven."

Peach Cobbler II

Submitted by: **Jannette Singleton**

"My grandmother's recipe makes a delicious cobbler with peaches, but you can also use blueberries. Hope you enjoy this as much as our family has all these years."

3	fresh peaches, peeled, pitted, and sliced	1½	cups all-purpose flour
1	teaspoon ground cinnamon	2	teaspoons baking powder
1½	cups white sugar	½	teaspoon salt
½	cup shortening	1	cup milk
1	cup white sugar	3	tablespoons butter
		2	cups boiling water

1. Preheat oven to 350°F (175°C). Grease a 7x11 inch baking dish.
2. Stir together peaches with cinnamon and 1½ cups sugar. Set aside.
3. In a medium bowl, beat shortening and 1 cup sugar. Mix in flour, baking powder, and salt alternately with milk. Pour into prepared pan. Top with peach mixture. Drop butter in boiling water and pour over peaches.
4. Bake in the preheated oven for 40 to 45 minutes or until golden brown. **Yield:** 6 to 8 servings.

Per serving: About 681 calories, 5g protein, 115g carbohydrate, 24g fat, 2g fiber, 19mg cholesterol, 359mg sodium

---

◄ Family Favorite

Prep Time: 20 minutes
Cook Time: 45 minutes
Average Rating: ★★★★★

32 Ratings ▲ 25 Reviews

What other cooks have done:
"This is an amazingly good recipe! I was a little worried about putting the topping on the bottom and pouring water over it at first, but it turned out great. I personally like mine to be a little more fruity, so I used 5 peaches instead of 3."

Cooking Basics: Real Ripeness ▼

It's happened to everyone—you feast your eyes upon the lush, dazzling fruits piled high in the produce aisle, and you buy your favorites, inspired by the vivid red, green, yellow, and orange hues you see sparkling enticingly from the bins. You feel excited and virtuous that you're eating something that's delicious and healthy, too. But then you get the produce home and start nibbling. Suddenly, you're not so excited. The tomatoes are chewy and bland. The peaches are hard as a rock. The melon is flavorless. The strawberries make you pucker. What went wrong?

Beauty: Only Skin Deep?

Consumers use their eyes more than other senses. Fruit growers know this, and so many have worked to develop fruit that looks deceptively alluring long before it's ripe. They go through this trouble instead of offering truly ripe fruit, because unripe fruit will not bruise during mechanized picking, and it will not be past its peak by the time it arrives in the grocery store. The problem for consumers: Unripe fruit does not taste very good. In fact, while many fruits improve in color or juiciness after being picked, most of it has no chance of improving in flavor once it's picked.

Use All Your Senses

Don't give up hope yet, though: It's still possible to get some delectable fruit if you use all your senses. One of your most important weapons for choosing wisely is your nose. When most fruit is truly ripe, it gives off a sweet, seductive aroma that cannot be faked by fruit growers or grocery stores. Ripe fruit also tends to be heavy for its size, so pick it up and heft it in your hand a little. And, while you've got the fruit in your hand, give it a gentle squeeze because another good indicator of ripeness for some fruit is its softness. When most fruits yield to gentle pressure, they're ready to eat.

Another good way to choose fruit is by season. Almost every variety of fruit has a specific time of year when the local crops are at their peak of perfection. Familiarize yourself with the seasons of your locale's crops so you can buy produce at its peak. A good clue as to what is at the peak of its season is to notice which items in the produce aisle are the cheapest and most plentiful.
- Jennifer Anderson

For more information, visit **Allrecipes.com**

Thai Up Your Backyard Barbecue

Wake up your taste buds with this enticing meal. Marinate the chicken overnight, and you can have the whole meal on the table in 30 minutes. Now that's exciting!

Serves 6 to 8

Barbecued Thai-Style Chicken
Asian Coleslaw
Skewered Cantaloupe

Barbecued Thai-Style Chicken

Submitted by: **Skye**
"Arrange cooked chicken pieces on a serving platter lined with salad greens or a banana leaf, and garnish with cilantro sprigs for an added touch."

Around-the-World Cuisine ▶

Prep Time: 15 minutes

Cook Time: 30 minutes

Average Rating: ★★★★★

14 Ratings ▲ 14 Reviews

What other cooks have done:
"Exotic, incredibly flavorful, and surprising! I have never tried anything like it before. I marinated sliced chicken breasts overnight, and it was great with jasmine rice. Next time I will try adding a little thai chili garlic sauce."

1	bunch fresh cilantro with roots, washed ★	1	teaspoon curry powder
3	cloves garlic, peeled	1	tablespoon white sugar
3	small red hot chile peppers, seeded and chopped		Dash of salt
1	teaspoon ground turmeric	3	tablespoons fish sauce
		3	pounds chicken pieces
		¼	cup coconut milk

1. Cut cilantro roots off at the stem and mince roots thoroughly, reserving a few leaves for garnish. In a blender or food processor, combine cilantro roots, garlic, chile peppers, turmeric, curry powder, sugar, and salt. Process to a coarse paste. Mix in fish sauce and blend until smooth.
2. Place chicken in a large shallow dish. Rub with the cilantro paste. Cover and marinate in the refrigerator at least 3 hours or overnight.
3. Preheat grill for high heat and lightly oil grate.
4. Place chicken on the prepared grill with the lid open. Brush liberally with coconut milk. Baste frequently with excess cilantro paste mixture up until last 5 minutes of grilling. Grill chicken until browned and tender, turning only once, or until a meat thermometer inserted in thickest part of meat registers 170°F (75°C) for white meat and 180°F (80°C) for dark meat. **Yield:** 6 servings.

★ Cilantro is sold with the roots attached in Asian markets, or you can pull the roots up from your herb garden. Cilantro stems will work as a substitute if you can't find cilantro roots.

Per serving: About 289 calories, 22g protein, 6g carbohydrate, 19g fat, 1g fiber, 85mg cholesterol, 700mg sodium

Asian Coleslaw

Submitted by: **Bobbi Ritcheske**

"Here's a great twist on cabbage salad. The peanut butter in the dressing is the secret."

6	tablespoons rice wine vinegar	2	cups thinly sliced red cabbage
6	tablespoons vegetable oil	2	cups shredded Napa cabbage
5	tablespoons smooth peanut butter	2	red bell peppers, thinly sliced
3	tablespoons soy sauce	2	carrots, julienned
3	tablespoons brown sugar	6	green onions, chopped
2	tablespoons minced fresh ginger root	½	cup chopped fresh cilantro
1½	tablespoons minced garlic		Salt, pepper, and/or sesame seeds
5	cups thinly sliced green cabbage		

1. Prepare the dressing by whisking together the rice vinegar, oil, peanut butter, soy sauce, brown sugar, ginger, and garlic.

2. In a large bowl, combine the green cabbage, red cabbage, Napa cabbage, bell peppers, carrots, green onions, and cilantro. Add dressing and toss. Season with salt and pepper and/or sesame seeds to taste. **Yield:** 8 to 10 servings.

Per serving: About 202 calories, 5g protein, 18g carbohydrate, 14g fat, 4g fiber, 0mg cholesterol, 554mg sodium

Skewered Cantaloupe

Submitted by: **Lol**

"Melon grills beautifully, and the minty sauce takes it to the next level. For a great dessert, serve it with big scoops of vanilla ice cream."

2	cantaloupes, cut into chunks	1	cup honey
½	cup butter	⅔	cup chopped fresh mint leaves

1. Preheat grill for medium heat and lightly oil grate.

2. Thread the cantaloupe chunks onto 8 metal skewers. In a small saucepan, heat butter with honey until melted. Stir in mint. Brush cantaloupe with honey mixture.

3. Place skewers on heated grill. Cook 4 to 6 minutes, turning to cook all sides. Serve with remaining sauce on the side. **Yield:** 8 servings.

Per serving: About 308 calories, 3g protein, 53g carbohydrate, 12g fat, 2g fiber, 31mg cholesterol, 138mg sodium

No-Sweat Tex-Mex

Treat your family to an evening of Tex-Mex fare with this simple, yet satisfying meal. Turn leftover cooked chicken into creamy enchiladas in no time. If you don't have any leftover chicken, buy packages of frozen, cooked, diced chicken breast, or you can cook your own. Three skinned, boned, cooked chicken breast halves yield about 1½ cups chopped meat—just enough to fill your enchiladas. The salad can be made ahead, or you can put it together while the enchiladas cook. Finish off the meal with a rich, decadent flan that's been chilled overnight.

Serves 6

Chicken Enchiladas II
Black Bean and Corn Salad II
Creamy Caramel Flan

Chicken Enchiladas II

Submitted by: **Steph**
"Here's a great way to use leftover chicken. Even kids love these enchiladas!"

1	tablespoon butter	½	cup sour cream
½	cup chopped green onions	1½	cups cubed cooked chicken breast
½	teaspoon garlic powder		
1	(4.5 ounce) can diced green chiles	1	cup shredded Cheddar cheese, divided
1	(10.75 ounce) can condensed cream of chicken or mushroom soup	6	(7 inch) flour tortillas
		¼	cup milk

1. Preheat oven to 350°F (175°C). Lightly grease a large baking dish.
2. In a medium saucepan over medium heat, melt the butter and sauté the green onions until tender, about 2 minutes. Add the garlic powder, then stir in the green chiles, cream of chicken soup, and sour cream. Mix well. Reserve about 1¾ cups of this sauce and set aside.
To the remaining sauce in the saucepan, add the chicken and ½ cup shredded Cheddar cheese. Stir together.
3. Fill each flour tortilla with the chicken mixture and roll up. Place seam side down in the prepared baking dish.
4. In a small bowl, combine the reserved sauce with the milk. Spoon mixture over rolled tortillas. Bake, uncovered, in the preheated oven for 20 minutes. Top with remaining ½ cup Cheddar cheese, and bake 10 more minutes or until cheese is bubbly. **Yield:** 6 servings.

Per serving: About 643 calories, 27g protein, 72g carbohydrate, 27g fat, 4g fiber, 61mg cholesterol, 1305mg sodium

Family Favorite ▶

Prep Time: 15 minutes
Cook Time: 30 minutes
Average Rating: ★★★★★
410 Ratings ▲ 292 Reviews
What other cooks have done:
"I used cream of chicken soup, added a few jalapeño peppers, ⅛ teaspoon cumin, and ¼ cup extra sour cream to the mix. I topped the final product with a bit of sour cream and some black olives, and served with Mexican rice."

Black Bean and Corn Salad II

Submitted by: **Jen**
"This salad is colorful and includes a zingy lime dressing."

⅓ cup fresh lime juice
½ cup olive oil
1 clove garlic, minced
1 teaspoon salt
⅛ teaspoon ground cayenne pepper
2 (15 ounce) cans black beans, rinsed and drained
1½ cups frozen corn kernels, thawed
1 avocado, peeled, pitted, and diced
1 red bell pepper, chopped
2 tomatoes, chopped
6 green onions, thinly sliced
½ cup chopped fresh cilantro

1. Place lime juice, olive oil, garlic, salt, and cayenne pepper in a small jar. Cover with lid and shake until ingredients are well mixed.
2. In a salad bowl, combine beans, corn, avocado, bell pepper, tomatoes, green onions, and cilantro. Shake lime dressing and pour it over the salad. Toss salad to coat vegetables and beans with dressing and serve, or cover and chill. **Yield:** 6 servings.

Per serving: About 392 calories, 11g protein, 35g carbohydrate, 25g fat, 11g fiber, 0mg cholesterol, 832mg sodium

◀ **Make-Ahead**

Prep Time: 25 minutes
Average Rating: ★★★★★
62 Ratings ▲ 46 Reviews
What other cooks have done:
"This salad is incredible! I used fresh corn and topped it off with avocado, and it was beautiful. Great color and flavor! Try it with nacho chips as a salsa."

Creamy Caramel Flan *(pictured on page 299)*

Submitted by: **Jo Poynor**
"This recipe is a cross between egg custard and cheesecake."

¾ cup white sugar
1 (8 ounce) package cream cheese, softened
5 eggs
1 (14 ounce) can sweetened condensed milk
1 (12 ounce) can evaporated milk
1 teaspoon vanilla extract

1. Preheat oven to 350°F (175°C).
2. In a heavy saucepan over medium-low heat, cook sugar, stirring until golden. Pour into a 9 inch round cake pan, tilting to coat bottom and sides. (Syrup will harden and crack.)
3. In a large bowl, beat cream cheese until smooth. Beat in eggs, 1 at a time, until well incorporated. Beat in condensed and evaporated milk and vanilla until smooth. Pour into caramel-coated pan. Cover cake pan and place in a roasting pan. Fill roasting pan with hot water to reach 1 inch up the sides of the cake pan.
4. Bake in the preheated oven for 60 minutes or until a knife inserted near center comes out clean. Remove pan from water bath and uncover. Cool 1 hour on wire rack; cover and chill 8 hours or overnight. To unmold, run a knife around edges of pan and invert on a rimmed serving platter, letting caramel drizzle over top. **Yield:** 10 servings.

Per serving: About 346 calories, 10g protein, 41g carbohydrate, 16g fat, 0g fiber, 154mg cholesterol, 183mg sodium

◀ **Restaurant Fare**

Prep Time: 15 minutes
Cook Time: 1 hour 15 minutes
Average Rating: ★★★★★
32 Ratings ▲ 24 Reviews
What other cooks have done:
"We each had a slice of the flan when it wasn't completely cooled, and it was very similar to a light custard. Then the next morning, my wife and I each had a refrigerated slice, and it was rich and smooth like cheesecake. It's very versatile in the texture department."

Pack the Picnic Basket

Throw together this simple meal on a beautiful spring evening and take dinner outside. Every recipe can be made ahead and stored in the refrigerator. Pack any leftovers for lunch the next day.

Serves 6

Becky's Chicken Salad
Italian Confetti Pasta Salad
Cappuccino Brownies

Becky's Chicken Salad

Submitted by: **Becky Riley**
"Whipped cream gives this chicken salad a lift. Serve on lettuce leaves or on sandwiches."

¼ cup heavy whipping cream	2 tablespoons chopped fresh parsley
2½ cups diced cooked chicken	
1 cup chopped celery	1 teaspoon salt
1 cup seedless grapes, halved	1 cup mayonnaise
½ cup sliced almonds	

1. In a medium bowl, whip cream to soft peaks.
2. Combine chicken, celery, grapes, almonds, parsley, salt, and mayonnaise with whipped cream. Cover and chill. **Yield:** 6 servings.

Per serving: About 286 calories, 11g protein, 5g carbohydrate, 25g fat, 1g fiber, 46mg cholesterol, 400mg sodium

---

Quick & Easy ▶

Prep Time: 15 minutes
Average Rating: ★★★★★
72 Ratings ▲ 58 Reviews

What other cooks have done:
"I used walnuts instead of almonds and apples instead of grapes in my chicken salad. I also substituted light mayo and fat-free frozen whipped topping to lighten it up."

Pack the Picnic Basket ▼

Don't set the table, pack the picnic basket! Picnicking lets us spend more time enjoying precious warm weather, and it breaks us out of our usual mealtime routines. Even eating a sandwich and a bag of chips takes on a new thrill when we're lounging on a blanket in a beautiful outdoor setting.

Picnic Precautions Some foods should not be left at room temperature for any period of time, including raw meats and anything containing raw eggs. It's better to take ready-to-eat foods on your picnics. If your destination is more than a few minutes away, put perishable foods in a cooler with ice or a frozen gel pack. If you're going to be in the car for a while before arriving at your picnic site and you don't want to hassle with a cooler, consider going vegetarian for the day, or buy perishable items once you near your destination.

Give Mayonnaise a Break! Mayonnaise has gained a reputation as the most dangerous food to take on a picnic. New research, however, tells us that's not the case. Store-bought mayonnaise contains pasteurized eggs and enough salt and lemon juice or vinegar to actually inhibit bacterial growth. So, while you should still be careful about keeping everything cool, don't let that stop you from using all the creamy mayo you like in your picnic sandwiches, salads, and dips!   *–Jennifer Anderson*
For more information, visit **Allrecipes.com**

Italian Confetti Pasta Salad

Submitted by: **Jeri Mortinson**
"This recipe is so easy to make and always such a hit! It's great for backyard barbecues. For best results, chill overnight."

2	cups tricolored rotini pasta	1	clove garlic, minced
1	cup mayonnaise	1½	tablespoons chopped fresh basil
1	tablespoon red wine vinegar	1	cup chopped tomatoes
1	teaspoon salt	½	cup chopped yellow bell pepper
¼	teaspoon ground black pepper	½	cup sliced black olives

1. Cook pasta according to package directions. Rinse in cold water and drain.
2. In a large bowl, whisk together mayonnaise, vinegar, salt, black pepper, and garlic until well blended. Mix in basil. Add pasta, tomatoes, bell pepper, and olives; fold gently until mixed. Cover and chill several hours. Stir gently before serving. **Yield:** 6 servings.

Per serving: About 376 calories, 4g protein, 17g carbohydrate, 34g fat, 1g fiber, 20mg cholesterol, 720mg sodium

◄ **Make-Ahead**

Prep Time: 15 minutes
Average Rating: ★★★★★
14 Ratings ▲ 7 Reviews
What other cooks have done:
"This is just what I was looking for! I didn't have tomatoes so I put what I had—pimentos and artichoke hearts. It was a hit at my work BBQ."

Cappuccino Brownies

Submitted by: **Mary Beth Davis**
"These luscious, creamy brownies freeze well, and they're wonderful to give as presents to teachers and friends."

2	pounds semisweet chocolate chips	8	large eggs
¼	cup instant coffee granules	3	tablespoons vanilla extract
1	cup unsalted butter, softened	1	teaspoon ground cinnamon
2	cups white sugar	1	teaspoon salt
		2	cups all-purpose flour

1. Preheat oven to 375°F (190°C). Grease 4 (8x8 inch) baking pans.
2. Place the chocolate chips and the coffee granules in top of a double boiler over simmering water. Cook over medium heat, stirring occasionally, until melted and smooth. Set aside.
3. In a large bowl, beat the butter and sugar together until light and fluffy. Beat in eggs, 2 at a time, mixing well after each addition. Stir in vanilla, cinnamon, and salt; mix in melted chocolate. Mix in flour until just blended. Divide batter equally into the prepared pans and spread smoothly.
4. Bake in the preheated oven for 35 minutes or until the edges pull from the sides of the pans. Cool on a wire rack. Cover and refrigerate 8 hours. Cut the cold brownies into bars to serve. **Yield:** 6 dozen.

Per serving: About 127 calories, 2g protein, 16g carbohydrate, 7g fat, 1g fiber, 31mg cholesterol, 41mg sodium

◄ **Crowd-Pleaser**

Prep Time: 30 minutes
Cook Time: 35 minutes
Average Rating: ★★★★☆
18 Ratings ▲ 9 Reviews
What other cooks have done:
"Since this recipe makes 4 pans of brownies, I froze 2 pans to have on hand for unexpected guests. Bake them in disposable pans, place in a freezer-safe plastic bag, and freeze up to 3 months."

A Good Ol' Chili Feed

This is no ordinary chili supper. Award-Winning Chili boasts carrots, bacon, and a few other secret ingredients to create a show-stopping meal. You can make the banana pudding ahead and chill it. Prepare sweet corn muffins while the chili simmers on the cooktop.

Serves 8

Award-Winning Chili
Best-Ever Corn Muffins
Banana Pudding IV

Award-Winning Chili

Submitted by: **Jennifer**
"This delicious chili took 2nd place at our local chili cook-off! If it's too thick, add water ¼ cup at a time until you reach desired consistency."

1	(14.5 ounce) can stewed tomatoes, chopped	⅓	cup steak sauce, (such as Heinz 57)
1	(6 ounce) can tomato paste	5	slices bacon
1	carrot, sliced	1½	pounds ground beef
1	onion, chopped	1	(1.25 ounce) package chili seasoning mix
2	stalks celery, chopped	1	teaspoon ground cumin
¼	cup dry white wine	1	(15 ounce) can kidney beans, drained
1	pinch crushed red pepper flakes	1	tablespoon chopped fresh cilantro
¼	cup chopped green bell pepper	1	tablespoon chopped fresh parsley
¼	cup chopped red bell pepper		

1. In a large pot over medium heat, combine tomatoes, tomato paste, carrot, onion, celery, wine, pepper flakes, bell peppers, and steak sauce. Bring to a boil; cover, reduce heat, and simmer.
2. While tomato mixture is simmering, in a large skillet over medium heat, cook bacon until crisp. Remove to paper towels to cool; crumble bacon. Cook beef in bacon drippings until brown; drain. Stir chili seasoning into ground beef.
3. Stir seasoned beef, cumin, and bacon into tomato mixture. Continue to simmer, covered, 15 minutes or until vegetables are tender.
4. Stir in beans, cilantro, and parsley. Heat through and serve. **Yield:** 8 servings.

Per serving: About 388 calories, 21g protein, 22g carbohydrate, 24g fat, 6g fiber, 64mg cholesterol, 1112mg sodium

Best-Ever Corn Muffins

Submitted by: **Kelly**
"This recipe was handed down to me from my mother. It's easy to make, and the ingredients are probably already in your kitchen."

¼	cup butter, softened	1½	cups biscuit baking mix
½	cup white sugar	¼	cup yellow cornmeal
2	eggs	⅔	cup milk
1	tablespoon vanilla extract		

1. Preheat oven to 375°F (190°C). Grease 12 muffin cups or line with paper muffin liners.
2. In a large bowl, beat together the butter and sugar until light and fluffy. Stir in the eggs, 1 at a time, beating well with each addition, then stir in the vanilla.
3. In a separate bowl, stir together baking mix and cornmeal. Blend this mixture into the butter/egg mixture alternately with the milk; stir just until combined. Spoon batter into prepared muffin cups.
4. Bake in the preheated oven for 20 to 30 minutes or until golden.
Yield: 12 muffins.

Per serving: About 164 calories, 3g protein, 22g carbohydrate, 7g fat, 1g fiber, 47mg cholesterol, 246mg sodium

◀ Family Favorite

Prep Time: 8 minutes
Cook Time: 30 minutes
Average Rating: ★★★★★
21 Ratings ▲ 17 Reviews
What other cooks have done:
"I used less sugar and added jalapeños and sun-dried tomatoes."

Banana Pudding IV

Submitted by: **Patricia Osborne**
"A quick and easy banana pudding recipe—enjoy!"

1	(8 ounce) package cream cheese, softened	1	teaspoon vanilla extract
1	(14 ounce) can sweetened condensed milk	1	(8 ounce) container frozen whipped topping, thawed and divided
1	(5 ounce) package instant vanilla pudding mix	½	(12 ounce) package vanilla wafers
3	cups cold milk	4	bananas, sliced

1. In a large bowl, beat cream cheese until fluffy. Beat in condensed milk, pudding mix, milk, and vanilla until smooth. Fold in ½ of the whipped topping.
2. Line the bottom of a 9x13 inch dish with vanilla wafers. Arrange sliced bananas evenly over wafers. Spread with pudding mixture. Top with remaining whipped topping. Cover and chill. **Yield:** 12 servings.

Per serving: About 405 calories, 7g protein, 56g carbohydrate, 17g fat, 1g fiber, 36mg cholesterol, 338mg sodium

◀ Kid-Friendly

Prep Time: 30 minutes
Average Rating: ★★★★★
98 Ratings ▲ 80 Reviews
What other cooks have done:
"This is great comfort food. I divided the recipe into 3 small loaf pans to take to some of my friends, and their families really enjoyed it. Try substituting banana pudding mix for the vanilla for a change. Either way, it's a definite keeper."

Fast French

Wow your family with Chicken Cordon Bleu, garlicky green beans, and an apple pie that's made even more decadent with a layer of cream cheese. Prepare the chicken first and simmer the green beans right before dinner is served. The chicken cooks on the cooktop, so bake your pie while the rest of the meal is being prepared, or you can make it ahead and chill until ready to serve.

Serves 6

Chicken Cordon Bleu II
Garlic Green Beans
French Apple Pie with
Cream Cheese Topping

Chicken Cordon Bleu II

Submitted by: **Behr Kleine**

"'Cordon Bleu' is a French term, translated as 'blue ribbon,' that originally referred to an award for culinary excellence given to women cooks. The term can now apply to any superior cook (yes, men, too), and also to this dish (breaded and sautéed chicken breasts with ham and Swiss cheese slices). This version adds paprika and a creamy white wine sauce worthy of its own blue ribbon."

6 skinless, boneless chicken breast halves	6 tablespoons butter
6 slices Swiss cheese	½ cup dry white wine
6 slices ham	1 teaspoon chicken bouillon granules
3 tablespoons all-purpose flour	1 tablespoon cornstarch
1 teaspoon paprika	1 cup heavy whipping cream

1. Pound chicken breasts to even thickness. Place a cheese and ham slice on each breast to within ½ inch of the edges. Fold the edges of the chicken over the filling and secure with wooden picks. Mix the flour and paprika in a small bowl and coat the chicken pieces.
2. Heat the butter in a large skillet over medium-high heat and cook the chicken until browned on all sides. Add the wine and bouillon. Reduce heat to low, cover, and simmer for 30 minutes, until chicken is no longer pink and juices run clear.
3. Remove the wooden picks and transfer the breasts to a warm platter. Blend the cornstarch with the cream in a small bowl and whisk slowly into the skillet. Cook, stirring constantly until thickened, and pour over the chicken. Serve warm. **Yield:** 6 servings.

Per serving: About 588 calories, 44g protein, 7g carbohydrate, 41g fat, 0g fiber, 207mg cholesterol, 363mg sodium

Garlic Green Beans

Submitted by: **Ericka Ettinger**

"Caramelized garlic and cheese! Is there anything better with green beans? You'd better make plenty for everyone."

1	tablespoon butter	2	(14.5 ounce) cans green
3	tablespoons olive oil		beans, drained
1	medium head garlic, peeled		Salt and pepper to taste
	and sliced	¼	cup grated Parmesan cheese

1. Melt butter in a large skillet, and stir in olive oil and garlic. Sauté over low heat until the garlic is slightly brown.

2. Stir in the green beans, and season with salt and pepper. Cook until beans are thoroughly heated, about 10 minutes. Turn off heat and sprinkle with Parmesan cheese. **Yield:** 6 servings.

Per serving: About 159 calories, 4g protein, 9g carbohydrate, 12g fat, 3g fiber, 10mg cholesterol, 579mg sodium

◀ Quick & Easy

Prep Time: 5 minutes
Cook Time: 20 minutes
Average Rating: ★★★★★
211 Ratings ▲ 143 Reviews
What other cooks have done:
"I cooked some bacon and used the drippings instead of oil, and I crumbled the bacon on top. I also made it once with green beans and corn, and it was just as good."

French Apple Pie with Cream Cheese Topping

Submitted by: **Holly**

"Take a delicious French apple pie and gild the lily by topping it with a cream cheese layer!"

¼	cup butter, softened	1	teaspoon vanilla extract
1	cup white sugar	2	tablespoons hot water
1	egg	1	(3 ounce) package cream
¼	teaspoon salt		cheese, softened
1	teaspoon ground cinnamon	3	tablespoons unsalted butter,
1	teaspoon ground nutmeg		softened
1	teaspoon baking soda	½	teaspoon vanilla extract
1	cup all-purpose flour	1½	cups sifted confectioners'
½	cup chopped walnuts		sugar
2½	cups diced apple, without		
	peel		

1. Preheat oven to 350°F (175°C). Grease a 9 inch pie pan.

2. Combine ¼ cup butter, white sugar, egg, salt, cinnamon, nutmeg, baking soda, flour, nuts, apple, 1 teaspoon vanilla, and hot water in the order given. (Batter will be thick.) Pour into pie pan.

3. Bake in the preheated oven for 45 minutes.

4. To make topping: Mix cream cheese, 3 tablespoons butter, ½ teaspoon vanilla, and sifted confectioners' sugar. Beat until smooth. Pour over pie. Serve hot or warm, or refrigerate and let cream cheese topping set up. **Yield:** 8 servings.

Per serving: About 458 calories, 5g protein, 68g carbohydrate, 20g fat, 2g fiber, 65mg cholesterol, 330mg sodium

◀ Holiday Fare

Prep Time: 15 minutes
Cook Time: 45 minutes
Average Rating: ★★★★★
19 Ratings ▲ 12 Reviews
What other cooks have done:
"I must say this is a quick, easy and very yummy recipe. I made it into muffins, and they were great. I tried the tiny muffin tins for a bite-sized dessert for entertaining, and they were a hit. If you use the small muffin tins, remember to dice the apples a bit smaller."

Better-Than-Takeout Chinese Dinner

Put the phone down and forgo boxes of take-out food . . . you'll have homemade stir-fry and fried rice in no time—straight from your kitchen. Pick up some fortune cookies at the supermarket for a fun finish to the meal.

Serves 4

Spicy Orange Beef
Fried Rice

Spicy Orange Beef *(pictured on page 44)*

Submitted by: **Christine Johnson**
"This stir-fry is a good weekday dinner recipe. It's ready in a flash and is sure to please the whole family."

2 tablespoons vegetable oil	2 tablespoons cornstarch
1 pound round steak, cut into thin strips on the diagonal	1 cup beef broth
	¼ cup soy sauce
¼ cup orange zest	¼ cup sherry
1 clove garlic, minced	¼ cup orange marmalade
½ teaspoon ground ginger	½ teaspoon crushed red pepper flakes

1. In a wok or skillet, heat oil over medium-high heat. Add beef strips, ⅓ at a time. Stir-fry for 3 minutes or until browned, removing the done pieces to a plate lined with paper towels.
2. Return all the beef to the wok. Stir in orange zest, garlic, and ginger; stir-fry 1 minute.
3. In a medium bowl, combine cornstarch, broth, soy sauce, sherry, marmalade, and red pepper. Pour this mixture into the beef, stirring constantly. Bring to a boil over medium heat and cook for 1 minute. Serve hot. **Yield:** 4 servings.

Per serving: About 396 calories, 25g protein, 20g carbohydrate, 22g fat, 1g fiber, 73mg cholesterol, 1229mg sodium

---

Quick & Easy ▶

Prep Time: 15 minutes
Cook Time: 15 minutes
Average Rating: ★★★★☆
26 Ratings ▲ 19 Reviews
What other cooks have done:
"Really yummy! I used a little less orange zest and added some veggies. I have also made it with chicken, and that's good, too!"

Fried Rice *(pictured on page 44)*

Submitted by: **homemaker**

"The best homemade fried rice you can make! The bacon may be nontraditional, but it adds a little extra crunch. It's great with chicken or beef."

2⅔	cups water	¼	pound bacon, cut into strips (6 slices)
1⅓	cups uncooked white rice	2	tablespoons soy sauce
3	eggs, lightly beaten	1	(10 ounce) package frozen green peas, thawed
¼	teaspoon salt		
⅛	teaspoon ground black pepper	2	green onions, chopped
1	teaspoon vegetable oil, divided		

1. In a saucepan, bring water to a boil. Add rice and stir. Reduce heat; cover and simmer for 20 minutes. Meanwhile, season eggs with salt and pepper.

2. Heat oil in a small skillet and pour in eggs. Coat the bottom of the skillet with the eggs in order to cook them evenly; cook for about 3 minutes. Flip the eggs, cook 1 more minute, and remove skillet to a cool surface. Let eggs cool, then cut into thin slices. Set aside.

3. Place bacon in a large, deep skillet. Cook over medium-high heat until evenly brown. Drain, crumble, and set aside. Reserve 2 teaspoons bacon drippings.

4. Place rice in skillet; break up any clumps and toss to coat with reserved bacon drippings. Stir in bacon, egg slices, soy sauce, peas, and green onions. Stir and cook until heated through, approximately 3 minutes. **Yield:** 4 servings.

Per serving: About 548 calories, 17g protein, 64g carbohydrate, 24g fat, 4g fiber, 178mg cholesterol, 919mg sodium

---

◄ Family Favorite

Prep Time: 10 minutes

Cook Time: 30 minutes

Average Rating: ★★★★★

50 Ratings ▲ 36 Reviews

What other cooks have done:

"This rice was great! I used a fresh stir-fry mix that I steamed and cut up, and I added some shrimp in place of the bacon. This recipe was wonderful, and the best part is you can really use anything you have around to make it."

Cooking Basics: **The Chinese Pantry** ▼

Check out these fundamental flavors of Chinese cooking. Most of these items can easily be found in the supermarket or at Asian markets. If your family keeps begging for Asian-inspired menus, you may want to keep some of these items on hand for quick weeknight meals.

Chili paste or sauce: A spicy seasoning made of crushed chile peppers, oil, vinegar, garlic, and other flavorings. You can substitute crushed red pepper, but because it's more potent, start with one-third the amount and add more to taste.

Dark sesame oil: Nutty and rich, it's made from roasted or toasted sesame seeds. Because it smokes at high temperatures, it's primarily used as a seasoning and not for stir-frying.

Ginger: One of the most widely used seasonings in Asian cooking. When buying fresh ginger, look for hefty, smooth, shiny knobs.

Hoisin sauce: A sauce made with soybeans, sugar, vinegar, and spices. Sweet and fairly thick, its main uses are in marinades for barbecuing and roasting and in dipping sauces.

Oyster sauce: Made from oysters, salt, and seasonings. It's often used in sauces for seafood, meat, and vegetable dishes. You can substitute an equal amount of soy sauce.

Plum sauce: Also known as duck sauce, this is made from plums, apricots, vinegar, and sugar. In China it's often served with roasted goose or duck; in the United States, it's the ubiquitous table sauce in American-Cantonese restaurants.

Rice wine: An all-purpose cooking wine made from fermented rice. Sake or Japanese rice wines are acceptable substitutes, as is a very high-quality dry sherry.

Soy sauce: Another essential ingredient in Asian cooking. Made from fermented soybeans and wheat, its flavor varies by manufacturer and aging process.

Monstrous Meatless Mushroom Meal

What's so monstrous about this meal? Start with wedges of potatoes doused in spices and then oven-fried. Next, assemble a garden-fresh salad and chill in the refrigerator. Thick, juicy portobellos are then quickly broiled and made into burger-sized sandwiches. For dessert, try sweet zucchini bread that's swirled with chocolate. You can make the bread ahead or let it bake while you eat your meal. We're talking about one mighty meatless meal!

Serves 4

Portobello Sandwiches
Baked French Fries
Good-for-You Greek Salad
Chocolate-Wave Zucchini Bread

Portobello Sandwiches

Submitted by: **Nicholle**
"Quick, juicy burgers. My friends and I eat them at least once a week!"

Quick & Easy ▶

Prep Time: 8 minutes
Cook Time: 9 minutes
Average Rating: ★★★★★
43 Ratings ▲ 27 Reviews
What other cooks have done:
"I put red onion, honey-Dijon mustard, and provolone cheese on it as well, and made it like a gourmet burger."

2	cloves garlic, minced	4	hamburger buns
6	tablespoons olive oil	¼	cup mayonnaise
½	teaspoon dried thyme	1	tablespoon capers, drained
2	tablespoons balsamic vinegar	1	large tomato, sliced
	Salt and pepper to taste	4	lettuce leaves
4	large portobello mushroom caps		

1. Turn on broiler, and adjust rack so it's as close to heat source as possible.
2. In a medium bowl, mix together garlic, olive oil, thyme, vinegar, salt, and pepper.
3. Put the mushroom caps, bottom side up, in a shallow baking pan. Brush the caps with ½ of the dressing. Put the caps under the broiler and broil for 5 minutes.
4. Turn the caps, and brush with the remaining dressing. Broil for 4 minutes. Toast the buns lightly.
5. In a small bowl, mix mayonnaise and capers. Spread mayonnaise mixture on the buns; top with mushroom caps, tomato, and lettuce.
Yield: 4 servings.

Per serving: About 409 calories, 7g protein, 35g carbohydrate, 28g fat, 4g fiber, 4mg cholesterol, 487mg sodium

Baked French Fries

Submitted by: **Ashlee**
"This is an easy way to make a great side dish for burgers!"

4	large baking potatoes	2	teaspoons garlic powder
¼	cup olive oil	2	teaspoons chili powder
2	teaspoons paprika	2	teaspoons onion powder

1. Preheat oven to 450°F (230°C).
2. Cut potatoes into wedges. Mix olive oil, paprika, garlic powder, chili powder, and onion powder together. Coat potatoes with oil mixture and place on a baking sheet.
3. Bake in the preheated oven for 45 minutes. **Yield:** 4 servings.

Per serving: About 246 calories, 3g protein, 29g carbohydrate, 14g fat, 3g fiber, 0mg cholesterol, 21mg sodium

◄ Kid-Friendly

Prep Time: 5 minutes
Cook Time: 45 minutes
Average Rating: ★★★★★
38 Ratings ▲ 29 Reviews
What other cooks have done:
"I added ⅛ teaspoon cayenne pepper, and I cut the cooking time from 45 to 30 minutes. My family loved them!"

Good-for-You Greek Salad

Submitted by: **Jen**
"You can use two green onions instead of the small red onion in this yummy salad, if you wish."

¼	cup olive oil	1	small red onion, chopped
4	teaspoons lemon juice	1	cup crumbled feta cheese
1½	teaspoons dried oregano	6	black Greek olives, pitted and sliced
	Salt and pepper to taste		
3	large ripe tomatoes, chopped		
2	cucumbers, peeled and chopped		

1. Whisk together oil, lemon juice, oregano, and salt and pepper to taste.
2. In a shallow bowl or on a serving platter, combine tomatoes, cucumber, and onion. Drizzle with dressing. Sprinkle feta cheese and olives over salad. Serve. **Yield:** 4 to 6 servings.

Per serving: About 185 calories, 5g protein, 8g carbohydrate, 16g fat, 2g fiber, 22mg cholesterol, 350mg sodium

◄ Restaurant Fare

Prep Time: 15 minutes
Average Rating: ★★★★★
13 Ratings ▲ 11 Reviews
What other cooks have done:
"Excellent salad. I increased the oregano by 1 teaspoon and used a 4 ounce can of sliced black olives instead of Greek olives. There were no leftovers!"

Chocolate-Wave Zucchini Bread

Submitted by: **Lisa Perry**

"The zucchini makes this cake moist and the chocolate, delicious."

⅓	cup shortening	¼	teaspoon baking powder
1⅓	cups white sugar	1	teaspoon pumpkin pie spice
2	eggs	⅓	cup chopped walnuts
1½	cups grated zucchini	3	tablespoons unsweetened cocoa powder
⅓	cup water		
1	teaspoon vanilla extract	⅓	cup mini semisweet chocolate chips
1⅔	cups all-purpose flour		
1	teaspoon baking soda		
½	teaspoon salt		

1. Preheat oven to 350°F (175°C). Grease 1 (9x5 inch) loaf pan.

2. In a large bowl, cream shortening and sugar together. Mix in eggs. Stir in zucchini, water, and vanilla. Blend in flour, baking soda, salt, baking powder, and pumpkin pie spice. Stir in nuts.

3. Divide batter in half and add cocoa powder and chocolate chips to one of the halves. Pour plain batter into the loaf pan. Pour chocolate batter on top of plain batter.

4. Bake in the preheated oven about 1 hour or until a wooden pick inserted in center comes out clean. Cool 10 minutes and remove from pan. Store in refrigerator. **Yield:** 12 servings.

Per serving: About 268 calories, 4g protein, 41g carbohydrate, 11g fat, 1g fiber, 35mg cholesterol, 224mg sodium

Cooking Basics: Baking Quality Quick Breads ▼

Blueberry muffins for a special brunch, zucchini bread from the monstrous squash your neighbor gave you last summer, banana bread any time you bought more fruit than you could handle, or pumpkin spice loaves for holiday gifts. Quick bread is popular year-round. It's versatile, it's a crowd-pleaser, it's easy, and, as the name implies, it's quick!

The term "quick bread" refers to any bread that uses chemical leaveners (baking powder and/or baking soda) as opposed to yeast, and requires no kneading or rising time. As fast and easy as quick breads are to make, there are a few pointers we have for you so you can make your muffins and loaves even better.

Additions and Substitutions

Quick bread recipes are fairly versatile—you can add and substitute ingredients with greater freedom than you can with most other baked goods. To lower the fat, you can substitute some of the oil with an equal amount of almost any fruit puree (applesauce, baby food prunes, pumpkin puree, mashed bananas). You can add nuts and dried fruits to your heart's content, and substitute one kind of nut, dried fruit, or fresh fruit for another.

Add a finishing touch and a burst of flavor to finished quick breads by glazing them. Allow them to cool somewhat, and then make a simple mixture of confectioners' sugar and a little milk or fruit juice. Some especially popular choices are orange and lemon juices for the fragrant, tart zing they add.

The Magic's in the Mixing

The real secret to perfectly moist, tender, and well-shaped quick bread is to be scrupulously careful in your mixing. Combine the dry ingredients—flour, leavener, salt, and spices—in one bowl and mix them thoroughly with a wire whisk. In another bowl, beat together the fat, sugar, and eggs in the order the recipe advises. Stir any other ingredients—fruit or fruit puree, nuts, flavorings—into the wet ingredients. Only when each bowl of ingredients is mixed thoroughly should they be combined. Pour the dry ingredients into the wet ones and fold them together gently. Do this part by hand rather than with a mixer so you can use a gentle touch. Stir only until all the dry ingredients are moistened. Don't worry about a few lumps—they will disappear during baking. *– Jennifer Anderson*

For more information, visit **Allrecipes.com**

Mediterranean Dreaming

A refreshing, Mediterranean-inspired meal is just a few steps away, thanks to this simple menu plan. Remember to let the shrimp marinate in the refrigerator for about an hour. If you're using wooden skewers, soak them in warm water for 10 to 15 minutes before threading and grilling the shrimp. Trim the asparagus and put it on the grill along with the shrimp. Remove the shrimp and asparagus from the grill and cover with aluminum foil to keep warm. Prepare the couscous, and dinner's ready. Finish it off with your favorite flavor of ice cream or sorbet.

Serves 4

Basil Shrimp
Couscous with Dried Cherries
Grilled Asparagus

Basil Shrimp *(pictured on page 37)*

Submitted by: **Gail Laulette**
"This is one of the most delicious shrimp recipes for the grill I have ever had, and it's so easy. My son would eat the whole recipe if I didn't watch him."

2½ tablespoons olive oil	3 cloves garlic, minced
¼ cup butter, melted	½ teaspoon salt
⅓ cup lemon juice (1½ lemons)	¼ teaspoon white or black pepper
3 tablespoons coarse-grained prepared mustard	3 pounds large, fresh shrimp, peeled and deveined
½ cup minced fresh basil	

1. In a shallow, nonporous dish or bowl, mix together olive oil and melted butter. Then stir in lemon juice, mustard, basil, and garlic, and season with salt and white pepper. Add shrimp and toss to coat. Cover and refrigerate for 1 hour.
2. Preheat grill to high heat.
3. Remove shrimp from marinade and thread onto skewers; discard marinade.
4. Lightly oil grate and arrange kabobs on grill. Cook for 4 to 5 minutes, turning once, until done. **Yield:** 4 servings.

Per serving: About 576 calories, 71g protein, 10g carbohydrate, 26g fat, 3g fiber, 549mg cholesterol, 802mg sodium

◄ From the Grill

Prep Time: 25 minutes
Cook Time: 5 minutes
Average Rating: ★★★★★
59 Ratings ▲ 41 Reviews
What other cooks have done:
"This marinade gave the shrimp a great flavor. I added zucchini, onions, mushrooms, and bell pepper to the skewers, and it was a great meal served with rice or noodles."

Couscous with Dried Cherries *(pictured on facing page)*

Submitted by: **Stephanie Moon**

"My family loves couscous, and this fruity variation is one of our favorites. This is also delicious with other dried fruit such as cranberries and apricots."

1¼	cups chicken broth	¼	teaspoon ground black
½	cup dried sour cherries		pepper
1	tablespoon butter	1	cup uncooked couscous
¼	teaspoon salt		

1. In a 2-quart saucepan, heat chicken broth, dried cherries, butter, salt, and pepper to boiling over high heat.
2. Stir in couscous; cover and remove from heat. Let stand 5 minutes. Fluff with a fork and serve immediately. **Yield:** 4 servings.

Per serving: About 257 calories, 9g protein, 46g carbohydrate, 4g fat, 2g fiber, 8mg cholesterol, 527mg sodium

Grilled Asparagus *(pictured on facing page)*

Submitted by: **Larry Lampert**

"The special thing about this recipe is that it's so simple. Fresh asparagus with a little oil, salt, and pepper is cooked quickly over high heat on the grill."

1	pound fresh asparagus	Salt and pepper to taste
1	tablespoon olive oil	

1. Preheat grill to high heat.
2. Trim bottoms of asparagus. Lightly coat the spears with the oil. Season with salt and pepper to taste.
3. Grill over high heat for 2 to 3 minutes or to desired tenderness. **Yield:** 4 servings.

Per serving: About 56 calories, 3g protein, 5g carbohydrate, 4g fat, 2g fiber, 0mg cholesterol, 2mg sodium

Basil Shrimp, page 35; Couscous with Dried Cherries, facing page; and Grilled Asparagus, facing page

Golden Rum Cake,
page 69

Apple Pork Chops, page 67; Candied Carrots, page 68; and Orzo with Mushrooms and Walnuts, page 68

Homestyle Turkey, the Michigander Way, page 70; Brandied Orange and Cranberry Sauce, page 72; Praline Sweet Potatoes, page 72; Cream Peas, page 73; Awesome Sausage, Apple, and Dried Cranberry Stuffing, page 71

Pumpkin Roll Cake, page 73

Chicken Marsala, page 46, and Orzo with
Parmesan and Basil, page 47

Cinnamon Hazelnut
Biscotti, page 48

Cinnamon Rolls III, page 66

Asparagus Quiche, page 65 and
Fabulous Fruit Salad, page 66

Spicy Orange Beef, page 30
and Fried Rice, page 31

Special Occasion Menus

Company's coming and you'd love to wow your guests with something new. Search no further. We've got the consummate menu for your next special occasion. Imagine a warm holiday feast, a romantic Valentine's meal, or a Mother's Day brunch . . . or make tonight a special occasion just because. We've planned everything—now you can have all the fun.

Just Add a Red-Checked Tablecloth

Throw a red-checked tablecloth on the dining room table, open a bottle of red wine, and you've got instant atmosphere with this simple, yet elegant, meal for four. The main event—classic Chicken Marsala and orzo enhanced with Parmesan and fresh basil—is best served immediately, but both dishes can be ready in 30 minutes or less. Prepare the salad ahead, chill in the refrigerator, and toss with dressing just before serving. Coffee or cappuccino paired with homemade biscotti serves as a memorable finale to an unforgettable meal.

Serves 4

Chicken Marsala
Orzo with Parmesan and Basil
Caesar Salad Supreme
Cinnamon Hazelnut Biscotti

Chicken Marsala *(pictured on page 42)*

Submitted by: **Lisa**
"A delicious, classic chicken dish—lightly coated chicken breasts braised in Marsala wine and mushrooms. Ideal for a weeknight entrée or company."

¼ cup all-purpose flour	¼ cup butter
½ teaspoon salt	¼ cup olive oil
¼ teaspoon ground black pepper	1 cup sliced mushrooms
½ teaspoon dried oregano	½ cup Marsala wine
4 skinless, boneless chicken breast halves, pounded ¼ inch thick	¼ cup cooking sherry

1. In a shallow dish or bowl, mix together the flour, salt, pepper, and oregano. Coat chicken pieces in flour mixture.
2. In a large skillet, melt butter in oil over medium heat. Place chicken in the pan and lightly brown. Turn chicken pieces and add mushrooms. Pour in wine and sherry. Cover skillet; simmer chicken 10 minutes, turning once, or until no longer pink and juices run clear.
Yield: 4 servings.

Per serving: About 399 calories, 29g protein, 7g carbohydrate, 27g fat, 1g fiber, 100mg cholesterol, 575mg sodium

---

Restaurant Fare ▶

Prep Time: 10 minutes
Cook Time: 20 minutes
Average Rating: ★★★★★
239 Ratings ▲ 154 Reviews
What other cooks have done:
"I cut the amount of butter and oil in half, tripled the mushrooms, and doubled the amount of Marsala wine and sherry. I didn't pound the chicken all the way to ¼ inch thick, but it still turned out great. My dinner guests ate up every last bite."

Orzo with Parmesan and Basil *(pictured on page 42)*

Submitted by: **Dodie Pajer**
"For a quick Mediterranean macaroni and cheese, omit the basil."

2 tablespoons butter	½ cup freshly grated Parmesan
1 cup uncooked orzo pasta	cheese
1 (14 ounce) can chicken	Salt and pepper to taste
broth	2 tablespoons fresh basil
¼ cup chopped fresh basil	sprigs or flat-leaf parsley

1. Melt butter in heavy skillet over medium-high heat. Stir in orzo and sauté until lightly browned.
2. Stir in chicken broth; bring to a boil. Cover, reduce heat, and simmer until orzo is tender and liquid is absorbed, about 15 to 20 minutes.
3. Mix in chopped basil and Parmesan cheese. Season with salt and pepper. Transfer to a shallow bowl. Garnish with basil sprigs or parsley, if desired. **Yield:** 4 servings.

Per serving: About 330 calories, 13g protein, 43g carbohydrate, 11g fat, 1g fiber, 25mg cholesterol, 734mg sodium

◄ Quick & Easy

Prep Time: 10 minutes
Cook Time: 20 minutes
Average Rating: ★★★★★
31 Ratings ▲ 20 Reviews
What other cooks have done:
"This recipe has become a once-a-week meal that I have all the ingredients for on hand. I add cooked, cubed chicken breasts and broccoli sometimes to make a whole meal."

Caesar Salad Supreme

Submitted by: **Karen Weir**
"A rich anchovy dressing makes this salad a meal. Serve with crusty bread."

6 cloves garlic, peeled	1 tablespoon lemon juice
¾ cup mayonnaise	Salt and ground black
5 anchovy fillets, rinsed	pepper to taste
6 tablespoons grated	¼ cup olive oil
Parmesan cheese, divided	4 cups day-old bread, cubed
1 teaspoon Worcestershire	1 head romaine lettuce,
sauce	rinsed, dried, and torn
1 teaspoon prepared Dijon-	into bite-size pieces
style mustard	

1. Mince 3 cloves of the garlic and combine in a small bowl with mayonnaise, anchovies, 2 tablespoons of the Parmesan cheese, Worcestershire sauce, mustard, and lemon juice. Season to taste with salt and black pepper. Refrigerate until ready to use.
2. In a large pan, heat oil over medium heat. Cut remaining 3 cloves of garlic into quarters and add to hot oil. Cook and stir until brown; remove garlic from pan. Add bread cubes to the hot oil. Cook, turning frequently, until lightly browned. Remove bread cubes from oil and season with salt and pepper to taste.
3. Place lettuce in a large bowl. Toss with dressing, remaining Parmesan cheese, and croutons. **Yield:** 6 servings.

Per serving: About 368 calories, 6g protein, 9g carbohydrate, 35g fat, 1g fiber, 22mg cholesterol, 495mg sodium

◄ Family Favorite

Prep Time: 20 minutes
Cook Time: 15 minutes
Average Rating: ★★★★★
51 Ratings ▲ 42 Reviews
What other cooks have done:
"I made this recipe without the anchovies and added an extra clove of garlic in their place. I also used store-bought croutons. My guests raved it was the best Caesar Salad they've had in a long time—better than restaurant quality."

Cinnamon Hazelnut Biscotti (pictured on page 42)

Submitted by: **Kris**

"These are delicious with coffee, and they smell wonderful!"

(pictured on page 42)

¾	cup butter, softened	1	teaspoon ground cinnamon
1	cup white sugar	¾	teaspoon baking powder
2	eggs	½	teaspoon salt
1½	teaspoons vanilla extract	1	cup chopped hazelnuts
2½	cups all–purpose flour		

1. Preheat oven to 350°F (175°C). Grease a baking sheet or line with parchment paper.

2. In a medium bowl, cream together butter and sugar until light and fluffy. Beat in eggs and vanilla. Sift together the flour, cinnamon, baking powder, and salt; mix into the egg mixture. Stir in the hazelnuts. Shape dough into 2 equal logs approximately 12 inches long. Place logs on prepared baking sheet and flatten out to about ½ inch thickness.

3. Bake in the preheated oven for 25 to 30 minutes or until edges are golden and the center is firm. Remove from oven to cool on the pans. When loaves are cool enough to handle, use a serrated knife to slice the loaves diagonally into ½ inch thick slices. Return the slices to the baking sheet.

4. Bake 10 more minutes, turning once. Cool completely and store in an airtight container at room temperature. **Yield:** 3 dozen.

Per cookie: About 116 calories, 2g protein, 13g carbohydrate, 7g fat, 0g fiber, 23mg cholesterol, 85mg sodium

---

Crowd-Pleaser ▶

Prep Time: 25 minutes

Cook Time: 40 minutes

Average Rating: ★★★★★

41 Ratings ▲ 31 Reviews

What other cooks have done:

"I used chopped pecans instead of hazelnuts. I also dipped the biscotti in melted white chocolate and sprinkled them with a cinnamon-sugar mixture."

Drizzling Chocolate ▼

To make chocolate drizzles over biscotti, microwave 1 cup semisweet chocolate chips at MEDIUM (50% power) in a glass bowl 2 to 3 minutes, stirring once. Place melted chocolate in a small heavy-duty, zip-top plastic bag and seal. Snip a tiny hole in 1 corner of bag and drizzle chocolate over biscotti.

Here's to Leisurely Luncheons

Ease into this luncheon menu that's fit for a bridal shower, a holiday open house, or any other gathering of friends and family. Everything in the menu, from hummus spread to the short-bread cookies, can be made ahead, giving you the opportunity to savor the "leisurely" occasion. If possible, serve the Bread Machine Rolls warm from the oven to welcome your guests with the comforting aroma of fresh-baked bread.

Serves 12

Hummus III
Holiday Chicken Salad
Bread Machine Rolls
Alyson's Broccoli Salad
Raspberry and Almond Shortbread Thumbprints

Hummus III

Submitted by: **Rhoda McIntosh**
"Hummus is a pureed garbanzo bean dip with Middle Eastern origins. Serve with pita bread and an assortment of fresh vegetables. This is the secret combination straight from a Boston restaurant. Tahini, or sesame seed paste, can be found in health food stores, gourmet shops, and even many grocery stores."

2 cups canned garbanzo beans, drained	1 tablespoon olive oil
⅓ cup tahini	1 pinch paprika
¼ cup lemon juice	1 teaspoon minced fresh parsley
1 teaspoon salt	Pita bread, cut into wedges, or assorted crackers
2 cloves garlic, halved	

1. Place the garbanzo beans, tahini, lemon juice, salt, and garlic in a blender or food processor. Blend until smooth. Transfer mixture to a serving bowl.
2. Drizzle olive oil over the garbanzo bean mixture. Sprinkle with paprika and parsley. Serve with pita wedges or crackers. **Yield:** 12 servings.

Per serving: About 77 calories, 3g protein, 8g carbohydrate, 4g fat, 2g fiber, 0mg cholesterol, 236mg sodium

◄ Healthy

Prep Time: 10 minutes
Average Rating: ★★★★★
78 Ratings ▲ 52 Reviews
What other cooks have done:
"I added a dash or two of cayenne pepper. Try saving some of the liquid from the garbanzo beans and add a little while pureeing if the consistency is too thick."

Holiday Chicken Salad

Submitted by: **Elaine**
"Serve on lettuce leaves or make sandwiches. Stand back and enjoy the applause!"

1	cup mayonnaise	2	green onions, chopped
1	teaspoon paprika	1	cup chopped pecans
1	teaspoon seasoning salt	4	cups cubed, cooked chicken
1½	cups dried cranberries		Ground black pepper to
1	cup chopped celery		taste
½	cup minced green bell pepper		

1. In a medium bowl, mix together mayonnaise with paprika and seasoning salt. Blend in dried cranberries, celery, bell pepper, onion, and nuts. Add cubed chicken and mix well. Season with black pepper to taste. Chill 1 hour. Serve on Bread Machine Rolls (recipe below), if desired. **Yield:** 12 servings.

Per serving: About 332 calories, 14g protein, 13g carbohydrate, 25g fat, 2g fiber, 45mg cholesterol, 223mg sodium

Bread Machine Rolls

Submitted by: **Kay**
"These are the best dinner rolls I've ever made. They also make great buns for sandwiches."

3	cups bread flour	2	tablespoons butter, softened
3	tablespoons white sugar	1	(.25 ounce) package active
1	teaspoon salt		dry yeast
¼	cup dry milk powder	1	egg white
1	cup warm water (110°F/45°C)	2	tablespoons cold water

1. Place all of the ingredients (except the egg white and cold water) in the pan of the bread machine in the order recommended by the manufacturer. Set on Dough cycle; press Start.
2. Remove risen dough from the machine, deflate, and turn out onto a lightly floured surface. Divide the dough into 12 equal pieces and form into rounds. Place the rounds on lightly greased baking sheets. Cover the rolls with a damp cloth and let rise until doubled in volume, about 40 minutes. Meanwhile, preheat oven to 350°F (175°C).
3. In a small bowl, lightly beat the egg white with the water; lightly brush the risen rolls with this mixture. Bake in the preheated oven for 15 minutes or until the rolls are golden brown. **Yield:** 12 servings.

Per serving: About 165 calories, 6g protein, 30g carbohydrate, 3g fat, 1g fiber, 6mg cholesterol, 233mg sodium

---

Make-Ahead ▶

Prep Time: 15 minutes
Cook Time: 20 minutes
Average Rating: ★★★★★
41 Ratings ▲ 34 Reviews
What other cooks have done:
"I used walnuts instead of pecans and apples instead of cranberries. Also, add flavor to the chicken by adding Italian seasoning, garlic, and parsley to the water when you boil it."

Family Favorite ▶

Prep Time: 1 hour 20 minutes
Cook Time: 15 minutes
Average Rating: ★★★★★
62 Ratings ▲ 45 Reviews
What other cooks have done:
"I added 1½ teaspoons salt and sprinkled sesame seeds on the rolls before baking. I served them with honey butter (2 tablespoons butter and 1 tablespoon honey), and they were wonderful."

Alyson's Broccoli Salad

Submitted by: **Eleanor Johnson**
"Confirmed broccoli haters have changed their minds after tasting this salad. I have used sugar substitutes for the white sugar and nonfat or low-fat mayonnaise, and it still tastes great!"

20	slices bacon	6	tablespoons white wine vinegar
2	heads fresh broccoli, cut into bite size pieces	¼	cup white sugar
½	cup chopped red onion	2	cups mayonnaise
1	cup raisins	2	cups sunflower seeds

1. Place bacon in a large, deep skillet. Cook over medium-high heat until evenly brown. Drain, crumble, and set aside.
2. In a medium bowl, combine the broccoli, onion, and raisins. In a small bowl, whisk together the vinegar, sugar, and mayonnaise. Pour over broccoli mixture; toss until well mixed. Refrigerate at least 2 hours.
3. Toss with bacon and sunflower seeds. **Yield:** 12 servings.

Per serving: About 746 calories, 12g protein, 21g carbohydrate, 71g fat, 5g fiber, 51mg cholesterol, 584mg sodium

◀ Covered-Dish Favorite

Prep Time: 15 minutes
Cook Time: 15 minutes
Average Rating: ★★★★
95 Ratings ▲ 71 Reviews
What other cooks have done:
"I bought pre-cut broccoli florets and pre-cooked bacon, so I had this salad ready in about 10 minutes. Make twice what you think you'll need because it will disappear in a hurry."

Raspberry and Almond Shortbread Thumbprints

Submitted by: **Dee**
"Shortbread thumbprint cookies filled with raspberry jam and drizzled with glaze are perfect for any gathering."

1	cup butter, softened	½	cup seedless raspberry jam
⅔	cup white sugar	½	cup confectioners' sugar
½	teaspoon almond extract	¾	teaspoon almond extract
2	cups all-purpose flour	1	teaspoon milk

1. Preheat oven to 350°F (175°C).
2. In a medium bowl, cream together butter and white sugar until smooth. Mix in ½ teaspoon almond extract. Mix in flour until dough comes together. Roll dough into 1½ inch balls and place on ungreased baking sheets. Make a small indentation in the center of each ball, using your thumb, and fill the hole with jam.
3. Bake in the preheated oven for 14 to 18 minutes or until lightly browned. Let cool 1 minute on the baking sheets. Remove cookies to wire racks to cool completely.
4. In a medium bowl, mix together the confectioners' sugar, ¾ teaspoon almond extract, and milk until smooth. Drizzle lightly over warm cookies. **Yield:** 3 dozen.

Per cookie: About 104 calories, 1g protein, 14g carbohydrate, 5g fat, 0g fiber, 14mg cholesterol, 55mg sodium

◀ Holiday Fare

Prep Time: 30 minutes
Cook Time: 18 minutes
Average Rating: ★★★★★
47 Ratings ▲ 36 Reviews
What other cooks have done:
"I filled a squeeze bottle with the raspberry preserves, which made filling the cookies really easy. I also drizzled with dark chocolate instead of the glaze."

A San Francisco Seafood Feast

This unique menu abounds with culinary treasures from beautiful San Francisco. Cioppino, a tomato-based fish stew, brimming on the cooktop, will certainly whet your guests' appetites. On the following page, get the full scoop on this stew that was created by Italian immigrants in the Bay area. Artichoke Bruschetta will get the party started, and sourdough bread that's up to San Francisco standards pairs perfectly with the hearty stew. Finish off the feast with glazed Amaretto Cake that you can make ahead.

Serves 12

Artichoke Bruschetta
Cioppino
San Francisco Sourdough Bread
Sourdough Starter II
Amaretto Cake

Artichoke Bruschetta

Submitted by: **Roxanne**
"This is a great bruschetta recipe based on an artichoke dip. It's always a huge hit! Try adding spinach or tomatoes."

1 (6.5 ounce) jar marinated artichoke hearts, drained and chopped	5 tablespoons mayonnaise
½ cup grated Romano cheese	1 French baguette, cut into ½ inch thick slices
⅓ cup finely chopped red onion	

1. Preheat the broiler.
2. In a medium bowl, mix chopped artichoke hearts, Romano cheese, red onion, and mayonnaise. Top French baguette slices with equal amounts of the artichoke heart mixture. Arrange slices in a single layer on a large baking sheet.
3. Broil in the preheated oven 2 minutes or until toppings are bubbly and lightly browned. **Yield:** 12 servings.

Per serving: About 162 calories, 5g protein, 23g carbohydrate, 5g fat, 2g fiber, 5mg cholesterol, 384mg sodium

Party Food ▶

Prep Time: 18 minutes
Cook Time: 2 minutes
Average Rating: ★★★★★
32 Ratings ▲ 27 Reviews
What other cooks have done:
"I added 1 clove of garlic, 1 tomato, 1 tablespoon of olive oil, and sprinkled Parmesan cheese on top. I then put the artichoke mixture in a big bowl and garlic bagel chips around the bowl for everyone to dip instead of putting it on the bread."

Cioppino

Submitted by: **Star Pooley**

"Serve this wonderful seafood stew with a loaf of warm, crusty bread for sopping up the delicious broth!"

¾	cup butter	½	teaspoon dried oregano
2	onions, chopped	1	cup water
2	cloves garlic, minced	1½	cups white wine
1	bunch fresh parsley, chopped	1½	pounds large shrimp, peeled and deveined
2	(14.5 ounce) cans stewed tomatoes	1½	pounds bay scallops
2	(14 ounce) cans chicken broth	18	small clams
		18	mussels, cleaned and debearded
2	bay leaves	1½	cups crabmeat
1	tablespoon dried basil	1½	pounds cod fillets, cubed, optional
½	teaspoon dried thyme		

1. Over medium-low heat, melt butter in a large stockpot; add onions, garlic, and parsley. Cook slowly, stirring occasionally, until onions are soft.
2. Add tomatoes (break them into chunks as you add them). Add chicken broth, bay leaves, basil, thyme, oregano, water, and wine. Mix well. Cover and simmer 30 minutes.
3. Stir in the shrimp, scallops, clams, mussels, and crabmeat. Stir in cod fillets, if desired. Bring to a boil. Lower heat; cover and simmer 5 to 7 minutes or until clams and mussels open (discard clams and mussels that don't open). Ladle soup into bowls and serve with warm, crusty bread. **Yield:** 13 servings.

Per serving: About 341 calories, 38g protein, 10g carbohydrate, 14g fat, 1g fiber, 170mg cholesterol, 854mg sodium

◄ Crowd-Pleaser

Prep Time: 10 minutes
Cook Time: 45 minutes
Average Rating: ★★★★★
44 Ratings ▲ 34 Reviews
What other cooks have done:
"I replaced the butter with extra-virgin olive oil. Other changes: I used crushed tomatoes and a can of diced tomatoes, no water was necessary, and I added ½ teaspoon crushed red pepper flakes to give it a little zip. I also used red wine instead of white and included squid and sea bass. It was a hit for a friend's birthday dinner party."

Cioppino: The Most Succulent of Seafood Stews ▼

You can always tell who has been lucky enough to have taken part in a cioppino feast before, because, at the very mention of this rich, tomato-laced seafood stew, their eyes will light up and their mouths will start to water. This dish with an Italian-sounding name never graced the kitchens of Italy—it was, in fact, first cooked by Italian fishermen in San Francisco, and was originally made to use up the odds and ends from everyone's daily catch.

A Seafood Sampler

Cioppino begins with a base of tomatoes, olive oil, garlic, onions, and white wine. Crab is usually the main ingredient, but cioppino almost always contains other kinds of fish and shellfish as well, such as shrimp, clams, mussels, scallops, squid, lobster, chunks of halibut or monkfish. There are as many "original" recipes for cioppino as there are people who love it.

Roll Up Your Sleeves and Dig In!

Cioppino is decidedly a delicacy with its bounty of precious seafood and is often reserved for special occasions; however, it's a hearty meal and almost impossible to eat daintily. Instead, have fun and give in to eating with your hands! Cover the table with butcher paper. Roll up your sleeves, pile napkins on the table, and get ready to enjoy yourself. Crack the crab shells and pick out the sweet meat inside; slurp the tender clams and mussels from their shells; and then pile up the empty shells in the middle of the table. Mop up the rich juices with a piece of fresh, crusty bread. When you're done, just wipe off your chin and roll up the butcher paper, shells and all, and toss it out for supereasy cleanup. Sigh with contentment. And feel good about yourself because this unbelievably wonderful feast is heavy on nutritious seafood, low in fat, and good for you!
– Jennifer Anderson
For more information, visit **Allrecipes.com**

San Francisco Sourdough Bread

Submitted by: **Donna**

"Using a good sourdough starter, like the one we've included, will guarantee delicious flavor."

4¾ cups bread flour
3 tablespoons white sugar
2½ teaspoons salt
1 (.25 ounce) package active dry yeast
1 cup warm milk
2 tablespoons butter, softened
1½ cups sourdough starter (see recipe on facing page)
1 large egg
1 tablespoon water
¼ cup chopped onion

1. In a large bowl, combine 1 cup flour, sugar, salt, and yeast. Add milk and softened butter. Stir in starter. Mix in up to 3¾ cups flour gradually (you may need more or less, depending on your climate).

2. Turn dough out onto a floured surface and knead for 8 to 10 minutes. Place in a greased bowl, turning once to oil surface, and cover. Allow to rise for 1 hour or until doubled in volume.

3. Punch down and let rest 15 minutes. Shape into 2 loaves. Place on a greased baking sheet. Allow to rise for 1 hour or until doubled.

4. Preheat oven to 375°F (190°C). In a small bowl, lightly beat the egg with the water; brush egg wash over tops of loaves and sprinkle with chopped onion.

5. Bake in the preheated oven for 30 minutes or until done. **Yield:** 2 loaves (24 servings).

Per serving: About 145 calories, 5g protein, 26g carbohydrate, 2g fat, 1g fiber, 11mg cholesterol, 267mg sodium

Sourdough Know-How ▼

Sourdough bread has been around for centuries, and today we still love the tangy, distinctive flavor of this age-old favorite. At the heart of good sourdough bread is a reliable sourdough starter, a yeast mixture used in the bread making process. A starter will last indefinitely if you keep "feeding" it with flour, milk (or water), and sugar. You may have a starter that's been passed along from a family member or friend, but if you're starting from scratch, these tips should help you get "started."

- Mix and store the starter in glass, stoneware, or plastic. Metal can cause a chemical reaction with the starter.
- Place the starter in a bowl large enough to allow it to double in volume as it ferments.
- Never cover the container too tightly because the yeast needs air to live and the gas from the fermentation process needs to escape. Punch a small hole in a plastic wrap cover or leave the lid ajar.
- If a clear liquid forms on top of the mixture, just stir it back in.
- Allow the starter to come to room temperature before using it.
- Remember to feed the starter each time you remove some for bread baking.

- Sydny Carter

For more information, visit **Allrecipes.com**

Sourdough Starter II

Submitted by: **Glenda**

"Prepare the starter in a glass container and store in the refrigerator."

2	cups all-purpose flour	1	cup milk
2	cups warm water	1	cup flour
	(110°F/45°C)	¼	cup sugar
1	(.25 ounce) package active		
	dry yeast		

1. Mix together flour, warm water, and yeast in a quart jar. Let stand, uncovered, in a warm place overnight or up to 48 hours. The longer the mixture stands, the stronger the ferment will be.

2. After fermenting, the starter is ready to use or to store, covered, in the refrigerator. Feed once or twice a week with 1 cup milk, 1 cup flour, and ¼ cup sugar; allow the starter to rest at room temperature for several hours after feeding. **Yield:** 3 cups.

Per serving: About 310 calories, 10g protein, 64g carbohydrate, 1g fat, 3g fiber, 0mg cholesterol, 8mg sodium

◄ Make-Ahead

Prep Time: 5 minutes
Average Rating: ★★★★★
7 Ratings ▲ 3 Reviews
What other cooks have done:
"The starter dough may smell very sour and liquid may form on its surface, but this is normal. Stir the starter before each use. Be sure to leave 1 cup of starter in the container after using some."

Amaretto Cake

Submitted by: **Shawn**

"The amaretto glaze is drizzled over the cake while it's still warm. The cake makes a moist, decadent finish to any meal."

1	(18.25 ounce) package	½	cup vegetable oil
	yellow cake mix	¼	teaspoon almond extract
4	eggs	2	tablespoons amaretto
1	(5 ounce) package instant		liqueur
	vanilla pudding mix	1	cup confectioners' sugar
½	cup water	½	cup amaretto liqueur

1. Preheat the oven to 350°F (175°C). Grease and flour a 10 inch Bundt pan.

2. Combine cake mix, eggs, pudding, water, oil, almond extract, and 2 tablespoons amaretto; blend together. Pour batter into prepared pan.

3. Bake in the preheated oven for 40 to 45 minutes or until a toothpick inserted into the center of cake comes out clean. Remove cake from oven and, while still warm, poke holes in the surface with a wooden pick. Drizzle with the Amaretto Glaze (see step 4), insuring that some of the glaze fills the holes. Let the cake cool for at least 2 hours before removing from the pan.

4. While the cake bakes, prepare Amaretto Glaze: Sift the confectioners' sugar and combine with ½ cup amaretto. Blend until smooth. Add more amaretto as needed. **Yield:** 1 (10 inch) Bundt cake (12 servings).

Per serving: About 428 calories, 4g protein, 62g carbohydrate, 16g fat, 1g fiber, 72mg cholesterol, 478mg sodium

◄ Holiday Fare

Prep Time: 30 minutes
Cook Time: 45 minutes
Average Rating: ★★★★★
62 Ratings ▲ 52 Reviews
What other cooks have done:
"The only thing that makes it better is to let it set for at least a day. The glaze soaks in and the cake is even more moist. I made it and immediately took it to someone's house, and it was a hit. But, I brought home the rest, and the next day it was twice as good."

Prime Rib Spread

Don't let this stately cut of beef intimidate you. Prime Rib, also called rib roast or standing rib roast, can be a magnificent centerpiece for your next special occasion. Your guests will definitely be impressed, and you'll be cool and collected with this simple recipe that involves minimal preparation time. A gratin of potatoes and exotic mushrooms bubbling from the oven and a crisp layered salad round out the exciting spread. Prepare the salad, dressing included, and chill a couple hours before dinner is served. An elegant cheesecake crowned with apples and pecans can be prepared the day before and chilled until your guests are ready for the grand finale.

Serves 12

Prime Rib
Potato and Shiitake Mushroom Gratin
Seven-Layer Salad
Autumn Cheesecake

Prime Rib

Submitted by: **Dale**
"What could be better!"

10	pounds prime rib roast	½	cup prepared Dijon-style
6	cloves garlic, sliced		mustard
	Salt and ground black		
	pepper to taste		

1. Preheat oven to 500°F (260°C). Line roasting pan with foil.
2. Make slits all over roast. Insert slivers of sliced garlic throughout the roast. Combine salt, pepper, and mustard. Spread over roast.
3. Put on rack in prepared roasting pan. Roast in the preheated oven for 60 to 90 minutes. Turn off oven. Leave oven closed, do not peek for 90 minutes, and check temperature with meat thermometer for desired doneness (145°F/63°C for medium-rare).
Yield: 12 servings.

Per serving: About 445 calories, 47g protein, 2g carbohydrate, 27g fat, 0g fiber, 132mg cholesterol, 367mg sodium

Potato and Shiitake Mushroom Gratin

Submitted by: **Christine L.**

"Fall mushrooms give this dish a hearty flavor. You can substitute vegetable broth for the chicken broth and make a perfect meal for that vegetarian girlfriend your son is bringing to the holiday dinner. The rest of the family will love it, too."

6	tablespoons butter			Ground black pepper to taste
1½	pounds fresh mushrooms, quartered		3	pounds Yukon gold potatoes, peeled and cut into ⅛ inch thick slices
1½	pounds shiitake mushrooms, chopped		2	cups Parmesan cheese
3	tablespoons minced garlic		2	cups half-and-half
2	teaspoons dried thyme		2	cups heavy whipping cream
1	teaspoon dried rosemary, crushed		1¼	teaspoons salt
2	cups chicken broth		1	teaspoon ground black pepper
	Salt to taste			

1. Melt butter in a large pot over high heat. Add fresh mushrooms and shiitake mushrooms and sauté until liquid evaporates, about 10 minutes. Add garlic, thyme, and rosemary; sauté 1 minute. Add chicken broth. Simmer until liquid evaporates, stirring often, about 18 minutes. Season with salt and pepper. Cool.

2. Preheat oven to 375°F (190°C). Butter a 9x13 inch baking dish.

3. Arrange ⅓ of the potatoes in prepared dish, overlapping slightly. Top potatoes with half of the mushroom mixture. Sprinkle ⅓ of the cheese over mushrooms. Repeat layering ⅓ of the potatoes, remaining mushroom mixture, and ⅓ of the cheese. Arrange remaining potatoes over cheese.

4. Whisk half-and-half, cream, 1¼ teaspoons salt, and 1 teaspoon pepper in a large bowl to blend. Pour mixture over potatoes. Cover loosely with foil.

5. Place baking dish on middle rack in oven. Bake in the preheated oven for 1 hour and 15 minutes or until potatoes are tender and liquid thickens.

6. Uncover. Sprinkle remaining ⅓ of the cheese over potatoes. Bake until cheese melts and gratin is golden at edges, about 15 minutes longer. Let stand 10 minutes before serving. **Yield:** 12 servings.

Per serving: About 509 calories, 17g protein, 50g carbohydrate, 31g fat, 7g fiber, 98mg cholesterol, 780mg sodium

◀ Company is Coming

Prep Time: 30 minutes

Cook Time: 2 hours

Average Rating: ★★★★★

54 Ratings ▲ 12 Reviews

What other cooks have done:
"Unbelievable! Even if you don't want to spend too much money on shiitake mushrooms, this dish is still great using only button mushrooms!"

Seven-Layer Salad

Submitted by: **Leah Mae**

"Feel free to substitute green onions for red, and Monterey Jack for Cheddar."

1	pound bacon	10	ounces shredded Cheddar cheese
1	large head iceberg lettuce, rinsed, dried, and chopped	1	cup chopped cauliflower
1	red onion, chopped	1¼	cups mayonnaise
1	(10 ounce) package frozen green peas, thawed	2	tablespoons white sugar
		⅔	cup grated Parmesan cheese

1. Place bacon in a large, deep skillet. Cook over medium-high heat until evenly brown. Crumble and set aside. Place lettuce in a large bowl and top with a layer of onion, peas, shredded cheese, cauliflower, and bacon.

2. Whisk together the mayonnaise, sugar, and Parmesan cheese. Drizzle dressing over salad and refrigerate until chilled. **Yield:** 12 servings.

Per serving: About 462 calories, 14g protein, 13g carbohydrate, 40g fat, 2g fiber, 61mg cholesterol, 735mg sodium

Crowd-Pleaser ▶

Prep Time: 15 minutes

Cook Time: 15 minutes

Average Rating: ★★★★★

30 Ratings ▲ 21 Reviews

What other cooks have done:

"I ignored the measurements and simply made sure there was an ample amount of each ingredient to make a layer to suit the bowl I used, and it worked out well."

Autumn Cheesecake

Submitted by: **Stephanie**

"This is a delicious apple cheesecake that's perfect any time of year."

1	cup graham cracker crumbs	2	eggs
½	cup finely chopped pecans	½	teaspoon vanilla extract
3	tablespoons white sugar	⅓	cup white sugar
½	teaspoon ground cinnamon	½	teaspoon ground cinnamon
¼	cup unsalted butter, melted	4	cups apples, peeled, cored, and thinly sliced
2	(8 ounce) packages cream cheese, softened	¼	cup chopped pecans
½	cup white sugar		

1. Preheat oven to 350°F (175°C). In a large bowl, stir together the graham cracker crumbs, ½ cup pecans, 3 tablespoons sugar, ½ teaspoon cinnamon, and melted butter; press into a 9 inch springform pan. Bake in the preheated oven for 10 minutes.

2. In a large bowl, combine cream cheese and ½ cup sugar. Mix at medium speed until smooth. Beat in eggs, 1 at a time, mixing well after each addition. Blend in vanilla; pour filling into the baked crust.

3. Stir together ⅓ cup sugar and ½ teaspoon cinnamon. Toss with the apples to coat. Spoon over filling; sprinkle with ¼ cup pecans.

4. Bake in the preheated oven for 60 to 70 minutes or until filling is set. With a knife, loosen cake from rim of pan. Let cool and remove the rim of pan. Chill cake before serving. **Yield:** 12 servings.

Per serving: About 349 calories, 5g protein, 31g carbohydrate, 24g fat, 2g fiber, 87mg cholesterol, 164mg sodium

Make-Ahead ▶

Prep Time: 30 minutes

Cook Time: 1 hour 10 minutes

Average Rating: ★★★★★

143 Ratings ▲ 108 Reviews

What other cooks have done:

"I used cinnamon graham crackers for the crust and added another 8 ounces of cream cheese and another egg to fill up my 10 inch pan."

All-American Bistro

Go Americana with this meal of family favorites. When special events pop up during the week, celebrate that soccer victory or the honor roll inductee with a special family feast. While the rosemary-crusted chicken roasts in the oven, prepare the glazed carrots and mashed potatoes. Polish off the meal with another American classic, Apple Crisp, served with vanilla ice cream. It's a menu fit for company but easy enough for any night of the week.

Serves 4

Roast Chicken with Rosemary
Garlic Mashed Potatoes
Buttery Cooked Carrots
Apple Crisp II

Roast Chicken with Rosemary *(pictured on page 2)*

Submitted by: **Nanette**
"When I was in Italy, I smelled the scrumptious aroma of roast chicken at a street stand. I bought one of the chickens and looked at what they stuffed in the cavity to make it taste so good. It was fragrant rosemary! I do my turkeys like this, too."

1	(3 pound) whole chicken, rinsed	1	teaspoon pepper
1	tablespoon olive oil	1	small onion, quartered
1	teaspoon salt	¼	cup chopped fresh rosemary

1. Preheat oven to 375°F (190°C).
2. Rub chicken with olive oil and season with salt and pepper. Stuff with onion and rub rosemary on inside and outside of chicken. If desired, tie ends of legs together with heavy string. Place chicken, breast side up, on a rack in a shallow roasting pan. Roast in the preheated oven for 1 hour and 15 minutes or until a meat thermometer inserted in thigh registers 180°F (82°C). **Yield:** 4 servings.

Per serving: About 187 calories, 16g protein, 1g carbohydrate, 13g fat, 0g fiber, 64mg cholesterol, 60mg sodium

◄ Family Favorite

Prep Time: 15 minutes
Cook Time: 1 hour 15 minutes
Average Rating: ★★★★★
41 Ratings ▲ 33 Reviews
What other cooks have done:
"Instead of cutting the onion into quarters, I diced it and also added a clove of minced garlic into the 'stuffing.' After the chicken was cooked, I tossed the onion, garlic, and rosemary mixture with some rice, and it was delicious as a side dish!"

Garlic Mashed Potatoes (pictured on page 2)

Submitted by: **Lorna**

"These garlic mashed potatoes are rich and very tasty. For a creamier texture, use heavy cream in place of the milk. These potatoes are also terrific topped with green onions."

8	potatoes, peeled and cubed (4 pounds)	½	teaspoon freshly ground black or white pepper
2	cloves garlic, minced	1	cup milk
¼	cup butter	2	tablespoons sesame seeds, toasted
1	teaspoon salt		

1. Bring a large pot of water to a boil, add potatoes, and boil 25 minutes or until soft. Drain well.

2. Place potatoes, garlic, butter, salt, pepper, and milk in an electric blender or mixer. Blend until smooth or to your desired consistency. Top the potatoes with sesame seeds before serving. **Yield:** 4 servings.

Per serving: About 300 calories, 8g protein, 34g carbohydrate, 15g fat, 5g fiber, 33mg cholesterol, 140mg sodium

Buttery Cooked Carrots (pictured on page 2)

Submitted by: **Rebecca**

"Sweet cooked carrots that even my carrot-hating family loves. There are never any leftovers."

1	pound baby carrots	⅓	cup light brown sugar
¼	cup butter or margarine	¼	teaspoon salt

1. Cook carrots in a large pot of boiling water 8 minutes or until tender. Drain off most of the liquid, leaving bottom of pan covered with water. Set the carrots aside.

2. Stir butter, brown sugar, and salt into the water. Simmer and stir until the butter melts. Return carrots to the pot and toss to coat. Cover and let sit for a few minutes to allow flavors to mingle. **Yield:** 4 servings.

Per serving: About 188 calories, 1g protein, 21g carbohydrate, 12g fat, 2g fiber, 0mg cholesterol, 175mg sodium

Apple Crisp II

Submitted by: **Diane Kester**

"Warm apple filling crowned with a crunchy brown sugar-oat topping gets even better when served with vanilla ice cream. It's a simple dessert with sophisticated flavor."

10	cups thinly sliced apples	1	cup all-purpose flour
1	cup white sugar	1	cup packed brown sugar
1	tablespoon all-purpose flour	¼	teaspoon baking powder
1	teaspoon ground cinnamon	¼	teaspoon baking soda
½	cup water	½	cup butter, melted
1	cup quick-cooking oats		

1. Preheat oven to 350°F (175°C).

2. Place the sliced apples in a 9x13 inch pan. Mix the white sugar, 1 tablespoon flour, and ground cinnamon together, and sprinkle over apples. Pour water evenly over apples.

3. Combine the oats, 1 cup flour, brown sugar, baking powder, baking soda, and melted butter. Crumble evenly over the apple mixture.

4. Bake in the preheated oven for about 45 minutes. **Yield:** 12 servings.

Per serving: About 329 calories, 3g protein, 64g carbohydrate, 9g fat, 4g fiber, 21mg cholesterol, 123mg sodium

◄ Crowd-Pleaser

Prep Time: 30 minutes
Cook Time: 45 minutes
Average Rating: ★★★★★
143 Ratings ▲ 97 Reviews
What other cooks have done:
"I did not use the ½ cup of water, but I sprinkled a little water on top of the apples. I also doubled the topping."

Cooking Basics: **No Bad Apples** ▼

In the wide world of fruit, apples are a constant and familiar presence. Unfortunately, this also means that, for many of us, apples have sunk to the status of the mundane when placed next to more exotic choices in the fruit bowl. Mushy, bland apples showed up in our school lunches, often abandoned after a few obliging bites. The reason that many apples are so uninspiring, however, is not because they're inherently blah, but because they're old. Many apples have been stored in a warehouse for a while before making their way to your grocery store. Try an apple that's been plucked straight from the tree: there's no going back once you've sunk your teeth into that resilient, crisp, sweet, juicy flesh.

There's a greater variety of apples available to us now than ever before, so you never need to eat a boring apple again. In fact, there are over 1,000 varieties of apple, and over 100 of them are commonly available in supermarkets, farmers' markets, roadside stands, and backyard trees across the nation.

Apple Picking
While there are so many apples to choose from, some tend to be more appropriate for certain kinds of dishes than others. Apples for cooking and baking should be firm and flavorful so their texture and taste can stand up to the heat. For making apple-

sauce, choose an apple with a softer composition that will break down into a smooth puree. For eating fresh, it's all a matter of preference: No matter whether you prefer honey-sweet apples or puckery-tart ones, bone-jarringly crunchy or soft and yielding, there's an apple out there for you. Check out the Apple Selection chart on page 316 for a complete guide to choosing the right apple for your needs.

No matter which branch of the apple family tree you prefer to nibble from, there are a few things that all good apples should have in common. Choose firm apples that are heavy for their size. You can steer clear of mushy, over-watered apples by checking the bottoms and choosing those that are closed, not open. The apples should have a fresh smell, not a musty one, and the skin should be smooth and taut with no soft spots. Wrinkled skin, mushy spots, and a hollow, spongy feel are traits of an old, improperly stored apple. Sometimes there will be a sign on the apple bin that says "New Crop." This means that they've been picked recently, and that's what you want. Apples are at their best from late summer to mid-autumn, so give these fall fruits their just desserts (and breakfasts, lunches, dinners, and snacks) while the season lasts!

– Jennifer Anderson

For more information, visit **Allrecipes.com**

A Springtime Spectacular

Whether it's Easter supper, or a graduation celebration, this meal will turn heads. Here's a game plan to get you started: Bake the potatoes and stuff them ahead, or you can microwave them for their first "bake." Pop the ham in the oven and keep basting it while you prepare the rest of the meal. Once the ham is finished cooking, increase the oven temperature to bake the potatoes while the ham rests on the counter. The salad will come together quickly just before the meal is served. Top it off with a springtime favorite—Awesome Carrot Cake with Cream Cheese Frosting—that's truly as awesome as it sounds.

Serves 12

Honey-Glazed Ham
Ultimate Twice-Baked Potatoes
Jamie's Cranberry-Spinach Salad
Awesome Carrot Cake with
Cream Cheese Frosting

Honey-Glazed Ham

Submitted by: **Colleen**

"This ham tastes very much like the famous honey-glazed ham, but costs much less, and there's no need to fight the crowds during the holidays. You can even buy presliced ham to make it easier and more like the original. It's very good. (I bake the ham while preparing the rest of the meal so that I don't forget to baste it!)"

1	(5 pound) smoked fully cooked ham half	¼	cup dark corn syrup
¼	cup whole cloves	2	cups honey
		⅔	cup butter

1. Preheat oven to 325°F (165°C).
2. Score ham and stud with the whole cloves. Place ham in a foil-lined pan.
3. In the top half of a double boiler, heat the corn syrup, honey, and butter. Keep glaze warm while baking ham.
4. Brush glaze over ham and bake for 1 hour and 15 minutes in pre-heated oven. Baste ham every 10 to 15 minutes with the honey glaze. During the last 4 to 5 minutes of baking, turn on broiler to caramelize the glaze. Remove from oven and let sit a few minutes before serving.
Yield: 12 servings.

Per serving: About 455 calories, 32g protein, 55g carbohydrate, 14g fat, 1g fiber, 115mg cholesterol, 2465mg sodium

Ultimate Twice-Baked Potatoes

Submitted by: **Debra Connors**

"These potatoes make a wonderful side dish for any meal and are terrific heated up the next day for lunch."

6	large baking potatoes	¾	teaspoon salt
12	slices bacon	¾	teaspoon pepper
1½	cups sour cream	1½	cups shredded Cheddar cheese, divided
¾	cup milk		
6	tablespoons butter	12	green onions, sliced, divided

1. Preheat oven to 350°F (175°C).

2. Bake potatoes in the preheated oven for 1 hour.

3. Meanwhile, place bacon in a large, deep skillet. Cook over medium-high heat until evenly brown. Drain, crumble, and set aside.

4. When potatoes are done, allow them to cool for 10 minutes. Slice potatoes in half lengthwise and scoop the flesh into a large bowl; save skins. To the potato flesh, add sour cream, milk, butter, salt, pepper, ¾ cup cheese, half the green onions, and half the bacon. Mix with a hand mixer until well blended and creamy. Spoon the mixture into the potato skins. Top each with remaining cheese, green onions, and remaining bacon.

5. Bake in the preheated oven 15 more minutes until cheese melts.

Yield: 12 servings.

Per serving: About 393 calories, 9g protein, 16g carbohydrate, 33g fat, 1g fiber, 63mg cholesterol, 524mg sodium

◄ Family Favorite

Prep Time: 15 minutes
Cook Time: 1 hour 15 minutes
Average Rating: ★★★★★
45 Ratings ▲ 36 Reviews
What other cooks have done:
"To cut down on time, I cooked the potatoes in the microwave (instead of the 1 hour in the oven), prepared them, and threw them in the oven as directed."

Jamie's Cranberry-Spinach Salad

Submitted by: **Jamie Hensley**

"Everyone I have made this for raves about it. It's different and easy to make!"

1	tablespoon butter	1	tablespoon poppy seeds
¾	cup blanched and slivered almonds	½	cup white sugar
		2	teaspoons minced onion
1	pound spinach, rinsed and torn into bite-size pieces	¼	teaspoon paprika
		¼	cup white wine vinegar
1	cup dried cranberries	¼	cup cider vinegar
2	tablespoons toasted sesame seeds	½	cup vegetable oil

1. In a medium saucepan, melt butter over medium heat. Cook almonds in butter until lightly toasted. Remove from heat and let cool.

2. In a large bowl, toss the spinach with the almonds and cranberries.

3. In a medium bowl, whisk together the sesame seeds, poppy seeds, sugar, onion, paprika, white wine vinegar, cider vinegar, and vegetable oil. Toss with spinach just before serving. **Yield:** 12 servings.

Per serving: About 224 calories, 3g protein, 19g carbohydrate, 16g fat, 3g fiber, 3mg cholesterol, 42mg sodium

◄ Quick & Easy

Prep Time: 10 minutes
Cook Time: 10 minutes
Average Rating: ★★★★★
302 Ratings ▲ 245 Reviews
What other cooks have done:
"I used baby spinach leaves, which are a little more tender and eliminates having to tear the spinach into pieces. I also added some crumbled Gorgonzola cheese. Save some cranberries, almonds, and cheese to sprinkle on the top of the salad for a pretty presentation."

Awesome Carrot Cake with Cream Cheese Frosting

Submitted by: **Tracy Kirk**

"The name says it all. It doesn't get much better than this 'awesome' carrot cake that's moist, rich, and simply delicious."

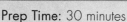
3	cups grated carrots	1	(8 ounce) can crushed
2	cups all-purpose flour		pineapple with juice
2	cups white sugar	¾	cup chopped pecans
2	teaspoons baking soda	3½	cups confectioners' sugar
1	teaspoon baking powder	1	(8 ounce) package cream
½	teaspoon salt		cheese, softened
1	teaspoon ground cinnamon	½	cup butter, softened
4	eggs	1¼	teaspoons vanilla extract
1½	cups vegetable oil	1	cup chopped pecans
1¼	teaspoons vanilla extract		

1. Preheat oven to 350°F (175°C). Grease and flour a 9x13 inch pan.
2. In a large bowl, combine carrot, flour, white sugar, baking soda, baking powder, salt, and cinnamon. Stir in eggs, oil, 1¼ teaspoons vanilla, pineapple, and ¾ cup chopped pecans. Spoon batter into prepared pan.
3. Bake in the preheated oven for 40 to 45 minutes or until a toothpick inserted into the center of the cake comes out clean. Allow to cool.
4. To make frosting: In a medium bowl, combine confectioners' sugar, cream cheese, ½ cup butter, and 1¼ teaspoons vanilla. Beat until smooth and stir in 1 cup chopped pecans. Spread on cooled cake.
Yield: 16 servings.

Per serving: About 435 calories, 4g protein, 47g carbohydrate, 27g fat, 2g fiber, 53mg cholesterol, 266mg sodium

Sunny Sunday Brunch

Nothing is too good for Mom, so make this Mother's Day memorable with a brunch that's fit for a queen. Make the fruit salad ahead, and allow enough time to let the quiche cool before serving. Spoil her with your own comfort food: warm, homemade cinnamon rolls. This delightful meal will give Mom something else to brag about for a whole year.

Serves 12

Asparagus Quiche
Fabulous Fruit Salad
Cinnamon Rolls III

Asparagus Quiche *(pictured on page 43)*

Submitted by: **Michele O'Sullivan**
"This delectable combination of ingredients results in a tasty quiche dish."

½ (15 ounce) package refrigerated pie crust	4 eggs
1 pound fresh asparagus, trimmed and cut into ½ inch pieces	1 cup half-and-half
	¼ teaspoon ground nutmeg
	½ teaspoon salt
10 slices bacon	¼ teaspoon pepper
1 egg white, lightly beaten	1¼ cups shredded Swiss cheese

1. Preheat the oven to 425°F (220°C). Fit pie crust into a 9 inch quiche dish. Prick bottom and sides of pie crust with a fork. Bake in the preheated oven for 9 minutes; set aside.
2. Reduce oven temperature to 400°F (200°C). Place asparagus in a steamer over 1 inch of boiling water and cover. Cook until tender but still firm, about 4 to 6 minutes. Drain and cool.
3. Place bacon in a large, deep skillet. Cook over medium-high heat until evenly brown. Drain, crumble, and set aside.
4. Brush prebaked pie crust with beaten egg white. Sprinkle crumbled bacon and asparagus into pie crust.
5. In a bowl, beat together eggs, half-and-half, nutmeg, salt, and pepper. Sprinkle Swiss cheese over bacon and asparagus. Pour egg mixture on top of cheese.
6. Bake, uncovered, in the preheated oven for 35 to 40 minutes or until firm. Cool to room temperature before serving. **Yield:** 12 servings.

Per serving: About 282 calories, 11g protein, 5g carbohydrate, 24g fat, 1g fiber, 115mg cholesterol, 267mg sodium

◄ Crowd-Pleaser

Prep Time: 25 minutes
Cook Time: 40 minutes
Average Rating: ★★★★★
36 Ratings ▲ 26 Reviews
What other cooks have done:
"This was a huge hit at our Mother's Day brunch. We actually ended up adding more bacon. One time-saver would be to cook the bacon the day before."

Fabulous Fruit Salad *(pictured on page 43)*

Submitted by: **Tracy Fall**

"This easy, healthy fruit salad will round out any meal perfectly."

Healthy ▶

Prep Time: 10 minutes
Average Rating: ★★★★★
19 Ratings ▲ 16 Reviews
What other cooks have done:
"If nectarines aren't available, use 1 cup chopped canned peaches instead. You can also leave the skin on the apples to add color, if you'd like."

2 red apples, peeled, cored, and chopped	4 stalks celery, chopped
2 green apples, peeled, cored, and chopped	1 cup dried cranberries
2 nectarines, pitted and sliced	1 cup chopped walnuts
	2 (8 ounce) containers nonfat lemon yogurt

1. In a large bowl, combine apples, nectarines, celery, cranberries, and walnuts. Mix in yogurt. Chill until ready to serve. **Yield:** 12 servings.

Per serving: About 167 calories, 4g protein, 24g carbohydrate, 7g fat, 3g fiber, 1mg cholesterol, 38mg sodium

Cinnamon Rolls III *(pictured on page 43)*

Submitted by: **Miss Alix**

"Here's an easy alternative to buying those famous cinnamon rolls in the mall. They taste exactly the same, and the dough is made in the bread machine."

Bread Machine Recipe ▶

Prep Time: 2 hours
Cook Time: 25 minutes
Average Rating: ★★★★★
36 Ratings ▲ 34 Reviews
What other cooks have done:
"I don't have a bread machine, so I made the dough by hand and kneaded it a few times. I let it rise for about one hour before forming the rolls and again afterward like the recipe calls for. I used walnuts instead of pecans."

¼ cup warm water	¼ cup butter, softened
¼ cup butter, melted	1 cup brown sugar
½ (3.4 ounce) package instant vanilla pudding mix	4 teaspoons ground cinnamon
1 cup warm milk	¾ cup chopped pecans
1 large egg	½ (8 ounce) package cream cheese, softened
1 tablespoon white sugar	
½ teaspoon salt	¼ cup butter, softened
4 cups bread flour	1 cup confectioners' sugar
1 (.25 ounce) package active dry yeast	½ teaspoon vanilla extract
	1½ teaspoons milk

1. In the pan of your bread machine, combine water, butter, vanilla pudding, warm milk, egg, sugar, salt, bread flour, and yeast. Set machine to Dough cycle; press Start. When Dough cycle has finished, turn dough out onto a lightly floured surface; roll into a 10x17 inch rectangle. Spread with ¼ cup softened butter. In a small bowl, stir together brown sugar, cinnamon, and pecans. Sprinkle brown sugar mixture over dough.
2. Roll up dough, beginning with long side. Slice into 15 (1 inch) slices and place in a 9x13 greased pan. Let rise in a warm place until doubled, about 45 minutes. Meanwhile, preheat oven to 350°F (175°C).
3. Bake in the preheated oven for 20 to 25 minutes or until golden brown. While rolls bake, stir together cream cheese, ¼ cup butter, confectioners' sugar, vanilla, and milk. Top with frosting. **Yield:** 15 rolls.

Per serving: About 350 calories, 6g protein, 45g carbohydrate, 16g fat, 2g fiber, 46mg cholesterol, 206mg sodium

Those Brisk Autumn Evenings

There's a chill in the air and the leaves are starting to fall. . . . It's time to welcome autumn with a casual, comforting meal shared with close friends or family. Apple cider, brown sugar, and sliced apples elevate everyday pork chops to company fare. Glazed carrots and nutty mushroom orzo can be ready in no time, while the chops finish in the oven. Golden Rum Cake served with coffee or hot tea makes a perfect ending to a cozy evening of bountiful food and good friends.

Serves 4

Apple Pork Chops
Orzo with Mushrooms and Walnuts
Candied Carrots
Golden Rum Cake

Apple Pork Chops *(pictured on page 39)*

Submitted by: **Marie**
"I started making this dish a few years ago after apple picking with my children. We all enjoy it and hope you do, too!"

2	tablespoons vegetable oil
½	cup chopped onion
4	(½ inch thick) bone–in pork chops
½	teaspoon salt
½	teaspoon ground black pepper

2	apples, cored and sliced into rings
2	tablespoons brown sugar
½	teaspoon ground mustard
⅛	teaspoon ground cloves
¾	cup hot water, apple cider, or apple juice

1. Preheat oven to 375°F (190°C).
2. Heat oil in a large skillet. Sauté onion in oil for 4 minutes or until tender. Remove onion with slotted spoon and set aside. Brown pork chops on both sides in oil.
3. Place chops in a 9x13 inch baking dish and sprinkle with salt and pepper. Cover the chops with the apples and cooked onion.
4. In a small bowl, combine brown sugar, mustard, cloves, and water. Pour over chops. Cover and bake in the preheated oven for 30 to 40 minutes. **Yield:** 4 servings.

Per serving: About 226 calories, 13g protein, 19g carbohydrate, 11g fat, 2g fiber, 33mg cholesterol, 314mg sodium

◀ Holiday Fare

Prep Time: 10 minutes
Cook Time: 44 minutes
Average Rating: ★★★★★
140 Ratings ▲ 87 Reviews
What other cooks have done:
"I substituted a few things, like spicy mustard, and I added cinnamon as well. I also quickly sautéed the apples with the onions just to help them acquire some more flavor. This was an overall winner!"

Orzo with Mushrooms and Walnuts *(pictured on page 39)*

Submitted by: **Amanda**

"This recipe makes quite a bit. Everyone I've prepared it for loves it. You can easily double the recipe, if needed."

1½	tablespoons olive oil	1	cup uncooked orzo pasta
1	onion, chopped	3	tablespoons chopped
½	pound fresh mushrooms,		walnuts, toasted
	sliced		Salt and pepper to taste
2	cups chicken broth		

1. Heat oil in a large heavy saucepan over medium-high heat. Sauté onion and mushrooms, until tender, about 8 to 10 minutes. Pour in broth and bring to a boil. Stir in orzo; reduce heat to medium, cover and simmer until orzo is tender and liquid is absorbed, about 10 to 12 minutes. Remove from heat and stir in walnuts. Season with salt and pepper to taste. **Yield:** 4 servings.

Per serving: About 323 calories, 10g protein, 48g carbohydrate, 10g fat, 3g fiber, 0mg cholesterol, 507mg sodium

Candied Carrots *(pictured on page 39)*

Submitted by: **Denyse**

"My family's favorite vegetable. They're great for the holidays, too!"

1	pound carrots, cut into 2 inch pieces	¼	cup packed brown sugar
		⅛	teaspoon salt
2	tablespoons butter, cut in pieces	⅛	teaspoon pepper

1. Place carrots in a pot of salted water. Bring water to a boil, reduce heat, and simmer about 20 to 25 minutes. Be careful not to overcook carrots.

2. Drain the carrots, reduce heat to low, and return the carrots to the pan. Stir in butter, brown sugar, salt, and pepper. Cook for about 3 to 5 minutes until sugar is bubbly. Serve warm. **Yield:** 4 servings.

Per serving: About 152 calories, 1g protein, 25g carbohydrate, 6g fat, 3g fiber, 16mg cholesterol, 201mg sodium

---

Quick & Easy ▶

Prep Time: 10 minutes

Cook Time: 25 minutes

Average Rating: ★★★★★

10 Ratings ▲ 7 Reviews

What other cooks have done:

"This was an excellent side dish. I added celery in addition to the onion and mushrooms, and it tasted great! I also added some herbs and spices to kick it up a bit."

Holiday Fare ▶

Prep Time: 10 minutes

Cook Time: 30 minutes

Average Rating: ★★★★★

26 Ratings ▲ 17 Reviews

What other cooks have done:

"I steamed the carrots instead of boiling them. Instead of turning the heat to low after adding the sauce ingredients, I recommend turning the heat up a bit and cooking until the sauce reduces and caramelizes."

Golden Rum Cake *(pictured on page 38)*

Submitted by: **Jackie Smith**

"My family requests this rummy Bundt cake at all our get-togethers. The butter rum glaze makes it special. An easy way to glaze your cake is to pour half of the glaze into Bundt pan, reinsert cake, then pour the rest of glaze over the cake. Let the glaze absorb well, then invert back onto platter."

1 cup chopped walnuts	½ cup water
1 (18.25 ounce) package yellow cake mix without pudding	½ cup vegetable oil
	½ cup dark rum
	½ cup butter
1 (3.4 ounce) package instant vanilla pudding mix	¼ cup water
	1 cup white sugar
4 eggs	½ cup dark rum

1. Preheat oven to 325°F (165°C). Grease and flour a 10 inch Bundt pan. Sprinkle chopped nuts evenly in the pan.

2. In a large bowl, combine cake mix and pudding mix. Mix in the eggs, ½ cup water, oil, and ½ cup rum. Blend well. Pour batter over chopped nuts in the pan.

3. Bake in the preheated oven for 1 hour or until a toothpick inserted into the cake comes out clean. Let sit for 10 minutes in pan; turn out onto a serving plate. Brush glaze over top and sides. Allow cake to absorb glaze and repeat until all glaze is used.

4. To make the glaze: Combine butter, ¼ cup water, and 1 cup sugar in a saucepan. Bring to a boil over medium heat and continue to boil for 5 minutes, stirring constantly. Remove from heat and stir in ½ cup rum. **Yield:** 12 servings.

Per serving: About 567 calories, 6g protein, 60g carbohydrate, 30g fat, 1g fiber, 92mg cholesterol, 502mg sodium

◄ Crowd-Pleaser

Prep Time: 30 minutes
Cook Time: 1 hour
Average Rating: ★★★★★
43 Ratings ▲ 34 Reviews
What other cooks have done:
"I tried this recipe with coconut rum for a different twist. Instead of using nuts, I toasted coconut flakes and used them as garnish around the cake. This is the easiest and best-tasting rum cake I've ever made!"

Holiday Feast

Gather around the table for a memorable holiday meal and start new family traditions with this feast featuring classics such as turkey, stuffing, and sweet potatoes. Mainstays such as cranberry sauce get a face-lift with orange zest and a splash of brandy. Consider baking the Pumpkin Roll Cake as an eye-pleasing alternative to the same pie served year after year. Your family will thank you for it!

Serves 8

Homestyle Turkey, the Michigander Way

Awesome Sausage, Apple, and Dried Cranberry Stuffing

Brandied Orange and Cranberry Sauce

Praline Sweet Potatoes

Cream Peas

Pumpkin Roll Cake

Homestyle Turkey, the Michigander Way *(pictured on pages 40-41)*

Submitted by: **Robin C.**
"A simple, down-to-basics recipe when it comes to the good ol' turkey."

1	(12-pound) whole turkey Awesome Sausage, Apple, and Dried Cranberry Stuffing (recipe follows)	3	tablespoons chicken bouillon
6	tablespoons butter, softened	2	tablespoons dried parsley
4	cups warm water	2	tablespoons dried minced onion
		2	tablespoons seasoning salt

1. Preheat oven to 350°F (175°C). Rinse turkey and pat dry. Discard the giblets or add to pan, if desired. Loosely stuff cavity with 4 cups Awesome Sausage, Apple, and Dried Cranberry Stuffing, if desired.
2. Place turkey in a roasting pan. Separate the skin over the breast to make pockets, running your fingers gently under skin to loosen it. Rub 3 tablespoons of butter on both sides between the skin and breast meat.
3. In a medium bowl, combine the water with the bouillon granules. Sprinkle in the parsley and minced onion. Pour over the turkey. Sprinkle seasoning salt over turkey.
4. Cover with a loose tent of foil and bake in the preheated oven 2½ hours or until a meat thermometer inserted in thigh registers 180°F (80°C) and in stuffing registers 165°F (75°C). For the last 45 minutes or so, remove the foil so the turkey will brown. **Yield:** 10 servings.

Per serving: About 940 calories, 112g protein, 2g carbohydrate, 51g fat, 0g fiber, 389mg cholesterol, 1008mg sodium

Awesome Sausage, Apple, and Dried Cranberry Stuffing *(pictured on pages 40-41)*

Submitted by: **Stacy M. Polcyn**

"This Thanksgiving stuffing is fantastic! It's very flavorful and fresh-tasting. I replaced the pork sausage with much healthier turkey sausage and substituted dried cranberries instead of chopped dried apricots for good flavor and color."
(Note: This stuffing can be prepared a day ahead. Keep covered and chilled in the refrigerator until ready to use. Do not stuff the turkey in advance for food safety reasons.)

1½	cups whole wheat bread cubes	1	medium Golden Delicious apple, peeled, cored, and chopped
3¾	cups white bread cubes	¾	cup dried cranberries
16	ounces bulk seasoned turkey sausage	⅓	cup chopped parsley
1	cup chopped onion	1	cooked chicken liver, finely chopped
¾	cup chopped celery	¾	cup turkey stock or chicken broth
2½	teaspoons dried sage		
1½	teaspoons dried rosemary	¼	cup unsalted butter, melted
½	teaspoon dried thyme		

1. Preheat oven to 350°F (175°C). Bake the whole wheat and white bread cubes 20 minutes or until evenly golden brown. Transfer toasted bread cubes to a large bowl and let cool.

2. In a large skillet, cook the sausage and chopped onion over medium heat, stirring and breaking up the lumps until fully cooked. Add the chopped celery, sage, rosemary, and thyme; cook for 2 minutes while stirring.

3. Add the sausage mixture to the bread; add the chopped apple, dried cranberries, parsley, and liver. Toss mixture well. Combine the stock and the melted butter, drizzle over the mixture, and toss stuffing well. Cover and refrigerate until ready to use.

4. Stuff 4 cups chilled stuffing into a 12-pound turkey just before roasting. Place remaining stuffing in an 8x8 inch square baking dish and bake separately at 350°F (175°C) for 30 minutes or until thoroughly heated and desired consistency. **Yield:** 10 servings.

Per serving: About 231 calories, 10g protein, 18g carbohydrate, 13g fat, 2g fiber, 99mg cholesterol, 344mg sodium

◄ Make-Ahead

Prep Time: 15 minutes
Cook Time: 55 minutes
Average Rating: ★★★★★
94 Ratings ▲ 67 Reviews
What other cooks have done:
"I made this recipe for Thanksgiving and will be making it again for Christmas. It really is 'awesome'! I used pork sausage instead of turkey, and the cranberries gave it color and great flavor. I cooked this in a 2 quart casserole dish instead of stuffing the turkey, and it came out moist and yummy!"

Brandied Orange and Cranberry Sauce *(pictured on page 40)*

Submitted by: **Claudia**
"This is the best cranberry sauce you'll ever eat!"

⅓ cup orange zest (about 3 large oranges)
2 cups water
2 cups white sugar
⅔ cup orange juice
1 tablespoon lemon juice
3 cups fresh or frozen cranberries
1 tablespoon brandy

1. In a small pan over medium heat, combine the orange zest and water. Cover and bring to a boil. Reduce heat and simmer for 15 minutes. Drain, reserving zest and ⅓ cup liquid.
2. To the reserved zest and liquid add the sugar, orange juice, and lemon juice. Bring to a boil; reduce heat and simmer for 3 minutes, uncovered, stirring often.
3. Add cranberries; increase heat to high and bring to a boil. Reduce heat and simmer, stirring often, about 5 minutes or until the cranberries have popped and a small spoonful of sauce sets on a cold plate.
4. Remove from heat and stir in brandy. Store in refrigerator. **Yield:** 8 servings.

Per serving: About 232 calories, 1g protein, 60g carbohydrate, 0g fat, 3g fiber, 0mg cholesterol, 3mg sodium

Praline Sweet Potatoes *(pictured on page 40)*

Submitted by: **Mike Kennon**
"The best sweet potatoes you will ever eat!"

4 cups mashed cooked sweet potatoes
½ cup white sugar
2 tablespoons vanilla extract
4 eggs, beaten
1 cup heavy whipping cream
½ cup butter, softened
1 cup packed brown sugar
½ cup all-purpose flour
1¼ cups chopped pecans

1. Preheat oven to 350°F (175°C). Butter a 2 quart baking dish.
2. In a bowl, combine the sweet potatoes, sugar, vanilla, eggs, and cream. Blend well and spread evenly in dish.
3. Prepare the topping by combining the softened butter, brown sugar, flour, and pecans. Mix until crumbly and sprinkle over sweet potato mixture.
4. Bake in the preheated oven for 30 minutes or until top is bubbly. **Yield:** 8 servings.

Per serving: About 689 calories, 9g protein, 79g carbohydrate, 39g fat, 5g fiber, 178mg cholesterol, 267mg sodium

Cream Peas *(pictured on page 40)*

Submitted by: **Stephanie Moon**
"We love these peas so much we have this as a side dish quite often."

4	cups frozen green peas	⅔	cup heavy whipping cream
1⅓	cups water	¼	cup all-purpose flour
¼	teaspoon salt	2	tablespoons white sugar
6	tablespoons butter		

1. In a medium saucepan, combine peas, water, and salt. Bring to a boil, then stir in butter. In a small bowl, whisk together cream, flour, and sugar. Stir mixture into peas. Cook over medium-high heat until thick and bubbly, about 5 minutes. **Yield:** 8 servings.

Per serving: About 235 calories, 5g protein, 19g carbohydrate, 16g fat, 4g fiber, 51mg cholesterol, 172mg sodium

◄ **Quick & Easy**

Prep Time: 5 minutes
Cook Time: 5 minutes
Average Rating: ★★★★★
26 Ratings ▲ 23 Reviews
What other cooks have done:
"My 2-year-old seemed to be on a hunger strike until she tried these peas. She loved them so much that I used mixed veggies the next night in the recipe and she gobbled them up, too."

Pumpkin Roll Cake *(pictured on page 41)*

Submitted by: **Stephanie**
"This can be frozen and served chilled."

3	eggs	½	teaspoon salt
1	cup white sugar	¼	teaspoon ground nutmeg
⅔	cup canned pumpkin	1	cup chopped walnuts
1	teaspoon lemon juice	2	(3 ounce) packages cream
¾	cup all-purpose flour		cheese, softened
1	teaspoon baking powder	1	cup confectioners' sugar
2	teaspoons ground	¼	cup butter, softened
	cinnamon	½	teaspoon vanilla extract

1. Preheat oven to 375°F (190°C).
2. In a mixing bowl, beat eggs on high for 5 minutes. Gradually beat in sugar until thick and lemon-colored. Add pumpkin and lemon juice.
3. In another bowl, combine flour, baking powder, cinnamon, salt, and nutmeg; fold into the pumpkin mixture.
4. Grease a 10x15 inch jellyroll pan; line with wax paper. Grease and flour the paper. Spread batter into pan; sprinkle with walnuts.
5. Bake in the preheated oven for 15 minutes or until cake springs back when lightly touched. Immediately turn out onto a linen towel dusted with confectioners' sugar. Peel off paper and roll up cake in the towel, starting with the short end. Cool.
6. Meanwhile, in a mixing bowl, beat cream cheese, 1 cup confectioners' sugar, butter, and vanilla until fluffy. Unroll cake. Spread filling to within 1 inch of edges. Roll up again and chill. Dust with additional confectioners' sugar before serving, if desired. **Yield:** 16 servings.

Per serving: About 230 calories, 4g protein, 27g carbohydrate, 13g fat, 1g fiber, 59mg cholesterol, 201mg sodium

◄ **Make-Ahead**

Prep Time: 30 minutes
Cook Time: 15 minutes
Average Rating: ★★★★★
16 Ratings ▲ 13 Reviews
What other cooks have done:
"This pumpkin roll was a big hit at a teacher appreciation luncheon. I used a full 8 ounces of cream cheese for the filling and also folded in 1 cup of whipped topping into the filling before spreading it."

Love Me Tenderloin

Throw a Valentine's Day dinner party and dine in style in your own home. Your guests are sure to fall in love with the beef tenderloin steaks, and the chocolate mousse cake will bring out the passion in everyone.

Serves 6 to 8

Lover's Beef Burgundy Filet
Rosemary Mashed Potatoes and Yams with Garlic and Parmesan
Brussels Sprouts in Mustard Sauce
Chocolate Mousse Cake IV

Lover's Beef Burgundy Filet

Submitted by: **Penelope Holmes**
"Pull out this fancy recipe for special occasions and wow your loved ones. Everyone seems to fall in love with this dish after just one bite."

4 cups Burgundy wine	½ cup butter, softened
1½ cups canola oil	1 teaspoon Burgundy wine
1½ cups soy sauce	1 tablespoon minced shallots
2 cups oyster sauce	1 tablespoon minced green
1 tablespoon garlic, minced	onions
1½ teaspoons dried oregano	1 teaspoon ground white
8 (6 ounce) beef tenderloin steaks	pepper

1. In a medium saucepan, mix together 4 cups wine, canola oil, soy sauce, oyster sauce, garlic, and oregano. Bring to a boil and remove from heat. Place in the refrigerator 1 hour or until chilled.
2. Place steaks in a 9x13 inch baking dish and pour the chilled marinade over them. Cover tightly with foil and refrigerate at least 5 hours.
3. In a medium bowl, beat butter and 1 teaspoon wine with a hand mixer. Mix in shallots, green onions, and white pepper by hand; cover tightly and refrigerate.
4. Lightly oil a cold grill rack and preheat a grill to high heat. Preheat oven to 200°F (95°C).
5. Grill marinated steaks to desired doneness, turning once. Place steaks in a clean 9x13 inch baking dish. Dollop with the butter-wine mixture and place in the preheated oven for 1 minute or until butter is melted. **Yield:** 8 servings.

Per serving: About 589 calories, 4g protein, 8g carbohydrate, 53g fat, 1g fiber, 31mg cholesterol, 3164mg sodium

---

Restaurant Fare ▶

Prep Time: 40 minutes
Cook Time: 20 minutes
Average Rating: ★★★★★
48 Ratings ▲ 33 Reviews
What other cooks have done:
"Absolutely mouthwatering! The marinade was very flavorful and delicious. I used sirloin steak since the store was out of filet, and it was juicy and scrumptious all the same!"

Rosemary Mashed Potatoes and Yams with Garlic and Parmesan

Submitted by: **Ibby**

"This is a truly unique twist on traditional mashed potatoes."

8	cloves garlic	¼	cup butter
3	tablespoons olive oil	½	teaspoon dried rosemary
1½	pounds baking potatoes, peeled and cubed	½	cup grated Parmesan cheese, divided
1½	pounds sweet potatoes, peeled and cubed		Salt to taste
½	cup milk		Ground black pepper to taste

1. Preheat oven to 350°F (175°C). Put garlic in a small ovenproof bowl and drizzle with olive oil. Roast for 30 minutes, until very soft. Cool, peel, and reserve oil.

2. Cook potatoes and sweet potatoes in a large pot of salted water until tender, about 20 to 30 minutes. Drain, reserving 1 cup liquid.

3. Place potatoes in a bowl. Add milk, butter, rosemary, garlic, and reserved olive oil. Mash until smooth, adding reserved cooking liquid as needed. Mix in ¼ cup cheese and salt and pepper to taste. Transfer to a greased 8x8 inch baking dish. Sprinkle with remaining cheese.

4. Bake for 45 minutes, until heated through and golden on top.

Yield: 8 servings.

Per serving: About 303 calories, 6g protein, 41g carbohydrate, 14g fat, 5g fiber, 21mg cholesterol, 196mg sodium

◀ Crowd-Pleaser

Prep Time: 30 minutes
Cook Time: 1 hour 45 minutes
Average Rating: ★★★★★
31 Ratings ▲ 26 Reviews
What other cooks have done:
"I didn't have time to roast the garlic, so I sautéed the minced garlic in olive oil before adding it to the mixture."

Brussels Sprouts in Mustard Sauce

Submitted by: **Marilyn**

"These Brussels sprouts are cooked in chicken broth, giving them a great depth of flavor. Even my children love this recipe."

2	tablespoons cornstarch	1	pound Brussels sprouts
¼	cup water	2	teaspoons prepared Dijon-style mustard
1	(14 ounce) can chicken broth	2	teaspoons lemon juice

1. Dissolve cornstarch in ¼ cup water; set aside.

2. In a small pot, bring chicken broth to a boil and cook Brussels sprouts until tender. Strain, reserving chicken broth and Brussels sprouts; place Brussels sprouts in a warm serving dish.

3. Return chicken broth to stove and add mustard and lemon juice; return to boil. Add cornstarch mixture and stir until thickened.

4. Pour over Brussels sprouts and serve. **Yield:** 6 servings.

Per serving: About 50 calories, 3g protein, 9g carbohydrates, 1g fat, 2g fiber, 0mg cholesterol, 353mg sodium

◀ Healthy

Prep Time: 15 minutes
Cook Time: 15 minutes
Average Rating: ★★★★☆
14 Ratings ▲ 7 Reviews
What other cooks have done:
"I used lemon-pepper in place of the lemon juice."

Chocolate Mousse Cake IV

Submitted by: **Stephanie**
"Chocolate cake with chocolate mousse filling. What could be better?"

1	(18.25 ounce) package chocolate cake mix	½	cup cold water
1	(14 ounce) can sweetened condensed milk	1	(3.9 ounce) package instant chocolate pudding mix
2	(1 ounce) squares unsweetened chocolate, melted	1	cup heavy cream, whipped

1. Preheat oven to 350°F (175°C). Prepare and bake cake mix as package directs for 2 (9 inch) layers. Cool and remove from pans.
2. In a large bowl, mix together sweetened condensed milk and melted chocolate. Gradually stir in the water and instant pudding until smooth. Chill for at least 30 minutes.
3. Remove the chocolate mixture from the refrigerator and stir to loosen. Fold in whipped cream and return to the refrigerator for at least another hour.
4. Place 1 layer of cake onto a serving plate. Top with 1½ cups of the mousse, then cover with the remaining cake layer. Frost with the remaining mousse and refrigerate until serving. Garnish with fresh fruit or chocolate shavings. **Yield:** 14 servings.

Per serving: About 322 calories, 5g protein, 50g carbohydrate, 14g fat, 2g fiber, 21mg cholesterol, 441mg sodium

Annie's Fruit Salsa and Cinnamon
Chips, page 85

Hot Mexican Spinach Dip, page 86
and Margaritas, page 104

Chicken Satay and Hot Peanut
Sauce, page 96

Double Tomato
Bruschetta,
page 89

Cosmopolitan,
page 104

Cheese Straws, page 82, and
Aileen's Punch, page 99

Appetizers & Beverages

Looking for something more than that same old bottled salsa and chips? Maybe it's time to try something new. Whether it's a New Year's Eve soirée, a child's birthday party, or a Friday movie night munch-fest, we've got all the right dips, nibbles, snacks, and cocktails to keep everyone happy.

Cheese Straws *(pictured on page 80)*

Submitted by: **Carol**

"I won't forget the cheese straws that my mother made for my father. The only difference was that she did not add cayenne pepper like I do here."

2	cups shredded sharp Cheddar cheese	1	teaspoon baking powder
¾	cup butter or margarine	¼	teaspoon cayenne pepper
2	cups all-purpose flour	½	teaspoon salt

1. Preheat oven to 400°F (205°C). Grease or line a baking sheet with parchment paper.
2. Process shredded cheese and butter in a food processor until blended. Add flour, baking powder, cayenne pepper, and salt; process until mixture forms a ball, stopping often to scrape down sides.
3. On a lightly floured surface, roll pieces of the dough to ¼ inch thickness. Cut sticks into 4 to 5 inch lengths. Arrange the pieces on the baking sheet.
4. Bake in the preheated oven for 5 minutes or until browned.
Yield: about 7 dozen.

Per cheese straw: About 34 calories, 1g protein, 2g carbohydrate, 2g fat, 0g fiber, 2mg cholesterol, 57mg sodium

Monterey Jack Salsa

Submitted by: **Debra D. Tate**

"This is a totally unique salsa that's great with tortilla chips, and it keeps for several days. It tastes even better the second day."

2	cups shredded Monterey Jack cheese	1	(6 ounce) can chopped black olives
5	green onions, chopped	1	cup Italian salad dressing
1	avocado, peeled, pitted, and diced	1	teaspoon monosodium glutamate (MSG) (optional)
1	tomato, chopped		
¼	cup chopped fresh cilantro		
1	(4.5 ounce) can diced green chiles		

1. In a medium bowl, mix together cheese, green onions, avocado, tomato, cilantro, chile peppers, olives, dressing, and monosodium glutamate. Serve immediately, or cover and chill. **Yield:** 3 cups.

Per 2 tablespoons: About 97 calories, 3g protein, 2g carbohydrate, 9g fat, 1g fiber, 8mg cholesterol, 357mg sodium

Spicy Bean Salsa

Submitted by: **Susan Navarrete**

"Black-eyed peas, black beans, tomatoes, and corn serve as a base for this chunky-style salsa. Serve it with tortilla chips, and watch it disappear."

1 (15 ounce) can black-eyed peas, drained
1 (15 ounce) can black beans, rinsed and drained
1 (15 ounce) can whole kernel corn, drained
½ cup chopped onion
½ cup chopped green bell pepper

1 (4 ounce) can diced jalapeño peppers
1 (14.5 ounce) can diced tomatoes, drained
1 cup Italian salad dressing
½ teaspoon garlic salt

1. In a medium bowl, combine black-eyed peas, black beans, corn, onion, bell pepper, jalapeño peppers, and tomatoes. Season with dressing and garlic salt; mix well. Cover and refrigerate overnight to blend flavors. **Yield:** 4 cups.

Per ⅓ cup: About 190 calories, 5g protein, 20g carbohydrate, 10g fat, 5g fiber, 0mg cholesterol, 768mg sodium

BLT Dip

Submitted by: **Kathy Walstrom**

"This dip is a hit at any party. It really tastes like a BLT. Use fat-free or low-fat mayonnaise and sour cream if you want to cut down on the fat. You could even use turkey bacon, if you'd like. Serve with crackers or chips."

1 pound bacon
1 cup mayonnaise
1 (8 ounce) container sour cream

1 tomato, peeled, seeded, and diced

1. Place bacon in a large, deep skillet. Cook over medium-high heat until evenly browned. Drain on paper towels.
2. In a medium bowl, combine mayonnaise and sour cream. Crumble bacon into the sour cream and mayonnaise mixture. Mix in tomato just before serving. **Yield:** 3 cups.

Per 3 tablespoons: About 296 calories, 3g protein, 1g carbohydrate, 31g fat, 0g fiber, 33mg cholesterol, 300mg sodium

Best Guacamole

Submitted by: **Kathy Shaw**

"The real trick to great guacamole is to use ripe avocados. Serve this dip with corn chips, fresh vegetables, or with any Mexican fare."

2	avocados	½	teaspoon salt
½	lemon, juiced	2	tablespoons olive oil
2	tablespoons chopped onion		

1. Cut the avocados into halves. Remove the seeds and scoop out the pulp into a small bowl. Use a fork to mash the avocado. Stir in lemon juice, onion, salt, and olive oil. Cover the bowl and refrigerate for 1 hour before serving. **Yield:** 2 cups.

Per 2 tablespoons: About 57 calories, 1g protein, 2g carbohydrate, 6g fat, 1g fiber, 0mg cholesterol, 75mg sodium

Restaurant Fare ▶

Prep Time: 5 minutes

Average Rating: ★★★★★

39 Ratings ▲ 20 Reviews

What other cooks have done:

"I omitted the olive oil and added chopped tomatoes, chopped jalapeños for spice, and a tiny bit of garlic. This recipe is so flexible; just mash up the avocados and add whatever you like."

Avocados 101 ▼

What they look like: Most varieties of avocado are oval- or round-shaped with thick, rough green skin. Depending on the type, an avocado can range from 3 ounces to 4 pounds.

Selection tips: Look for fruit that's firm, yet gives when gently squeezed. If it's still hard, it's not ready to be eaten yet. Two medium avocados should yield about 1 pound, or 2½ cups sliced, diced, or chopped.

Storage tips: You may refrigerate ripe avocados until you're ready to eat them, but only for a few days. Placing an avocado in a paper bag with an apple or banana and storing it at room temperature will accelerate the ripening process, if needed. Since cut and exposed avocados tend to discolor quickly, add cubed or sliced avocado to your dish as late as possible in the preparation process. Or add a dash of lemon or lime juice to fresh guacamole to help prevent discoloration.

Health benefits: While avocados are known to be high in unsaturated fat, many believe they are worth the splurge for their great buttery taste. They are also a good source for fiber, vitamin C, and other nutrients such as thiamin and riboflavin.

Annie's Fruit Salsa and Cinnamon Chips *(pictured on page 77)*

Submitted by: **Ann Renzino Page**

"Tasty fruit salsa and cinnamon tortilla chips make a great appetizer or snack. You can use any flavor fruit preserves, and feel free to use whatever fruit is in season."

2   kiwis, peeled and diced
2   Golden Delicious apples, peeled, cored, and diced
1   (8 ounce) package raspberries
1   pound strawberries, coarsely chopped
2   tablespoons white sugar
1   tablespoon brown sugar
3   tablespoons raspberry preserves
10 (10 inch) flour tortillas
    Butter flavored cooking spray
1   cup cinnamon sugar

1. In a large bowl, thoroughly mix kiwi, apple, raspberries, strawberries, white sugar, brown sugar, and preserves. Cover and chill in the refrigerator at least 15 minutes.

2. Preheat oven to 350°F (175°C).

3. Coat one side of each flour tortilla with butter flavored cooking spray. Cut each tortilla into 6 wedges and arrange in a single layer on a large baking sheet. Sprinkle wedges with desired amount of cinnamon sugar. Spray again with cooking spray.

4. Bake tortillas, in batches, in the preheated oven for 8 to 10 minutes. Allow to cool approximately 15 minutes. Serve with chilled fruit mixture. **Yield:** 7 cups salsa and 60 chips.

Per ¾ cup salsa and 6 chips: About 471 calories, 7g protein, 100g carbohydrate, 6g fat, 6g fiber, 0mg cholesterol, 347mg sodium

◄ Healthy

Prep Time: 15 minutes
Cook Time: 1 hour
Average Rating: ★★★★★
235 Ratings ▲ 186 Reviews
What other cooks have done:
"We used the leftovers as a topping for vanilla ice cream. It was even better than with the chips."

Seven-Layer Dip

Submitted by: **Dee Dee Perez**
"This is a great party dip because you can make it ahead and store in the refrigerator. You can also throw it together and serve immediately."

1½	pounds ground beef	1	cup guacamole
1	(16 ounce) can refried beans	1	cup salsa
4	cups shredded Mexican-style cheese, divided	1	(6 ounce) can black olives, chopped
1	(8 ounce) container sour cream	½	cup chopped tomatoes
		½	cup chopped green onions

1. In a large skillet, brown ground beef. Drain and set aside to cool to room temperature.
2. Spread the beans into a 9x13 inch dish. Sprinkle 2 cups shredded cheese over beans. Sprinkle beef on top of cheese. Layer sour cream, guacamole, and salsa evenly over beef. Sprinkle remaining cheese, olives, tomatoes, and green onions over top.
3. Serve immediately, or refrigerate overnight and serve cold. **Yield:** 12 servings.

Per serving: About 300 calories, 13g protein, 11g carbohydrate, 23g fat, 3g fiber, 60mg cholesterol, 287mg sodium

---

Make-Ahead ▶

Prep Time: 15 minutes
Average Rating: ★★★★★
63 Ratings ▲ 40 Reviews
What other cooks have done:
"What a terrific quick and easy recipe. The kids and adults loved it. This will be a regular around our house. I added taco seasoning mix to the beef and added chopped jalapeños in the layers. I served it later that evening rolled up in a soft tortilla."

Hot Mexican Spinach Dip *(pictured on page 78)*

Submitted by: **Linda**
"Take your taste buds on a joyride to old Mexico with this hot, creamy dip. Enjoy the fiesta of flavors of spinach, salsa, and Monterey Jack cheese. This dip's great with tortilla chips."

1	(16 ounce) jar salsa	1	(5 ounce) can evaporated milk
1	(10 ounce) package frozen chopped spinach, thawed and drained	1	(2.25 ounce) can chopped black olives, drained
2	cups shredded Monterey Jack cheese	1	tablespoon red wine vinegar
1	(8 ounce) package cream cheese, diced and softened		Salt and pepper to taste

1. Preheat oven to 400°F (200°C).
2. Mix together salsa, chopped spinach, Monterey Jack cheese, cream cheese, evaporated milk, black olives, red wine vinegar, salt, and pepper. Pour into a greased 7x11 inch baking dish.
3. Bake mixture in the preheated oven for 12 to 15 minutes or until bubbly. **Yield:** 7 cups.

Per 2 tablespoons: About 40 calories, 2g protein, 1g carbohydrate, 3g fat, 0g fiber, 9mg cholesterol, 52mg sodium

Party Food ▶

Prep Time: 15 minutes
Cook Time: 15 minutes
Average Rating: ★★★★★
48 Ratings ▲ 36 Reviews
What other cooks have done:
"I use Cheddar cheese instead of the Jack, and half-and-half instead of the evaporated milk. Be sure to use hot salsa, and let the dip get hot and bubbly in the oven!"

Hot Artichoke-Spinach Dip

Submitted by: **Sherrie D.**
"This is a delicious dip, but it's very rich! Serve warm with tortilla chips. Garnish with extra sour cream and salsa, if you'd like."

1 (14 ounce) can artichoke hearts, drained	⅓ cup heavy cream
⅓ cup grated Romano cheese	½ cup sour cream
¼ cup grated Parmesan cheese	1 cup shredded mozzarella cheese
½ teaspoon minced garlic	
1 (10 ounce) package frozen chopped spinach, thawed and drained	

1. Preheat oven to 350°F (175°C). Lightly grease an 8x8 inch square baking dish.
2. In a blender or food processor, place artichoke hearts, Romano cheese, Parmesan cheese, and garlic. Pulse until chopped, but not ground. Set aside.
3. In a medium bowl, mix together spinach, heavy cream, sour cream, and mozzarella cheese. Stir in artichoke mixture. Spoon into prepared baking dish.
4. Bake in the preheated oven for 20 to 25 minutes or until cheese is melted and bubbly. **Yield:** 4 cups.

Per ¼ cup: About 89 calories, 4g protein, 4g carbohydrate, 6g fat, 1g fiber, 19mg cholesterol, 249mg sodium

◄ Crowd-Pleaser

Prep Time: 20 minutes
Cook Time: 25 minutes
Average Rating: ★★★★★
62 Ratings ▲ 44 Reviews
What other cooks have done:
"I used artichoke bottoms instead of hearts because I like the texture better, and it turned out great. I served it with a baguette that had been sliced, brushed with a touch of olive oil, and broiled. This is a great recipe for parties."

Baked Brie in Puff Pastry

Submitted by: **Nancy**
"This wonderful, light puff pastry is filled with melted Brie cheese. Serve with crackers on the side."

1 (8 ounce) round Brie	¼ cup sliced almonds
½ (17.3 ounce) package frozen puff pastry, thawed	

1. Preheat oven to 350°F (175°C). Lightly grease a 9 inch pie dish.
2. Slice Brie in half, horizontally. Lay the puff pastry in the pie dish. Place half of the Brie (rind-side down) onto the pastry dough. Sprinkle almonds evenly over the top. Place the other half of the Brie (rind-side up) over the almonds. Bundle the pastry dough around the Brie.
3. Bake in the preheated oven for 15 to 20 minutes. Let cool for 5 minutes before serving. **Yield:** 10 servings.

Per serving: About 225 calories, 7g protein, 12g carbohydrate, 17g fat, 1g fiber, 23mg cholesterol, 203mg sodium

◄ Quick & Easy

Prep Time: 5 minutes
Cook Time: 20 minutes
Average Rating: ★★★★☆
27 Ratings ▲ 21 Reviews
What other cooks have done:
"I fill the center with seedless raspberry jam (I put the jam through a sieve) and fresh raspberries, and I brush the pastry with beaten egg before baking. I also put fresh raspberries on top and serve alongside water crackers."

Garden Veggie Pizza Squares

Submitted by: **Meghan Brand**

"This is a must-make appetizer for every event in my house. I received it from a friend years ago and everyone loves it."

1. Preheat oven to 375°F (190°C).

2. Roll out crescent rolls onto a large ungreased baking sheet. Stretch and flatten to form a single 10x13 inch rectangle on the baking sheet. Bake 10 minutes in the preheated oven or until golden brown. Allow to cool.

3. Place cream cheese in a medium bowl. Mix cream cheese with ½ of the Ranch dressing mix. Adjust the amount of dressing mix to taste. Spread the mixture over the cooled crust. Arrange carrot, red bell pepper, green bell pepper, broccoli, and green onions on top. Chill in the refrigerator approximately 1 hour. Cut into bite-size squares to serve.
Yield: 24 servings.

Per serving: About 75 calories, 2g protein, 6g carbohydrate, 5g fat, 1g fiber, 15mg cholesterol, 162mg sodium

Mexican Cream Cheese Roll-ups

Submitted by: **Kathy Jenkins**

"I got this one from my best friend's mom. They are so delicious—nobody believes how easy they are."

1. In a medium bowl, mix together cream cheese, mayonnaise, green olives, black olives, and green onions.

2. Spread cream cheese mixture in a thin layer onto each tortilla. Roll up tortillas. Chill about 1 hour or until the filling is firm.

3. Slice chilled roll-ups into 1 inch pieces. Serve with salsa for dipping. **Yield:** 8 servings.

Per serving: About 433 calories, 9g protein, 43g carbohydrate, 20g fat, 3g fiber, 36mg cholesterol, 834mg sodium

Creamy Dill Cucumber Toasties

Submitted by: **Dianne McKenzie**
"I got this recipe years ago from a friend of a friend. I love it and make it all the time for parties. It looks great on the platter, and it's super easy! Everyone loves it!"

1 (8 ounce) package cream cheese, softened	½ cup mayonnaise
1 (0.7 ounce) package Italian-style salad dressing mix	1 French baguette, cut into ½ inch thick slices
	1 cucumber, sliced
	2 teaspoons dried dill weed

1. In a medium bowl, mix together cream cheese, dressing mix, and mayonnaise.
2. Spread a thin layer of the cream cheese mixture on bread slices and top each with a slice of cucumber. Sprinkle with dill. **Yield:** 12 servings.

Per serving: About 247 calories, 5g protein, 22g carbohydrate, 16g fat, 1g fiber, 25mg cholesterol, 593mg sodium

◄ **Quick & Easy**

Prep Time: 15 minutes
Average Rating: ★★★★★
74 Ratings ▲ 55 Reviews
What other cooks have done:
"I used fresh dill instead of the dried and mixed 1 tablespoon in with the cream cheese mixture in addition to the dill I sprinkled on top."

Double Tomato Bruschetta *(pictured on page 79)*

Submitted by: **Loll**
"A delicious and easy appetizer. The balsamic vinegar gives it a little bite. Dried basil can be substituted, but it's best with fresh."

6 roma (plum) tomatoes, chopped	¼ cup fresh basil, chopped
½ cup sun dried tomatoes, packed in oil, chopped	¼ teaspoon salt
3 cloves garlic, minced	¼ teaspoon ground black pepper
¼ cup olive oil	1 French baguette
2 tablespoons balsamic vinegar	1 cup shredded mozzarella cheese

1. Preheat the broiler.
2. In a large bowl, combine the roma tomatoes, sun dried tomatoes, garlic, olive oil, vinegar, basil, salt, and pepper. Allow the mixture to sit for 10 minutes.
3. Cut the baguette into ½ inch thick slices. On a baking sheet, arrange the baguette slices in a single layer. Broil for 1 to 2 minutes, until slightly brown, and remove from oven.
4. Divide the tomato mixture evenly over the baguette slices. Top with mozzarella cheese.
5. Broil for 5 minutes or until the cheese is melted. **Yield:** 8 servings.

Per serving: About 404 calories, 20g protein, 39g carbohydrate, 19g fat, 3g fiber, 33mg cholesterol, 741mg sodium

◄ **Party Food**

Prep Time: 20 minutes
Cook Time: 7 minutes
Average Rating: ★★★★★
29 Ratings ▲ 22 Reviews
What other cooks have done:
"I've made this recipe many times now. For added appeal for the kids, I add slices of pepperoni. It's better than pizza!"

Easy Sausage Cheese Balls

Submitted by: **Michelle**

"These are great for appetizers or for breakfast. Sausage cheese balls may be frozen before or after baking. Keep extras in the freezer and pull them out when company comes."

1	pound ground sausage	3	cups biscuit mix
4	cups shredded Cheddar cheese		

1. Preheat oven to 400°F (200°C).

2. In a medium bowl, combine the sausage, cheese, and biscuit mix. Shape mixture into walnut-sized balls. Place on a foil-lined baking sheet.

3. Bake in the preheated oven for 12 to 15 minutes. Serve hot. **Yield:** 3 dozen.

Per cheese ball: About 137 calories, 6g protein, 8g carbohydrate, 9g fat, 0g fiber, 22mg cholesterol, 354mg sodium

Bacon and Tomato Cups

Submitted by: **Kelli**

"Little buttermilk biscuit cups are baked with a savory mixture of bacon and tomato resting inside."

8	slices bacon	½	cup mayonnaise
1	tomato, chopped	1	teaspoon dried basil
½	onion, chopped	1	(12 ounce) can refrigerated
1	cup shredded Swiss cheese		buttermilk biscuits

1. Preheat oven to 375°F (190°C). Lightly grease a mini muffin pan.

2. In a skillet over medium heat, cook bacon until evenly browned. Drain on paper towels. Crumble bacon into a medium mixing bowl, and mix with tomato, onion, Swiss cheese, mayonnaise, and basil.

3. Separate biscuits into halves horizontally. Place each half into cups of the prepared mini muffin pan. Fill each biscuit half with the bacon mixture.

4. Bake in the preheated oven for 10 to 12 minutes or until golden brown. **Yield:** 15 servings.

Per serving: About 235 calories, 5g protein, 15g carbohydrate, 17g fat, 1g fiber, 19mg cholesterol, 422mg sodium

Flaky Crescent Mushroom Turnovers

Submitted by: **Paula**

"If you love mushrooms, you'll love this easy, hot appetizer. Sautéed mushrooms are baked with cheese inside a flaky crust. Poppy seeds can be substituted for sesame seeds."

¼	pound fresh mushrooms, coarsely chopped	1	(8 ounce) can refrigerated crescent roll dough
2	tablespoons minced fresh parsley	2½	tablespoons grated Parmesan cheese
2	tablespoons minced onion	2	tablespoons sesame seeds
3	tablespoons butter, divided		

1. Preheat oven to 375°F (190°C).

2. In a medium saucepan over medium heat, slowly cook and stir the mushrooms, parsley, and onion in 2 tablespoons butter until tender. Drain and set aside.

3. Separate the dough into 4 rectangles. Cut rectangles in half, forming 8 squares, and arrange on a large baking sheet. Place 1 tablespoon mushroom mixture on each square. Top each square with 1 teaspoon Parmesan cheese. Fold the squares into triangles.

4. In a small saucepan, melt remaining butter. Brush triangles with butter and sprinkle with sesame seeds.

5. Bake in the preheated oven for 10 to 15 minutes or until golden brown. Serve warm. **Yield:** 8 servings.

Per serving: About 173 calories, 4g protein, 12g carbohydrate, 12g fat, 1g fiber, 13mg cholesterol, 294mg sodium

◄ Crowd-Pleaser

Prep Time: 20 minutes
Cook Time: 15 minutes
Average Rating: ★★★★★
14 Ratings ▲ 10 Reviews
What other cooks have done:
"I made this recipe as a project with my children, and they ate up a double recipe of these goodies. It's easy and fun to make with kids if you cook the mushrooms in advance and let them fill and fold the dough. I used a fork to seal the edges before baking so they wouldn't pull apart, and that really helped the second batch. Kids went crazy over these."

Brown Sugar Smokies

Submitted by: **Tina Clinkenbeard**
"Bacon-wrapped yummies! You can make these little smokies on skewers or secure them with toothpicks."

1 pound bacon	1 teaspoon brown sugar
1 (16 ounce) package little smokie sausages	

1. Preheat oven to 350°F (175°C). Soak wooden skewers in water for 10 to 15 minutes.
2. Cut bacon into thirds and wrap each strip around a little sausage. Thread wrapped sausages onto wooden skewers. Arrange the skewers on a baking sheet and sprinkle with brown sugar.
3. Bake in the preheated oven about 20 minutes or until bacon is crisp and the brown sugar is melted. **Yield:** 8 servings.

Per serving: About 433 calories, 11g protein, 1g carbohydrate, 43g fat, 0g fiber, 65mg cholesterol, 870mg sodium

Cocktail Meatballs

Submitted by: **Jennie**
"These simple meatballs have a delightful combination of tastes and textures. After cooking, I like to keep the meatballs warm in a slow cooker until ready to serve."

1 pound ground beef	⅛ teaspoon ground black pepper
½ cup dried breadcrumbs	
⅓ cup chopped onion	¼ cup shortening
¼ cup milk	1 (12 ounce) bottle chili sauce
1 egg	
1 teaspoon salt	1¼ cups grape jelly
½ teaspoon Worcestershire sauce	

1. In a large bowl, combine ground beef, breadcrumbs, onion, milk, egg, salt, Worcestershire sauce, and ground black pepper. Mix together and shape into meatballs.
2. In a large skillet, heat shortening over medium heat. Add meatballs and cook until browned, about 5 to 7 minutes. Remove from skillet and drain on paper towels.
3. Add chili sauce and jelly to skillet; heat, stirring until jelly is melted. Return meatballs to skillet and stir until coated. Reduce heat to low. Simmer, uncovered, for 30 minutes. **Yield:** 8 servings.

Per serving: About 458 calories, 13g protein, 55g carbohydrate, 23g fat, 1g fiber, 75mg cholesterol, 1077mg sodium

Jalapeño Poppers

Submitted by: **Paula P**

"Sharp Cheddar cheese is the rich, delicious filling for these spicy favorites that are baked rather than deep-fried. You'll want to pop them down one after another!"

1 (8 ounce) package cream cheese, softened	2 eggs, beaten
1 (8 ounce) package shredded sharp Cheddar cheese	½ tablespoon milk
¼ cup mayonnaise	1½ cups crushed corn flake cereal
15 fresh jalapeño peppers, halved lengthwise and seeded	

1. Preheat oven to 350°F (175°C). Lightly grease a medium baking sheet.

2. In a medium bowl, mix together cream cheese, sharp Cheddar cheese, and mayonnaise. Stuff jalapeño halves with the mixture.

3. Whisk together eggs and milk in a small bowl. Place crushed corn flake cereal in a separate small bowl.

4. Dip each stuffed jalapeño half into the egg and milk mixture, then roll in corn flake cereal to coat.

5. Arrange in a single layer on the prepared baking sheet. Bake in the preheated oven 30 minutes or until filling is bubbly and lightly browned. **Yield:** 15 servings.

Per serving: About 176 calories, 7g protein, 10g carbohydrate, 12g fat, 0g fiber, 275mg sodium

---

◀ Hot & Spicy

Prep Time: 30 minutes
Cook Time: 30 minutes
Average Rating: ★★★★★
33 Ratings ▲ 27 Reviews

What other cooks have done:
"The peppers were very hot, so be sure to wash and seed them with gloves on. But after baking the peppers, they were much milder. They were great the day after as well—very cheesy and yummy."

Bacon and Cheddar Stuffed Mushrooms

Submitted by: **Krista Hughes**

"Cremini mushrooms (also known as portobellini mushrooms) are stuffed with Cheddar cheese and bacon for an impressive accompaniment with any meal."

3	slices bacon	1	tablespoon chopped onion
8	cremini mushrooms	¾	cup shredded Cheddar
1	tablespoon butter		cheese, divided

1. Place bacon in a large, deep skillet. Cook over medium-high heat until evenly browned. Drain, dice, and set aside.
2. Preheat oven to 400°F (200°C).
3. Remove mushroom stems, setting aside caps. Chop the stems.
4. Melt the butter in a large saucepan over medium heat. Add mushroom stems and onion; slowly cook, stirring until the onion is soft. Remove from heat.
5. In a medium bowl, stir together the mushroom stem mixture, bacon, and ½ cup Cheddar cheese. Mix well and scoop the mixture into the mushroom caps.
6. Bake in the preheated oven 15 minutes or until the cheese has melted. Remove the mushrooms from the oven and sprinkle with the remaining cheese. **Yield:** 8 servings.

Per mushroom: About 120 calories, 4g protein, 1g carbohydrate, 11g fat, 0g fiber, 22mg cholesterol, 164mg sodium

Restaurant-Style Potato Skins

Submitted by: **Misty**

"A wonderful appetizer for you and your family to enjoy."

6	potatoes	⅛	cup bacon bits
1	cup vegetable oil	1	(16 ounce) package sour
1	(8 ounce) package shredded		cream
	Cheddar cheese		

1. Preheat oven to 375°F (190°C). Grease a 9x13 inch baking pan.
2. Pierce potatoes with a fork. Microwave the potatoes on High 10 to 12 minutes or until soft. Cut the potatoes in half vertically. Scoop out the inside of the potatoes until ¼ inch of the potato shell remains. Reserve removed potato for another use.
3. Heat oil to 365°F (180°C) in a deep fryer or a deep saucepan. Place potato in hot oil; fry for 5 minutes. Drain shells on paper towels.
4. Fill the potato shells with cheese and bacon bits. Arrange on the prepared baking pan.
5. Bake in the preheated oven for 7 minutes or until the cheese is melted. Serve hot with sour cream. **Yield:** 6 servings.

Per serving: About 740 calories, 15g protein, 26g carbohydrate, 65g fat, 2g fiber, 75mg cholesterol, 357mg sodium

Bread Pot Fondue

Submitted by: **Laurie**

"This creamy, cheesy, spicy appetizer is a real treat for your palate. It's easy to put together and well worth the time in the oven. Bake the scooped-out pieces of bread and use them for dipping."

1 (1 pound) loaf round bread	½ cup chopped green onions
1 (8 ounce) package shredded Cheddar cheese	1 (4.5 ounce) can chopped green chiles
2 (3 ounce) packages cream cheese	1 teaspoon Worcestershire sauce
1½ cups sour cream	2 tablespoons vegetable oil
1 cup cooked ham, diced	1 tablespoon butter, melted

1. Preheat oven to 350°F (175°C).

2. Cut a hole in the top of the bread and hollow out the loaf, leaving a bowl. Reserve removed bread.

3. In a medium bowl, mix together the Cheddar cheese, cream cheese, sour cream, ham, green onions, green chiles, and Worcestershire sauce. Spoon the mixture into the bread bowl. Replace the top of the bread. Wrap tightly with foil and place on a medium baking sheet.

4. Bake in the preheated oven 60 to 70 minutes.

5. Tear the reserved bread into bite-sized pieces. In a small bowl, mix the bread, oil, and butter. Place on a medium baking sheet.

6. Bake in the preheated oven 10 to 15 minutes or until browned, turning occasionally. **Yield:** 40 servings.

Per serving: About 90 calories, 3g protein, 4g carbohydrate, 7g fat, 0g fiber, 18mg cholesterol, 123mg sodium

◀ Crowd-Pleaser

Prep Time: 20 minutes
Cook Time: 1 hour 25 minutes
Average Rating: ★★★★★
12 Ratings ▲ 8 Reviews
What other cooks have done:
"I have made this many times, and it's the hit of the party. Leave out the chiles to make it kid-friendly . . . just as good!"

Candied Kielbasa

Submitted by: **Nancy**

"Kielbasa, or Polish sausage, is a spicy sausage usually made with pork (though beef is sometimes added). It comes in chunky links and is sold pre-cooked. I haven't met anyone yet who didn't like this dish."

1 cup packed brown sugar	2 pounds kielbasa sausage, sliced thinly
½ cup ketchup	
¼ cup prepared horseradish	

1. In a slow cooker, combine the sugar, ketchup, and horseradish. Add the sausage and mix well. Cook on High until sauce starts to boil. Reduce heat to Low and cook until sauce thickens, about 45 minutes to 1 hour. **Yield:** 8 servings.

Per serving: About 474 calories, 15g protein, 34g carbohydrate, 31g fat, 0g fiber, 76mg cholesterol, 1433mg sodium

◀ Slow-Cooker Creation

Prep Time: 5 minutes
Cook Time: 1 hour
Average Rating: ★★★★★
24 Ratings ▲ 21 Reviews
What other cooks have done:
"I did this on the stove, cooking slowly for about an hour and a half, and it was perfect."

Chicken Satay *(pictured on page 79)*

Submitted by: **Keira**

"Why go out for Thai food when you can make it at home? These delicious Thai-style chicken satay are made of chicken marinated in a peanutty sauce and then grilled. They are great served with Hot Peanut Sauce (recipe follows)."

(pictured on page 79)

2	tablespoons creamy peanut butter		2	cloves garlic, chopped
½	cup soy sauce		1	teaspoon hot sauce
½	cup lime or lemon juice		6	skinless, boneless chicken
1	tablespoon brown sugar			breast halves, cut into
2	tablespoons curry powder			¼ inch wide strips

1. In a bowl, combine peanut butter, soy sauce, lime juice, brown sugar, curry powder, garlic, and hot sauce. Place the chicken strips in the marinade and refrigerate at least 2 hours or overnight.
2. Preheat a grill to high heat.
3. Remove chicken from marinade, discarding marinade. Thread the chicken onto metal skewers and grill for 5 minutes per side. **Yield:** 4 servings.

Per serving: About 489 calories, 87g protein, 12g carbohydrate, 9g fat, 2g fiber, 205mg cholesterol, 2015mg sodium

Hot Peanut Sauce *(pictured on page 79)*

Submitted by: **Dee Lowman**

"You can also serve this over rice noodles because they're sweet and offer a good foil for the hot sauce. Adjust the hotness of this dish according to your taste."

¼	cup peanut butter		1½	tablespoons brown sugar
¼	cup hot water		¼	teaspoon cayenne pepper
2	tablespoons soy sauce		1½	teaspoons lemon juice

1. In a small bowl, combine peanut butter and water; mix until a smooth paste forms. Stir in soy sauce, brown sugar, cayenne, and lemon juice. Mix until well combined and smooth. **Yield:** 6 servings.

Per serving: About 81 calories, 3g protein, 6g carbohydrate, 6g fat, 1g fiber, 0mg cholesterol, 343mg sodium

---

From the Grill ▶

Prep Time: 2 hours 10 minutes
Cook Time: 20 minutes
Average Rating: ★★★★☆
44 Ratings ▲ 31 Reviews
What other cooks have done:
"I put the chicken on skewers, along with pieces of onion, green and red peppers, tomatoes, and portobello mushrooms."

Quick & Easy ▶

Prep Time: 10 minutes
Average Rating: ★★★★★
5 Ratings ▲ 4 Reviews
What other cooks have done:
"Quick and easy to make with ingredients I had on hand. I added a bit more hot sauce for a little more zing."

Chicken Quesadillas

Submitted by: **Heather**

"The zesty chicken and cooked peppers are a succulent delight when mixed with the melted cheeses. Cut into wedges and serve with sour cream and salsa."

1 pound skinless, boneless chicken breast halves
1 (1.1 oz) package dry fajita seasoning mix
1 tablespoon vegetable oil
2 green bell peppers, chopped
2 red bell peppers, chopped
1 onion, chopped
10 (10 inch) flour tortillas
1 (8 ounce) package shredded Cheddar cheese
Bacon bits
1 (8 ounce) package shredded Monterey Jack cheese

1. Preheat the broiler.
2. Cut the chicken into small cubes; toss with the fajita seasoning mix. Broil 5 minutes or until the chicken is no longer pink on the inside.
3. Preheat oven to 350°F (175°C).
4. Heat the oil in a large saucepan over medium heat. Mix in the seasoned chicken, green bell peppers, red bell peppers, and onion. Slowly cook and stir 10 minutes or until the vegetables are tender.
5. Place tortillas on greased baking sheets. Layer half of each tortilla with Cheddar cheese, chicken mixture, and desired amount of bacon bits. Top with Monterey Jack cheese. Fold the tortillas.
6. Bake in the preheated oven for 10 minutes or until the cheese melts. **Yield:** 10 quesadillas.

Per serving: About 248 calories, 14g protein, 23g carbohydrate, 11g fat, 2g fiber, 35mg cholesterol, 468mg sodium

◄ Family Favorite

Prep Time: 20 minutes
Cook Time: 25 minutes
Average Rating: ★★★★★
36 Ratings ▲ 18 Reviews
What other cooks have done:
"I made this recipe for a Cinco de Mayo celebration that I hosted. Everyone loved them. I made a couple of extras, heated them the next day, and they were still great. My sons thought they were yummy with sour cream and salsa."

Mahogany Chicken Wings

Submitted by: **Christinet**

"These sweet, succulent wings look as delicious as they taste!"

3 pounds chicken wings, split and tips discarded
½ cup soy sauce
½ cup honey
¼ cup molasses
2 tablespoons chili sauce
1 teaspoon ground ginger
2 cloves garlic, finely chopped

1. Place chicken in a shallow dish. In a medium bowl, mix soy sauce, honey, molasses, chili sauce, ground ginger, and garlic. Pour mixture over the chicken. Cover and refrigerate about 1 hour, turning occasionally.
2. Preheat oven to 375°F (190°C).
3. In a large baking dish, arrange chicken in a single layer. Bake in the preheated oven for about 50 minutes, brushing with remaining soy sauce mixture often and turning once until meat is no longer pink and juices run clear. **Yield:** 8 servings.

Per serving: About 771 calories, 52g protein, 42g carbohydrate, 44g fat, 0g fiber, 210mg cholesterol, 1595mg sodium

◄ Crowd-Pleaser

Prep Time: 15 minutes
Cook Time: 50 minutes
Average Rating: ★★★★★
18 Ratings ▲ 18 Reviews
What other cooks have done:
"If you want them to be a little bit spicier, I suggest increasing the chili sauce. I cooked these on a baking sheet, and they came out good and crispy."

Orange Cream Milk Punch

Submitted by: **Bea**
"This quick and easy punch is excellent for kids' parties."

1   quart vanilla ice cream
2   pints orange sherbet
1   quart cold milk
1   (16 ounce) can lemon–lime flavored carbonated beverage

1. Place the ice cream and sherbet in a punch bowl. Pour in the milk and lemon–lime soda. Stir gently and serve immediately. **Yield:** 24 servings.

Per serving: About 117 calories, 3g protein, 19g carbohydrate, 4g fat, 0g fiber, 15mg cholesterol, 55mg sodium

Very Fruity Rum Punch

Submitted by: **Jeff**
"You'll love this rum punch I invented with some extra kick. It has been a hit at more than one party."

1   (6 ounce) can frozen orange juice concentrate
1   (6 ounce) can frozen pineapple juice concentrate
1½ cups rum
⅓   cup banana liqueur
    Dash grenadine syrup
1   orange, sliced into rounds
1   lime, sliced into rounds
1   lemon, sliced into rounds

1. In a large punch bowl, prepare the orange and pineapple juices according to package directions. Stir in the rum, banana liqueur, and grenadine. Float slices of orange, lime, and lemon on top. **Yield:** 24 servings.

Per serving: About 64 calories, 0g protein, 7g carbohydrate, 0g fat, 0g fiber, 0mg cholesterol, 1mg sodium

Incredible Punch

Submitted by: **Mary Lynn**

"Absolutely the best punch! A hit at showers, teas, and kids' birthday parties. It's made with cran-raspberry juice, ginger ale, and piña colada mixer and has a beautiful pink color."

2 (46 ounce) bottles cranberry-raspberry juice	2 liters raspberry ginger ale
1 (32 ounce) bottle piña colada mix	

1. In a large plastic container, combine cranberry-raspberry juice with the piña colada mix. Freeze overnight.

2. Remove from freezer 30 minutes prior to serving. To serve, place frozen slush in a punch bowl and slowly add raspberry ginger ale. **Yield:** 50 servings.

Per serving: About 44 calories, 0g protein, 10g carbohydrate, 0g fat, 0g fiber, 0mg cholesterol, 7mg sodium

◄ Make-Ahead

Prep Time: 10 minutes
Average Rating: ★★★★★
61 Ratings ▲ 51 Reviews
What other cooks have done:
"I made this for a wedding reception, and it was the first thing gone. I used one-third of a two-liter bottle of raspberry soda with regular ginger ale for every batch, and it was wonderful! I broke it up with a knife before adding the ginger ale, and it was the right slushy texture."

Aileen's Punch *(pictured on page 80)*

Submitted by: **Lisa Rosenkrans**

"This punch is very refreshing and so easy to put together. I recommend making an ice ring out of extra pineapple juice or apricot nectar."

1 (46 ounce) can pineapple juice, chilled	2 liters lemon-lime flavored carbonated beverage, chilled
1 (46 ounce) can apricot nectar, chilled	
1 (6 ounce) can frozen limeade concentrate, thawed and undiluted	

1. In a punch bowl, combine pineapple juice, apricot nectar, and limeade. Pour in the lemon-lime soda. **Yield:** 30 servings.

Per serving: About 90 calories, 0g protein, 23g carbohydrate, 0g fat, 0g fiber, 0mg cholesterol, 9mg sodium

◄ Family Favorite

Prep Time: 5 minutes
Average Rating: ★★★★★
16 Ratings ▲ 13 Reviews
What other cooks have done:
"I made this for a friend's baby shower, and it was delicious. I made an ice ring with pineapple rings and edible flowers to go with it, and it was beautiful to look at, too!"

Warm and Spicy Autumn Punch

Submitted by: **Michele O'Sullivan**
"The aroma of this punch tells you that fall is in the air. Make a batch and your home will have a fragrance that will get everyone's attention."

2	oranges	¼	teaspoon ground nutmeg
8	whole cloves	¼	cup honey
6	cups apple juice	3	tablespoons lemon juice
1	cinnamon stick	2¼	cups pineapple juice

1. Preheat oven to 350°F (175°C). Stud the oranges with cloves and bake in the preheated oven for 30 minutes. Remove from oven.
2. In a large saucepan, combine the apple juice and cinnamon stick; bring to a boil. Reduce heat and simmer 5 minutes. Remove from heat and stir in the nutmeg, honey, lemon juice, and pineapple juice.
3. Serve hot in a punch bowl with the 2 clove-studded, baked oranges floating on top. **Yield:** 16 servings.

Per serving: About 93 calories, 0g protein, 23g carbohydrate, 0g fat, 1g fiber, 0mg cholesterol, 11mg sodium

Creamy Hot Cocoa

Submitted by: **Jeanie Bean**
"It's old-fashioned, it's comforting, it makes the kitchen smell wonderful, and it's good for the soul."

⅓	cup unsweetened cocoa powder	⅓	cup boiling water
¾	cup white sugar	3½	cups milk
	Pinch salt	¾	teaspoon vanilla extract
		½	cup half-and-half

1. Combine the cocoa, sugar, and pinch of salt in a saucepan. Blend in the boiling water. Bring this mixture to an easy boil while you stir. Simmer and stir for about 2 minutes. Watch that it doesn't scorch.
2. Stir in 3½ cups of milk and heat until very hot, but do not boil. Remove from heat and add vanilla. Divide among 4 mugs. Add the half-and-half to the mugs of cocoa to cool it to drinking temperature. **Yield:** 4 servings.

Per serving: About 309 calories, 9g protein, 53g carbohydrate, 9g fat, 2g fiber, 27mg cholesterol, 218mg sodium

Mocha au Lait Mix

Submitted by: **Amy Beth**
"This Mocha au Lait Mix makes a great holiday gift when presented in a decorative holiday container or mug. Just make sure you remember to include the directions on a gift tag."

1½ cups dry milk powder	⅔ cup miniature chocolate chips
½ cup instant coffee granules	
⅓ cup brown sugar	

1. In a medium bowl, combine milk powder, instant coffee, brown sugar, and mini chocolate chips. Mix well and store in an airtight container.
2. Instructions per serving: In a blender, combine ⅔ cup boiling water with ¼ cup mix. Blend until frothy and serve in a mug. **Yield:** 12 servings.

Per serving: About 127 calories, 6g protein, 21g carbohydrate, 3g fat, 1g fiber, 3mg cholesterol, 84mg sodium

◄ Holiday Gift Giving

Prep Time: 10 minutes
Average Rating: ★★★★★
6 Ratings ▲ 4 Reviews
What other cooks have done:
"My whole family loved this. I didn't have mini chocolate chips, so I used candy-coated chocolate pieces instead. I think it would be great either way."

Hot Buttered Rum Batter

Submitted by: **Sheri Marr**
"For absolutely delicious and buttery hot buttered rums, this is the batter to use!"

2 cups butter	1 quart vanilla ice cream
1 (16 ounce) package brown sugar	1 teaspoon ground nutmeg
1 (16 ounce) package confectioners' sugar	1 tablespoon ground cinnamon
	Rum

1. Melt butter in large pot over medium heat. Blend in brown sugar and confectioners' sugar. Remove from heat and whisk in the ice cream, 1 teaspoon nutmeg, and cinnamon.
2. Pour mixture into a sealable plastic container and freeze up to 3 months.
3. To mix one drink: In a coffee mug, add 1 tablespoon Hot Buttered Rum Batter and 1 ounce rum; fill cup with boiling water. Stir and sprinkle drink with dash of nutmeg. **Yield:** 100 servings.

Per serving: About 78 calories, 0g protein, 10g carbohydrate, 4g fat, 0g fiber, 12mg cholesterol, 44mg sodium

◄ Make-Ahead

Prep Time: 10 minutes
Cook Time: 10 minutes
Average Rating: ★★★★★
11 Ratings ▲ 8 Reviews
What other cooks have done:
"I like using more of the batter per cup. I used equal amounts of rum and batter, then filled the cup with the boiling water."

Gluehwein

Submitted by: **Else**

"Gluehwein is a German/Austrian winter-holiday drink that most tourists know as an after-ski drink. After you come in out of the snow, it's supposed to make you glow with warmth again."

¾	cup water	10	whole cloves
¾	cup white sugar	1	(750 milliliter) bottle red
1	cinnamon stick		wine
1	orange		

1. In a saucepan, combine the water, sugar, and cinnamon. Bring to a boil, then reduce heat and let simmer about 12 minutes.
2. Cut the orange in half and squeeze the juice into the simmering water. Push the cloves into the outside of the orange peel and place into the simmering water. Continue simmering for 30 minutes, until thick and syrupy.
3. Pour in the wine and heat until steaming, but not simmering. Remove the clove-studded orange halves. Serve wine warm in glasses that have been preheated in warm water (cold glasses will break).
Yield: 6 servings.

Per serving: About 202 calories, 1g protein, 31g carbohydrate, 1g fat, 1g fiber, 0mg cholesterol, 15mg sodium

B and L's Strawberry Smoothie

Submitted by: **Brittany and Lisa**

"You'll love this icy-cold strawberry smoothie."

8	strawberries, hulled	3	tablespoons white sugar
½	cup skim milk	2	teaspoons vanilla extract
½	cup plain yogurt	6	cubes ice, crushed

1. In a blender, combine strawberries, milk, yogurt, sugar, and vanilla. Toss in the ice. Blend until smooth and creamy. Pour into glasses and serve. **Yield:** 2 servings.

Per serving: About 160 calories, 6g protein, 30g carbohydrate, 1g fat, 1g fiber, 5mg cholesterol, 77mg sodium

Classic Spanish Sangría

Submitted by: **Lisa**

"This is an authentic version of the popular wine drink. You can add any fruit that you want, but I find that apples and pears absorb too much rum. I like to use red Burgundy wine and white rum, but spiced rum is nice, too."

1	lemon	1	(750 milliliter) bottle dry red wine
1	lime	1	cup orange juice
1	orange	½	cup white sugar
1½	cups rum		

1. Chill the fruit, rum, wine, and orange juice. Slice the lemon, lime, and orange into thin rounds and place in a large glass pitcher. Pour in the rum and sugar. Chill in refrigerator for 2 hours to develop the flavors.

2. When ready to serve, crush the fruit lightly with a wooden spoon and stir in the wine and orange juice. Adjust sweetness to taste. **Yield:** 6 servings.

Per serving: About 322 calories, 1g protein, 26g carbohydrate, 0g fat, 1g fiber, 0mg cholesterol, 12mg sodium

◄ Make-Ahead

Prep Time: 10 minutes
Average Rating: ★★★★★
21 Ratings ▲ 16 Reviews
What other cooks have done:
"I doubled the recipe for a party of 12, put it in a punch bowl, and it made a great presentation. It was delicious and looked good. Just make sure you stir it whenever you're walking by after mixing all the ingredients to dissolve all the sugar."

Original Irish Cream

Submitted by: **Mom**

"Irish whiskey is mixed with cream and sugar with hints of coffee, chocolate, vanilla, and almond. You can keep it for one month, if refrigerated."

1	cup heavy cream	2	tablespoons chocolate syrup
1	(14 ounce) can sweetened condensed milk	1	teaspoon vanilla extract
1⅔	cups Irish whiskey	1	teaspoon almond extract
1	teaspoon instant coffee granules		

1. In a blender, combine cream, sweetened condensed milk, Irish whiskey, instant coffee, and chocolate syrup. Add vanilla and almond extracts.

2. Blend on high for 20 to 30 seconds. Store in a tightly sealed container and refrigerate. Shake well before serving. Will keep up to one month if refrigerated. **Yield:** 12 servings.

Per serving: About 299 calories, 4g protein, 27g carbohydrate, 11g fat, 0g fiber, 42mg cholesterol, 66mg sodium

◄ Crowd-Pleaser

Prep Time: 15 minutes
Average Rating: ★★★★★
27 Ratings ▲ 25 Reviews
What other cooks have done:
"I've made this recipe several times for Christmas gifts, and it's always a huge hit. Since I'm not crazy about coffee, I left out the instant coffee and doubled the chocolate syrup. It makes a fabulous after-dinner drink and a great addition to hot chocolate!"

Cosmopolitan *(pictured on page 79)*

Submitted by: **Goldie**
"This is a civil cocktail, mon cherie!"

3   tablespoons vodka
1   tablespoon Cointreau
1   teaspoon fresh lime juice

3   tablespoons cranberry juice
    Lime twist for garnish

1. Pour vodka, Cointreau, lime juice, and cranberry juice into a cocktail mixer with lots of ice. Shake vigorously for several seconds and strain into a cocktail glass. Garnish with a lime twist. **Yield:** 1 serving.

Per serving: About 185 calories, 0g protein, 13g carbohydrate, 0g fat, 0g fiber, 0mg cholesterol, 7mg sodium

Margaritas *(pictured on page 78)*

Submitted by: **Katherine**
"I have been asked by everyone, 'How do you make your margaritas?' Everyone says I make the best. I like them—maybe you will, too."

1   (6 ounce) can frozen
    limeade concentrate,
    thawed and undiluted

¾   cup tequila
¼   cup triple sec

1. Fill blender with crushed ice. Pour in limeade concentrate, tequila, and triple sec. Blend until smooth. Pour into glasses and serve. **Yield:** 4 servings.

Per serving: About 259 calories, 0g protein, 33g carbohydrate, 0g fat, 0g fiber, 0mg cholesterol, 1mg sodium

Chocolate Martini à la Laren

Submitted by: **TMoore**
"Chocolate heaven! I used to work at a fine dining restaurant. The bartender concocted this recipe and I've been hooked ever since!"

½   cup chocolate liqueur
⅓   cup vodka

1   (1 ounce) square semisweet
    chocolate, grated

1. In a cocktail mixer full of ice, combine chocolate liqueur and vodka. Shake vigorously and strain into 2 chilled martini glasses. Garnish with grated chocolate. **Yield:** 2 servings.

Per serving: About 302 calories, 1g protein, 9g carbohydrate, 4g fat, 2g fiber, 0mg cholesterol, 1mg sodium

---

Quick & Easy ▶

Prep Time: 3 minutes
Average Rating: ★★★★★
8 Ratings ▲ 5 Reviews
What other cooks have done:
"I ran out of cranberry juice, but had raspberry-cranberry juice on hand. It made a nice variation."

Crowd-Pleaser ▶

Prep Time: 5 minutes
Average Rating: ★★★★★
8 Ratings ▲ 7 Reviews
What other cooks have done:
"Try freezing 2 to 3 cups watermelon that's been seeded and cut into chunks. Add frozen watermelon chunks with the ice when making these margaritas. You can also puree the seeded watermelon and freeze in ice cube trays for later use."

Out-of-the-Ordinary ▶

Prep Time: 5 minutes
Average Rating: ★★★★★
4 Ratings ▲ 1 Review
What other cooks think:
"Sinfully delicious!"

Breads

Nothing starts the weekend better than a stack of homemade pancakes or warm blueberry muffins. And how about homemade cornbread to serve with dinner tonight? Quick breads are just a few steps away with our easy recipes. And who says yeast breads are only for the experienced baker? We've got just the recipe for you—whatever the occasion—for homemade breads that will impress your family and friends every time.

Cheddar Bay Biscuits

Submitted by: **Cookie**

"These biscuits are cheesy and rich, and fairly close to the ones a famous seafood restaurant chain serves."

4	cups biscuit mix	1	teaspoon garlic powder
3	ounces Cheddar cheese, shredded	¼	teaspoon salt
1⅓	cups water	⅛	teaspoon onion powder
½	cup melted butter	⅛	teaspoon dried parsley

1. Preheat oven to 375°F (190°C). Lightly grease a baking sheet or line with parchment paper.

2. In a bowl, combine the biscuit mix, cheese, and water. Mix just until dough is firm. Using a small scoop, drop dough onto prepared pan.

3. Bake in the preheated oven for 10 to 12 minutes or until golden brown.

4. Combine the melted butter, garlic powder, salt, onion powder, and parsley. Brush over baked biscuits immediately upon removing from oven. **Yield:** 20 biscuits.

Per biscuit: About 139 calories, 3g protein, 18g carbohydrate, 6g fat, 0g fiber, 17mg cholesterol, 565mg sodium

Restaurant Fare ▶

Prep Time: 10 minutes

Cook Time: 12 minutes

Average Rating: ★★★★★

113 Ratings ▲ 83 Reviews

What other cooks have done:

"Super-easy and the family just raved! I did modify this recipe by adding 1 teaspoon each of garlic powder and parsley and ½ teaspoon onion powder to the biscuit mixture. I also returned the biscuits to the oven for about 2 minutes after brushing with the butter mixture, which gave them a nice golden color."

J.P.'s Big Daddy Biscuits *(pictured on page 113)*

Submitted by: **John Pickett**

"Serve these gems with butter, preserves, honey, gravy, or as dinner rolls. The dough can also be prepared several hours or up to a day ahead. If so, turn dough out onto aluminum foil that has been either floured or lightly greased. Roll up foil and refrigerate. Don't be surprised if your biscuits rise even higher because the baking powder has had more time to act in the dough."

2	cups all-purpose flour	1	tablespoon white sugar
1	tablespoon baking powder	⅓	cup shortening
1	teaspoon salt	1	cup milk

1. Preheat oven to 425°F (220°C).

2. In a large bowl, whisk together the flour, baking powder, salt, and sugar. Cut in the shortening until the mixture resembles coarse crumbs. Gradually stir in milk until dough pulls away from the side of the bowl.

3. Turn out onto a floured surface and knead 15 to 20 times. Pat or roll dough out to 1 inch thickness. Cut biscuits with a large cutter or juice glass dipped in flour. Repeat until all dough is used. Brush off the excess flour, and place biscuits onto an ungreased baking sheet.

4. Bake in the preheated oven for 12 to 15 minutes or until edges begin to brown. **Yield:** 6 biscuits.

Per biscuit: About 282 calories, 6g protein, 36g carbohydrate, 13g fat, 1g fiber, 3mg cholesterol, 636mg sodium

Family Favorite ▶

Prep Time: 30 minutes

Cook Time: 15 minutes

Average Rating: ★★★★★

167 Ratings ▲ 134 Reviews

What other cooks have done:

"When I made my second batch of these I didn't knead them at all. I just mixed the dough until it formed a ball and rolled it out and cut it. They turned out better this way—light and fluffy, which is what I wanted."

Grandma Johnson's Scones

Submitted by: **Rob**
"Tried and tested through three generations of kids. Add one cup of raisins, if desired, and remember—too much handling will kill them."

1	cup sour cream	¼	teaspoon cream of tartar
1	teaspoon baking soda	1	teaspoon salt
4	cups all-purpose flour	1	cup butter, chilled
1	cup white sugar	1	egg
2	teaspoons baking powder		

1. Preheat oven to 350°F (175°C). Lightly grease a baking sheet. In a small bowl, stir together sour cream and baking soda and set aside.
2. In a large bowl, combine flour, sugar, baking powder, cream of tartar, and salt. Cut in butter with a knife or pastry blender until crumbly. Combine egg with sour cream mixture; stir into flour mixture just until moistened. Turn dough out onto a lightly floured surface and knead briefly. Roll dough out into a ¾ inch thick round. Cut into 12 wedge shaped pieces and place pieces on prepared baking sheet.
3. Bake in the preheated oven for 12 to 15 minutes or until golden brown. **Yield:** 12 scones.

Per scone: About 400 calories, 6g protein, 50g carbohydrate, 20g fat, 1g fiber, 68mg cholesterol, 513mg sodium

◄ Quick & Easy

Prep Time: 15 minutes
Cook Time: 15 minutes
Average Rating: ★★★★
38 Ratings ▲ 33 Reviews
What other cooks have done:
"I added an extra ½ cup sugar, 1 teaspoon ground cinnamon, ½ teaspoon ground nutmeg, and 1 teaspoon vanilla. I brushed the top with milk and sprinkled with cinnamon, sugar, and sliced almonds. I was looking for an outstanding scone recipe, and I found it."

Apple Scones

Submitted by: **Carol**
"These scones have a terrific aroma and taste. They are perfect for tea."

2	cups all-purpose flour	1	apple, peeled, cored, and shredded
¼	cup white sugar		
2	teaspoons baking powder	½	cup milk
½	teaspoon baking soda	2	tablespoons milk
½	teaspoon salt	2	tablespoons white sugar
¼	cup butter, chilled	½	teaspoon ground cinnamon

1. Preheat oven to 425°F (220°C). Lightly grease a baking sheet. Measure flour, sugar, baking powder, baking soda, and salt into a large bowl. Cut in butter with a knife or pastry blender until crumbly. Add shredded apple and ½ cup milk. Stir to form a soft dough.
2. Turn dough out onto a lightly floured surface. Knead gently 8 to 10 times. Pat into 2 (6 inch) circles. Place on prepared baking sheet. Brush tops with 2 tablespoons milk and sprinkle with sugar and cinnamon. Score each into 6 pie-shaped wedges.
3. Bake in the preheated oven for 15 minutes or until browned and risen. Serve warm with butter. **Yield:** 12 scones.

Per scone: About 148 calories, 3g protein, 25g carbohydrate, 4g fat, 1g fiber, 11mg cholesterol, 277mg sodium

◄ Kid-Friendly

Prep Time: 15 minutes
Cook Time: 15 minutes
Average Rating: ★★★★
63 Ratings ▲ 45 Reviews
What other cooks have done:
"These scones are wonderful. I added cinnamon to the dough, and instead of apples, I used peaches. They turned out just delicious."

Pumpkin-Apple Streusel Muffins *(pictured on page 116)*

Submitted by: **Jan**

"What better way to celebrate fall than with delicious muffins that combine the wonderful texture of apples with the warm taste of pumpkin. A simple streusel topping gives them a little something extra."

Holiday Fare ▶

Prep Time: 15 minutes

Cook Time: 25 minutes

Average Rating: ★★★★★

39 Ratings ▲ 32 Reviews

What other cooks have done:

"Instead of muffins, I spooned the batter into a 10 inch greased tube pan, and sprinkled the streusel over it. I baked it at 350° for just under an hour (58 minutes). What a fabulous coffee cake! Moist, deep flavor, and with melt-in-your-mouth texture."

2½	cups all-purpose flour	½	cup vegetable oil
2	cups white sugar	2	cups peeled, cored, and chopped apple
1	tablespoon pumpkin pie spice	2	tablespoons all-purpose flour
1	teaspoon baking soda	¼	cup white sugar
½	teaspoon salt	½	teaspoon ground cinnamon
2	eggs, lightly beaten	4	teaspoons butter
1	cup canned pumpkin		

1. Preheat oven to 350°F (175°C). Lightly grease a muffin pan or line with 24 muffin papers.

2. In a large bowl, sift together 2½ cups flour, 2 cups sugar, pumpkin pie spice, baking soda, and salt. In a separate bowl, mix together eggs, pumpkin, and oil. Add pumpkin mixture to flour mixture, stirring just to moisten. Fold in apples. Spoon the batter into prepared muffin cups.

3. In a small bowl, mix together 2 tablespoons flour, ¼ cup sugar, and cinnamon. Cut in butter until mixture resembles coarse crumbs. Sprinkle topping evenly over muffin batter.

4. Bake in the preheated oven for 20 to 25 minutes or until a toothpick inserted into a muffin comes out clean. **Yield:** 24 muffins.

Per muffin: About 248 calories, 3g protein, 43g carbohydrate, 8g fat, 1g fiber, 26mg cholesterol, 184mg sodium

Muffin Magic ▼

Follow our pointers to get the perfect muffin every time:
- For perfectly rounded muffins, a lumpy batter is desirable. Stir gently just until dry ingredients are moistened. Don't overstir the batter or your muffins will be peaked and will have a coarse, tough texture.
- Muffins that contain more sugar require an electric mixer and have a cake-like texture. Don't use a mixer unless the recipe specifies using one.
- Remove muffins from pans as soon as they're baked to keep condensation from forming and making them soggy on the bottom.

Banana Crumb Muffins

Submitted by: **Lisa Kreft**

"The crumb topping makes these banana muffins stand apart from the ordinary."

1½	cups all-purpose flour	1	egg, lightly beaten
1	teaspoon baking soda	⅓	cup butter, melted
1	teaspoon baking powder	⅓	cup packed brown sugar
½	teaspoon salt	2	tablespoons all-purpose flour
3	bananas, mashed	⅛	teaspoon ground cinnamon
¾	cup white sugar	1	tablespoon butter

1. Preheat oven to 375°F (190°C). Lightly grease a muffin pan or line with 10 muffin papers.

2. In a large bowl, mix together 1½ cups flour, baking soda, baking powder, and salt. In another bowl, beat together bananas, white sugar, egg, and melted butter. Stir the banana mixture into the flour mixture just until moistened. Spoon batter into prepared muffin cups.

3. In a bowl, combine brown sugar, 2 tablespoons flour, and cinnamon. Cut in butter until mixture resembles coarse crumbs. Sprinkle over muffins.

4. Bake in the preheated oven for 18 to 20 minutes or until a toothpick inserted into a muffin comes out clean. **Yield:** 10 muffins.

Per muffin: About 261 calories, 3g protein, 46g carbohydrate, 8g fat, 1g fiber, 41mg cholesterol, 375mg sodium

Chocolate Chocolate Chip Nut Muffins

Submitted by: **Marais Leon**

"These are the best chocolate muffins you will ever have!"

2	cups all-purpose flour	1	egg
½	cup unsweetened cocoa powder	2	tablespoons vegetable oil
		1	teaspoon vanilla extract
1½	cups white sugar	1	cup semisweet chocolate chips
2	teaspoons baking powder		
½	teaspoon baking soda	¾	cup chopped walnuts
¼	teaspoon salt	⅓	cup whole almonds
1¼	cups milk	¼	cup white sugar

1. Preheat oven to 350°F (175°C). Lightly grease a muffin pan or line with 12 muffin papers.

2. In a medium bowl, sift together flour, cocoa, sugar, baking powder, baking soda, and salt. In a large bowl, combine milk, egg, oil, and vanilla. Add dry ingredients to mixture in large bowl; stir well. Add chocolate chips and walnuts; stir well. Fill muffin cups ¾ full. Poke almonds into tops of unbaked muffins. Sprinkle with sugar.

3. Bake in the preheated oven for 20 to 25 minutes or until toothpick inserted into a muffin comes out clean. **Yield:** 12 muffins.

Per muffin: About 376 calories, 7g protein, 59g carbohydrate, 15g fat, 4g fiber, 20mg cholesterol, 163mg sodium

To-Die-For Blueberry Muffins

Submitted by: **Colleen**

"These muffins are extralarge and yummy with a sugary-cinnamon crumb topping. I usually double the recipe and fill the muffin cups just to the top edge for a wonderful, generous-sized, deli-style muffin. Add extra blueberries too, if you want!"

Prep Time: 15 minutes

Cook Time: 25 minutes

Average Rating: ★★★★★

254 Ratings ▲ 182 Reviews

What other cooks have done:

"This recipe lives up to its name. They are to-die-for. They disappeared as soon as they came out of the oven. I doubled the blueberries, which made them even better, and I also used wheat flour. They still turned out wonderfully."

1½ cups all-purpose flour	1 cup fresh blueberries
¾ cup white sugar	½ cup white sugar
½ teaspoon salt	⅓ cup all-purpose flour
2 teaspoons baking powder	1½ teaspoons ground
⅓ cup vegetable oil	cinnamon
1 egg, beaten	¼ cup butter, cubed
⅓ cup milk	

1. Preheat oven to 400°F (200°C). Grease a muffin pan or line with 8 muffin papers.

2. Combine 1½ cups flour, ¾ cup sugar, salt, and baking powder. Place vegetable oil into a 1 cup measuring cup; add the egg and enough milk to fill the cup. Add to flour mixture, stirring just until moist. Fold in blueberries. Fill muffin cups right to the top and set aside.

3. Mix together ½ cup sugar, ⅓ cup flour, and 1½ teaspoons cinnamon. Cut in butter until mixture resembles coarse crumbs. Sprinkle topping over muffins.

4. Bake in the preheated oven for 20 to 25 minutes or until done.

Yield: 8 muffins.

Per muffin: About 383 calories, 4g protein, 57g carbohydrate, 16g fat, 2g fiber, 43mg cholesterol, 341mg sodium

Lemon-Blueberry Bread *(pictured on page 114)*

Submitted by: **Felicia**
"I make this quick bread often. It's one of my family's favorites."

⅓	cup melted butter	2	tablespoons grated lemon zest
1	cup white sugar		
3	tablespoons fresh lemon juice	½	cup milk
		½	cup chopped walnuts
2	eggs	1	cup fresh or frozen blueberries
1½	cups all-purpose flour		
1	teaspoon baking powder	2	tablespoons lemon juice
1	teaspoon salt	¼	cup confectioners' sugar

1. Preheat oven to 350°F (175°C). Lightly grease an 8x4 inch loaf pan.
2. In a bowl, beat butter, 1 cup sugar, juice, and eggs. Combine flour, baking powder, salt, and lemon zest; stir into egg mixture alternately with milk. Fold in nuts and blueberries. Pour batter into prepared pan.
3. Bake in the preheated oven for 60 to 70 minutes or until a toothpick inserted in center of the loaf comes out clean. Cool bread in pan for 10 minutes. Meanwhile, combine lemon juice and ¼ cup sugar in a small bowl. Cool bread in pan 10 minutes and turn out onto a wire rack to cool. Remove bread from pan and drizzle with glaze. Cool on a wire rack. **Yield:** 1 (8x4 inch) loaf (12 servings).

Per serving: About 242 calories, 4g protein, 37g carbohydrate, 10g fat, 1g fiber, 50mg cholesterol, 284mg sodium

◄ **Kid-Friendly**

Prep Time: 30 minutes
Cook Time: 1 hour 10 minutes
Average Rating: ★★★★★
19 Ratings ▲ 12 Reviews
What other cooks have done:
"This bread is delicious. Everyone at the potluck loved it. Next time I will use cranberries—I think it will be just as good, if not better!"

Downeast Maine Pumpkin Bread

Submitted by: **Laurie Bennett**
"This moist and spicy bread actually tastes even better the day after it's baked."

1	(15 ounce) can pumpkin	2	teaspoons baking soda
4	eggs	1½	teaspoons salt
1	cup vegetable oil	1	teaspoon ground cinnamon
⅔	cup water	1	teaspoon ground nutmeg
3	cups white sugar	½	teaspoon ground cloves
3½	cups all-purpose flour	¼	teaspoon ground ginger

1. Preheat oven to 350°F (175°C). Grease and flour 3 (7x3 inch) loaf pans.
2. In a large bowl, mix together pumpkin, eggs, oil, water, and sugar until well blended. In a separate bowl, whisk together the flour, baking soda, salt, cinnamon, nutmeg, cloves, and ginger. Stir the dry ingredients into the pumpkin mixture until just blended. Pour into prepared pans.
3. Bake in the preheated oven for about 50 minutes or until a toothpick inserted in center comes out clean. Cool in pan 10 minutes and turn out onto a wire rack. **Yield:** 3 (7x3 inch) loaves (24 servings).

Per serving: About 263 calories, 3g protein, 41g carbohydrate, 10g fat, 1g fiber, 35mg cholesterol, 304mg sodium

◄ **Holiday Fare**

Prep Time: 15 minutes
Cook Time: 50 minutes
Average Rating: ★★★★★
210 Ratings ▲ 183 Reviews
What other cooks have done:
"I topped this with a glaze of confectioners' sugar mixed with a touch of orange juice. I also substituted pumpkin pie spice for all the spices to help in the quickness of the making, and it turned out great. You must try this one!"

Rhubarb Bread

Submitted by: **Lori**

"Rhubarb is one of the wonderful gifts of spring. This bread will turn it into a delicious treat for the whole family."

1	cup milk	1	teaspoon salt
1	tablespoon lemon juice	1	teaspoon baking soda
1	teaspoon vanilla extract	1½	cups chopped rhubarb
1½	cups packed brown sugar	½	cup chopped walnuts
⅔	cup vegetable oil	½	cup brown sugar
1	egg	1	teaspoon ground cinnamon
2½	cups all-purpose flour	2	tablespoons butter, melted

1. Preheat oven to 325°F (165°C). Lightly grease 2 (7x3 inch) loaf pans. In a small bowl, stir together milk, lemon juice, and vanilla; let stand for 10 minutes.

2. In a large bowl, mix together 1½ cups brown sugar, oil, and egg. Combine the flour, salt, and baking soda; stir into sugar mixture alternately with the milk mixture just until combined. Fold in rhubarb and nuts. Pour batter into prepared loaf pans.

3. In a small bowl, combine ½ cup brown sugar, cinnamon, and butter. Sprinkle this mixture over the unbaked loaves.

4. Bake in the preheated oven for 40 minutes or until a toothpick inserted in center comes out clean. Cool in pan 10 minutes and turn out onto a wire rack. **Yield:** 2 (7x3 inch) loaves (20 servings).

Per serving: About 206 calories, 3g protein, 26g carbohydrate, 10g fat, 1g fiber, 13mg cholesterol, 200mg sodium

Banana Banana Bread

Submitted by: **Shelley Albeluhn**

"This moist and delicious banana bread is wonderful toasted."

2	cups all-purpose flour	¾	cup brown sugar
1	teaspoon baking soda	2	eggs, beaten
¼	teaspoon salt	2⅓	cups mashed, overripe
½	cup butter		bananas

1. Preheat oven to 350°F (175°C). Lightly grease a 9x5 inch loaf pan.

2. In a large bowl, combine flour, baking soda, and salt. In a separate bowl, beat butter and brown sugar. Stir in eggs and mashed bananas until well blended. Stir banana mixture into flour mixture until moist. Pour batter into prepared loaf pan.

3. Bake in the preheated oven for 60 to 65 minutes or until a toothpick inserted in center comes out clean. Cool in pan for 10 minutes and turn out onto a wire rack. **Yield:** 1 (9x5 inch) loaf (12 servings).

Per serving: About 230 calories, 4g protein, 35g carbohydrate, 9g fat, 2g fiber, 56mg cholesterol, 246mg sodium

J.P.'s Big Daddy Biscuits,
page 106

Lemon-Blueberry Bread,
page 111

Focaccia Bread, page 128

Honey Wheat Bread, page 126

Breads 115

Pumpkin-Apple Streusel Muffins,
page 108

Cranberry-Orange Loaf

Submitted by: **Carol**

"This moist, fruity bread tastes better the next day."

2	cups all-purpose flour	½	cup pecans, coarsely chopped
1½	teaspoons baking powder		
½	teaspoon baking soda	¼	cup butter or margarine
½	teaspoon salt	1	cup white sugar
1	tablespoon grated orange zest	1	egg
		¾	cup orange juice
1½	cups fresh or frozen cranberries		

1. Preheat oven to 350°F (180°C). Lightly grease a 9x5 inch loaf pan.

2. Whisk together flour, baking powder, soda, and salt. Stir in orange zest, cranberries, and nuts. In a large bowl, beat butter, sugar, and egg until smooth. Stir in juice. Add flour mixture, stirring until just moistened. Pour into prepared pan.

3. Bake in the preheated oven for 1 hour or until a toothpick inserted in center comes out clean. Cool in pan 10 minutes and turn out onto a wire rack. **Yield:** 1 (9x5 inch) loaf (12 servings).

Per serving: About 228 calories, 3g protein, 37g carbohydrate, 8g fat, 2g fiber, 18mg cholesterol, 260mg sodium

◄ Holiday Fare

Prep Time: 15 minutes

Cook Time: 1 hour

Average Rating: ★★★★★

26 Ratings ▲ 24 Reviews

What other cooks have done:

"I've made this recipe several times this season—for work potlucks, family dinners—and it's always a big hit. I have to make a double batch each time so I've got a loaf for me. I always slice the cranberries in half. While it's a bit more work, they make a lovely 'star' pattern in the loaf when it's cut."

Zucchini Bread IV

Submitted by: **Kristen**

"Thanks to my mother, this is the best zucchini bread recipe."

3	eggs	3	teaspoons ground cinnamon
1	cup vegetable oil		
2	cups white sugar	1	teaspoon baking soda
2	cups grated zucchini	¼	teaspoon baking powder
2	teaspoons vanilla extract	1	teaspoon salt
3	cups all-purpose flour	½	cup chopped walnuts

1. Preheat oven to 325°F (165°C). Grease and flour 2 (8x4 inch) loaf pans.

2. In a large bowl, beat eggs until light and frothy. Mix in oil and sugar. Stir in zucchini and vanilla. Combine flour, cinnamon, baking soda, baking powder, salt, and nuts; stir into the egg mixture. Divide batter into prepared pans.

3. Bake in the preheated oven for 60 to 70 minutes or until a toothpick inserted in center comes out clean. Cool in pan 10 minutes and turn out onto a wire rack. **Yield:** 2 (8x4 inch) loaves (24 servings).

Per serving: About 230 calories, 3g protein, 30g carbohydrate, 12g fat, 1g fiber, 27mg cholesterol, 163mg sodium

◄ Family Favorite

Prep Time: 15 minutes

Cook Time: 1 hour 10 minutes

Average Rating: ★★★★★

57 Ratings ▲ 42 Reviews

What other cooks have done:

"I whipped this up while the rest of my dinner was cooking. It was really good, quick, and easy. Even the kids liked it. I added ½ cup chocolate chips to the second loaf (yum). It's a good way to use up excess zucchini."

Cinnamon Bread

Submitted by: **Carol**

"What a lovely way to start off your morning when you want a little something different. Note: If you don't have buttermilk, substitute milk with 1 tablespoon vinegar to measure 1 cup."

2	cups all-purpose flour	¼	cup vegetable oil
1	cup white sugar	2	eggs
2	teaspoons baking powder	2	teaspoons vanilla extract
½	teaspoon baking soda	2	tablespoons white sugar
1½	teaspoons ground cinnamon	1	teaspoon ground cinnamon
1	teaspoon salt	2	teaspoons butter or margarine
1	cup buttermilk		

1. Preheat oven to 350°F (175°C). Grease a 9x5 inch loaf pan.
2. Combine flour, 1 cup sugar, baking powder, baking soda, 1½ teaspoons cinnamon, salt, buttermilk, oil, eggs, and vanilla in a large bowl. Beat 3 minutes. Pour into prepared loaf pan. Smooth top.
3. Combine 2 tablespoons white sugar, 1 teaspoon cinnamon, and butter, mixing until crumbly. Sprinkle topping over smoothed batter. Using knife, cut in a light swirling motion to give a marbled effect.
4. Bake in the preheated oven for about 50 minutes or until a toothpick inserted in center comes out clean. Cool in pan 10 minutes and turn out onto a wire rack. **Yield:** 1 (9x5 inch) loaf (12 servings).

Per serving: About 219 calories, 4g protein, 36g carbohydrate, 6g fat, 1g fiber, 36mg cholesterol, 368mg sodium

Irresistible Irish Soda Bread

Submitted by: **Karin Christian**

"This easy bread is best made the day before or several hours before serving."

3	cups all-purpose flour	1	teaspoon baking soda
1	tablespoon baking powder	1	egg, lightly beaten
⅓	cup white sugar	2	cups buttermilk
1	teaspoon salt	¼	cup butter, melted

1. Preheat oven to 325°F (160°C). Grease a 9x5 inch loaf pan.
2. Combine flour, baking powder, sugar, salt, and baking soda. Blend egg and buttermilk and add to the flour mixture. Mix just until moistened. Stir in butter. Pour into prepared pan.
3. Bake in the preheated oven for 65 to 70 minutes or until a toothpick inserted in center comes out clean. Cool in pan 10 minutes and turn out onto a wire rack. Wrap in foil for several hours, or overnight, for best flavor. **Yield:** 1 (9x5 inch) loaf (12 servings).

Per serving: About 192 calories, 5g protein, 32g carbohydrate, 5g fat, 1g fiber, 29mg cholesterol, 500mg sodium

Eggnog Quick Bread

Submitted by: **Mary E. Crain**
"This tastes like Christmas and gets better with age! Smaller loaves make excellent gifts. Use refrigerated eggnog, not the canned stuff."

2	eggs	1	teaspoon vanilla extract
1	cup white sugar	2¼	cups all-purpose flour
1	cup eggnog	2	teaspoons baking powder
½	cup butter, melted	½	teaspoon salt
2	teaspoons rum flavored extract	¼	teaspoon ground nutmeg

1. Preheat oven to 350°F (175°C). Grease bottom only of a 9x5 inch loaf pan.
2. Beat eggs in a large bowl. Blend in sugar, eggnog, butter, rum extract, and vanilla.
3. Stir together flour, baking powder, salt, and nutmeg. Mix into eggnog mixture; stir to just moisten dry ingredients. Pour batter into prepared pan.
4. Bake in the preheated oven for 40 to 60 minutes or until a toothpick inserted in center comes out clean. Cool 10 minutes and remove bread from pan. Cool completely. Wrap tightly and store in the refrigerator. **Yield:** 1 (9x5 inch) loaf (12 servings).

Note: Pour batter into 3 (5¾x3¼ inch) loaf pans for smaller loaves that are perfect for gift giving. Grease the pans, pour the batter evenly into the pans, and bake at 350°F (175°C) for 35 to 40 minutes or until a toothpick inserted in center of loaf comes out clean.

Per serving: About 262 calories, 4g protein, 38g carbohydrate, 10g fat, 1g fiber, 69mg cholesterol, 279mg sodium

◄ Holiday Fare

Prep Time: 10 minutes
Cook Time: 60 minutes
Average Rating: ★★★★★
25 Ratings ▲ 21 Reviews
What other cooks have done:
"I made this bread and gave small loaves away at Christmas. I made 2 batches—one with rum extract, and one with real rum, and you couldn't really tell the difference—both were excellent. I topped them with confectioners' sugar and added cinnamon to one batch."

Homesteader Cornbread

Submitted by: **Patricia Bergstrom**

"This recipe comes from my mother-in-law in Canada. It's the moistest cornbread that I have ever tasted. It's great with chili con carne or as stuffing for your holiday turkey."

1½	cups cornmeal	1	teaspoon salt
2½	cups milk	⅔	cup white sugar
2	cups all-purpose flour	2	eggs, beaten
1	tablespoon baking powder	½	cup vegetable oil

1. Preheat oven to 400°F (200°C). Grease an 8x8 inch square pan or cast iron skillet.

2. In a small bowl, combine cornmeal and milk; let stand for 5 minutes.

3. In a large bowl, whisk together flour, baking powder, salt, and sugar. Mix in the cornmeal mixture, eggs, and oil just until moistened. Pour batter into prepared pan.

4. Bake in the preheated oven for 30 to 35 minutes or until a knife inserted in the center of the cornbread comes out clean. **Yield:** 6 servings.

Per serving: About 585 calories, 12g protein, 83g carbohydrate, 23g fat, 3g fiber, 78mg cholesterol, 588mg sodium

Good Old-Fashioned Pancakes

Submitted by: **Verona**

"I found this great recipe in my grandma's recipe book. Judging from the weathered look of this recipe card, this was a family favorite."

1½	cups all-purpose flour	1¼	cups milk
3½	teaspoons baking powder	1	egg, beaten
1	tablespoon white sugar	3	tablespoons butter, melted
1	teaspoon salt		

1. In a large bowl, sift together the flour, baking powder, sugar, and salt. Make a well in the center and pour in the milk, egg, and melted butter; mix until smooth.

2. Heat a lightly oiled griddle or skillet over medium-high heat. Pour or scoop the batter onto the griddle, using approximately ¼ cup for each pancake. Brown on both sides and serve hot. **Yield:** 8 servings.

Per serving: About 159 calories, 5g protein, 22g carbohydrate, 6g fat, 1g fiber, 41mg cholesterol, 470mg sodium

Mom's Best Waffles

Submitted by: **Love**

"My mom makes the best waffles, and I thought I'd share the recipe with the world!"

2	cups all-purpose flour	2	cups milk
2	teaspoons baking powder	2	eggs, beaten
2	tablespoons white sugar	2	tablespoons vegetable oil
1	teaspoon salt		

1. In a large bowl, stir together flour, baking powder, sugar, and salt. Add milk, eggs, and oil; mix well.

2. Spray waffle iron with cooking spray. Pour mix onto hot waffle iron. Cook until golden brown. **Yield:** 4 servings.

Per serving: About 411 calories, 14g protein, 60g carbohydrate, 12g fat, 2g fiber, 115mg cholesterol, 799mg sodium

Almond French Toast

Submitted by: **The Princess**

"This French toast is perfect for Mother's Day. It's a delicious twist on the traditional breakfast dish and makes a nice addition to any brunch. Serve with fresh fruit, fruit preserves, or warm maple syrup."

1	cup slivered almonds	½	teaspoon almond extract
3	eggs	1	teaspoon vanilla extract
1	cup milk	12	thick slices French bread
3	tablespoons all-purpose flour	3	tablespoons canola oil
¼	teaspoon salt	3	tablespoons butter
½	teaspoon baking powder		Confectioners' sugar for dusting (optional)

1. Place almonds in a small saucepan over low heat. Tossing frequently, toast until lightly browned, 5 to 10 minutes. Remove from heat and set aside.

2. In a large bowl, whisk together eggs, milk, flour, salt, baking powder, almond extract, and vanilla. Soak bread slices in the mixture until saturated. Place slices in a shallow pan. Refrigerate slices approximately 1 hour.

3. Heat oil and butter in a large skillet over medium heat. Working with 1 slice at a time, press 1 side of soaked bread slices in the almonds to coat. Fry bread slices on both sides until golden brown. Dust with confectioners' sugar before serving, if desired. **Yield:** 6 servings.

Per serving: About 517 calories, 16g protein, 46g carbohydrate, 30g fat, 5g fiber, 125mg cholesterol, 655mg sodium

Fluffy French Toast

Submitted by: **Bonnie**

"This French toast recipe is different because it uses flour. I have given it to some friends, and they've all liked it better than the French toast they usually make."

¼	cup all-purpose flour	½	teaspoon ground cinnamon
1	cup milk	1	teaspoon vanilla extract
	Pinch of salt	1	tablespoon white sugar
3	eggs	12	thick slices bread

1. Measure flour into a large bowl. Slowly whisk in the milk. Whisk in the salt, eggs, cinnamon, vanilla extract, and sugar until smooth.
2. Heat a lightly oiled griddle or skillet over medium heat.
3. Soak bread slices in mixture until saturated. Cook bread on each side until golden brown. Serve hot. **Yield:** 6 servings.

Per serving: About 84 calories, 4g protein, 12g carbohydrate, 2g fat, 1g fiber, 55mg cholesterol, 139mg sodium

Monkey Bread

Submitted by: **LuAnn Connolly**

"Refrigerated biscuits with cinnamon bake in a tube pan. My 7-year-old daughter, Leah, loves her Monkey Bread."

1	cup white sugar	½	cup chopped walnuts (optional)
2	teaspoons ground cinnamon	½	cup raisins (optional)
3	(12 ounce) cans refrigerated biscuits	½	cup butter or margarine
		1	cup packed brown sugar

1. Preheat oven to 350°F (175°C). Grease a 9 or 10 inch tube pan.
2. Mix white sugar and cinnamon in a plastic bag. Cut biscuits into quarters. Shake 6 to 8 biscuit pieces in the sugar cinnamon mix. Arrange pieces in the prepared pan. Continue until all biscuit pieces are coated and placed in pan. If using nuts and raisins, arrange them among the biscuit pieces as you go along.
3. In a small saucepan, melt the butter and the brown sugar over medium heat. Boil for 1 minute. Pour over the biscuits.
4. Bake in the preheated oven for 35 minutes. Let bread cool in pan for 10 minutes and turn out onto a plate. **Yield:** 15 servings.

Per serving: About 415 calories, 5g protein, 62g carbohydrate, 18g fat, 2g fiber, 0mg cholesterol, 820mg sodium

Raspberry-Almond Coffee Cake

Submitted by: **Melissa Marsh**
"A winner! Moist, light cake is 'berry' delicious as a dessert or for breakfast. Your house will smell just wonderful while it's baking and cooling."

1	cup fresh raspberries	2	tablespoons butter, melted
3	tablespoons brown sugar	1	teaspoon vanilla extract
1	cup all-purpose flour	1	egg
⅓	cup white sugar	¼	cup sliced almonds
½	teaspoon baking powder	¼	cup sifted confectioners' sugar
¼	teaspoon baking soda		
⅛	teaspoon salt	1	teaspoon milk
½	cup sour cream	¼	teaspoon vanilla extract

1. Preheat oven to 350°F (175°C). Spray an 8 inch round cake pan with cooking spray.

2. Combine raspberries and brown sugar in a bowl. Set aside.

3. In a large bowl, combine flour, sugar, baking powder, baking soda, and salt. Combine sour cream, butter, 1 teaspoon vanilla, and egg; add to flour mixture. Stir just until moist. Spoon ⅔ of the batter into the prepared pan. Spread raspberry mixture evenly over the batter. Spoon remaining batter over raspberry mixture. Top with almonds.

4. Bake in the preheated oven for 40 minutes or until a toothpick inserted in center comes out clean. Let cool in pan for 10 minutes on a wire rack.

5. Combine confectioners' sugar, milk, and ¼ teaspoon vanilla. Stir well. Drizzle glaze over cake. Serve warm or at room temperature.

Yield: 6 servings.

Per serving: About 173 calories, 3g protein, 26g carbohydrate, 7g fat, 1g fiber, 33mg cholesterol, 123mg sodium

◄ Holiday Fare

Prep Time: 30 minutes
Cook Time: 40 minutes
Average Rating: ★★★★★
21 Ratings ▲ 17 Reviews

What other cooks have done:
"What an amazing coffee cake! And it's super-easy, too: All you need are a few bowls and a big wooden spoon (no need for your mixer). I skipped the glaze given in this recipe and instead came up with my own chocolate glaze: 2 ounces Belgian dark chocolate and 4 ounces Belgian milk chocolate melted in the microwave and whisked together with ½ cup hot whipping cream. The combination of raspberry, almond, and chocolate was heavenly. Possibly the best coffee cake I've ever made."

Cold-Oven Popovers

Submitted by: **Christine**

"These popovers turn out every time, and the best part is, you don't need a popover pan! Add any seasoning you wish to these popovers."

3	eggs	1	cup all-purpose flour
1	cup milk	½	teaspoon salt

1. Grease muffin pan or line with muffin papers. Chill muffin pan in refrigerator while mixing batter.

2. In a bowl, beat eggs well. Add milk, flour, and salt. Beat with a wire whisk or spoon, disregarding lumps. Pour batter into prepared muffin cups, filling each cup ¾ full.

3. Place popovers in cold oven. Set oven to 450°F (230°C) and bake for 30 minutes until golden and puffed. Serve immediately. If you must hold them, pierce and keep warm in a 170°F (75°C) oven. **Yield:** 1 dozen popovers.

Per popover: About 133 calories, 7g protein, 18g carbohydrate, 4g fat, 1g fiber, 109mg cholesterol, 246mg sodium

Diana's Hawaiian Bread Rolls

Submitted by: **Diana Kotlinski**

"After years of trying to perfect the recipe, I finally did it! This recipe makes the best dinner rolls. They're sweet and full of flavor."

1½	cups warm water (110°F/45°C)	5	tablespoons white sugar
1	egg	2	tablespoons instant nonfat dry milk powder
1	teaspoon salt	2	tablespoons butter-flavored shortening
1	teaspoon vanilla extract		
1	teaspoon lemon extract	4½	cups bread flour
1	tablespoon molasses	2	teaspoons active dry yeast
1	tablespoon honey		

1. Place all ingredients into the bread machine pan in the order recommended by the manufacturer. Select Dough setting for a 2 pound batch; press Start. The dough may be sticky, so add more bread flour as needed as it mixes.

2. When the dough cycle is complete, turn the risen dough out on a lightly floured surface and divide into 12 pieces. Form the pieces into rounds and place on lightly greased baking sheets. Cover the rolls with a damp cloth and let rise until doubled in volume, about 40 minutes. Meanwhile, preheat oven to 350°F (175°C).

3. Bake in the preheated oven for 15 minutes or until golden brown. **Yield:** 1 dozen rolls.

Per roll: About 249 calories, 7g protein, 46g carbohydrate, 3g fat, 1g fiber, 18mg cholesterol, 209mg sodium

Hot Cross Buns

Submitted by: **Sue Litster**
"Let your bread machine do all the work for these traditional sweet rolls."

¾	cup warm water (110°F/45°C)	1	tablespoon active dry yeast
3	tablespoons butter	¾	cup currants
1	tablespoon instant nonfat dry milk powder	1	teaspoon ground cinnamon
¼	cup white sugar	1	egg yolk
½	teaspoon salt	2	tablespoons water
1	egg	½	cup confectioners' sugar
1	egg white	¼	teaspoon vanilla extract
3	cups all-purpose flour	2	teaspoons milk

1. Put warm water, butter, milk powder, ¼ cup sugar, salt, egg, egg white, flour, and yeast into the bread machine. Select Dough setting and press Start.
2. When 5 minutes of kneading are left, add currants and cinnamon. Leave in machine until doubled in size.
3. Punch down on a floured surface, cover, and let rest 10 minutes.
4. Shape into 12 balls and place on a greased baking sheet. Cover and let rise in a warm place until doubled in size, about 35 to 40 minutes.
5. Preheat oven to 375°F (190°C). Whisk egg yolk and 2 tablespoons water. Brush on buns.
6. Bake in the preheated oven for 20 minutes. Remove from pan immediately and cool on a wire rack.
7. To make crosses: Mix together confectioners' sugar, vanilla, and milk. Make an "X" on each cooled bun. **Yield:** 1 dozen buns.

Per bun: About 197 calories, 5g protein, 35g carbohydrate, 4g fat, 2g fiber, 43mg cholesterol, 117mg sodium

Bread Machine Challah

Submitted by: **Suzy**
"Here's an easy recipe for challah or egg bread using a bread machine."

¾	cup milk	¼	cup white sugar
2	eggs, beaten	1½	teaspoons salt
3	tablespoons butter	1½	teaspoons active dry yeast
3	cups bread flour		

1. Place all ingredients into the bread machine pan in the order suggested by the manufacturer.
2. Select Basic Bread and Light Crust settings; press Start. **Yield:** 1 (1½ pound) loaf (12 servings).

Per serving: About 185 calories, 6g protein, 30g carbohydrate, 4g fat, 1g fiber, 37mg cholesterol, 341mg sodium

Honey Wheat Bread *(pictured on page 115)*

Submitted by: **Kristin Zaharias**
"This is a county fair blue ribbon winning loaf—it's delicate and soft."

Prep Time: 25 minutes
Cook Time: 35 minutes
Average Rating: ★★★★★
62 Ratings ▲ 56 Reviews

What other cooks have done:
"This bread is outstanding. I've made it a few times now, and it has great taste and texture. I add about ¼ cup extra honey. The last time I made it, I added ¼ cup wheat germ, which turned out great, too. Next time, I'm going to try replacing all the honey with maple syrup to make Maple Wheat Bread. I think some other additions such as oats, rye flour, and sunflower, pumpkin, or sesame seeds might be good to try, too."

1	(.25 ounce) package rapid rise yeast	¼	cup water
1	teaspoon white sugar	¼	cup melted shortening
½	cup warm water (110°F/45°C)	¼	cup honey
1	(12 ounce) can evaporated milk	2	teaspoons salt
		2	cups whole wheat flour
		3	cups bread flour
		4	tablespoons butter, divided

1. Dissolve yeast and sugar in ½ cup warm water.
2. Combine evaporated milk, ¼ cup water, shortening, honey, salt, and wheat flour in a food processor or bowl. Mix in yeast mixture and let rest 15 minutes. Add bread flour and process until dough forms a ball. Knead dough by processing 80 more seconds in food processor or mix and knead by hand 10 minutes. Place the dough in a buttered bowl and turn to coat. Cover the bowl with plastic wrap. Let dough rise for 1 hour or until almost doubled.
3. Punch down and divide in half. Roll out each half and pound out bubbles. Form into 2 loaves and place in 2 buttered 9x5 inch loaf pans. Butter the tops of the dough; cover loosely with plastic wrap. Let rise in a warm area until doubled (second rise will take about 45 minutes).
4. Place a small pan of water on the bottom shelf of the oven. Preheat oven to 375°F (190°C).
5. Bake in the preheated oven for 25 to 35 minutes or until tops are dark golden brown. Butter crusts while warm. Slice when cool. **Yield:** 2 (9x5 inch) loaves (24 servings).

Per serving: About 154 calories, 5g protein, 24g carbohydrate, 5g fat, 2g fiber, 7mg cholesterol, 220mg sodium

Honey-of-an-Oatmeal Bread

Submitted by: **Merrilee**
"Our family goes through a loaf of this every day. It's slightly sweet, great with dinner, and a favorite for sandwiches."

Prep Time: 5 minutes
Cook Time: 3 hours
Average Rating: ★★★★★
56 Ratings ▲ 43 Reviews

What other cooks have done:
"I added a heaping teaspoon of cinnamon and ¾ cup raisins on the Sweet Cycle of my bread machine."

1	cup water	½	cup rolled oats
1	tablespoon vegetable oil	2⅓	cups bread flour
¼	cup honey	1	teaspoon active dry yeast
1	teaspoon salt		

1. Place all ingredients into bread machine pan in the order suggested by the manufacturer. Select Light Crust or Basic setting and press Start. **Yield:** 1 (1 pound) loaf (10 servings).

Per serving: About 185 calories, 5g protein, 36g carbohydrate, 2g fat, 2g fiber, 0mg cholesterol, 235mg sodium

Cheese Herb Bread

Submitted by: **D. Reichel**

"I use fresh herbs from my garden when they're available. The aroma will make it almost impossible to wait."

1¼	cups warm water (110°F/45°C)	3	tablespoons grated Parmesan cheese
3	cups bread flour	1½	teaspoons dried marjoram
2	tablespoons nonfat dry milk powder	1½	teaspoons dried thyme
2	tablespoons white sugar	1	teaspoon dried basil
1½	teaspoons salt	1	teaspoon dried oregano
2	tablespoons butter, softened	1	tablespoon active dry yeast

1. Place all ingredients into bread machine pan in the order suggested by the manufacturer. Select the Basic or White Bread setting and press Start. **Yield:** 1 (1½ pound) loaf (12 servings).

Per serving: About 163 calories, 6g protein, 28g carbohydrate, 3g fat, 1g fiber, 6mg cholesterol, 342mg sodium

Mama D's Italian Bread

Submitted by: **Christine Darrock**

"Here's a basic, delicious Italian bread that everyone is bound to love. I let my dough rise in a cold oven with the light on—it's the perfect temperature."

1	teaspoon white sugar	7	cups all-purpose flour, divided
1	tablespoon active dry yeast		
3	cups warm water (110°F/45°C)	1	tablespoon salt, divided
		1	tablespoon cornmeal

1. Add the sugar and yeast to the warm water and allow to proof until yeast resembles a creamy foam.
2. Stir in 4 cups of flour and beat until smooth. Cover and let rest for 15 minutes. Beat in the salt and then add enough remaining flour to make a stiff dough. Knead until soft. Place dough in a greased bowl, turning to coat. Cover and let rise until doubled.
3. Once doubled, punch down and divide into 3 pieces. Place back in the bowl, cover, and let rise.
4. Once doubled again, punch down and form into 3 fat oval-shaped loaves. Grease baking sheets and sprinkle with cornmeal. Place the bread on the sheets, cover with a towel, and let rise.
5. Preheat oven to 450°F (230°C). Once risen, mist loaves with water and bake in the preheated oven. Mist loaves again with water and turn occasionally while they bake. Bread is done in about 1 hour or until loaves are golden brown and sound hollow when tapped. **Yield:** 3 loaves (36 servings).

Per serving: About 90 calories, 3g protein, 19g carbohydrate, 0g fat, 1g fiber, 0mg cholesterol, 195mg sodium

Amish White Bread

Submitted by: **Peg**

"Eat one loaf with dinner and give the second as a gift."

⅔ cup white sugar	1½ teaspoons salt
2 cups warm water	¼ cup vegetable oil
(110°F/45°C)	6 cups bread flour
1½ tablespoons active dry yeast	

1. In a large bowl, dissolve the sugar in warm water and stir in yeast. Allow to proof until yeast resembles a creamy foam.

2. Mix salt and oil into the yeast. Mix in flour 1 cup at a time. Knead dough on a lightly floured surface until smooth. Place in a well oiled bowl and turn dough to coat. Cover with a damp cloth. Allow to rise until doubled, about 1 hour.

3. Preheat oven to 350°F (175°C). Punch dough down. Knead for a few minutes and divide in half. Shape into loaves and place into 2 well oiled 9x5 inch loaf pans. Allow to rise for 30 minutes or until dough has risen 1 inch above pans.

4. Bake in the preheated oven for 30 minutes. **Yield:** 2 (9x5 inch) loaves (24 servings).

Per serving: About 167 calories, 4g protein, 31g carbohydrate, 3g fat, 1g fiber, 0mg cholesterol, 147mg sodium

Focaccia Bread *(pictured on page 115)*

Submitted by: **Terri McCarrell**

"A quick alternative to garlic bread. Lots of herbs and lots of flavor!"

2¾ cups all-purpose flour	Pinch ground black pepper
1 teaspoon salt	1 tablespoon vegetable oil
1 teaspoon white sugar	1 cup water
1 tablespoon active dry yeast	2 tablespoons olive oil
1 teaspoon garlic powder	1 cup shredded mozzarella
1 teaspoon dried oregano	1 tablespoon grated Parmesan
1 teaspoon dried thyme	cheese
½ teaspoon dried basil	

1. In a large bowl, stir together the flour, salt, sugar, yeast, garlic powder, oregano, thyme, basil, and black pepper. Mix in vegetable oil and water.

2. When dough has pulled together, turn it out onto a lightly floured surface; knead until smooth and elastic. Place in an oiled bowl and turn to coat. Cover with a damp cloth; let rise in warm place for 20 minutes.

3. Preheat oven to 450°F (230°C). Punch dough down; place on greased baking sheet. Pat into a ½ inch thick rectangle. Brush top with olive oil. Sprinkle with mozzarella cheese and Parmesan cheese.

4. Bake in the preheated oven for 15 minutes or until golden brown. Serve warm. **Yield:** 12 servings.

Per serving: About 168 calories, 6g protein, 23g carbohydrate, 6g fat, 1g fiber, 5mg cholesterol, 252mg sodium

---

Jay's Signature Pizza Crust

Submitted by: **Jason Sharp**

"This recipe yields a crust that's soft and doughy on the inside and slightly crusty on the outside. Cover with your favorite sauce and topping to make a delicious pizza."

1	(.25 ounce) package active dry yeast	1	teaspoon salt
½	teaspoon brown sugar	2	tablespoons olive oil
1½	cups warm water (110°F/45°C)	3⅓	cups all-purpose flour, divided

1. In a large bowl, dissolve the yeast and brown sugar in the water and let stand for 10 minutes.

2. Stir the salt and oil into the yeast solution. Mix in 2½ cups of the flour.

3. Turn dough out onto a clean, well floured surface, and knead in more flour until the dough is no longer sticky. Place the dough in a well oiled bowl, turning to coat, and cover with a cloth. Let the dough rise until doubled (this should take about 1 hour). Punch down the dough and form a tight ball. Allow the dough to rest for a minute before rolling out.

4. Preheat oven to 425°F (220°C). If you are baking the dough on a pizza stone, you may place your toppings on the dough and bake immediately. If you are baking your pizza in a pan, lightly oil the pan and let the dough rise for 15 or 20 minutes before topping and baking it.

5. Bake pizza in the preheated oven until the cheese and crust are golden brown, about 15 to 20 minutes. **Yield:** 15 servings.

Per serving: About 119 calories, 3g protein, 22g carbohydrate, 2g fat, 1g fiber, 0mg cholesterol, 157mg sodium

◄ Party Food

Prep Time: 30 minutes
Cook Time: 20 minutes
Average Rating: ★★★★★
270 Ratings ▲ 204 Reviews
What other cooks have done:
"This is a great crust! I added some garlic and fresh basil to the dough. Also, you can divide the dough into five pieces and make personal pizzas. I'm thinking of making a few different flavor crusts: garlic and basil, crushed red pepper flakes, sun-dried tomato, and Parmesan. I found that you need to add a little more all-purpose flour to make it easier to handle."

Give It a Little Lift—with Yeast! ▼

Your bread is given life by a wonderful one-celled plant called yeast. Yeast feeds on sugars and starches in the dough. When it grows, it produces carbon dioxide that makes the dough rise. Yeast is a living organism with a finite life expectancy. It's also very sensitive. Too much heat (at the wrong time), sugar, or salt can kill it.

If you want to check whether your yeast is still usable, you need to proof it. To proof yeast, place 1 cup of warm (110°F/45°C) water in a bowl. Add 2 teaspoons of sugar, stir to dissolve, and then sprinkle with 1 teaspoon of yeast. Let it sit for a few minutes, then stir until it dissolves. Cover the bowl with plastic wrap and set it in a warm, draft-free place (inside your turned-off oven, for example). Within 5 to 10 minutes the top of the mixture should have turned foamy, which means the yeast is working. If there is no activity, throw away the yeast and buy a new supply.

Cooking Basics: Bread Machine Baking ▼

Whether you're making bread by hand or with a bread machine, you need only three ingredients to make a loaf: yeast (or a starter), flour, and liquid. Once you have those basics, you can add any number of other ingredients to make a great variety of breads. Making bread with a bread machine follows the same process as making bread by hand. The only difference is that the mixing, rising, and baking all take place within the machine. Once you take a peek at these bread machine basics, getting a nice golden loaf out of your bread machine will be a breeze!

It's the "Yeast" of Your Worries

Bread machine yeast and rapid-rise yeast are specially formulated for the bread machine. They also become active more quickly than active dry yeast. Active dry yeast should be dissolved in water before being used, but bread machine yeast can be mixed in with other dry ingredients. This is particularly important when using the timed mixing function on your machine.

The Skinny on Flours and Gluten

There's more to flour than meets the eye. There is a protein in flour called gluten, which provides the structure for your bread. Strands of gluten are woven together by mixing and then inflated as the yeast multiplies. Hard wheat yields the highest amount of protein, or gluten. "Bread machine bread flour" is identical to bread flour. Both have more gluten than all-purpose flour. High protein flours help to give yeast bread a chewy texture. Look for flour ground from hard wheat with 13 or more grams of protein per cup.

The Lowdown on Liquids

Many liquids can be used in bread making—water, milk, and buttermilk are the most popular. All liquids that you use in your recipe (including eggs) should be at room temperature when you put them into the bread machine. Yeast needs a warm (but not hot!) environment to grow. Since many people use the timer on their bread machine, most recipes do not use fresh milk. Who wants milk sitting in their bread machine overnight? Instead, recipes call for nonfat dry milk powder or powdered buttermilk. If you're mixing your dough right away, you can use fresh milk in your bread machine recipes. Simply replace the water with milk or buttermilk and omit the powdered milk.

Size Matters

When reading bread machine recipes, remember that all bread machines are not created equal. Some machines make 1 pound loaves; others make 1½ pound loaves or 2 pound loaves. Some machines have a variety of settings while others simply have an on/off button. Make sure you read your machine's manual and follow its guidelines.

When trying a new recipe, compare the amounts of ingredients to the recipes you usually use in your bread machine. It's important not to exceed the capacity of your bread machine pan. Use only recipes with the appropriate quantities of ingredients for your machine, or adjust the amounts accordingly. Small loaf machines generally use about 2 cups of flour, while large loaf machines use 3 cups. It's also very important that you measure ingredients correctly. Be exact. Even a teaspoon more or less of water could make a difference.

That Perfect Climate

After you've got all your ingredients measured out, don't be too quick to load the bread machine. Ideally, ingredients should be at room temperature when they go into the pan. However, due to potential health risks, it's a bad idea to store eggs at room temperature. To bring eggs to room temperature quickly and safely, place the whole (uncracked) egg in a cup of hot tap water for four or five minutes. If your recipe calls for milk, you should not use a delayed mix cycle. Cut butter or margarine into small pieces before adding it to the machine.

Follow Orders

When you're ready to let the bread machine work its magic, check the instructions for your machine regarding the order of loading ingredients. In some machines the wet ingredients go first; in others, the dry ingredients. And some machines have a separate yeast dispenser. When trying a new recipe, remember that yeast will activate when it comes in contact with water or any other moist ingredient, including eggs, fruit, cheese, vegetables, or butter.

– *Stephen Carroll* and *Ursula Dalzell*
For more information, visit **Allrecipes.com**

Bread Machine Bagels

Submitted by: **Cristy Chu**

"You'll love these quick and easy bagels you can make with your bread machine! You can use whatever topping that you wish. Many like poppy seeds."

1 cup warm water (110°F/45°C)	3 quarts water
1½ teaspoons salt	3 tablespoons white sugar
2 tablespoons white sugar	1 tablespoon cornmeal
3 cups bread flour	1 egg white, beaten
1 (.25 ounce) package active dry yeast	3 tablespoons poppy seeds

1. Place water, salt, sugar, flour, and yeast in the bread machine pan in the order recommended by the manufacturer. Select Dough setting; press Start.

2. When cycle is complete, let dough rest on a lightly floured surface. Meanwhile, in a large pot, bring 3 quarts of water to a boil. Stir in 3 tablespoons sugar.

3. Cut dough into 9 equal pieces and roll each piece into a small ball. Flatten balls. Poke a hole in the middle of each with your thumb. Twirl the dough on your finger or thumb to enlarge the hole and to even out the dough around the hole. Cover bagels with a clean cloth and let rest for 10 minutes.

4. Preheat oven to 375°F (190°C). Sprinkle an ungreased baking sheet with cornmeal. Carefully transfer bagels to boiling water. Boil for 1 minute, turning halfway through. Drain briefly on clean towel. Arrange boiled bagels on baking sheet. Brush tops with egg white and sprinkle with poppy seeds.

5. Bake in the preheated oven for 20 to 25 minutes or until well browned. **Yield:** 9 bagels.

Per bagel: About 215 calories, 7g protein, 42g carbohydrate, 2g fat, 2g fiber, 0mg cholesterol, 406mg sodium

◄ Healthy

Prep Time: 30 minutes
Cook Time: 3 hours 25 minutes
Average Rating: ★★★★★
47 Ratings ▲ 36 Reviews
What other cooks have done:
"I added sun-dried tomatoes and chopped black olives to the dough, cut out like doughnuts, and omitted the sugar in the boiling water. They make a great snack bread."

French Baguettes

Submitted by: **Judy Taubert**

"Great eaten fresh from oven. Used to make sub sandwiches or bruschetta, or have them with dinner tonight."

1	cup water	1½	teaspoons bread machine yeast
2½	cups bread flour		
1	tablespoon white sugar	1	egg yolk
1	teaspoon salt	1	tablespoon water

1. Place 1 cup water, bread flour, sugar, salt, and yeast into bread machine pan in the order recommended by manufacturer. Select Dough setting and press Start.

2. When the cycle has completed, place dough in a greased bowl, turning to coat all sides. Cover and let rise in a warm place for about 30 minutes or until doubled in bulk. Dough is ready if indentation remains when touched.

3. Punch down dough. On a lightly floured surface, roll into a 16x12 inch rectangle. Cut dough in half, creating 2 (8x12 inch) rectangles. Roll up each dough half tightly, beginning at 12 inch side, pounding out any air bubbles as you go. Roll gently back and forth to taper end. Place 3 inches apart on a greased baking sheet. Make deep diagonal slashes across loaves every 2 inches, or make 1 lengthwise slash on each loaf. Cover and let rise in a warm place for 30 to 40 minutes or until doubled in bulk.

4. Preheat oven to 375°F (190°C). Beat egg yolk with 1 tablespoon water; brush over tops of loaves.

5. Bake in the preheated oven for 20 to 25 minutes or until golden brown. **Yield:** 12 servings.

Per serving: About 112 calories, 4g protein, 22g carbohydrate, 1g fat, 1g fiber, 18mg cholesterol, 196mg sodium

# Entrées

Solve your dinner dilemmas with our collection of top-rated entrées. Splurge with elegant Prime Rib Roast or Crab Stuffed Flounder, break out the grill with Blue Cheese Burgers or Jay's Jerk Chicken, and wow your kids with Burrito Pie or Breaded Chicken Fingers. This bounty of family favorites includes recipes for classic comfort food, company-worthy fare, meatless main dishes, and many more unforgettable meals.

Prime Rib Roast

Submitted by: **William Anatooskin**
"Use this marinade to tenderize the roast."

⅓ cup orange marmalade
2 tablespoons brown sugar
1 tablespoon powdered mustard
1 tablespoon grated fresh ginger root
3 tablespoons soy sauce
¼ teaspoon hot sauce
4 cloves garlic, minced
1 cup beer
1 (8 pound) prime rib roast
¼ cup olive oil
Freshly ground black pepper

1. In a bowl, combine marmalade, brown sugar, mustard, ginger, soy sauce, hot sauce, and garlic. Mix well and gently stir in beer.
2. Prick holes in the roast with a 2-pronged fork. Place roast in a large bowl or in the roasting pan. Pour marinade over roast; cover and marinate in the refrigerator for at least 2 hours, basting at least twice.
3. Preheat oven to 400°F (200°C).
4. Place roast on a rack in a roasting pan. Add about 1 cup of marinade to roasting pan. Pour olive oil over roast. Sprinkle roast with freshly ground black pepper. Insert meat thermometer into the middle of the roast, making sure that the thermometer does not touch any bone. Cover pan with aluminum foil and seal edges tightly around pan.
5. Cook roast in the preheated oven for 1 hour. Remove foil and baste after 1 hour of cooking. Do not replace foil cover. Reduce heat to 325°F (165°C) and cook 1 more hour or until thermometer registers 145°F (63°C). Remove roasting pan from oven, place foil over roast, and let the roast stand for about 15 minutes before slicing. **Yield:** 12 servings.

Per serving: About 798 calories, 53g protein, 10g carbohydrate, 59g fat, 0g fiber, 215mg cholesterol, 433mg sodium

---

Cooking Basics: **Perfect Prime Rib** ▼

A rib roast (a.k.a. prime rib or standing rib roast) is a magnificent centerpiece for any meal. This cut of beef is unbelievably tender and juicy, and boasts a bold flavor that needs no dressing up.

Solve the Meat Mystery
Shopping for a roast can be confusing. The same cut of meat can be called by several different names. "Prime rib" is the most famous moniker for this cut, but the word "prime" actually describes the grade of the meat, not the cut. The top three grades of beef are Prime, Choice, and Select. Meats graded 'Prime' are sold almost exclusively to restaurants, so, while you may have eaten Prime rib in a restaurant before, you probably won't be able to buy a Prime rib roast at the grocery store. Instead, look for a Choice cut by the name of 'rib roast,' 'eye of the rib roast,' or 'standing rib roast.' A rib roast can be boneless, in which case it may be called an 'eye of the rib' roast, or it can

have the ribs still attached and may be called a 'standing rib' roast. The meat will be more flavorful if you roast it with the ribs still attached, but a boneless roast is definitely easier to carve.

The Real Secret to a Perfect Prime Rib
Once you've splurged for an expensive cut of meat, spend a few more dollars on a meat thermometer. A thermometer is the best way to guarantee the roast turns out just the way you want it. For an accurate reading, push the thermometer into the middle of the roast, making sure the tip is not touching fat or bone (or the pan!). We recommend you cook this cut of meat to medium-rare (145°F/63°C) or medium (160°F/70°C). Remember that the roast's temperature will rise at least 5 degrees after you remove it from the oven. Let the roast stand 15 to 20 minutes before carving to let the juices return to the center.   *- Jennifer Anderson*

For more information, visit **Allrecipes.com**

Beef Wellington

Submitted by: **Normala**

"This is a very easy recipe that I learned to make when I was living in England. Note that Beef Wellington should be served with the center slightly pink."

1	(2 to 3 pound) beef tenderloin
2	tablespoons butter, softened
2	tablespoons butter
1	onion, chopped
½	cup sliced fresh mushrooms
2	ounces liver pâté

2	tablespoons butter, softened
	Salt and pepper to taste
1	(17.3 ounce) package frozen puff pastry, thawed
1	egg yolk, beaten
1	(10.5 ounce) can beef broth
2	tablespoons red wine

1. Preheat oven to 425°F (220°C). Place beef in a 7x11 inch baking dish and spread with 2 tablespoons softened butter. Bake in the preheated oven for 10 to 15 minutes or until browned. Remove from pan and allow to cool completely. Reserve pan juices.

2. Melt 2 tablespoons butter in a skillet over medium heat. Sauté onion and mushrooms in butter for 5 minutes. Remove from heat and cool.

3. Increase heat to 450°F (230°C). Mix together pâté and 2 tablespoons softened butter and season with salt and pepper to taste. Spread pâté over beef.

4. Roll out the puff pastry dough and place beef in the center. Top with onion and mushroom mixture. Fold up and seal all the edges, making sure the seams are not too thick. Place beef in a lightly greased 9x13 inch baking dish, cut a few slits in the top of the dough, and brush with egg yolk.

5. Bake in the preheated oven for 10 minutes. Reduce heat to 425°F (220°C) and bake for 10 to 15 more minutes or until pastry is a rich, golden brown and meat thermometer inserted into thickest part of tenderloin registers 145°F (63°C) for medium-rare or 160°F (70°C) for medium. Set aside and keep warm.

6. Place all reserved juices in a small saucepan over high heat. Stir in beef broth and red wine; boil for 10 to 15 minutes or until slightly reduced. Strain and serve with beef. **Yield:** 6 servings.

Per serving: About 1156 calories, 42g protein, 39g carbohydrate, 91g fat, 2g fiber, 215mg cholesterol, 641mg sodium

◄ Restaurant Fare

Prep Time: 30 minutes
Cook Time: 1 hour
Average Rating: ★★★★★
32 Ratings ▲ 24 Reviews
What other cooks have done:
"I would recommend using this recipe for individual fillets for a very impressive, fine-dining restaurant look. I also suggest placing the pastry-covered meat on a rack in the baking pan. This allows the juices to run to the pan, away from the puff pastry-wrapped meat."

Beef Tenderloin with Roasted Shallots

Submitted by: **Christine**

"The shallot sauce takes some time but is well worth it. This is definitely a company dish, and the recipe doubles well for a larger party. Serve with a green salad and roasted vegetables."

Prep Time: 15 minutes
Cook Time: 1 hour 40 minutes
Average Rating: ★★★★★
85 Ratings ▲ 64 Reviews
What other cooks have done:
"I made this for a dinner party of 15 people last night with a 5½ pound tenderloin. I was worried about timing the preparation of the meat along with the other side dishes, so I prepared some of this ahead. I roasted the shallots and boiled the wine/broth combination the day before and stored these in the refrigerator. Then I cooked the bacon a couple of hours ahead, set it aside to cool, and allowed the pan it cooked in to sit on the cooktop. I put the wine/broth mixture, bacon, and shallots into the blender to make a smooth sauce. After roasting the tenderloin, I poured the smooth sauce into the pan, whisked in the butter and flour, and voilà—incredible tasting gravy to spoon over a moist and tender cut of meat. I did roast the tenderloin longer because many of my guests like beef well done. Even with that, it still could be cut with a fork."

¾	pound shallots, halved lengthwise and peeled	1	tablespoon fresh thyme or 1 teaspoon dried thyme
1½	tablespoons olive oil	½	teaspoon salt
½	teaspoon salt	½	teaspoon pepper
½	teaspoon pepper	3	slices bacon, diced
3	cups beef broth	3	tablespoons butter
¾	cup port wine	1	tablespoon all-purpose flour
1½	teaspoons tomato paste	¼	teaspoon pepper
2	pounds beef tenderloin roast, trimmed	4	sprigs watercress or fresh thyme for garnish

1. Preheat oven to 375°F (190°C). In a 9 inch pie dish, toss shallots with oil to coat. Season with salt and pepper. Roast in the preheated oven about 30 minutes or until shallots are deep brown and very tender, stirring occasionally.

2. In a large saucepan, combine beef broth and port. Bring to a boil. Cook over high heat until the volume is reduced by half, about 30 minutes. Whisk in tomato paste. Set aside.

3. Pat beef dry; sprinkle with thyme, ½ teaspoon salt, and ½ teaspoon pepper. Set a large roasting pan over medium heat on the cooktop and sauté bacon until done. Using a slotted spoon, transfer bacon to paper towels, reserving drippings in pan. Add beef to pan; brown on all sides over medium-high heat, about 7 minutes.

4. Transfer pan to oven. Roast beef until meat thermometer inserted into center registers 145°F (63°C) for medium-rare, about 25 minutes. Transfer beef to platter. Tent loosely with foil.

5. Skim off fat from pan drippings in roasting pan. Place pan over high heat on cooktop. Add broth mixture and bring to boil; stir to scrape up any browned bits. Melt 3 tablespoons butter in a saucepan; add flour and cook 1 minute. Add pan drippings and simmer 5 minutes or until sauce thickens. Stir in roasted shallots and reserved bacon. Season with ¼ teaspoon pepper.

6. Cut beef into ½ inch thick slices. Serve with sauce and garnish with watercress or thyme. **Yield:** 6 servings.

Per serving: About 663 calories, 31g protein, 12g carbohydrate, 52g fat, 0g fiber, 132mg cholesterol, 649mg sodium

BBQ Steak

Submitted by: **Silau**

"Get ready for the most tasteful and delicious steak you could ever imagine."

1	small onion, chopped	2	tablespoons Dijon-style
7	cloves garlic		prepared mustard
½	cup olive oil	2	teaspoons salt
½	cup white vinegar	1	teaspoon black pepper
½	cup soy sauce	2	pounds tri-tip steak or top
2	tablespoons chopped fresh		round steak
	rosemary		

1. Process onion, garlic, olive oil, vinegar, soy sauce, rosemary, mustard, salt, and pepper in a food processor until smooth. Pour over steak in a heavy-duty, zip-top plastic bag and refrigerate several hours.
2. Brush cold grill rack with oil and preheat the grill for high heat.
3. Place steak on the prepared grill. Grill for 3 to 7 minutes per side or to desired doneness. Slice to serve. **Yield:** 8 servings.

Per serving: About 397 calories, 24g protein, 4g carbohydrate, 32g fat, 1g fiber, 75mg cholesterol, 1608mg sodium

◀ From the Grill

Prep Time: 15 minutes
Cook Time: 14 minutes
Average Rating: ★★★★★
9 Ratings ▲ 4 Reviews
What other cooks have done:
"Goodbye to all store-bought marinades. This recipe is actually for the BBQ, but it works great even if you're broiling or pan-frying your steaks. It's really easy, too—put everything in the blender, and you're done. For a sweeter variation, add 2 tablespoons of brown sugar."

Rib Eye Steaks with a Soy and Ginger Marinade

Submitted by: **William Anatooskin**

"You'll use this marinade often. It's great for steaks or beef strips for stir-fries."

½	cup soy sauce	1	teaspoon powdered mustard
¼	cup maple syrup	½	teaspoon sesame oil
6	cloves garlic, minced	¼	teaspoon hot sauce
1	tablespoon grated fresh	½	cup beer
	ginger root	4	(10 ounce) rib eye steaks

1. In a medium bowl, combine soy sauce, syrup, garlic, ginger, mustard, sesame oil, and hot sauce; mix well. Add beer and stir lightly.
2. Prepare steaks by scoring any fatty areas with a knife (this prevents the steaks from curling when grilling). Place steaks in a 7x11 inch baking dish and pour marinade over top. Using a fork, punch holes in steaks to allow marinade to penetrate into the steaks. Turn steaks and punch holes on other side. Cover with plastic wrap and let marinate in the refrigerator for at least 1 hour or overnight.
3. Preheat the grill for high heat. Place steaks directly on grill and sear 1 side for about 15 seconds. Turn steaks over and cook for about 5 minutes; turn and cook for 5 more minutes or to desired degree of doneness. **Yield:** 4 servings.

Per serving: About 468 calories, 34g protein, 19g carbohydrate, 27g fat, 1g fiber, 100mg cholesterol, 1826mg sodium

◀ Quick & Easy

Prep Time: 10 minutes
Cook Time: 10 minutes
Average Rating: ★★★★★
40 Ratings ▲ 24 Reviews
What other cooks have done:
"By far, this is the best marinade recipe I've ever used! The steaks are great, and our guests are raving. I've also adjusted the recipe to make a good basic stir-fry sauce. You can't go wrong with this one!"

Awesome Slow-Cooker Pot Roast

Submitted by: **Brenda Arnold**

"This is a very easy recipe for a delicious pot roast. It makes its own gravy. It's designed especially for the working person who doesn't have time to cook all day, but it tastes like you did."

2 (10.75 ounce) cans condensed cream of mushroom soup
1 (1 ounce) package dry onion soup mix
1¼ cups water
1 (5½ pound) chuck roast

1. In a slow cooker, mix cream of mushroom soup, dry onion soup mix, and water. Cut chuck roast in half crosswise to ensure even doneness. Place pot roast in slow cooker and coat with soup mixture.
2. Cook on High setting for 3 to 4 hours or on Low setting for 6 to 8 hours. **Yield:** 12 servings.

Per serving: About 435 calories, 46g protein, 5g carbohydrate, 25g fat, 0g fiber, 127mg cholesterol, 663mg sodium

Ronaldo's Beef Carnitas

Submitted by: **Miss Annie**

"I use this recipe all the time. It's the best! The meat just falls apart, and it's delicious served in flour tortillas with guacamole and salsa. It also freezes well."

1 (4 pound) chuck roast
1 (4.5 ounce) can chopped green chiles
2 tablespoons chili powder
½ teaspoon dried oregano
½ teaspoon ground cumin
2 cloves garlic, minced
Salt to taste

1. Preheat oven to 300°F (150°C).
2. Place roast on heavy-duty foil large enough to enclose the meat. In a small bowl, combine the green chiles, chili powder, oregano, cumin, garlic, and salt to taste. Mix well and rub over the meat.
3. Totally wrap the meat in the foil and place in a roasting pan.
4. Bake in the preheated oven for 3½ to 4 hours or until the roast just falls apart with a fork. Remove from oven and shred using 2 forks. **Yield:** 8 servings.

Per serving: About 472 calories, 44g protein, 2g carbohydrate, 31g fat, 1g fiber, 148mg cholesterol, 359mg sodium

Slow-Cooker Beef Stroganoff

Submitted by: **Jessica**

"For an easy variation of a favorite, try this recipe. I used to prepare it the traditional way, with sour cream, but I didn't have any one night, so I used cream cheese instead. My husband and I liked it even better! Serve over hot, cooked egg noodles or rice."

1	pound cubed beef stew meat	½	cup chopped onion
1	(10.75 ounce) can condensed golden mushroom soup	1	tablespoon Worcestershire sauce
		¼	cup water
		4	ounces cream cheese

1. In a slow cooker, combine the meat, soup, onion, Worcestershire sauce, and water.
2. Cook on High setting for 4 to 5 hours or on Low setting for 8 hours. Stir in cream cheese just before serving. **Yield:** 4 servings.

Per serving: About 442 calories, 24g protein, 9g carbohydrate, 34g fat, 1g fiber, 110mg cholesterol, 800mg sodium

◄ **Slow-Cooker Creation**

Prep Time: 10 minutes
Cook Time: 8 hours
Average Rating: ★★★★★
153 Ratings ▲ 113 Reviews
What other cooks have done:
"I thickened the sauce with cornstarch before adding the cream cheese, and I also used red wine in place of the water. I also added an 8 ounce container of pre-sliced fresh mushrooms and quite a bit of pepper for extra flavor."

Cola Pot Roast II

Submitted by: **Sher Garfield**

"The rich gravy this makes is wonderful, with just a hint of sweetness. Everyone asks for the recipe, and no one ever guesses the secret ingredient ...cola!"

1	(4 pound) beef sirloin roast	1	(1 ounce) package dry onion soup mix
3	carrots, chopped		
3	stalks celery, chopped	1	(10.75 ounce) can condensed cream of mushroom soup
1	clove garlic, minced		
½	(.75 ounce) package dry brown gravy mix		
2	tablespoons water	10	ounces cola-flavored carbonated beverage

1. Preheat oven to 350°F (175°C).
2. Place meat in a roasting pan. Sprinkle carrots, celery, and minced garlic around roast.
3. In a small bowl, combine the brown gravy mix and water, mixing into a smooth paste. Add onion soup mix, cream of mushroom soup, and cola-flavored carbonated beverage. Pour over the roast.
4. Cover pan and cook in the preheated oven for 1 hour. Reduce oven temperature to 225°F (110°C) and continue cooking 2 hours. Remove from oven and turn roast over so that the top is now covered with the gravy. Cover pan and return to oven for 2 hours.
5. Remove from oven and let meat stand for 10 minutes before slicing. **Yield:** 14 servings.

Per serving: About 246 calories, 22g protein, 8g carbohydrate, 14g fat, 1g fiber, 70mg cholesterol, 426mg sodium

◄ **Family Favorite**

Prep Time: 15 minutes
Cook Time: 5 hours
Average Rating: ★★★★★
131 Ratings ▲ 83 Reviews
What other cooks have done:
"I've tried both sirloin and chuck roasts in this dish, and I've found that the less-expensive chuck roast actually has more flavor and is juicier and more tender than the sirloin. Instead of ½ package brown gravy mix, we use the whole thing. This dish makes a pan full of very tasty gravy, so be sure to make a big bowl of mashed potatoes to go with it!"

Slow-Cooker Pepper Steak

Submitted by: **Marge**

"Very tender and flavorful, this recipe is one of our family's favorites. It's great to make ahead in a slow cooker and then serve over rice, egg noodles, or chow mein."

2 pounds beef sirloin, cut into 2 inch strips	2 large green bell peppers, coarsely chopped
1 teaspoon garlic powder	1 (14.5 ounce) can stewed tomatoes, undrained
3 tablespoons vegetable oil	3 tablespoons soy sauce
1 beef bouillon cube	1 teaspoon white sugar
¼ cup hot water	1 teaspoon salt
1 tablespoon cornstarch	
½ cup chopped onion	

1. Sprinkle strips of sirloin with garlic powder. In a large skillet over medium heat, heat the vegetable oil and brown the seasoned beef strips. Transfer to a slow cooker.

2. Mix bouillon cube with hot water until dissolved, then mix in cornstarch until dissolved. Pour into the slow cooker with meat. Add onion, bell pepper, stewed tomatoes, soy sauce, sugar, and salt.

3. Cover and cook on High for 3 to 4 hours or on Low for 6 to 8 hours. **Yield:** 4 servings.

Per serving: About 459 calories, 43g protein, 18g carbohydrate, 24g fat, 3g fiber, 120mg cholesterol, 1765mg sodium

Slow Cooking Is Good Cooking ▼

Imagine walking in the door tonight and being stopped in your tracks by the enticing aroma of what can only be dinner. You can't believe it—someone has been home all day cooking for you! Then you remember—it's your slow cooker. All you had to do last night was chop up some meat and veggies, and all you had to do this morning was toss them in that magical appliance and switch it on. Slow cooking is hip again! Dust off that pot and get ready to rediscover just how easy a slow cooker can make your life.

Go Easy on the Juice

Because slow cookers work at low heat and with their lids on, there is hardly any liquid lost during cooking. In fact, it may appear that you have even more liquid than you started with. That's because almost all food, especially meats and vegetables, contain water. As they cook, they begin to release water. With most cooking methods, the water turns to steam and evaporates. But, since the lid is on the slow cooker, there's nowhere for the steam to go; it just collects on the lid and drips back into the food. So, if you're inventing your own slow cooker recipes or adapting your favorite stovetop and oven recipes for the slow cooker, decrease the amount of liquid you use.

Be Nice to the Spice

Whole spices such as bay leaves, peppercorns, or cinnamon sticks will give slow cooker items a very intense flavor if left in the pot for the entire cooking time, so use them sparingly. Ground spices as well as fresh and dried herbs, on the other hand, can lose much of their flavor if allowed to simmer for several hours in the slow cooker. It's better to add these during the last two hours of cooking if you can manage it. Dairy products such as milk, sour cream, and cheese also do not hold up well to several hours of simmering. To avoid curdling, wait until the last hour of cooking time to stir in these items.

Sooner or Later . . .

The slow cooker is one of the few cooking methods where you can cut the cooking time in half by turning up the temperature, and still get great results. Food will not burn in a slow cooker because it retains moisture so well, and because the heat is so evenly distributed around the sides as well as the bottom of the pot. If something takes 10 hours on the "low" setting, you can safely cook it for 5 hours on the "high" setting with very similar results.
- *Jennifer Anderson*

For more information, visit **Allrecipes.com**

Sensational Sirloin Kabobs *(pictured on page 151)*

Submitted by: **Kimber**

"After a wild night marinating in a slightly sweet soy sauce and lemon-lime mixture, sirloin steak chunks are skewered with veggies and grilled. You'll want to make these again and again!"

¼ cup soy sauce	2 pounds beef sirloin steak, cut into 1½ inch cubes
3 tablespoons light brown sugar	2 green bell peppers, cut into 2 inch pieces
3 tablespoons white vinegar	½ pound fresh mushrooms, stems removed
½ teaspoon garlic powder	1 pint cherry tomatoes
½ teaspoon seasoning salt	1 fresh pineapple, peeled, cored, and cubed
½ teaspoon garlic pepper seasoning	
4 ounces lemon-lime flavored carbonated beverage	

1. In a medium bowl, mix soy sauce, light brown sugar, white vinegar, garlic powder, seasoning salt, garlic pepper seasoning, and lemon-lime flavored carbonated beverage. Cover and chill 3 tablespoons soy mixture for basting.

2. Place beef sirloin steak in a heavy-duty, zip-top plastic bag. Cover with the remaining soy sauce mixture and seal. Marinate in the refrigerator 8 hours or overnight.

3. Lightly oil cold grill rack and preheat an outdoor grill for high heat.

4. Place green bell peppers in a medium saucepan with enough water to cover. Bring to a boil and cook approximately 1 minute.

5. On metal skewers, alternately place steak, parboiled green peppers, mushrooms, cherry tomatoes, and pineapple. Cook on the prepared grill 10 to 15 minutes or to desired doneness, basting frequently with 3 tablespoons reserved soy mixture. **Yield:** 4 servings.

Per serving: About 650 calories, 48g protein, 37g carbohydrate, 35g fat, 4g fiber, 152mg cholesterol, 1176mg sodium

---

◄ From the Grill

Prep Time: 15 minutes

Cook Time: 15 minutes

Average Rating: ★★★★★

13 Ratings ▲ 7 Reviews

What other cooks have done:

"If you like your green bell pepper a little crunchy, you may not want to parboil the pieces since they come out great when grilling the kabobs."

Beef Tips and Noodles

Submitted by: **Julie**

"This is a great dish that's very easy to make with just a few ingredients. I got this recipe from my mom years ago, and it's a family favorite."

1 (10.75 ounce) can condensed cream of mushroom soup	1 cup water
1 (1.25 ounce) package dry beef and onion soup mix	1 pound boneless top sirloin roast, cubed
1 (4.5 ounce) can mushrooms, drained	1 (16 ounce) package wide egg noodles

1. Preheat oven to 400°F (200°C).

2. In a 9x13 inch baking dish, combine the mushroom soup, beef and onion soup mix, canned mushrooms, and water. Mix thoroughly and add beef tips. Turn to coat well.

3. Bake in the preheated oven for 1 hour.

4. While beef tips are baking, bring a large pot of lightly salted water to a boil. Add pasta and cook for 8 to 10 minutes or until al dente; drain. Serve beef tips and sauce over noodles. **Yield:** 4 servings.

Per serving: About 629 calories, 36g protein, 82g carbohydrate, 17g fat, 4g fiber, 153mg cholesterol, 1240mg sodium

China Lake Barbecued Steak

Submitted by: **Bobbie**

"I made this for my family when I was a Navy wife with three children with healthy appetites. This recipe will make the most inexpensive cuts of meat very tender."

½ cup soy sauce	1½ teaspoons garlic powder
1 lemon, juiced	1 (1½ pound) flank steak
¼ cup vegetable oil	

1. Mix together soy sauce, lemon juice, and oil in a large heavy-duty, zip-top plastic bag. Rub garlic powder onto meat and add to bag. Marinate in the refrigerator for at least 4 hours, turning bag over every 2 hours.

2. Lightly oil cold grill rack and preheat grill for medium heat.

3. Place meat on grill. Cook over medium heat for 5 to 7 minutes per side or until done. **Yield:** 4 servings.

Per serving: About 455 calories, 37g protein, 6g carbohydrate, 32g fat, 2g fiber, 89mg cholesterol, 1858mg sodium

Flank Steak with Garlic Wine Sauce *(pictured on page 152)*

Submitted by: **Warner Beatty**

"Great on a cold winter day, and a real heart warmer. For best results, the meat should be quite rare."

1	medium head garlic	4	tablespoons butter, divided
1	tablespoon olive oil	¼	cup chopped green onions
1	(1½ pound) flank steak	1	cup dry red wine
1	teaspoon salt		
2	teaspoons freshly ground black pepper		

1. Preheat the oven to 400°F (200°C). Cut head of garlic in half, place on a square of foil, and drizzle with olive oil. Wrap and bake in the preheated oven for 45 minutes. Squeeze roasted garlic cloves out of skins and mash into a puree. Set aside.

2. Sprinkle steak with salt and freshly ground pepper. Heat a large heavy skillet over medium-high heat and cook seasoned steak until seared and well browned on both sides, about 2 minutes per side. Reduce heat to medium and add 2 tablespoons of the butter. Continue to cook for 10 to 12 minutes, turning often, or to desired degree of doneness. Remove meat, cover loosely, and let stand 10 minutes.

3. Pour off the fat in the skillet and add the green onions and red wine. Bring to a boil and whisk in the garlic puree. Boil about 3 to 4 minutes or until the wine is reduced by half and mixture is thick and syrupy. As it boils, scrape up browned bits with a wooden spoon. Stir in the meat juices that have accumulated under the steak. Remove from the heat and stir in the remaining 2 tablespoons of butter.

4. Slice the steak diagonally across the grain into thin strips. Arrange on a hot platter and pour the sauce down the center of the slices. Serve immediately. **Yield:** 4 servings.

Per serving: About 476 calories, 35g protein, 7g carbohydrate, 30g fat, 1g fiber, 120mg cholesterol, 245mg sodium

◄ Family Favorite

Prep Time: 55 minutes

Cook Time: 1 hour

Average Rating: ★★★★★

32 Ratings ▲ 21 Reviews

What other cooks have done:

"I added sliced mushrooms after the beef had been pan seared, and after removing the meat and pouring in the wine, I also added a cube of beef bouillon."

Lana's Sweet-and-Sour Meatballs

Submitted by: **Lana**

"You can use this wonderful savory meatball and sweet sauce recipe as a main dish, or you can use just the meatball recipe part for parties. I recommend serving over white rice."

2	pounds lean ground beef	⅓	cup water
2	eggs	3	tablespoons white vinegar
1	cup dry breadcrumbs	1	tablespoon soy sauce
½	cup finely chopped onion	½	cup packed brown sugar
½	teaspoon ground ginger	3	tablespoons cornstarch
1	teaspoon seasoning salt	½	teaspoon ground ginger
½	teaspoon ground black pepper	½	teaspoon seasoning salt
2	teaspoons Worcestershire sauce	1	large carrot, diced
2	teaspoons white sugar	1	large green bell pepper, cut into ½ inch pieces
1	(20 ounce) can pineapple chunks, drained with juice reserved		

1. Preheat oven to 400°F (200°C). Lightly grease a large, shallow baking pan.

2. In a large bowl, thoroughly mix the ground beef, eggs, breadcrumbs, and onion. Sprinkle with ½ teaspoon ginger, 1 teaspoon seasoning salt, pepper, Worcestershire sauce, and white sugar. Shape into 1 inch balls.

3. Place meatballs in a single layer in prepared pan. Bake in the preheated oven for 10 to 15 minutes; set aside.

4. To make the sauce, mix enough water with the reserved pineapple juice to make 1 cup. In a large pot over medium heat, combine the juice mixture, ⅓ cup water, vinegar, soy sauce, and brown sugar. Stir in cornstarch, ½ teaspoon ginger, and ½ teaspoon seasoning salt until smooth. Cover and cook until thickened.

5. Stir pineapple chunks, carrot, green pepper, and meatballs into the sauce. Gently stir to coat the meatballs with the sauce. Simmer, uncovered, for about 20 minutes or until meatballs are thoroughly cooked.

Yield: 8 servings.

Per serving: About 499 calories, 24g protein, 42g carbohydrate, 26g fat, 2g fiber, 138mg cholesterol, 531mg sodium

Burrito Pie *(pictured on page 191)*

Submitted by: **Kathi J. McClaren**

"This is a lot like a lasagna, only Mexican style! Cut into squares and garnish with sour cream, salsa, lettuce, and tomato. Make sure you like spicy foods before trying this one. It's hot!"

2	pounds ground chuck
1	onion, chopped
2	teaspoons minced garlic
1	(2¼ ounce) can sliced black olives, drained
1	(4.5 ounce) can chopped green chiles, undrained
1	(10 ounce) can diced tomatoes and green chiles, drained
1	(16 ounce) jar taco sauce
2	(16 ounce) cans refried beans
12	(8 inch) flour tortillas
1	(12 ounce) package shredded Colby cheese

1. Preheat oven to 350°F (175°C).

2. In a large skillet over medium heat, sauté the ground chuck for 5 minutes. Add the onion and garlic and sauté for 5 more minutes. Drain any excess fat. Mix in the olives, green chiles, tomatoes with green chiles, taco sauce, and refried beans. Stir mixture thoroughly, reduce heat to low, and let simmer for 15 to 20 minutes.

3. Spread a thin layer of the meat mixture in a 9x13 inch baking dish. Cover with a layer of tortillas followed by more meat mixture, then a layer of cheese. Repeat tortilla, meat, cheese pattern until all the tortillas are used, topping off with a layer of meat mixture and cheese.

4. Bake in the preheated oven for 20 to 30 minutes or until cheese is slightly brown and bubbly. **Yield:** 15 servings.

Per serving: About 460 calories, 21g protein, 36g carbohydrate, 25g fat, 5g fiber, 73mg cholesterol, 863mg sodium

◄ Covered-Dish Favorite

Prep Time: 30 minutes

Cook Time: 1 hour

Average Rating: ★★★★★

403 Ratings ▲ 272 Reviews

What other cooks have done:

"I made this with chicken and used fat-free refried beans, part-skim cheese, and low-fat sour cream. Cut the chicken into strips and do everything the same except use only 1½ cups taco sauce. It was still very yummy and cuts down on the fat grams."

Glazed Meatloaf

Submitted by: **Delia Martinez**

"Everyone will enjoy this succulent meatloaf glazed with a sweet-and-sour sauce."

½	cup ketchup	3	slices bread, broken up into small pieces
⅓	cup packed brown sugar		
¼	cup lemon juice, divided	1	egg, beaten
1	teaspoon powdered mustard	1	teaspoon beef bouillon granules
2	pounds ground beef		
¼	cup chopped onion		

1. Preheat oven to 350°F (175°C).

2. In a small bowl, combine the ketchup, brown sugar, 1 tablespoon lemon juice, and mustard.

3. In a large bowl, combine the ground beef, onion, bread, egg, bouillon, remaining lemon juice, and ⅓ of the ketchup mixture from the small bowl. Mix well and place in a lightly greased 5x9 inch loaf pan.

4. Bake in the preheated oven for 1 hour, drain any excess fat, coat with remaining ketchup mixture, and bake 10 more minutes. **Yield:** 6 servings.

Per serving: About 573 calories, 27g protein, 22g carbohydrate, 42g fat, 1g fiber, 164mg cholesterol, 394mg sodium

Blue Cheese Burgers

Submitted by: **Poni**

"Hamburgers? Yes. But basic fare? Definitely not! What a treat they are, and the wise cook will make up a dozen or so for the freezer. If you like blue cheese, you'll never forget these burgers."

¼	pound blue cheese	1	teaspoon coarsely ground black pepper
3	pounds ground round		
½	cup minced fresh chives	1½	teaspoons salt
¼	teaspoon hot sauce	1	teaspoon powdered mustard
1	teaspoon Worcestershire sauce	12	hamburger buns

1. Crumble the blue cheese into a large bowl and thoroughly combine with ground round, chives, hot sauce, Worcestershire sauce, black pepper, salt, and mustard. Cover and refrigerate for 2 hours.

2. Lightly oil cold grill rack and preheat grill for high heat.

3. Lightly press the meat into 12 patties. Cook on preheated grill until browned on both sides and to desired doneness. Serve on hamburger buns. **Yield:** 12 servings.

Per serving: About 459 calories, 26g protein, 22g carbohydrate, 29g fat, 1g fiber, 92mg cholesterol, 754mg sodium

American Lasagna

Submitted by: **Rosemary Stoker**
"Making this lasagna a day ahead and refrigerating overnight allow the spices to meld to give it exceptional flavor."

1½	pounds ground beef	12	dried lasagna noodles
1	onion, chopped	2	eggs, beaten
2	cloves garlic, minced	2	cups part–skim ricotta cheese
1	tablespoon chopped fresh basil	½	cup grated Parmesan cheese
1	teaspoon dried oregano	2	tablespoons dried parsley
2	tablespoons brown sugar	1	teaspoon salt
1½	teaspoons salt	1	pound mozzarella cheese, shredded
1	(28 ounce) can diced tomatoes	2	tablespoons grated Parmesan cheese
2	(6 ounce) cans tomato paste		

1. In a medium skillet over medium heat, brown ground beef, onion, and garlic; drain fat. Mix in basil, oregano, brown sugar, 1½ teaspoons salt, diced tomatoes, and tomato paste. Simmer for 30 to 45 minutes, stirring occasionally.

2. Preheat oven to 375°F (190°C). Bring a large pot of lightly salted water to a boil. Add lasagna noodles and cook for 5 to 8 minutes or until al dente; drain. Lay noodles flat on towels and blot dry.

3. In a medium bowl, mix together eggs, ricotta, ½ cup Parmesan cheese, parsley, and 1 teaspoon salt.

4. Layer 4 lasagna noodles in a 9x13 inch baking dish. Cover noodles with half ricotta mixture, half of the mozzarella cheese, and one-third of the sauce. Repeat. Top with remaining noodles and sauce. Sprinkle 2 tablespoons Parmesan cheese over the top.

5. Bake in the preheated oven 30 minutes. Let stand 10 minutes before serving. **Yield:** 8 servings.

Per serving: About 725 calories, 49g protein, 49g carbohydrate, 37g fat, 5g fiber, 178mg cholesterol, 1929mg sodium

---

◄ Make-Ahead

Prep Time: 30 minutes
Cook Time: 1 hour 30 minutes
Average Rating: ★★★★★
342 Ratings ▲ 238 Reviews
What other cooks have done:
"Instead of ricotta cheese, I used cottage cheese. I also rubbed each noodle with olive oil after I cooked them. I added some crushed red pepper flakes and mushrooms to the sauce."

Manicotti alla Romana *(pictured on facing page)*

Submitted by: **Mark Blau**

"White and red sauces cover this rich meat, spinach, and cheese-filled manicotti dish. I offer this on the catering menu at my catering company, and it's the most popular for casual dinner parties. It's a bit of work, but well worth the effort."

Restaurant Fare ▶

Prep Time: 1 hour

Cook Time: 50 minutes

Average Rating: ★★★★★

37 Ratings ▲ 25 Reviews

What other cooks have done:

"I made this for a casual dinner party and served it with herbed focaccia and a green salad. I received many compliments on the entire meal. I also filled the shells the day before and made the white sauce on the morning of the party. The best part of all—no pots to clean while guests were here!"

2	tablespoons olive oil	2	tablespoons butter
½	cup chopped onion	2	tablespoons all-purpose flour
6	cloves garlic, finely chopped		
1	pound ground beef	2	tablespoons chicken bouillon granules
1	tablespoon salt (or to taste)		
1	(10 ounce) package frozen chopped spinach	2	cups half-and-half
		¼	cup chopped fresh parsley
1	(12 ounce) package dried manicotti shells	1	tablespoon chopped fresh basil
2	cups ricotta cheese	½	cup grated Parmesan cheese
2	eggs, beaten		
3	cups spaghetti sauce, divided		

1. Heat oil in a large skillet over medium heat. Sauté onion until translucent. Add garlic and sauté for 1 minute; stir in ground beef. Cook until well browned and crumbled. Season with salt and set aside to cool.

2. Thaw spinach according to package directions and drain well. Meanwhile, bring a large pot of lightly salted water to a boil. Add manicotti shells and parboil for half of the time recommended on the package. Drain and cover with cool water to stop the cooking process and to prevent the shells from cracking.

3. Add the thawed spinach and ricotta cheese to the ground beef mixture. When the mixture is cool, add the beaten eggs. Spread ¼ cup spaghetti sauce in a lightly greased 9x13 inch baking dish. Gently drain the manicotti shells and carefully stuff each one with the meat and cheese mixture; place shells in prepared dish. Lightly cover the dish with plastic wrap or a clean, damp towel to prevent shells from cracking.

4. Preheat oven to 350°F (175°C).

5. Prepare the white sauce by melting the butter in a small saucepan over medium heat. Stir in flour and bouillon. Increase heat to medium high and cook, stirring constantly, until it begins to bubble. Stir in half-and-half and bring to a boil, stirring frequently. Cook for 1 minute, stirring constantly. Remove from heat and stir in parsley. Pour or ladle the sauce evenly over the stuffed shells.

6. Stir the basil into the remaining spaghetti sauce. Carefully pour or ladle spaghetti sauce over the white sauce, trying to layer the sauces without mixing.

7. Cover and bake in the preheated oven for 40 minutes. Remove from oven, uncover, and sprinkle with Parmesan cheese. Bake, uncovered, for 10 more minutes. **Yield:** 6 to 8 servings.

Per serving: About 693 calories, 37g protein, 56g carbohydrate, 36g fat, 5g fiber, 165mg cholesterol, 2133mg sodium

Manicotti alla Romana, facing page

Turkey Pot Pie, page 181

Greek Chicken, page 167

Sensational Sirloin
Kabobs, page 141

Lemon-Horseradish New
Potatoes, page 242

Flank Steak with Garlic
Wine Sauce, page 143

Almond-Crusted Halibut Crystal
Symphony, page 185

Spaghetti Carbonara II, page 165

Gourmet Chicken Pizza, page 175

Sesame Shrimp Stir-Fry, page 193

Chicken Danielle, page 174

Sea Bass, Cuban Style, page 187

Veal Marsala

Submitted by: **Christine**

"Stir in a few tablespoons of cream before serving, if desired. This dish can be made 24 hours ahead. To reheat, cover with foil and bake in a 350° oven for 30 minutes. Garnish with cherry tomatoes and parsley."

2	pounds veal cutlets	2	tablespoons olive oil
¼	cup all-purpose flour	¾	pound fresh mushrooms,
½	teaspoon seasoning salt		quartered
½	cup butter	¼	cup Marsala wine

1. Place cutlets between 2 sheets of plastic wrap and pound thinly with a meat mallet or rolling pin.

2. In shallow dish, combine flour and seasoning salt. Dredge cutlets in flour mixture and let stand 15 minutes on a wire rack.

3. In a large skillet over medium-high heat, melt butter with oil. Cook floured cutlets on both sides until brown. Add mushrooms and reduce heat to low; cover and cook 10 minutes.

4. Pour in Marsala and simmer 5 more minutes until veal is tender and sauce is hot. Serve immediately. **Yield:** 6 servings.

Per serving: About 360 calories, 21g protein, 14g carbohydrate, 24g fat, 1g fiber, 116mg cholesterol, 537mg sodium

◄ Quick & Easy

Prep Time: 10 minutes
Cook Time: 30 minutes
Average Rating: ★★★★★
17 Ratings ▲ 14 Reviews
What other cooks have done:
"I used large chicken breast tenders instead of veal, which worked out very well. I did add a tablespoon of cream to the sauce at the end, but it was thick enough without it."

Roast Leg of Lamb with Rosemary

Submitted by: **jmass**

"Marinating this leg of lamb overnight with fresh rosemary, garlic, mustard, honey, and lemon zest is key. Be prepared for many requests for seconds!"

¼	cup honey	1	teaspoon lemon zest
2	tablespoons prepared	3	cloves garlic, minced
	Dijon-style mustard	1	(5 pound) whole leg of
2	tablespoons chopped fresh		lamb
	rosemary	1	teaspoon coarse salt
1	teaspoon freshly ground		
	black pepper		

1. In a small bowl, combine the honey, mustard, rosemary, ground black pepper, lemon zest, and garlic. Mix well and apply to the lamb. Cover and marinate in the refrigerator overnight.

2. Preheat oven to 450°F (230°C).

3. Place lamb on a greased rack in a roasting pan and sprinkle with salt.

4. Bake in the preheated oven for 20 minutes; reduce heat to 400°F (200°C) and roast for 55 to 60 more minutes or until a meat thermometer registers 150°F (65°C) for medium-rare or 160°F (70°C) for medium. **Yield:** 7 servings.

Per serving: About 791 calories, 59g protein, 11g carbohydrate, 56g fat, 0g fiber, 224mg cholesterol, 642mg sodium

◄ Holiday Fare

Prep Time: 15 minutes
Cook Time: 1 hour 20 minutes
Average Rating: ★★★★★
27 Ratings ▲ 21 Reviews
What other cooks have done:
"Great recipe for first time lamb cooks. I served this for Easter dinner to rave reviews! The flavor of the marinade is fabulous and marinating overnight is a must. I made small slits in the meat and stuffed with slices of garlic that had been tossed in the marinade."

Rosemary-Braised Lamb Shanks

Submitted by: **S. Hodge**

"These lamb shanks are slowly simmered with fresh rosemary, garlic, tomatoes, and red wine and are great served with polenta or with my family's favorite, roasted garlic mashed potatoes. You need something to soak up the wonderful sauce that's created with these."

6	pounds lamb shanks	1	(28 ounce) can whole peeled tomatoes with juice
½	teaspoon salt		
½	teaspoon pepper		
2	tablespoons olive oil	1	(10.5 ounce) can chicken broth
2	onions, chopped		
3	large carrots, cut into ¼ inch rounds	1	(10.5 ounce) can beef broth
		5	teaspoons chopped fresh rosemary
10	cloves garlic, minced		
1	(750 milliliter) bottle red wine	2	teaspoons chopped fresh thyme

1. Sprinkle shanks with salt and pepper. Heat oil in a large heavy pot over medium-high heat. Working in batches, cook shanks until brown on all sides, about 8 minutes. Transfer shanks to a plate.

2. Add onion, carrot, and garlic to pot and sauté until golden brown, about 10 minutes. Stir in wine, tomatoes, chicken broth, and beef broth. Season with rosemary and thyme. Return shanks to pot, pressing down to submerge. Bring to a boil and reduce heat to medium low. Cover and simmer until meat is tender, about 2 hours.

3. Remove cover from pot. Simmer about 20 minutes longer. Transfer shanks to a platter and place in a warm oven. Boil juices in pot until thickened, about 15 minutes. Spoon over shanks. **Yield:** 4 servings.

Per serving: About 458 calories, 29g protein, 17g carbohydrate, 22g fat, 3g fiber, 92mg cholesterol, 648mg sodium

Overnight Pork Roast with Cabbage

Submitted by: **Holly**

"It's well worth the effort that goes into making this delicious pork loin and cabbage recipe topped with mashed potatoes. Make sure you have a meat thermometer handy for this one. Substitute sauerkraut for the cabbage for that Old World touch."

4	teaspoons caraway seeds, crushed and divided	2	bay leaves
2	cloves garlic, minced		Salt and pepper to taste
2	teaspoons salt	2½	pounds shredded fresh cabbage
1	teaspoon ground black pepper	1	(12 ounce) can or bottle beer
1	(3 pound) center cut pork loin roast	2	tablespoons molasses
3	tablespoons olive oil, divided	1	cup beef broth
1	onion, thinly sliced		Salt and pepper to taste
4	carrots	4	potatoes, cooked and mashed

1. In a small bowl, combine 2 teaspoons of the crushed caraway seeds, garlic, salt, and ground black pepper. Rub the pork with the dry rub mixture, cover, and refrigerate for 24 hours.

2. Preheat oven to 350°F (175°C).

3. Heat 1 tablespoon of the oil in a large skillet over medium-high heat. Add the onion, carrots, bay leaves, 1 teaspoon of the crushed caraway seeds, and salt and pepper to taste. Sauté for 8 minutes or until vegetables are tender. Transfer to a 10x15 inch roasting pan.

4. In the same skillet over high heat, combine ½ tablespoon of the olive oil, half of the cabbage, and ½ teaspoon crushed caraway seeds. Sauté, stirring often, until this cooks down, about 5 to 10 minutes. Transfer to the roasting pan and repeat with another ½ tablespoon of oil, the remaining half of the cabbage, and the remaining crushed caraway seeds. Once cooked down, transfer to the roasting pan.

5. Heat the remaining olive oil in the same skillet over medium-high heat. Place the pork in the heated oil and brown well on all sides. Set the roast on top of all the vegetables in the roasting pan. Add the beer and molasses to the skillet and bring to a boil, scraping up all the browned bits on the bottom of the skillet. Pour beer mixture and the broth over the roast and vegetables. Season with salt and pepper to taste.

6. Bake in the preheated oven for 45 minutes. Turn pork over and bake until a meat thermometer inserted in thickest part registers 160°F (70°C). At this point, remove the pan from the oven and let the pork sit on a cutting board for 5 minutes. Then slice the pork into serving size pieces. Discard the bay leaves. Return the sliced pork to the pan resting over the vegetables. Top with the mashed potatoes.

7. Bake at 350°F (175°C) for 10 to 15 minutes or until potatoes are lightly browned. **Yield:** 9 servings.

Per serving: About 373 calories, 35g protein, 26g carbohydrate, 13g fat, 6g fiber, 100mg cholesterol, 719mg sodium

Grecian Pork Tenderloin

Submitted by: **Dave Nash**

"Lean and tender, pork tenderloins are perfect for the grill. This recipe calls for marinating the meat in a mixture of lime juice and olive oil."

¾	cup fresh lime juice	3	tablespoons dried oregano leaves
⅓	cup olive oil		
3	cloves garlic, sliced	2	(1 pound) pork tenderloins
1	teaspoon salt		

1. In a large heavy-duty, zip-top plastic bag, combine lime juice, olive oil, garlic, salt, and oregano. Add tenderloins and marinate in the refrigerator for 2 to 5 hours.
2. Brush cold grill rack with oil and preheat grill for medium heat.
3. Place meat on the grill. Cook over medium heat for 15 to 25 minutes or until a meat thermometer inserted in thickest part registers 160°F (70°C), turning once. Let stand 5 to 10 minutes before slicing.
Yield: 5 servings.

Per serving: About 575 calories, 39g protein, 11g carbohydrate, 43g fat, 3g fiber, 120mg cholesterol, 1021mg sodium

Baked Pork Chops

Submitted by: **Dawn Edberg**

"A pork chop recipe that's quick and easy. You may have all the ingredients already in the house. Try serving over rice."

6	bone-in pork chops	¼	cup olive oil
1	teaspoon garlic powder	1	(10.75 ounce) can condensed cream of mushroom soup
1	teaspoon seasoning salt		
2	eggs, beaten		
¼	cup all-purpose flour	½	cup milk
2	cups Italian-style seasoned breadcrumbs	⅓	cup white wine

1. Preheat oven to 350°F (175°C).
2. Rinse pork chops, pat dry, and season with garlic powder and seasoning salt to taste. Place the beaten eggs in a small bowl. Dredge the pork chops lightly in flour, dip in egg, and coat liberally with breadcrumbs.
3. Heat the oil in a medium skillet over medium-high heat. Fry the pork chops 5 minutes per side or until the breading appears well browned. Transfer the chops to a 9x13 inch baking dish and cover with foil.
4. Bake in the preheated oven for 1 hour. While baking, combine the cream of mushroom soup, milk, and white wine in a medium bowl. After the pork chops have baked for an hour, cover them with the soup mixture. Replace foil and bake for 30 more minutes. **Yield:** 6 servings.

Per serving: About 478 calories, 29g protein, 36g carbohydrate, 22g fat, 2g fiber, 132mg cholesterol, 1158mg sodium

Honey Mustard BBQ Pork Chops

Submitted by: **Jody Champion**
"These pork chops are great! I accidentally left them in the marinade overnight, and they were even better! They're very tender and tasty."

⅓	cup honey	2	tablespoons onion powder
3	tablespoons orange juice	¼	teaspoon dried tarragon
1	tablespoon apple cider vinegar	3	tablespoons Dijon-style prepared mustard
1	teaspoon white wine	8	(½ to ¾ inch thick) boneless pork chops
1	teaspoon Worcestershire sauce		

1. Place honey, orange juice, apple cider vinegar, white wine, Worcestershire sauce, onion powder, tarragon, and mustard in a heavy-duty, zip-top plastic bag. Slash fatty edge of each chop in about three places without cutting into the meat; this will prevent the meat from curling during cooking. Add chops to the plastic bag and marinate for at least 2 hours in the refrigerator.
2. Lightly oil cold grill rack and preheat grill for high heat.
3. Place meat on the grill over high heat. Cook for 6 to 8 minutes turning once or until done. **Yield:** 8 servings.

Per serving: About 463 calories, 31g protein, 14g carbohydrate, 32g fat, 0g fiber, 79mg cholesterol, 229mg sodium

◀ **Family Favorite**

Prep Time: 15 minutes
Cook Time: 8 minutes
Average Rating: ★★★★★
17 Ratings ▲ 12 Reviews
What other cooks have done:
"The honey does make the chops deceptively darker than usual, so use a meat thermometer to get the meat to the right temperature."

Honey Garlic Ribs

Submitted by: **Loll**
"These ribs are delicious served either hot or at room temperature, so this is a great recipe for a casual dinner party that you can make ahead. The sauce is delicious served over rice."

4	pounds pork spareribs	2	cloves garlic, minced
½	cup honey	2	tablespoons brown sugar
¼	cup soy sauce	1	teaspoon baking soda
¼	cup distilled white vinegar	1	teaspoon garlic salt

1. Preheat oven to 375°F (190°C).
2. Slice the ribs into individual pieces. In a large bowl, combine the honey, soy sauce, vinegar, garlic, and brown sugar. Stir until honey and sugar are completely dissolved, then stir in the baking soda. The mixture will begin to foam. Transfer ribs to the bowl and turn to coat.
3. Line a shallow roasting pan with foil and arrange the ribs, meat side up, on the pan. Pour excess sauce over all and sprinkle with the garlic salt.
4. Bake in the preheated oven for 1 hour, turning every 20 minutes.
Yield: 4 servings.

Per serving: About 478 calories, 30g protein, 22g carbohydrate, 30g fat, 0g fiber, 120mg cholesterol, 912mg sodium

◀ **Party Food**

Prep Time: 20 minutes
Cook Time: 1 hour
Average Rating: ★★★★★
97 Ratings ▲ 74 Reviews
What other cooks have done:
"I used country style pork ribs and doubled the sauce. I cooked the ribs for almost 2 hours, and they were fabulous. I stir-fried some veggies and steamed some rice, and the meal was a hit."

Skillet Ham, Cabbage, and Potatoes

Submitted by: **Priscilla Eibl**

"You'll love this old-fashioned, one-skillet meal with sliced potatoes, cabbage, and ham."

One-Dish Meal ▶

Prep Time: 20 minutes

Cook Time: 40 minutes

Average Rating: ★★★★★

11 Ratings ▲ 9 Reviews

What other cooks have done:

"I had a huge bag of shredded cabbage to use, so it worked out perfectly. I did modify the spices a little by using garlic powder, salt, pepper, oregano, and basil instead of what's called for in the recipe. My 3-year-old daughter didn't even know she was eating cabbage!"

1	onion, chopped	3	large potatoes, scrubbed and sliced
2	tablespoons butter or margarine	1	dash seasoning salt
1	small head cabbage, coarsely chopped	1	dash paprika
¼	cup water	2	cups cubed cooked ham

1. In a large skillet over medium heat, sauté onion in the butter. When tender, add cabbage and stir. Pour water over cabbage, cover, and simmer gently on medium-low heat for 10 minutes.

2. Add potatoes and stir. Cover again and allow to simmer for 10 more minutes. Additional water may be needed. Sprinkle seasoning salt and paprika over cabbage and potatoes. Allow to simmer, covered, 5 to 10 more minutes until cabbage is soft and potatoes are nearly cooked. Mix in ham and finish cooking until ham is hot and potatoes are done. **Yield:** 4 servings.

Per serving: About 215 calories, 6g protein, 35g carbohydrate, 7g fat, 6g fiber, 4mg cholesterol, 141mg sodium

Cheesy Ham-Hash Brown Casserole

Submitted by: **Melissa Wardell**

"I mostly use this as a breakfast casserole, but it's great any time. It can be served without diced ham. It's quick and easy, not to mention delicious!"

Kid-Friendly ▶

Prep Time: 10 minutes

Cook Time: 1 hour

Average Rating: ★★★★★

85 Ratings ▲ 68 Reviews

What other cooks have done:

"I used 1 can of cheese soup and 1 can of cream of potato soup. I sautéed some green onions and added a little bacon and black pepper—it was full of flavor! This is also a great recipe for throwing in the microwave for part of the cooking time, if you're running late like me."

1	(32 ounce) package frozen hash brown potatoes, thawed	1	(16 ounce) container sour cream
1	(8 ounce) package sliced ham, chopped	2	cups shredded sharp Cheddar cheese
2	(10.75 ounce) cans cream of potato soup	1½	cups grated Parmesan cheese

1. Preheat oven to 375°F (190°C). Lightly grease a 9x13 inch baking pan.

2. In a large bowl, combine potatoes, ham, potato soup, sour cream, and Cheddar cheese. Sprinkle with Parmesan cheese. Pour into prepared pan.

3. Bake in the preheated oven about 1 hour or until sauce is bubbling and top is browned. Serve immediately. **Yield:** 12 servings.

Per serving: About 343 calories, 17g protein, 20g carbohydrate, 26g fat, 1g fiber, 57mg cholesterol, 834mg sodium

Breakfast Casserole II

Submitted by: **Sue Schuler**

"Make this holiday casserole the night before and bake while opening presents."

1 pound ground pork sausage	1 (4.5 ounce) can sliced mushrooms, drained
12 eggs	
1 (10.75 ounce) can condensed cream of mushroom soup	1 pound potato nuggets, thawed
	½ cup shredded Cheddar cheese
1 (12 ounce) can evaporated milk	

1. Place sausage in a large, deep skillet. Cook over medium-high heat until evenly browned. Drain, crumble, and set aside.
2. Preheat oven to 350°F (175°C). Lightly grease a 9x13 inch baking pan.
3. In a large bowl, beat together eggs, soup, and milk. Stir in sausage and mushrooms; pour into prepared pan. Add potato nuggets evenly to pan.
4. Bake in the preheated oven for 45 to 50 minutes. Remove from oven and sprinkle on cheese; bake 10 more minutes. **Yield:** 12 servings.

Per serving: About 271 calories, 16g protein, 14g carbohydrate, 17g fat, 1g fiber, 240mg cholesterol, 677mg sodium

Broccoli and Cheese Brunch Casserole

Submitted by: **Linda K.**

"Delicious for a brunch or weekend breakfast."

8 ounces ground pork sausage	8 eggs, lightly beaten
	1 cup ricotta cheese
1 (10 ounce) package frozen chopped broccoli, thawed and drained	¼ cup milk
	1 teaspoon black pepper
	½ teaspoon salt
1½ cups shredded Cheddar cheese, divided	1 Roma (plum) tomato, thinly sliced

1. Place sausage in a large, deep skillet. Cook over medium-high heat until evenly browned. Drain, crumble, and set aside.
2. Preheat oven to 350°F (175°C). Lightly grease a 7x11 inch baking dish.
3. In a bowl, combine cooked sausage, broccoli, and ½ cup Cheddar cheese. Spoon into prepared baking dish.
4. Stir together ½ cup Cheddar cheese, eggs, ricotta cheese, milk, pepper, and salt; pour over broccoli mixture. Sprinkle with remaining ½ cup Cheddar cheese. Arrange tomato slices on top.
5. Cover with aluminum foil and bake in the preheated oven for 30 minutes. Uncover and bake for 15 more minutes. Let stand for 10 minutes before serving. **Yield:** 9 servings.

Per serving: About 236 calories, 19g protein, 5g carbohydrate, 16g fat, 1g fiber, 231mg cholesterol, 465mg sodium

Italian Sausage and Zucchini

Submitted by: **Michelle W**

"This goes in the quick and easy category . . . and yummy, too! Serve over cooked rice or pasta."

1½ pounds Italian sausage links, cut into ¼ inch slices	½ cup chopped onion
2 small zucchini, sliced	1 (14.5 ounce) can stewed tomatoes, undrained
1 small yellow squash, sliced	

1. In a large skillet over medium heat, brown the sausage slices until the inside is no longer pink.
2. Stir in the zucchini, yellow squash, and onion; cook and stir for 2 minutes. Pour in the undrained tomatoes. Reduce heat, cover, and simmer for 10 to 15 minutes. **Yield:** 6 servings.

Per serving: About 287 calories, 17g protein, 9g carbohydrate, 20g fat, 2g fiber, 61mg cholesterol, 874mg sodium

Quick & Easy ▶

Prep Time: 20 minutes
Cook Time: 25 minutes
Average Rating: ★★★★★
15 Ratings ▲ 10 Reviews

What other cooks have done:
"I used a can of diced Italian-style tomatoes with olive oil and basil. I served this over angel hair pasta. I'm going to try this next time with blackened chicken."

Vikki's Red Bean Sausage

Submitted by: **Victoria Caylor**

"I went to a great restaurant in Savannah, Georgia, one summer and had red beans and rice. When I came home, I tried to figure out just how they made it. I haven't figured it out exactly, but this recipe is a pretty good imitation. Serve with hot, cooked white rice, fried potatoes, and cornbread, if desired."

2 tablespoons vegetable oil	2 (15 ounce) cans dark red kidney beans
1 pound smoked sausage of your choice, sliced	1 (15 ounce) can light red kidney beans
1 onion, chopped	2 (14.5 ounce) cans diced tomatoes
1 green bell pepper, chopped	5 green chile peppers, chopped
½ teaspoon minced garlic	1 teaspoon salt
2 tablespoons dried parsley	
1 teaspoon paprika	
1 teaspoon cayenne pepper	
1 tablespoon ground black pepper	

1. Heat oil in a large skillet over medium–high heat. Add sausage and onion and sauté until onion is translucent. Add bell pepper, garlic, parsley, paprika, cayenne pepper, and ground black pepper. Sauté until bell pepper is slightly tender, about 10 minutes.
2. Rinse and drain kidney beans. Add all kidney beans, tomatoes, and chile peppers. Stir together, reduce heat to medium, and let simmer for 25 to 30 minutes. Add salt while simmering. Serve hot. **Yield:** 14 servings.

Per serving: About 206 calories, 10g protein, 21g carbohydrate, 9g fat, 7g fiber, 28mg cholesterol, 991mg sodium

Hot & Spicy ▶

Prep Time: 20 minutes
Cook Time: 45 minutes
Average Rating: ★★★★★
14 Ratings ▲ 11 Reviews

What other cooks have done:
"This is very easy and good served over white rice. I left out the chili peppers and bought the tomatoes with the chiles already in them. You can also cut the cayenne pepper in half to make it more kid-friendly."

Spaghetti Carbonara II *(pictured on page 153)*

Submitted by: **Sandy T.**
"A super-rich, classic bacon and egg spaghetti dish. Great to serve for company. This recipe also makes an unusual brunch offering."

1	(16 ounce) package dried spaghetti	4	eggs, lightly beaten
1	tablespoon olive oil	½	cup grated Parmesan cheese
8	slices bacon, diced	¼	teaspoon salt
1	tablespoon olive oil	¼	teaspoon ground black pepper
1	onion, chopped	2	tablespoons chopped fresh parsley
1	clove garlic, minced		
¼	cup dry white wine (optional)	2	tablespoons grated Parmesan cheese

1. In a large pot of boiling salted water, cook spaghetti until al dente. Drain well. Toss with 1 tablespoon of olive oil and set aside.

2. Meanwhile in a large skillet, cook bacon until slightly crisp; remove and drain on paper towels. Reserve 2 tablespoons of drippings in skillet; add 1 tablespoon olive oil to skillet and heat. Add chopped onion and cook over medium heat until onion is translucent. Add minced garlic and cook 1 more minute. Add wine, if desired; cook 1 more minute.

3. Return cooked bacon to pan; add cooked and drained spaghetti. Toss to coat and heat through, adding more olive oil if it seems dry or is sticking together. Add beaten eggs and cook, tossing constantly with tongs or a large fork, until eggs are barely set. Quickly add ½ cup Parmesan cheese and toss again. Add salt and pepper.

4. Serve immediately with chopped parsley and 2 tablespoons Parmesan cheese. **Yield:** 5 servings.

Per serving: About 766 calories, 26g protein, 71g carbohydrate, 40g fat, 3g fiber, 209mg cholesterol, 609mg sodium

◄ Quick & Easy

Prep Time: 15 minutes
Cook Time: 30 minutes
Average Rating: ★★★★★
19 Ratings ▲ 17 Reviews
What other cooks have done:
"I added a package of sliced mushrooms to it and a wee bit more bacon than called for. Freezes pretty well, too."

Fried Chicken with Creamy Gravy

Submitted by: **Gina**

"Seasoned fried chicken is served with a rich gravy made from the pan drippings. It takes some preparation, but is definitely worth it."

½	cup milk	¼	teaspoon poultry seasoning
1	egg, beaten	1	(4 pound) whole chicken, cut into pieces
1	cup all-purpose flour		
2	teaspoons garlic salt	3	cups vegetable oil
1	teaspoon paprika	1	cup chicken broth
1	teaspoon ground black pepper	1	cup milk

1. In a medium bowl, beat together ½ cup milk and egg. In a heavy-duty, zip-top plastic bag, mix together the flour, garlic salt, paprika, pepper, and poultry seasoning. Place chicken in bag, seal, and shake to coat. Dip chicken in milk and egg mixture, then once more in flour mixture. Reserve any remaining flour mixture.

2. In a large skillet, heat oil to 365°F (185°C). Place coated chicken in the hot oil and brown on all sides. Reduce heat to medium low and continue cooking chicken until tender, about 30 minutes, turning it as needed for even browning. Remove from skillet and drain on paper towels.

3. Discard all but 2 tablespoons of the frying oil. Over low heat, stir in 2 tablespoons of the reserved flour mixture. Cook about 2 minutes, stirring constantly. Whisk in chicken broth, scraping browned bits off bottom of skillet. Stir in 1 cup milk and bring all to a boil over high heat, stirring constantly. Reduce heat to low and simmer for about 5 minutes. Serve immediately with the chicken. **Yield:** 4 servings.

Per serving: About 1062 calories, 25g protein, 15g carbohydrate, 101g fat, 1g fiber, 115mg cholesterol, 689mg sodium

Cooking Basics: **Chicken Pointers** ▼

Chicken is a favorite and healthy eating choice for many people. Like all fresh meats, it's perishable and care needs to be taken in its handling and preparation. To help you stay on the path to a delectable and safe meal, we recommend the following procedures for handling chicken.

Keep It Cold!

Never leave raw or frozen chicken at room temperature. Raw chicken should be stored in the coldest part of your refrigerator and used within 2 days. Freeze any chicken that won't be used in 2 days. Frozen chicken can be stored in the freezer for up to 1 year without sacrificing quality. When thawing frozen chicken do so slowly, ideally in your refrigerator but, if in a hurry, a cold water bath will be fine. In the refrigerator it will take about 24 hours to thaw a whole roaster chicken and about 2 to 9 hours for cut-up chicken parts.

Keep It Clean!

Always rinse chicken with cold water (inside and out) then pat dry with paper towels before preparing. To prevent cross contamination, thoroughly clean all surfaces, utensils, plates, cutting boards, knives, and hands with warm soapy water that have come in contact with raw chicken before they come in contact with any other raw or cooked foods.

Get It Done!

Always cook chicken to the proper temperature. The internal temperature of a whole chicken should reach 180°F (82°C), chicken breasts should be cooked to 170° F (77°C), and ground chicken should reach 165°F (74°C). Another check for doneness is to pierce or make a slit in the thickest part of the meat to see if the juices run clear. If they're clear and not pink, the chicken is done.

- Sivan Steffens

For more information, visit **Allrecipes.com**

Greek Chicken *(pictured on page 151)*

Submitted by: **Karen**

"I serve this summer dish with sliced tomatoes, feta cheese, and garlic bread."

½ cup olive oil	1 tablespoon chopped fresh oregano
3 cloves garlic, chopped	
1 tablespoon chopped fresh rosemary	2 lemons, juiced
1 tablespoon chopped fresh thyme	1 (4 pound) whole chicken, cut into pieces

1. In a glass dish, combine the olive oil, garlic, rosemary, thyme, oregano, and lemon juice. Add chicken pieces, cover, and marinate overnight in refrigerator.

2. Lightly oil a cold grill rack; preheat grill for medium-high heat.

3. Reduce heat to medium, remove chicken from marinade, and grill for 40 to 45 minutes or until a meat thermometer inserted in a thigh registers 180°F (80°C). **Yield:** 4 servings.

Per serving: About 824 calories, 62g protein, 7g carbohydrate, 61g fat, 3g fiber, 194mg cholesterol, 189mg sodium

Coq au Vin alla Italiana

Submitted by: **Richard**

"You can add your own favorite spices, herbs, or veggies to this to suit your taste. Serve with rice or mashed potatoes and cooked greens, if desired. You can use breast meat, but be careful not to overcook it, or it will dry out!"

1 tablespoon vegetable oil	1 cup chopped onion
5 cloves crushed garlic, divided	3 carrots, sliced
½ cup all-purpose flour	½ pound fresh mushrooms, sliced
1 teaspoon poultry seasoning	½ teaspoon dried rosemary
4 pounds dark meat chicken pieces	1 cup red wine
3 (4 ounce) links mild Italian sausage, sliced	1 (14.5 ounce) can whole peeled tomatoes
	Salt and pepper to taste

1. In a large skillet, heat oil and sauté half of the garlic. Season flour with poultry seasoning. Dredge chicken parts in flour and brown in the skillet for 4 to 5 minutes. Add the sausage and sauté for a few minutes. Add the onion, carrot, mushrooms, rosemary, and remaining garlic. Stir together.

2. Add the wine and tomatoes, cover, and let simmer over low heat for 25 minutes. Season with salt and pepper to taste; simmer for another 10 minutes. Let stand covered for 10 minutes and serve. **Yield:** 8 servings.

Per serving: About 615 calories, 44g protein, 21g carbohydrate, 37g fat, 2g fiber, 150mg cholesterol, 512mg sodium

Chicken Savoy

Submitted by: **Joe**

"A whole chicken cut into pieces is baked with a simple mixture of olive oil, chicken stock, garlic, spices, and cheese and then topped with balsamic vinegar just before serving. This is a recipe to eat with your fingers and get juices on your hands."

Restaurant Fare ▶

Prep Time: 10 minutes
Cook Time: 1 hour
Average Rating: ★★★★★
58 Ratings ▲ 42 Reviews
What other cooks have done:
"I added fresh garlic, some rosemary, paprika, and Parmesan cheese. It's very good served with linguine tossed with olive oil, garlic, and parsley."

1	(2 to 3 pound) whole chicken, cut into pieces	1	teaspoon dried oregano
2	tablespoons extra virgin olive oil		Salt and pepper to taste
1	cup chicken broth	¼	cup grated Romano cheese
1	clove garlic, crushed	3	tablespoons balsamic vinegar

1. Preheat oven to 450°F (230°C).
2. Place chicken pieces in a 9x13 inch baking dish. Pour oil and broth over chicken and sprinkle with garlic. Season with oregano, salt, and pepper and top with cheese.
3. Bake in the preheated oven for about 45 to 60 minutes or until chicken is cooked through and no longer pink inside.
4. Pour vinegar over chicken and serve. **Yield:** 4 servings.

Per serving: About 478 calories, 45g protein, 3g carbohydrate, 30g fat, 0g fiber, 176mg cholesterol, 380mg sodium

Chicken Parmigiana

Submitted by: **Candy**

"This is a very nice dinner for two. Serve it with your favorite pasta and tossed greens."

Family Favorite ▶

Prep Time: 30 minutes
Cook Time: 1 hour
Average Rating: ★★★★★
116 Ratings ▲ 66 Reviews
What other cooks have done:
"This recipe is wonderful and so easy. I made it with four breasts by just increasing the other ingredients slightly. Also, I pounded the chicken to tenderize and added some garlic to the sauce. This will be a new standard for me!"

1	egg, beaten	2	ounces shredded mozzarella cheese
2	ounces dry breadcrumbs		
2	skinless, boneless chicken breast halves	¼	cup grated Parmesan cheese
¾	(16 ounce) jar spaghetti sauce		

1. Preheat oven to 350°F (175°C). Lightly grease a medium baking sheet.
2. Pour egg into a small, shallow bowl. Place breadcrumbs in a separate shallow bowl. Dip chicken into egg, then into the breadcrumbs. Place coated chicken on the prepared baking sheet and bake in the preheated oven for 40 minutes or until no longer pink and juices run clear.
3. Pour half of the spaghetti sauce into a 7x11 inch baking dish. Place chicken over sauce and cover with remaining sauce. Sprinkle mozzarella and Parmesan cheeses on top and return to the preheated oven for 20 more minutes. **Yield:** 2 servings.

Per serving: About 541 calories, 52g protein, 36g carbohydrate, 20g fat, 3g fiber, 307mg cholesterol, 1441mg sodium

Apricot Chicken

Submitted by: **Shirley Rickey**

"Tangy, fruity chicken made in just three easy steps! It's great served with rice."

6   skinless, boneless chicken
    breast halves
1½ (1 ounce) packages dry
    onion soup mix
1   (10 ounce) bottle Russian-
    style salad dressing
1   cup apricot preserves

1. Preheat oven to 350°F (175°C).

2. Place the chicken pieces in a 9x13 inch baking dish. Combine the soup mix, dressing, and preserves, and pour over the chicken.

3. Cover and bake in the preheated oven for 1 hour. **Yield:** 6 servings.

Per serving: About 461 calories, 28g protein, 65g carbohydrate, 11g fat, 0g fiber, 68mg cholesterol, 1268mg sodium

Cajun Chicken Pasta

Submitted by: **Tammy Schill**

"Try this when you're feeling daring and want to mix things up a bit. A Southern-inspired recipe that's sure to add a little fun to your dinner table. Serve it in a bowl with crusty bread or cornbread."

4   ounces uncooked linguine
    pasta
2   boneless, skinless chicken
    breast halves, sliced into
    thin strips
2   teaspoons Cajun seasoning
2   tablespoons butter
1   green bell pepper, diced
½   red bell pepper, diced
4   fresh mushrooms, sliced
1   green onion, sliced
1½ cups heavy whipping cream
¼   teaspoon dried basil
¼   teaspoon lemon pepper
¼   teaspoon salt
⅛   teaspoon garlic powder
⅛   teaspoon ground black
    pepper
2   tablespoons freshly
    shredded Parmesan
    cheese

1. Bring a large pot of lightly salted water to a boil. Add linguine and cook for 8 to 10 minutes or until al dente; drain.

2. Meanwhile, place chicken and Cajun seasoning in a bowl and turn to coat. In a large skillet over medium heat, sauté chicken in butter until no longer pink and juices run clear, about 5 to 7 minutes. Add green and red bell peppers, sliced mushrooms, and green onion; cook for 2 to 3 minutes. Reduce heat and stir in heavy cream. Season the sauce with basil, lemon pepper, salt, garlic powder, and ground black pepper and heat through. Let stand, covered, 10 minutes.

3. In a large bowl, toss linguine with sauce. Sprinkle with shredded Parmesan cheese. **Yield:** 2 servings.

Per serving: About 1156 calories, 43g protein, 56g carbohydrate, 87g fat, 5g fiber, 365mg cholesterol, 1189mg sodium

Famous Butter Chicken

Submitted by: **Heather**

"Chicken breasts are dipped in beaten eggs and cracker crumbs, then baked with butter. These chicken breasts are really tender and moist. I never have leftovers."

2	eggs, beaten	4	skinless, boneless chicken breast halves
1	cup crushed buttery round cracker crumbs	½	cup butter, cut into pieces
½	teaspoon garlic salt		
	Ground black pepper to taste		

1. Preheat oven to 375°F (190°C).
2. Place eggs and cracker crumbs in 2 separate shallow bowls. Mix cracker crumbs with garlic salt and pepper. Dip chicken in the eggs, then dredge in the crumb mixture to coat.
3. Arrange coated chicken in a 9x13 inch baking dish. Place pieces of butter around the chicken.
4. Bake in the preheated oven for 40 minutes or until chicken is no longer pink and juices run clear. **Yield:** 4 servings.

Per serving: About 449 calories, 32g protein, 9g carbohydrate, 31g fat, 0g fiber, 237mg cholesterol, 707mg sodium

Garlic Ranch Chicken

Submitted by: **Trudi Davidoff**

"This is very easy and fast to make; using fat-free dressing keeps the calories down and helps prevent the chicken from burning."

1	cup fat-free Ranch dressing	4	skinless, boneless chicken breast halves
2	tablespoons chopped garlic		
1	tablespoon chopped fresh basil		

1. Combine the dressing, garlic, and basil in a heavy-duty, zip-top plastic bag. Add chicken, turning to coat. Squeeze out air and seal bag. Place in refrigerator for 30 minutes.
2. Preheat grill for medium heat.
3. Grill chicken breasts for 6 to 8 minutes on each side, turning occasionally, until juices run clear when pierced with a fork. **Yield:** 4 servings.

Per serving: About 227 calories, 27g protein, 23g carbohydrate, 2g fat, 1g fiber, 67mg cholesterol, 776mg sodium

Jenny's Grilled Chicken Breasts

Submitted by: **Jenny English**

"My friends and family beg me to make this. I like it with scalloped potatoes, baked potatoes, or rice pilaf. Try it with cilantro or oregano instead of parsley. Save leftovers for salad the next day."

4	skinless, boneless chicken breast halves		Ground black pepper to taste
½	cup lemon juice		Seasoning salt to taste
½	teaspoon onion powder	2	teaspoons dried parsley

1. Lightly oil grill rack and preheat grill for medium-high heat.
2. Dip chicken in lemon juice and sprinkle with the onion powder, ground black pepper, seasoning salt, and parsley. Discard any remaining lemon juice mixture.
3. Grill chicken breasts 10 to 15 minutes per side or until no longer pink and juices run clear. **Yield:** 4 servings.

Per serving: About 139 calories, 27g protein, 3g carbohydrate, 2g fat, 0g fiber, 68mg cholesterol, 78mg sodium

◄ From the Grill

Prep Time: 15 minutes
Cook Time: 30 minutes
Average Rating: ★★★★★
38 Ratings ▲ 22 Reviews
What other cooks have done:
"I doubled the recipe and used the leftover breasts for grilled chicken salads and sandwiches—they were great, too!"

Grilled Asian Chicken

Submitted by: **Janet M.**

"Great for last minute company or a quick dinner by rounding it out with a baked potato and tossed salad."

¼	cup soy sauce	2	cloves garlic, crushed
4	teaspoons sesame oil	4	boneless chicken breast halves
2	tablespoons honey		
3	slices fresh ginger root		

1. In a small microwave-safe bowl, combine the soy sauce, oil, honey, ginger root, and garlic. Heat in microwave on medium (50% power) for 1 minute, then stir. Heat again for 30 seconds, watching closely to prevent boiling.
2. Pour soy sauce mixture over chicken breasts in a shallow, medium dish or bowl and marinate in refrigerator for 15 minutes.
3. Lightly oil grill rack and preheat grill for medium-high heat.
4. Remove chicken from marinade, reserving marinade. Cook chicken on the prepared grill 10 to 15 minutes per side or until no longer pink and juices run clear. Bring marinade to a boil. Baste frequently with remaining marinade. **Yield:** 4 servings.

Per serving: About 269 calories, 25g protein, 9g carbohydrate, 15g fat, 0g fiber, 74mg cholesterol, 768mg sodium

◄ Quick & Easy

Prep Time: 15 minutes
Cook Time: 31 minutes
Average Rating: ★★★★★
37 Ratings ▲ 23 Reviews
What other cooks have done:
"I didn't make any changes other than marinating the meat longer than 15 minutes. After the chicken was done, I sliced it and added it to a bag of stir-fry veggies with noodles."

Carol's Arroz con Pollo

Submitted by: **Carol Alter**

"Translated as 'rice with chicken,' this dish will become a family favorite."

4	skinless, boneless chicken breast halves	1	cup long-grain white rice
½	teaspoon salt, divided	1	(14 ounce) can chicken broth
½	teaspoon ground black pepper, divided	½	cup white wine
½	teaspoon paprika, divided	⅛	teaspoon saffron
3	tablespoons vegetable oil	1	(14.5 ounce) can stewed tomatoes
1	green bell pepper, chopped	1	tablespoon chopped fresh parsley
¾	cup chopped onion		
1½	teaspoons minced garlic		

1. Cut each breast into 1 inch pieces. Sprinkle chicken with ¼ teaspoon each of salt, pepper, and paprika. Heal oil in a large skillet over medium heat. Add chicken; cook until golden. Remove chicken and set aside.
2. Add green bell pepper, onion, and garlic to oil in skillet. Cook for 5 minutes. Add rice; cook and stir until rice is opaque, 1 to 2 minutes. Stir in broth, white wine, saffron, and tomatoes. Stir in remaining salt, pepper, and paprika. Return to a boil. Cover and simmer for 20 minutes.
3. Return chicken to the skillet and cook to reheat. Stir in parsley.
Yield: 4 servings.

Per serving: About 475 calories, 33g protein, 50g carbohydrate, 13g fat, 3g fiber, 69mg cholesterol, 1036mg sodium

Salsa Chicken

Submitted by: **Faye**

"You can use mild, medium, or hot salsa depending on your taste. I usually serve it with Spanish rice and Mexican-style canned corn."

4	skinless, boneless chicken breast halves	1	cup salsa
4	teaspoons taco seasoning mix	1	cup shredded Cheddar cheese
		2	tablespoons sour cream

1. Preheat oven to 375°F (190°C).
2. Place chicken in a lightly greased 9x13 inch baking dish. Sprinkle taco seasoning on both sides of chicken and pour salsa over chicken.
3. Bake in the preheated oven for 25 to 35 minutes or until chicken is tender and juices run clear.
4. Sprinkle chicken evenly with cheese and continue baking 3 to 5 more minutes or until cheese is melted and bubbly. Top with sour cream and serve. **Yield:** 4 servings.

Per serving: About 283 calories, 36g protein, 6g carbohydrate, 13g fat, 1g fiber, 101mg cholesterol, 619mg sodium

Jay's Jerk Chicken

Submitted by: **R.H. Solomon**

"This well rounded flavor of sweet, hot, herbal, and spicy chicken can be served with rice, beans, or pasta. I also add garlic and a kiwi to the marinade."

6 green onions, chopped	1 tablespoon chopped fresh thyme
1 onion, chopped	½ teaspoon ground cloves
1 jalapeño pepper, seeded and minced	½ teaspoon ground nutmeg
¾ cup soy sauce	½ teaspoon ground allspice
½ cup white vinegar	4 skinless, boneless chicken breast halves
¼ cup vegetable oil	
2 tablespoons brown sugar	

1. In a food processor or blender, combine the green onions, onion, jalapeño pepper, soy sauce, vinegar, vegetable oil, brown sugar, thyme, cloves, nutmeg, and allspice. Mix for about 15 seconds.

2. Place the chicken in a medium bowl and cover with the marinade. Refrigerate for 4 to 6 hours or overnight.

3. Lightly oil grill rack and preheat grill for high heat.

4. Cook chicken on the prepared grill 10 to 15 minutes per side until no longer pink and juices run clear. **Yield:** 4 servings.

Per serving: About 285 calories, 31g protein, 22g carbohydrate, 8g fat, 5g fiber, 66mg cholesterol, 1400mg sodium

◄ Make-Ahead

Prep Time: 15 minutes
Cook Time: 30 minutes
Average Rating: ★★★★★
71 Ratings ▲ 54 Reviews
What other cooks have done:
"I omitted the green onion, but I added several cloves of garlic. After removing the chicken from the marinade, I brought the remaining marinade to a slow boil on the stovetop, spooned it over basmati rice, and served it all with grilled zucchini."

A Taste of the Caribbean: Jamaican Jerk ▼

A vacation to the Caribbean may not be in the cards just now, but you can bring the flavors to you by grilling some fragrant and spicy Jamaican jerk. The word "jerk" refers to a seasoning blend, a cooking method, and to the meat that has been treated to the jerk seasoning and cooking processes. Jerk was first created by the Arawak Indians, the original natives of Jamaica. The liberal amounts of indigenous spices and peppers preserved meats in the island heat, and also made them taste delicious when cooked over an open fire.

Island Blend

The number of recipes for jerk seasoning are infinite, and many have an ingredient list a mile long, but most Jamaican food lovers agree that there are three ingredients that all jerk seasoning mixes must have: allspice, Scotch bonnet peppers, and thyme. The allspice berry, also known as "Jamaica pepper" is native to the island and has a rich, spicy flavor reminiscent of a mingling of cloves, cinnamon, and nutmeg. Scotch bonnet peppers are small, orange, wrinkly, and hot! Thyme is widely used in Caribbean cooking and adds complexity to the flavor of the meat. Additional ingredients that are often added include garlic, brown sugar, green onions, soy sauce, lime juice, orange juice, rum, bay leaves, ginger, cloves, nutmeg, cinnamon, and black pepper.

Do the Grind

For the most flavorful seasoning, buy the spices whole, toast them lightly in a dry skillet, just until they begin to give off their aromas, and then grind them in a clean coffee grinder or, if you want to be really authentic, a mortar and pestle. If you want to decrease the heat of the peppers, remove the white membranes and seeds. Do not handle Scotch bonnet peppers without wearing plastic or latex gloves; the oils can irritate and burn your hands. If you're a bit apprehensive about eating something that hot, substitute a milder pepper—your jerked meats will still taste great!

Rub It In

Pork and chicken are the two most traditional meats to jerk, but the seasoning is wonderful on beef, lamb, and fish as well. If you want to do an all-day, slow-cooked barbecue, choose pork butt or whole chickens; for quick grilling, opt for boneless chicken, fish, or pork loin. Whichever one you choose, start by making shallow scores in the surface using a sharp knife, and then rub the seasoning paste over the surface of the food. It's a good idea to wear plastic or latex gloves while handling the seasoning. Wrap the food tightly in plastic wrap and refrigerate overnight to allow the spices to really permeate it.
- Jennifer Anderson

For more information, visit **Allrecipes.com**

Chicken Danielle *(pictured on page 155)*

Submitted by: **Danielle McQueen**

"A thick, creamy mushroom sauce served over golden brown chicken breasts and linguine is easy and satisfying. Crusty bread is always good for dipping in the sauce as well."

⅓ cup butter

4 skinless, boneless chicken breast halves

Salt and pepper to taste

1 (8 ounce) package sliced fresh mushrooms

¾ cup Marsala wine, divided

1 (10.75 ounce) can condensed cream of chicken soup

1 (10.75 ounce) can condensed cream of mushroom soup

¾ cup heavy whipping cream

1 teaspoon chopped fresh rosemary

½ teaspoon chopped fresh thyme

1 (16 ounce) package uncooked linguine pasta

Garnish: fresh thyme leaves, fresh rosemary sprigs, fresh ground pepper

1. Melt butter in a large skillet over medium heat. Season chicken with salt and pepper and add to skillet. Cook until golden brown on both sides, about 3 to 5 minutes each side. When browned, remove chicken to a 9x13 inch baking dish, reserving drippings.

2. In the same skillet, sauté mushrooms in pan drippings. Add wine and stir; simmer over medium-high heat for 5 minutes.

3. Preheat oven to 375°F (190°C).

4. Add cream of chicken soup and cream of mushroom soup to mushroom mixture. Slowly add cream, stirring constantly, until smooth. Season with rosemary and thyme.

5. Pour soup mixture over chicken in baking dish, cover, and bake in the preheated oven for 30 to 45 minutes.

6. About 15 minutes before serving chicken, bring a large pot of lightly salted water to a boil. Add linguine and cook for 8 to 10 minutes or until al dente; drain. Serve chicken breasts and sauce over the hot cooked pasta. Garnish, if desired. **Yield:** 4 servings.

Per serving: About 1029 calories, 44g protein, 81g carbohydrate, 55g fat, 4g fiber, 203mg cholesterol, 1466mg sodium

Pineapple Chicken Tenders

Submitted by: **Hillary Roberts**

"Delicious little bites for an appetizer or a light meal with a salad! The chicken tenders cook quickly on the grill, so watch them closely."

1 cup unsweetened pineapple juice	⅓ cup light soy sauce
½ cup packed brown sugar	2 pounds chicken breast tenders

1. In a small saucepan over medium heat, mix pineapple juice, brown sugar, and soy sauce. Remove from heat just before the mixture comes to a boil.

2. Place chicken tenders in a medium bowl. Cover with juice mixture and marinate in the refrigerator at least 30 minutes. Soak 8 to 10 wooden skewers in water for 30 minutes.

3. Lightly oil grill rack and preheat grill for medium heat. Thread chicken onto skewers. Grill chicken tenders about 5 minutes per side or until no longer pink and juices run clear. **Yield:** 4 to 5 servings.

Per serving: About 155 calories, 21g protein, 14g carbohydrate, 1g fat, 0g fiber, 53mg cholesterol, 539mg sodium

◀ Quick & Easy

Prep Time: 30 minutes
Cook Time: 10 minutes
Average Rating: ★★★★★
87 Ratings ▲ 46 Reviews
What other cooks have done:
"I added 1 clove of minced garlic and about ¼ teaspoon ground ginger. I grilled pineapple chunks on the skewers along with the chicken."

Gourmet Chicken Pizza *(pictured on page 154)*

Submitted by: **Lessalee**

"Here is a chicken pizza recipe that you'll love. We used to purchase this already prepared for the oven, but I came up with my own recipe."

2 skinless, boneless chicken breast halves	1 cup chopped tomatoes
1 (10 ounce) can refrigerated pizza crust dough	¼ cup chopped green onions
½ cup Ranch dressing	1 cup shredded Cheddar cheese
1 cup shredded mozzarella cheese	

1. Preheat oven to 425°F (220°C). Lightly grease a pizza pan or medium baking sheet.

2. Place chicken in a large skillet over medium-high heat. Cook until no longer pink and juices run clear. Cool and either shred or chop chicken into small pieces.

3. Unroll dough and press into the prepared pizza pan or baking sheet. Bake crust in the preheated oven for 7 minutes or until crust begins to turn golden brown. Remove from oven.

4. Spread Ranch dressing over partially baked crust. Sprinkle on mozzarella cheese. Place tomato, green onions, and chicken on mozzarella cheese; top with Cheddar cheese. Return to the oven for 20 to 25 minutes or until cheese is melted and bubbly. **Yield:** 8 servings.

Per serving: About 311 calories, 16g protein, 19g carbohydrate, 18g fat, 1g fiber, 48mg cholesterol, 506mg sodium

◀ Crowd-Pleaser

Prep Time: 15 minutes
Cook Time: 40 minutes
Average Rating: ★★★★★
88 Ratings ▲ 66 Reviews
What other cooks have done:
"I used Alfredo sauce instead of Ranch dressing, and added red onions, artichokes, and mushrooms. I also sautéed the shredded chicken with olive oil and garlic."

Pico de Gallo Chicken Quesadillas *(pictured on page 191)*

Submitted by: **Tony Cortez**

"Flour tortillas filled with chicken breast, onions, peppers, pico de gallo, and Monterey Jack cheese make a quick dinner everyone will enjoy. Homemade pico de gallo makes it extra special."

Prep Time: 25 minutes

Cook Time: 30 minutes

Average Rating: ★★★★★

98 Ratings ▲ 65 Reviews

What other cooks have done:

"Don't skip making the pico de gallo because that's what makes this recipe so good. Here's a quick and easy way to flip the tortilla: When the tortilla is ready to flip, take a dinner plate and place it upside down in the pan on top of the tortilla. Put your hand on top of the plate and flip the entire pan over so that the tortilla is on the plate. Now simply slide the tortilla back into the pan without any mess."

1 tomato, diced	¼ onion, thinly sliced
½ onion, finely chopped	½ green bell pepper, thinly sliced
1 lime, juiced	
1 tablespoon chopped fresh cilantro	1 clove garlic, minced
	2 (12 inch) flour tortillas
½ jalapeño pepper, seeded and minced	4 ounces shredded Monterey Jack cheese
Salt and pepper to taste	Salt and pepper to taste
1 tablespoon olive oil, divided	1 (8 ounce) container sour cream
1 skinless, boneless chicken breast half, cut into strips	

1. In a small bowl, combine the tomato, chopped onion, lime juice, cilantro, jalapeño, salt, and pepper. Set the pico de gallo aside.

2. In a large skillet, heat ½ tablespoon olive oil. Add the chicken and sauté about 8 minutes or until cooked through and juices run clear. Remove chicken from skillet and set aside.

3. Put the remaining ½ tablespoon of olive oil in the hot skillet and sauté the sliced onion and green bell pepper until tender. Stir in the minced garlic and sauté 1 minute. Finally, mix in half of the pico de gallo and the previously sautéed chicken breast meat. Set this mixture aside; keep warm.

4. In a heavy skillet, heat 1 flour tortilla. Spread half of the shredded cheese on the tortilla and top with the chicken mixture. Sprinkle remaining cheese and salt and pepper over the chicken and top with the remaining tortilla. Flip and cook on the opposite side. Remove quesadilla from skillet and cut into wedges. Serve with sour cream and remaining pico de gallo. **Yield:** 2 servings.

Per serving: About 692 calories, 32g protein, 79g carbohydrate, 29g fat, 7g fiber, 65mg cholesterol, 757mg sodium

Breaded Chicken Fingers

Submitted by: **Janet Shannon**
"If you like the taste of garlic, this recipe is for you."

6	skinless, boneless chicken breast halves, cut into ½ inch strips	1	cup all-purpose flour
		1	cup seasoned breadcrumbs
1	egg, beaten	1	teaspoon salt
1	cup buttermilk	1	teaspoon baking powder
1½	teaspoons garlic powder	1	quart oil for frying

1. Place chicken strips into a heavy-duty, zip-top plastic bag. In a small bowl, mix the egg, buttermilk, and garlic powder. Pour mixture into bag with chicken. Seal and refrigerate 2 to 4 hours.
2. In another large, zip-top plastic bag, mix together the flour, breadcrumbs, salt, and baking powder. Remove chicken from refrigerator and drain, discarding buttermilk mixture. Place chicken in flour mixture in bag. Seal and shake to coat.
3. Heat oil in a large, heavy skillet to 375°F (190°C).
4. Carefully place coated chicken in hot oil. Fry until golden brown and juices run clear. Drain on paper towels. **Yield:** 8 servings.

Per serving: About 233 calories, 26g protein, 25g carbohydrate, 3g fat, 1g fiber, 79mg cholesterol, 847mg sodium

◄ Kid-Friendly

Prep Time: 20 minutes
Cook Time: 10 minutes
Average Rating: ★★★★★
115 Ratings ▲ 85 Reviews
What other cooks have done:
"Instead of garlic powder and salt, I used Old Bay seasoning powder in the marinade and coating. Instead of half flour and half breadcrumbs, I used ⅓ cup each of flour, cornmeal, and breadcrumbs for a very crunchy crust. Boy, my meat-and-potatoes hubby didn't leave me any leftovers."

Yummy Honey Chicken Kabobs

Submitted by: **Ann Marie Lockwood**
"You can make these kabobs and marinate overnight for an outdoor barbecue as a tasty alternative to the usual barbecue fare."

¼	cup vegetable oil	2	cloves garlic
⅓	cup honey	5	small onions, cut into 2 inch pieces
⅓	cup soy sauce		
¼	teaspoon ground black pepper	2	red bell peppers, cut into 2 inch pieces
2	pounds skinless, boneless chicken breast halves, cut into 1 inch cubes		

1. Whisk together oil, honey, soy sauce, and pepper. Before adding chicken, reserve a small amount of marinade for basting. Add the chicken, garlic, onion, and peppers; marinate for 2 or more hours.
2. Soak 10 to 12 wooden skewers in water for 30 minutes. Drain chicken and divide chicken and vegetables evenly among the skewers.
3. Cook the skewers on the grill, turning and brushing with reserved marinade, about 12 to 15 minutes or until the chicken is cooked (this can also be done in the broiler). **Yield:** 6 servings.

Per serving: About 347 calories, 37g protein, 25g carbohydrate, 11g fat, 2g fiber, 88mg cholesterol, 873mg sodium

◄ Family Favorite

Prep Time: 20 minutes
Cook Time: 15 minutes
Average Rating: ★★★★★
59 Ratings ▲ 44 Reviews
What other cooks have done:
"I changed the vegetables according to what I had on hand. I made them with baby portobello mushrooms and red and green bell peppers."

Fresh Asparagus and Chicken Casserole

Submitted by: **Kathy Sauers**

"Great in the spring when asparagus first comes in and you can get it fresh."

1	(8 ounce) package egg noodles	1	cup chicken broth
4	teaspoons olive oil	1½	cups sour cream
1	onion, chopped	½	teaspoon dried oregano
1	cup chopped, cooked chicken	1	pound fresh asparagus, trimmed and cut into ½ inch pieces
1	red bell pepper, chopped	½	cup grated Parmesan cheese
2	stalks celery, chopped		

1. Preheat oven to 350°F (175°C). Lightly grease a 1½ quart baking dish.
2. Cook noodles in a large pot of boiling water for 5 minutes or until almost tender. Drain and set aside.
3. Heat the oil in a heavy skillet over medium heat. Sauté onion 4 to 5 minutes, until softened. Add chicken, red bell pepper, celery, and broth. Bring to a boil; simmer 5 minutes. Stir in sour cream and oregano.
4. Spread half of the chicken mixture into the prepared dish. Sprinkle the asparagus over the top. Add the cooked noodles; top with the remaining chicken mixture. Sprinkle with Parmesan cheese. Bake in the preheated oven for 30 minutes or until cheese is bubbly. **Yield:** 4 servings.

Per serving: About 566 calories, 27g protein, 49g carbohydrate, 30g fat, 5g fiber, 119mg cholesterol, 531mg sodium

Pollo Fajitas

Submitted by: **Teresa C. Rouzer**

"Serve with warm flour tortillas, salsa, and sour cream."

1	tablespoon Worcestershire sauce	1½	pounds boneless, skinless chicken thighs, cut into strips
1	tablespoon cider vinegar		
1	tablespoon soy sauce	1	tablespoon vegetable oil
1	teaspoon chili powder	1	onion, thinly sliced
1	clove garlic, minced	1	green bell pepper, sliced
	Dash hot sauce	½	lemon, juiced

1. In a bowl, combine Worcestershire sauce, vinegar, soy sauce, chili powder, garlic, and hot sauce. Add chicken; turn to coat. Marinate in refrigerator 30 minutes or cover and refrigerate for several hours.
2. Heat oil in a large skillet over high heat. Add chicken and sauté for 5 minutes. Add the onion and green bell pepper; sauté 3 more minutes. Remove from heat and sprinkle with lemon juice. **Yield:** 5 servings.

Per serving: About 335 calories, 25g protein, 6g carbohydrate, 24g fat, 2g fiber, 114mg cholesterol, 360mg sodium

Cottage Cheese Chicken Enchiladas

Submitted by: **Crystal**

"Ever tried chicken enchiladas made with cottage cheese? Now's your chance! This takes some prep time, but it's well worth it. You can make it a day ahead and serve it the next day."

1 tablespoon vegetable oil	½ cup sour cream
2 skinless, boneless chicken breast halves, boiled and shredded	2 cups cottage cheese
	1 teaspoon salt
	Pinch ground black pepper
½ cup chopped onion	12 (6 inch) corn tortillas
1 (4.5 ounce) can chopped green chiles	2 cups shredded Monterey Jack cheese
1 (1 ounce) package taco seasoning mix	1 (10 ounce) can red enchilada sauce

1. To make meat mixture: Heat oil in a medium skillet over medium-high heat. Add chicken, onion, and green chiles and sauté until browned. Add taco seasoning and prepare meat mixture according to package directions.

2. To make cheese mixture: In a medium bowl, mix sour cream with cottage cheese and season with salt and pepper; stir until well blended.

3. Preheat oven to 350°F (175°C).

4. To assemble enchiladas: Heat tortillas until soft. In each tortilla, place a spoonful of meat mixture, a spoonful of cottage cheese mixture, and 2 tablespoons shredded cheese. Roll tortillas and place in a lightly greased 9x13 inch baking dish. Top with any remaining meat and cottage cheese mixture, enchilada sauce, and remaining shredded cheese.

5. Bake in the preheated oven for 30 minutes or until cheese is melted and bubbly. **Yield:** 6 servings.

Per serving: About 549 calories, 34g protein, 35g carbohydrate, 31g fat, 4g fiber, 98mg cholesterol, 1603mg sodium

◄ Make-Ahead

Prep Time: 30 minutes
Cook Time: 30 minutes
Average Rating: ★★★★★
86 Ratings ▲ 60 Reviews

What other cooks have done:
"I substituted 4 cups of leftover shredded pork from a roast I served the night before, and it tasted fabulous. Also, I baked the enchiladas on a bed of Spanish rice mixed with Mexican corn, and the rice kept the enchiladas from getting soggy. Plus the rice absorbed the extra sauce and made a great side dish."

Rosemary Roasted Turkey

Submitted by: **Star Pooley**

"You can also use this recipe for roasting Cornish game hens, chicken breasts, or a whole chicken."

¾	cup olive oil	1	tablespoon Italian seasoning
3	tablespoons minced garlic	1	teaspoon ground black pepper
2	tablespoons chopped fresh rosemary		Salt to taste
1	tablespoon chopped fresh basil	1	(12 pound) turkey

1. Preheat oven to 325°F (165°C).

2. In a small bowl, mix the olive oil, garlic, rosemary, basil, Italian seasoning, black pepper, and salt. Set aside.

3. Rinse the turkey inside and out; pat dry. Loosen the skin from the breast by slowly working your fingers between the breast and the skin. Work it loose to the end of the drumstick, being careful not to tear skin.

4. Using your hand, spread a generous amount of the rosemary mixture under the breast skin and down the thigh and leg. Rub the remainder of the rosemary mixture over the outside of the breast. Use toothpicks to seal skin over any exposed breast meat.

5. Place turkey on a rack in a roasting pan. Add about ¼ inch of water to pan. Roast in the preheated oven 3 to 4 hours or until a meat thermometer inserted in thigh registers 180°F (80°C). **Yield:** 12 servings.

Per serving: About 851 calories, 93g protein, 1g carbohydrate, 50g fat, 0g fiber, 309mg cholesterol, 296mg sodium

Healthy Turkey Loaf

Submitted by: **Susan**

"I whipped up this low-fat number while on a diet program. My husband, the meatloaf lover, just loves this loaf, and it's so easy to mix up, freeze, and bake later for a quick meal!"

½	pound ground turkey	2	tablespoons chopped yellow bell pepper
1	egg		
¼	cup salsa	¼	cup chopped onion
2	tablespoons chopped red bell pepper	¼	cup dry breadcrumbs
			Lemon pepper to taste

1. Preheat oven to 350°F (175°C).

2. In a bowl combine the turkey, egg, salsa, red bell pepper, yellow bell pepper, onion, breadcrumbs, and lemon pepper. Mix well with hands until blended. Press mixture into a 5x3 inch loaf pan.

3. Bake in the preheated oven for 25 minutes. **Yield:** 4 servings.

Per serving: About 141 calories, 13g protein, 8g carbohydrate, 6g fat, 1g fiber, 98mg cholesterol, 198mg sodium

Turkey Pot Pie *(pictured on page 150)*

Submitted by: **Linda**

"A perfect way to use leftover turkey. This pie tastes yummy and will feed up to eight hungry people."

1	(15 ounce) package refrigerated pie crust dough	½	teaspoon pepper
		2	cubes chicken bouillon
		2	cups water
4	tablespoons butter, divided	2	potatoes, peeled and cubed (about 1 pound)
1	onion, minced		
2	stalks celery, chopped	3	tablespoons all-purpose flour
2	carrots, diced		
3	tablespoons dried parsley	½	cup milk
1	teaspoon dried oregano	1½	cups cubed cooked turkey
¼	teaspoon salt		

1. Preheat oven to 425°F (220°C). Roll out 1 pie crust and place into a 10 inch pie dish; set aside.

2. Place 2 tablespoons of the butter in a large skillet. Add the onion, celery, carrot, parsley, oregano, salt, and pepper. Cook and stir 5 minutes or until the vegetables are soft. Stir in the bouillon and water. Bring mixture to a boil. Stir in the potato and cook 10 minutes or until tender but still firm.

3. In a small saucepan, melt the remaining 2 tablespoons butter. Stir in the flour. Add the milk and stir until smooth. Add the turkey and the vegetable mixture, and cook until thickened, about 2 minutes. Pour mixture into the unbaked pie crust. Roll out the top crust and place on filling. Flute edges and make 4 slits in the top crust to let out steam.

4. Bake in the preheated oven for 10 minutes. Reduce oven temperature to 350°F (175°C) and continue baking for 20 more minutes or until crust is golden brown. **Yield:** 8 servings.

Per serving: About 459 calories, 13g protein, 41g carbohydrate, 27g fat, 4g fiber, 38mg cholesterol, 682mg sodium

---

◄ **Classic Comfort Food**

Prep Time: 20 minutes
Cook Time: 30 minutes
Average Rating: ★★★★★
51 Ratings ▲ 40 Reviews
What other cooks have done:
"I cut up all the veggies the night before so it was easy to throw together the next day. I won't wait for leftover turkey next time—I'll try using cooked chicken."

Goat Cheese and Spinach Turkey Burgers

Submitted by: **Nicole**

"This fast and easy recipe is perfect to make after a long day at work. The goat cheese adds a creamy flavor to sometimes bland turkey burgers."

1½	pounds ground turkey breast	2	tablespoons goat cheese, crumbled
1	cup frozen chopped spinach, thawed and drained		

1. Preheat the oven to Broil.

2. In a medium bowl, mix ground turkey, spinach, and goat cheese. Form the mixture into 4 patties.

3. Arrange patties on a broiler pan and cook in the center of the preheated oven 15 minutes or until a meat thermometer inserted in patties registers 180°F (85°C). **Yield:** 4 servings.

Per serving: About 276 calories, 32g protein, 2g carbohydrate, 15g fat, 1g fiber, 137mg cholesterol, 207mg sodium

Honey Duck

Submitted by: **Kaylee**

"Orange-stuffed duck is sprinkled with fresh basil and ginger and basted with a honey citrus glaze. Delicious, flavorful, moist duck recipe!"

1	teaspoon chopped fresh basil	2	cups water
1	teaspoon chopped fresh ginger root	1	cup honey
1	teaspoon salt	½	cup butter
1	(4 pound) duck, rinsed	1	teaspoon lemon juice
½	orange, quartered	½	cup undiluted, thawed orange juice concentrate

1. Preheat oven to 350°F (175°C).

2. In a small bowl, mix together the basil, ginger, and salt and sprinkle mixture on inside and outside of duck. Stuff duck with orange quarters and place in a roasting pan. Add water.

3. In a small saucepan, combine the honey, butter, lemon juice, and orange juice concentrate. Simmer over low heat until syrupy; pour a little of the mixture over the duck, saving the rest for basting. Cover pan.

4. Bake the duck in the preheated oven for 30 minutes. Turn duck breast down, reduce heat to 300°F (150°C), and roast, covered, for 2 to 2½ hours more or until very tender, basting frequently with honey mixture. If desired, turn duck breast up during last few minutes of cooking to brown. **Yield:** 8 servings.

Per serving: About 382 calories, 15g protein, 43g carbohydrate, 18g fat, 1g fiber, 93mg cholesterol, 472mg sodium

Cheesy Catfish

Submitted by: **Deborah Westbrook**
"Even your kids will love this savory catfish dish that's coated in Parmesan cheese and baked."

1	egg	1½	teaspoons ground black pepper
1	tablespoon milk	1	teaspoon paprika
¾	cup grated Parmesan cheese	8	(4 ounce) catfish fillets
1¼	cups all-purpose flour	¼	cup butter or margarine, melted
1½	teaspoons salt		

1. Preheat oven to 350°F (175°C).
2. Beat the egg together with milk in a medium bowl. In another bowl, stir together the cheese, flour, salt, pepper, and paprika.
3. Dip catfish in the egg mixture, then dredge in the cheese mixture until coated. Arrange fish in a single layer in a 9x13 inch baking dish. Pour melted butter over the fish.
4. Bake in the preheated oven for 15 minutes or until golden brown.
Yield: 8 servings.

Per serving: About 431 calories, 23g protein, 27g carbohydrate, 25g fat, 1g fiber, 105mg cholesterol, 872mg sodium

◄ Family Favorite

Prep Time: 20 minutes
Cook Time: 15 minutes
Average Rating: ★★★★☆
52 Ratings ▲ 30 Reviews
What other cooks have done:
"I experimented and substituted about ¼ teaspoon of Old Bay seasoning and some garlic powder for the salt and pepper."

Mexican Baked Fish

Submitted by: **Christine Johnson**
"You get to choose the heat for this baked fish dish. Use mild salsa for a little heat and extra-hot salsa for lots of heat. Serve with rice, black beans, warm tortillas, and lime Margaritas for a festive meal."

6	cod fillets (1½ pounds)	1	avocado, peeled, pitted, and sliced
1	cup salsa	¼	cup sour cream
1	cup shredded sharp Cheddar cheese		
½	cup coarsely crushed corn chips		

1. Preheat oven to 400°F (200°C). Lightly grease a 9x13 inch baking dish.
2. Rinse fish fillets under cold water and pat dry with paper towels. Place fillets side by side in the prepared baking dish. Pour the salsa over the top and sprinkle with the shredded cheese. Top with the crushed corn chips.
3. Bake, uncovered, in the preheated oven for 15 minutes or until fish flakes easily with a fork. Serve topped with sliced avocado and sour cream. **Yield:** 6 servings.

Per serving: About 279 calories, 28g protein, 11g carbohydrate, 14g fat, 3g fiber, 56mg cholesterol, 448mg sodium

◄ Quick & Easy

Prep Time: 15 minutes
Cook Time: 15 minutes
Average Rating: ★★★★★
147 Ratings ▲ 93 Reviews
What other cooks have done:
"I used tilapia instead of cod and combined Cheddar and pepper Jack cheeses for a little spice. Once baked, I put the fish under the broiler for a few minutes to really crisp up the corn chips. Kids loved it!"

Crab Stuffed Flounder

Submitted by: **Diana**

"An easy recipe! My children enjoy it and they're not big fish eaters either!"

6	flounder fillets (1½ pounds)	¼	teaspoon salt
			Ground white pepper to taste
1	cup crabmeat, drained, flaked, and cartilage removed	3	saltine crackers, crushed
		1	egg, separated
1	tablespoon finely chopped green bell pepper	1	tablespoon mayonnaise
¼	teaspoon powdered mustard	¼	cup butter, melted
¼	teaspoon Worcestershire sauce	5	tablespoons mayonnaise
		½	teaspoon paprika
		1	tablespoon dried parsley

1. Preheat oven to 400°F (200°C). Rinse the fillets and pat dry with paper towels.

2. Combine crabmeat, green bell pepper, mustard, Worcestershire sauce, salt, white pepper, and the crushed saltines. Combine the egg white and 1 tablespoon mayonnaise. Stir into the crabmeat mixture.

3. Brush the flounder fillets with melted butter. Place in a lightly greased, shallow baking dish. Spoon the crab mixture over the fillets and drizzle with any remaining butter.

4. Bake the fillets in the preheated oven for 15 minutes.

5. While the fish is baking, lightly beat the egg yolk in a small bowl. Stir in 5 tablespoons of mayonnaise. Remove fish from the oven and spread this mixture over the stuffing; sprinkle with paprika and parsley.

6. Increase oven temperature to 450°F (230°C) and bake until golden and bubbly, about 6 minutes. **Yield:** 6 servings.

Per serving: About 267 calories, 26g protein, 5g carbohydrate, 15g fat, 0g fiber, 127mg cholesterol, 463mg sodium

Almond-Crusted Halibut Crystal Symphony *(pictured on page 152)*

Submitted by: **Susan W.**

"This halibut dish melts in your mouth! If you can find crème fraîche, substitute it for the heavy cream. Each fillet should be between ¾ and 1 inch thick."

⅓ cup dry white wine
2 tablespoons cider vinegar
2 tablespoons minced shallots
1 sprig fresh thyme
1 bay leaf
  Ground black pepper to taste
⅓ cup heavy whipping cream
10 tablespoons unsalted butter, chilled and cut into pieces
3 tablespoons chopped fresh chives
2 teaspoons fresh lemon juice
  Salt to taste
  Ground black pepper to taste
6 (6 ounce) halibut fillets
  Salt and ground black pepper to taste
2 tablespoons vegetable oil
2 tablespoons unsalted butter, melted and divided
¼ cup fresh breadcrumbs
⅔ cup minced blanched almonds
1 egg, lightly beaten
  Lemon zest, fresh thyme for garnish

◄ Company is Coming

Prep Time: 20 minutes
Cook Time: 25 minutes
Average Rating: ★★★★★
22 Ratings ▲ 19 Reviews
What other cooks have done:
"I made this with Chilean sea bass and served it with rice pilaf and steamed cauliflower. I like to double the sauce to serve it over the vegetables."

1. In a small, heavy saucepan, boil wine, vinegar, shallots, thyme, bay leaf, and pepper until liquid is evaporated. Add cream and bring to a boil. Reduce heat and simmer until reduced by half. Reduce heat to low and whisk in butter, 1 piece at a time, lifting pan off heat occasionally to cool mixture. Add each new piece of butter before previous one has melted completely. Do not allow sauce to simmer.

2. Strain sauce through a fine sieve into a heat-proof bowl; add chives, lemon juice, salt, and pepper. Keep beurre blanc warm by setting bowl in a larger pan of very warm water.

3. Preheat oven to Broil. Pat fillets dry and season with salt and pepper.

4. In a large nonstick skillet, heat oil and 1 tablespoon butter over medium-high heat until foam subsides. Sauté fillets in 2 batches for 2 to 3 minutes on each side or until golden and just cooked through. Transfer fillets with a slotted spatula to a baking sheet and cool 5 minutes. In a small bowl, using a fork, stir together breadcrumbs, almonds, and remaining tablespoon butter. Brush tops of fillets with egg and spread with almond mixture.

5. Broil fillets in the preheated oven about 3 inches from heat 2 to 3 minutes or until browned (watch closely—every broiler has its own personality). Arrange each fillet on a plate and spoon beurre blanc around it. Garnish, if desired. **Yield:** 6 servings.

Per serving: About 611 calories, 41g protein, 8g carbohydrate, 46g fat, 2g fiber, 170mg cholesterol, 154mg sodium

Baked Orange Roughy, Italian Style

Submitted by: **Tonya Dennis**
"Italian-style seasonings enhance the flavor of this delicate fish that's sure to please even the pickiest eater."

¼	cup Italian seasoned breadcrumbs	¼	teaspoon garlic powder
2	tablespoons grated Parmesan cheese	½	teaspoon salt
		4	orange roughy fillets (1 pound)
2	tablespoons grated Romano cheese	¼	cup butter, melted
		2	teaspoons dried parsley

1. Preheat oven to 400°F (200°C). Lightly grease a 7x11 inch baking dish.
2. In a medium, shallow bowl, mix Italian seasoned breadcrumbs, Parmesan cheese, Romano cheese, garlic powder, and salt.
3. Brush both sides of orange roughy fillets with butter and dredge in the breadcrumb mixture to lightly coat.
4. Arrange fillets in a single layer in the prepared baking dish. Sprinkle fillets with parsley. Bake in the preheated oven for 10 to 15 minutes or until the fish flakes easily with a fork. **Yield:** 4 servings.

Per serving: About 235 calories, 20g protein, 5g carbohydrate, 14g fat, 0g fiber, 58mg cholesterol, 671mg sodium

Baked Dijon Salmon

Submitted by: **Arnie Williams**
"A wonderful way to prepare fresh salmon fillets in the oven. Be sure to make extra because your family will be begging for more!"

¼	cup butter, melted	4	teaspoons chopped fresh parsley
3	tablespoons prepared Dijon-style mustard	4	(4 ounce) salmon fillets
1½	tablespoons honey		Salt and pepper to taste
¼	cup dry breadcrumbs	1	lemon for garnish
¼	cup finely chopped pecans		

1. Preheat oven to 400°F (200°C).
2. In a small bowl, stir together butter, mustard, and honey. Set aside. In another bowl, mix together breadcrumbs, pecans, and parsley.
3. Brush each salmon fillet lightly with honey mustard mixture and sprinkle the fillets with the breadcrumb mixture.
4. Bake salmon in the preheated oven for 10 to 15 minutes or until it flakes easily with a fork. Season with salt and pepper and garnish, if desired. **Yield:** 4 servings.

Per serving: About 429 calories, 25g protein, 17g carbohydrate, 31g fat, 2g fiber, 97mg cholesterol, 543mg sodium

Sea Bass, Cuban Style *(pictured on page 156)*

Submitted by: **Kiki Hahn**
"This dish will save you time in the kitchen—it's easy to prepare and sure to please."

2	tablespoons extra virgin olive oil	¼	cup drained capers
1½	cups thinly sliced white onion	⅛	teaspoon crushed red pepper flakes
2	tablespoons minced garlic	1½	cups dry white wine
4	cups seeded, chopped roma (plum) tomatoes	4	(6 ounce) sea bass fillets
⅔	cup sliced stuffed green olives	2	tablespoons butter
		¼	cup finely chopped cilantro
			Fresh cilantro sprigs for garnish

1. In a large skillet, heat oil over medium heat and sauté onion and garlic until the onion becomes soft. Add tomatoes; sauté until they begin to soften. Add olives, capers, red pepper flakes, and wine. Heat to a simmer.
2. Add fillets to sauce and reduce heat to low. Cover and gently simmer 8 minutes until fish is cooked through and flakes easily with a fork.
3. Remove fillets and keep warm. Add butter to sauce and increase the heat. Simmer until the sauce thickens. Stir in cilantro. Spoon tomato mixture evenly on each plate and top each with a fillet and more tomato mixture. Garnish, if desired. **Yield:** 4 servings.

Per serving: About 441 calories, 34g protein, 17g carbohydrate, 20g fat, 4g fiber, 84mg cholesterol, 1013mg sodium

---

◀ Quick & Easy

Prep Time: 20 minutes
Cook Time: 25 minutes
Average Rating: ★★★★★
15 Ratings ▲ 11 Reviews
What other cooks have done:
"Try doing pork chops this way, but simmer them longer. Also try adding a few extra red pepper flakes to make the delicious sauce a little spicier."

Cajun Style Blackened Snapper

Submitted by: **Sandra**
"Serve this fish with a dish of melted butter on the side."

2	tablespoons paprika	1½	teaspoons ground black pepper
1	tablespoon salt	1½	teaspoons ground white pepper
2	teaspoons onion powder		
2	teaspoons garlic powder	4	(6 ounce) red snapper fillets
1	teaspoon dried thyme	1½	cups butter, melted and divided
1	teaspoon dried oregano		
2	teaspoons cayenne pepper		

1. Heat a large cast iron skillet over high heat for 10 minutes.
2. Mix paprika, salt, onion powder, garlic powder, thyme, oregano, cayenne pepper, black pepper, and white pepper together in a small bowl.
3. Dip fish fillets into melted butter; sprinkle each fillet generously with the seasoning mixture. Place the fillets in the skillet. Pour 1 tablespoon of butter over each fillet. Cook 3 to 5 minutes or until the underside of the fillet looks charred. Flip the fish over, pour 1 tablespoon of butter over each fillet, and cook 2 more minutes. **Yield:** 4 servings.

Per serving: About 806 calories, 36g protein, 6g carbohydrate, 72g fat, 2g fiber, 248mg cholesterol, 2525mg sodium

---

◀ Hot & Spicy

Prep Time: 15 minutes
Cook Time: 7 minutes
Average Rating: ★★★★★
20 Ratings ▲ 17 Reviews
What other cooks have done:
"I make up the spice in advance and have a whole batch ready for anytime, making dinner preparation so much faster."

Angel Hair Pasta with Shrimp and Basil

Submitted by: **Pat Lowe**

"Freshly grated Parmesan cheese makes this dish complete."

¼ cup olive oil, divided	½ cup dry white wine
1 (8 ounce) package angel hair pasta	¼ cup chopped parsley
1 teaspoon chopped garlic	3 tablespoons chopped fresh basil
1 pound large shrimp, peeled and deveined	3 tablespoons grated Parmesan cheese
2 (28 ounce) cans Italian-style diced tomatoes, drained	

1. Add 1 tablespoon olive oil to a large pot of lightly salted water and bring to a boil. Add pasta and cook until al dente; drain.
2. Heat remaining olive oil in a 10 inch skillet. Add garlic and cook over medium heat, stirring constantly until garlic is tender, about 1 minute. Do not let the garlic burn. Add shrimp and continue stirring until pink, about 3 to 5 minutes. Remove shrimp from the skillet; set aside.
3. Add tomatoes, wine, parsley, and basil to the skillet. Cook for 8 to 12 minutes, stirring occasionally or until liquid is reduced by half. Return shrimp to the skillet and cook until heated, 2 to 3 minutes. Serve over the pasta. Top with Parmesan cheese. **Yield:** 4 servings.

Per serving: About 525 calories, 35g protein, 47g carbohydrate, 18g fat, 5g fiber, 175mg cholesterol, 1059mg sodium

---

Family Favorite ▶

Prep Time: 10 minutes
Cook Time: 25 minutes
Average Rating: ★★★★★
195 Ratings ▲ 120 Reviews

What other cooks have done:

"I added extra garlic, used just one 28 ounce can of crushed tomatoes, increased the wine a tad, and added a bit of whipping cream to the sauce to thicken and add richness."

Grilled Shrimp Scampi

Submitted by: **Holly Murphy**

"Shrimp marinated in lemon, garlic, and parsley are grilled to perfection. Serve as an appetizer or main dish. Scallops can also be used."

¼ cup olive oil	Ground black pepper to taste
¼ cup lemon juice	¼ teaspoon crushed red pepper flakes
3 tablespoons chopped fresh parsley	1½ pounds medium shrimp, peeled and deveined
1 tablespoon minced garlic	

1. In a medium bowl, combine the olive oil, lemon juice, parsley, garlic, black pepper, and crushed red pepper. Stir in shrimp to coat. Marinate in the refrigerator for 30 minutes or less. Soak 10 to 12 wooden skewers in water for 30 minutes.
2. Preheat grill for high heat. Remove shrimp from marinade, discarding marinade, and thread shrimp onto skewers. Grill for 2 to 3 minutes on each side or until done. **Yield:** 6 servings.

Per serving: About 206 calories, 23g protein, 3g carbohydrate, 11g fat, 0g fiber, 173mg cholesterol, 169mg sodium

---

From the Grill ▶

Prep Time: 35 minutes
Cook Time: 6 minutes
Average Rating: ★★★★★
72 Ratings ▲ 48 Reviews

What other cooks have done:

"To devein shrimp, take a fork and put one tine just under the shell at the head end and hold the tail and push the fork all the way to the tail end. This will take the shell off and devein it at the same time."

Asparagus Cashew Rice Pilaf, page 197

Maryland Crab Cakes, page 195

Burrito Pie, page 145

Pico de Gallo Chicken Quesadillas, page 176

Mostaccioli with Spinach and Feta,
page 197

Sesame Shrimp Stir-Fry *(pictured on page 155)*

Submitted by: **Debbie**

"This quick and tasty main dish has a double hit of sesame flavor—from oil and seeds that add nutty flavor to crisp peppers and shrimp."

2	cups water	2	tablespoons sesame oil
1	cup rice	1	red bell pepper, sliced into thin strips
1	pound medium shrimp, peeled and deveined	3	green onions, sliced
¼	teaspoon ground ginger	3	tablespoons teriyaki sauce
¼	teaspoon cayenne pepper	½	pound sugar snap peas
1	clove garlic, minced	⅛	cup cornstarch
1	tablespoon sesame seeds	¾	cup chicken broth
¼	teaspoon ground black pepper	¼	teaspoon salt

1. In a medium saucepan, bring 2 cups salted water to a boil. Add rice, reduce heat, cover, and simmer for 20 minutes.

2. While rice is simmering, combine shrimp, ginger, cayenne pepper, garlic, sesame seeds, and black pepper in a heavy-duty, zip-top plastic bag. Allow to marinate in the refrigerator for 15 minutes.

3. Heat sesame oil in a large wok or skillet. Add red bell pepper and green onions; sauté 3 to 4 minutes to soften slightly. Add teriyaki sauce. Add peas and shrimp with seasoning; sauté 4 minutes or until shrimp turn pink.

4. Stir cornstarch into chicken broth and add to wok; cook, stirring until mixture boils. Sprinkle with salt. Spoon shrimp mixture over rice. **Yield:** 4 servings.

Per serving: About 411 calories, 25g protein, 53g carbohydrate, 10g fat, 4g fiber, 173mg cholesterol, 1072mg sodium

---

◄ **One-Dish Meal**

Prep Time: 15 minutes

Cook Time: 40 minutes

Average Rating: ★★★★☆

12 Ratings ▲ 12 Reviews

What other cooks have done:

"I used frozen baby pea pods, reduced the amount of cayenne pepper, and added a bit more teriyaki sauce. I served this over bulghur wheat instead of white rice for more fiber and a slightly nutty taste."

Coquilles St. Jacques

Submitted by: **Doreen**

"This is a great elegant dish for a dinner party and can be made ahead."

½	cup dry breadcrumbs	1	tablespoon chopped fresh parsley
5	tablespoons melted butter, divided	1	pound sea scallops, quartered
6	ounces shredded Gruyère cheese	1	(8 ounce) package sliced fresh mushrooms
1	cup mayonnaise	½	cup chopped onion
¼	cup dry white wine		

1. In small mixing bowl, toss the breadcrumbs with 1 tablespoon of melted butter; mix thoroughly and set aside.
2. In another small bowl, combine the cheese, mayonnaise, wine, and parsley; mix thoroughly and set aside.
3. In a skillet over medium heat, sauté scallops in 2 tablespoons of melted butter until opaque. Transfer to a plate lined with paper towels. Preheat oven to Broil.
4. Reheat the skillet over medium heat and cook the mushrooms and onion in remaining 2 tablespoons of melted butter until tender. Add cheese mixture and return the scallops to the skillet. Cook until heated through and the cheese is melted. Spoon the mixture into individual ramekins. Sprinkle the tops with breadcrumb mixture.
5. Broil in the preheated oven 6 inches from heat for 2 to 4 minutes or until browned. **Yield:** 4 servings.

Per serving: About 719 calories, 36g protein, 32g carbohydrate, 50g fat, 2g fiber, 138mg cholesterol, 1009mg sodium

Scallops One - Two - Three

Submitted by: **Joelle Flynn**

"With three ingredients and three simple steps, you'll have a dish fit for company."

6	slices bacon	3	tablespoons fresh lemon juice
12	sea scallops, rinsed and drained		

1. Preheat oven to 350°F (175°C).
2. Cut the bacon slices in half and wrap each half around a scallop. Use a toothpick to secure in place. Drizzle lemon juice over scallops. Place on a baking sheet.
3. Bake in the preheated oven for 15 to 20 minutes or until bacon is cooked. Serve warm. **Yield:** 4 servings.

Per serving: About 276 calories, 11g protein, 2g carbohydrate, 25g fat, 0g fiber, 43mg cholesterol, 379mg sodium

Maryland Crab Cakes *(pictured on page 190)*

Submitted by: **John L.**
"Growing up near the Chesapeake Bay, you learn that crabs are as valuable as gold. My mom made crab cakes every Friday in the summer months, but I like my recipe just a tad better. Don't tell Mom!"

1	pound crabmeat	1	teaspoon Worcestershire sauce
2	slices white bread, crusts trimmed	1	tablespoon Old Bay seasoning
1	egg, beaten	2	tablespoons butter
1	tablespoon mayonnaise		
1	teaspoon Dijon-style prepared mustard		

1. Remove any remaining pieces of shell in crab.
2. Break bread into small pieces and place in a medium bowl with crabmeat. Add egg, mayonnaise, mustard, Worcestershire sauce, and Old Bay seasoning. Mix ingredients by hand to avoid overworking the crabmeat (you want to keep the lumps of meat as much as possible). Form into 6 patties.
3. Heat butter in a skillet and fry cakes for about 4 minutes on each side or until a brown crust forms on both sides of the crab cakes.
Yield: 6 servings.

Per serving: About 144 calories, 17g protein, 3g carbohydrate, 7g fat, 0g fiber, 114mg cholesterol, 982mg sodium

◄ Restaurant Fare

Prep Time: 12 minutes
Cook Time: 8 minutes
Average Rating: ★★★★★
15 Ratings ▲ 14 Reviews
What other cooks have done:
"Best crab cakes I've made, and I've tried a lot of recipes. To keep them from falling apart, I shape the mixture into balls for the first side of cooking and after I turn them, I flatten into patties."

Clams Italiano

Submitted by: **Bonnie Dailey**
"These clams are steamed in wine, butter, and spices. When the clams are gone, dip Italian bread in the broth."

½	cup butter	1	teaspoon crushed red pepper flakes (optional)
5	cloves garlic, minced	36	small clams in shell, scrubbed
2	cups dry white wine		
1	tablespoon dried oregano		
1	tablespoon dried parsley		

1. In a large frying pan, melt butter over medium heat. Add garlic and sauté briefly. Stir in wine, oregano, and parsley. Stir in crushed red pepper.
2. Add clams to the broth mixture and cover. Steam until all the clams have opened; discard any that do not open. Serve in soup bowls and ladle broth generously over them. **Yield:** 6 servings.

Per serving: About 263 calories, 11g protein, 5g carbohydrate, 16g fat, 1g fiber, 70mg cholesterol, 209mg sodium

◄ Out-of-the-Ordinary

Prep Time: 15 minutes
Cook Time: 15 minutes
Average Rating: ★★★★★
7 Ratings ▲ 5 Reviews
What other cooks have done:
"I served the clams and sauce over linguine, and it was wonderful. My father used to make linguine and clam sauce all the time; it took me a long time to find a recipe that's nearly as good and this is it."

Mussels Marinière

Submitted by: **Christine**

"Most of the work in this simple recipe comes with preparing the mussels; cooking takes very little time. Dip crusty bread in the buttery wine sauce."

4	quarts mussels	1	bay leaf
1	onion, chopped	¼	teaspoon dried thyme
2	cloves garlic, minced	2	cups white wine
6	tablespoons chopped fresh parsley, divided	3	tablespoons butter, divided

1. Rinse and scrub mussels. Pull off beards, the tuft of fibers that attach each mussel to its shell, cutting them at the base with a paring knife. Discard those that do not close when you handle them and any with broken shells. Set aside.

2. Combine onion, garlic, 4 tablespoons parsley, bay leaf, thyme, wine, and 2 tablespoons butter in a large pot. Bring to a boil. Lower heat and cook 2 minutes. Add mussels and cover. Cook just until shells open, 3 to 4 minutes. Do not overcook. Remove mussels from sauce and place in bowls.

3. Strain liquid and return to pot. Add remaining butter and parsley. Heat until butter melts. Pour over mussels. **Yield:** 4 servings.

Per serving: About 689 calories, 72g protein, 26g carbohydrate, 22g fat, 1g fiber, 190mg cholesterol, 1804mg sodium

Lobster de Jonghe

Submitted by: **Gina Owens-Stanley**

"Individual servings of lobster are baked with a breadcrumb topping."

½	cup breadcrumbs	1	tablespoon lemon juice
½	cup grated Parmesan cheese	24	ounces lobster meat, cooked and cubed
2	tablespoons thinly sliced green onions	½	cup butter, melted
¼	cup butter, melted		

1. Preheat oven to 350°F (175°C).

2. In a small bowl, mix together breadcrumbs, cheese, green onions, ¼ cup melted butter, and lemon juice. Set aside.

3. Divide lobster meat among 6 ramekins. Pour ½ cup melted butter evenly over lobster and top with breadcrumb mixture.

4. Bake in the preheated oven for 25 minutes or until topping is browned. **Yield:** 6 servings.

Per serving: About 388 calories, 28g protein, 9g carbohydrate, 27g fat, 0g fiber, 149mg cholesterol, 893mg sodium

Asparagus Cashew Rice Pilaf *(pictured on page 189)*

Submitted by: **Sandy T.**

"This is an adaptation of an old Armenian recipe, and this variation is so delicious I can't stop eating it. It's a great way to stretch expensive seasonal asparagus and pricey cashews. It's terrific as a vegetarian entrée or side dish."

¼	cup butter	2¼	cups vegetable broth
2	ounces uncooked spaghetti, broken into 1 inch pieces		Salt and pepper to taste
¼	cup minced onion	½	pound fresh asparagus, trimmed and cut into 2 inch pieces
½	teaspoon minced garlic		
1¼	cups uncooked jasmine rice	½	cup cashew halves

1. Melt butter in a medium saucepan over medium-low heat. Increase heat to medium and stir in spaghetti, cooking until coated with the melted butter and lightly browned.
2. Stir onion and garlic into the saucepan and cook about 2 minutes or until tender. Stir in jasmine rice and cook about 5 minutes. Pour in vegetable broth. Season with salt and pepper. Bring the mixture to a boil, cover, and cook 20 minutes or until rice is tender and liquid is absorbed.
3. Place asparagus in a separate medium saucepan with enough water to cover. Bring to a boil and cook 1 to 2 minutes or until crisp-tender.
4. Mix asparagus and cashew halves into the rice mixture and serve warm. **Yield:** 8 servings.

Per serving: About 246 calories, 5g protein, 34g carbohydrate, 10g fat, 2g fiber, 16mg cholesterol, 937mg sodium

◄ Family Favorite

Prep Time: 25 minutes
Cook Time: 25 minutes
Average Rating: ★★★★★
27 Ratings ▲ 19 Reviews
What other cooks have done:
"I used peas instead of asparagus to save on cost. Choose a vegetable broth you really like since this provides much of the flavor to the dish."

Mostaccioli with Spinach and Feta *(pictured on page 192)*

Submitted by: **Cathy Burghardt**

"I use mostaccioli or penne, whichever is available. I've served this hot and cold."

8	ounces uncooked mostaccioli or penne pasta	1	clove garlic, minced
		8	ounces tomato basil feta cheese
2	tablespoons olive oil		Salt to taste
3	cups chopped tomatoes		Ground black pepper to taste
10	ounces fresh spinach, washed and chopped		

1. Cook pasta according to package directions. Drain and set aside.
2. Heat oil in a large pot. Add tomato, spinach, and garlic; cook and stir 2 minutes or until spinach is wilted and mixture is thoroughly heated. Add pasta and cheese; cook 1 minute. Season to taste with salt and pepper. **Yield:** 6 servings.

Per serving: About 305 calories, 12g protein, 35g carbohydrate, 14g fat, 3g fiber, 34mg cholesterol, 464mg sodium

◄ Quick & Easy

Prep Time: 15 minutes
Cook Time: 10 minutes
Average Rating: ★★★★★
33 Ratings ▲ 21 Reviews
What other cooks have done:
"I added onions and mushrooms and used canned whole tomatoes instead of fresh."

Connie's Zucchini "Crab" Cakes

Submitted by: **Patti Jo**
"These really taste like crab cakes, but without the crab. This is a really good way to utilize that bumper crop of zucchini!"

2½	cups grated zucchini	1	teaspoon Old Bay
1	egg, beaten		seasoning
2	tablespoons butter, melted	¼	cup all-purpose flour
1	cup breadcrumbs	½	cup vegetable oil
¼	cup minced onion		

1. In a large bowl, combine zucchini, egg, and butter. Stir in breadcrumbs, minced onion, and seasoning. Mix well.
2. Shape mixture into patties. Dredge in flour.
3. In a medium skillet, heat oil over medium-high heat until hot. Fry patties in oil until golden brown on both sides. **Yield:** 5 servings.

Per serving: About 276 calories, 6g protein, 25g carbohydrate, 17g fat, 2g fiber, 55mg cholesterol, 752mg sodium

Mexican Bean Pie

Submitted by: **Adele**
"Add extra fiber to your diet by using whole wheat tortillas."

1	(15 ounce) can black beans, rinsed and drained	1	jalapeño pepper, seeded and minced
1	(15 ounce) can pinto beans	1	tablespoon cumin
1	(16 ounce) can refried beans	1	teaspoon chili powder
1	(2 ounce) can sliced black olives		Ground black pepper to taste
½	(15 ounce) can whole kernel corn, drained	5	(9 inch) flour tortillas
½	cup chopped green bell pepper	1½	cups shredded Cheddar cheese
		½	cup salsa
		½	cup sour cream

1. Preheat oven to 350°F (175°C).
2. Combine black beans, pinto beans, refried beans, olives, corn, bell pepper, jalapeño pepper, cumin, chili powder, and black pepper in a medium pot. Cook on medium-high heat until thickened, about 10 minutes.
3. Lightly grease a round cake pan. Place 1 tortilla in the pan. Spread bean mixture on the tortilla. Sprinkle ¼ cup cheese over the bean mixture. Top with another tortilla; repeat this layering process 3 times. Top with the remaining ½ cup cheese.
4. Bake in the preheated oven for 20 minutes. Allow pie to cool slightly before serving. Serve with salsa and sour cream. **Yield:** 6 servings.

Per serving: About 487 calories, 25g protein, 63g carbohydrate, 19g fat, 16g fiber, 49mg cholesterol, 1322mg sodium

---

Crowd-Pleaser ▶

Prep Time: 20 minutes
Cook Time: 10 minutes
Average Rating: ★★★★★
135 Ratings ▲ 103 Reviews
What other cooks have done:
"I suggest you drain the zucchini very well by sprinkling with 1 teaspoon of salt and place on a plate. Mix it with your hands to evenly distribute the salt. Place a heavy saucepan on top of the zucchini and allow it to stand for 20 minutes to purge the liquid. It makes the 'crab' cakes lighter and flakier."

One-Dish Meal ▶

Prep Time: 15 minutes
Cook Time: 30 minutes
Average Rating: ★★★★★
38 Ratings ▲ 23 Reviews
What other cooks have done:
"This filling can also be used for burritos. I had enough filling to fill two pie dishes instead of using pans. Also, try and look for 9 inch tortillas so they fit perfectly in the cake pan. This saves a lot of time cutting the tortillas to fit the pan."

Vegetarian Moussaka

Submitted by: **Anne Buchanan**

"This recipe always gets rave reviews from vegetarians and non-vegetarians alike. It's easy to make, but takes time. Serve with salad."

1	eggplant, thinly sliced	2	tablespoons chopped fresh parsley
¼	teaspoon salt		
1	tablespoon olive oil	1	cup crumbled feta cheese
1	large zucchini, thinly sliced	1½	tablespoons butter
2	potatoes, thinly sliced	2	tablespoons all–purpose flour
1	onion, sliced		
1	clove garlic, chopped	1¼	cups milk
1	tablespoon white vinegar		Ground black pepper to taste
1	(14.5 ounce) can whole peeled tomatoes, chopped		Pinch ground nutmeg
½	(14.5 ounce) can lentils, drained, juice reserved	1	egg, beaten
1	teaspoon dried oregano	¼	cup grated Parmesan cheese

1. Sprinkle eggplant slices with salt and set aside for 30 minutes. Rinse and pat dry.

2. Preheat oven to 375°F (190°C).

3. Heat oil in a large skillet over medium–high heat. Lightly brown eggplant and zucchini slices on both sides; drain. Adding more oil if necessary, brown potato slices; drain.

4. Sauté onion and garlic in oil in skillet until lightly browned. Pour in vinegar and reduce. Stir in tomatoes, lentils, half the juice from lentils, oregano, and parsley. Cover, reduce heat to medium low, and simmer for 15 minutes.

5. In a 9x13 inch baking dish, layer eggplant, zucchini, potatoes, onion, and feta. Pour tomato mixture over vegetables; repeat layering, finishing with a layer of eggplant and zucchini.

6. Cover and bake in the preheated oven for 25 minutes.

7. Meanwhile, in a small saucepan, combine butter, flour, and milk. Bring to a slow boil, whisking constantly until thick and smooth. Season with pepper and add nutmeg. Remove from heat, cool for 5 minutes, and stir in beaten egg.

8. Pour sauce over vegetables and sprinkle with Parmesan cheese. Bake, uncovered, for another 25 to 30 minutes. **Yield:** 7 servings.

Per serving: About 230 calories, 10g protein, 23g carbohydrate, 12g fat, 4g fiber, 62mg cholesterol, 459mg sodium

Veggie Pot Pie

Submitted by: **Pam Smith**
"A mouth-watering vegetable pot pie perfect for any night of the week."

2	tablespoons olive oil	2	cups cauliflower florets
1	onion, chopped	1	cup fresh green beans, trimmed and snapped into ½ inch pieces
1	(8 ounce) package sliced fresh mushrooms	3	cups vegetable broth
1	clove garlic, minced	2	tablespoons cornstarch
2	large carrots, diced	2	tablespoons soy sauce
2	potatoes, peeled and diced	¼	cup water
2	stalks celery, sliced ¼ inch wide		Pastry for 9 inch double-crust pie
1	teaspoon salt		
1	teaspoon ground black pepper		

1. Preheat oven to 425°F (220°C).

2. Heat oil in a large skillet or saucepan. Add the onion, mushrooms, and garlic; sauté briefly. Mix in the carrot, potato, and celery. Sprinkle with salt and pepper; stir well.

3. Mix in the cauliflower, green beans, and vegetable broth. Bring to a boil and turn down heat to a simmer; cook until vegetables are crisp-tender, about 5 minutes.

4. In a small bowl, mix the cornstarch, soy sauce, and ¼ cup water until cornstarch is completely dissolved. Add this mixture to the veg-etables and stir until sauce thickens, about 3 minutes.

5. Press the crust into a 7x11 inch baking dish. Pour the filling into the crust and cover the pie filling with the top crust.

6. Bake in the preheated oven for 30 minutes or until the crust is golden brown. **Yield:** 6 servings.

Per serving: About 291 calories, 7g protein, 34g carbohydrate, 15g fat, 6g fiber, 0mg cholesterol, 2480mg sodium

Tofu Parmigiana

Submitted by: **Jill B. Mittelstadt**

"This breaded tofu alla Parmigiana is one of my husband's favorites. Serve with a simple crisp green salad, angel hair pasta, and garlic bread."

½ cup seasoned breadcrumbs
5 tablespoons grated Parmesan cheese, divided
2 teaspoons dried oregano, divided
Salt to taste
Ground black pepper to taste

1 (12 ounce) package firm tofu
¼ cup olive oil, divided
1 (8 ounce) can tomato sauce
½ teaspoon dried basil
1 clove garlic, minced
4 ounces shredded mozzarella cheese

1. Preheat oven to 400°F (200°C).

2. In a small bowl, combine breadcrumbs, 2 tablespoons Parmesan cheese, 1 teaspoon oregano, salt, and pepper.

3. Slice tofu into ¼ inch thick slices; place in bowl of cold water. One at a time, press tofu slices into crumb mixture, turning to coat both sides.

4. Heat 2 tablespoons oil in a medium skillet over medium heat. Cook tofu slices until crisp on 1 side. Drizzle with remaining 2 tablespoons olive oil, turn, and brown on the other side.

5. Combine tomato sauce, basil, garlic, and remaining oregano. Place a thin layer of sauce in an 8 inch square pan. Arrange tofu slices in the pan. Spoon remaining sauce over tofu. Top with shredded mozzarella and remaining 3 tablespoons Parmesan.

6. Bake in the preheated oven for 20 minutes. **Yield:** 4 servings.

Per serving: About 300 calories, 19g protein, 18g carbohydrate, 18g fat, 2g fiber, 21mg cholesterol, 991mg sodium

◄ Out-of-the-Ordinary

Prep Time: 25 minutes
Cook Time: 20 minutes
Average Rating: ★★★★★
92 Ratings ▲ 59 Reviews
What other cooks have done:
"To make your tofu have a more chicken-like texture, choose the firmest tofu you can find. Cut the tofu into the size and thickness you prefer, and pat the tofu dry with a paper towel. Place tofu in freezer bags or plastic wrap and freeze at least 8 hours or overnight. When ready to use, place the tofu in a deep bowl and pour boiling water over the tofu. Pat dry and coat with the breadcrumbs. If the breadcrumbs won't stick, spray the tofu cuts with cooking spray. I baked mine in the oven on a baking sheet sprayed with cooking spray."

Making Meatless Meals ▼

More and more people are making the choice to become vegetarians. And a great deal more people have made it a goal to eat less meat, often by cooking one or more meatless dinners every week. Not only can a plant-based diet be beneficial to your health and create a lower impact on the environment, but cutting out meat can cut your grocery bill way back, too.

No More Missing Meat

Vegetarian cooking may seem a little mysterious to people who have never dabbled with it. Most of us were raised to think of a proper meal as one that contains three elements: meat, starch, and vegetables—usually arranged into three neat sections on a dinner plate. Some other common misconceptions about vegetarian meals is that they all contain baffling, obscure ingredients; that they involve complicated and time-consuming cooking techniques; or that the food is just bland and unappetizing. None of these things is true, though. A meatless meal can be just as satisfying and just as nutritious—if not more so—than a meat-centered one.

"Meat" Your Alternatives

As vegetarianism becomes more mainstream, it's much easier to find vegetarian recipes and meal ideas. Not only that, but most grocery stores now carry an array of meat alternatives, not to mention a gorgeous variety of fruits, vegetables, whole grains, legumes, and spices. There are vegetarian substitutes for most of your favorite meats, including hamburgers, hot dogs, sausages, chicken, and even bacon. But you don't even need to use meat substitutes to cook a wonderful vegetarian meal. Ingredients to put protein, bulk, and that gratifying texture you can sink your teeth into, without resorting to meat, include tofu, legumes, nuts, tempeh, seitan, and vegetables.

- Jennifer Anderson
For more information, visit **Allrecipes.com**

Spinach and Potato Frittata

Submitted by: **Cheryl**
"I make this for Saturday family brunches and get-togethers. It's a big hit."

2	tablespoons olive oil		Salt and pepper to taste
6	small red potatoes, sliced	6	eggs
1	cup torn fresh spinach	⅓	cup milk
2	tablespoons sliced green onions	½	cup shredded Cheddar cheese
1	teaspoon crushed garlic		

1. Heat olive oil in a medium skillet over medium heat. Place potato in the skillet, cover, and cook about 10 minutes, until tender but firm. Mix in spinach, green onions, and garlic. Season with salt and pepper. Continue cooking 1 to 2 minutes, until spinach is wilted.
2. In a medium bowl, beat together eggs and milk. Pour into the skillet over the vegetables. Sprinkle with Cheddar cheese. Reduce heat to low, cover, and cook 5 to 7 minutes or until eggs are firm. **Yield:** 6 servings.

Per serving: About 187 calories, 11g protein, 7g carbohydrate, 13g fat, 3g fiber, 223mg cholesterol, 202mg sodium

Spinach Mushroom Quiche

Submitted by: **Mindy Spearman**
"This is fast and easy, thanks to the crescent roll crust and soup mix spice packet."

2	tablespoons butter	1	(1 ounce) package herb and lemon soup mix
2	cups sliced fresh mushrooms	½	cup half-and-half
2	cups torn spinach leaves	4	eggs, beaten
6	green onions, chopped	1	cup shredded Monterey Jack cheese
1	(8 ounce) package refrigerated crescent rolls		

1. Preheat oven to 375°F (190°C).
2. Melt butter in a skillet over medium heat and cook mushrooms, spinach, and green onions for 5 minutes or until tender, stirring constantly. Remove the skillet from heat.
3. In a 9 inch pie dish coated with nonstick cooking spray, arrange crescent roll triangles in a circle, with narrow tips hung over the rim of the pie dish about 2 inches. Press dough onto the bottom and up sides of the pie dish to fill in any gaps.
4. In a medium bowl, stir together the soup mix, half-and-half, and eggs. Stir the cheese and cooked vegetables into the egg mixture until blended. Pour into the prepared crust. Fold the points of dough that are hanging over the edge back over the filling.
5. Bake in the preheated oven for 30 minutes or until a knife inserted into the center comes out clean. **Yield:** 6 servings.

Per serving: About 345 calories, 15g protein, 23g carbohydrate, 22g fat, 3g fiber, 195mg cholesterol, 712mg sodium

---

 Salads

Nothing rounds out a meal like a crisp salad that's packed full of seasonal vegetables. And for busy nights, a main-dish salad can be a healthy, stress-free alternative to meat and potatoes. In this chapter, you'll find all the best time-honored recipes that will make the salad the star of your next meal.

California Salad Bowl

Submitted by: **Lori Guilderson**

"I often bring this to our family dinners. I get lots of requests for the recipe."

1	avocado, peeled and pitted
1	tablespoon lemon juice
½	cup mayonnaise
¼	teaspoon hot sauce
¼	cup olive oil
1	clove garlic, quartered
½	teaspoon salt
1	head romaine lettuce, rinsed, dried, and torn into bite size pieces
3	ounces Cheddar cheese, shredded
2	tomatoes, diced
2	green onions, chopped
½	(2.25 ounce) can sliced green olives
1	cup coarsely crushed corn chips

1. In a blender or food processor, process avocado, lemon juice, mayonnaise, hot sauce, olive oil, garlic, and salt until smooth.
2. In a large bowl, toss together romaine lettuce, Cheddar cheese, tomatoes, green onions, green olives, and corn chips. Toss with the avocado dressing mixture just before serving. **Yield:** 8 servings.

Per serving: About 282 calories, 5g protein, 15g carbohydrate, 24g fat, 3g fiber, 15mg cholesterol, 449mg sodium

Mandarin Almond Salad

Submitted by: **Bonnie A. Deger**

"A wonderful medley of flavors and textures!"

1	head romaine lettuce, rinsed, dried, and chopped
2	(11 ounce) cans mandarin oranges, drained
6	green onions, thinly sliced
2	tablespoons white sugar
½	cup sliced almonds
¼	cup red wine vinegar
½	cup olive oil
1	tablespoon white sugar
⅛	teaspoon crushed red pepper flakes
	Ground black pepper to taste

1. In a large bowl, combine the lettuce, oranges, and green onions.
2. Heat 2 tablespoons sugar with the almonds in a saucepan over medium heat. Cook and stir while sugar starts to melt and coat almonds. Stir constantly until almonds are light brown. Turn onto a plate and cool for 10 minutes.
3. Combine red wine vinegar, olive oil, 1 tablespoon white sugar, red pepper flakes, and black pepper in a jar with a tight fitting lid. Shake vigorously until sugar is dissolved.
4. Before serving, toss lettuce with salad dressing until coated. Transfer to a serving bowl; sprinkle with sugared almonds. **Yield:** 8 servings.

Per serving: About 231 calories, 2g protein, 20g carbohydrate, 17g fat, 2g fiber, 0mg cholesterol, 11mg sodium

Salad with Prosciutto and Caramelized Pears and Walnuts

Submitted by: **J. Craig**

"This amazing salad blends different flavors that will impress your guests. Try to use Asian pears in this salad, but if you can't find them in your area, you can substitute Bosc or Anjou."

2 cups fresh orange juice
2 tablespoons red wine vinegar
2 tablespoons finely chopped red onion
1 tablespoon white sugar
1 tablespoon white wine
Salt and pepper to taste
¾ cup extra virgin olive oil
1 tablespoon butter
2 pears, peeled, cored, and sliced
1 cup walnut halves
½ cup white sugar
¼ cup water
¼ pound prosciutto, cut into thin strips
2 romaine hearts, rinsed and torn (8 cups)

1. In a medium saucepan, heat orange juice over medium-high heat, whisking often for 25 minutes or until reduced by ¼.

2. Blend vinegar, onion, 1 tablespoon sugar, wine, salt, and pepper until smooth. Then, while blending on a low speed, remove cap and slowly drizzle in the olive oil to thicken the dressing. Chill until ready to use.

3. Melt butter in a nonstick skillet over medium heat. Sauté pears and nuts in butter for 3 minutes. Add ½ cup sugar and water and cook, stirring constantly, until golden brown and caramelized, about 10 minutes. Remove from heat and set aside to cool.

4. In a large bowl, combine prosciutto, romaine hearts, and vinaigrette; toss to coat. Top with pear mixture. **Yield:** 6 servings.

Per serving: About 548 calories, 9g protein, 39g carbohydrate, 42g fat, 3g fiber, 15mg cholesterol, 537mg sodium

◀ Company is Coming

Prep Time: 25 minutes
Cook Time: 40 minutes
Average Rating: ★★★★★
13 Ratings ▲ 13 Reviews
What other cooks have done:
"The flavors in the salad blend together so perfectly that it's a party for your mouth. It's also beautiful . . . the colors are all really different. My friends were so impressed they deemed the dinner I served the salad with 'the best ever'! I topped the salad with crumbled goat cheese, and it was good that way, too."

Mixed Greens with Walnut and Roasted Onion Dressing

Submitted by: **Barrett**

"The best part of this salad is the dressing. It's great on any salad. I prefer using yellow onions that are strong in flavor. Add a bit of goat cheese for extra flavor."

2   large onions, sliced into wedges
1   cup olive oil, divided
1   tablespoon white sugar
½   cup chicken broth
6   tablespoons sherry wine vinegar
   Salt and pepper to taste
2   (10 ounce) packages mixed greens
1   cup toasted chopped walnuts
½   red onion, thinly sliced

1. Preheat oven to 400°F (200°C).

2. Place onions cut side down on a baking sheet. Drizzle with 2 tablespoons oil and sprinkle with sugar. Bake in the preheated oven for 30 minutes. Turn onions over and bake 30 more minutes or until brown and caramelized. Set aside to cool.

3. Puree onions, remaining oil, broth, and vinegar in a food processor until smooth. Season with salt and pepper. Cover and chill.

4. In a large salad bowl, combine greens, ½ cup walnuts, and half of red onion. Add enough dressing to coat greens and toss well. Sprinkle with remaining walnuts and red onion and serve. **Yield:** 10 servings.

Per serving: About 300 calories, 3g protein, 8g carbohydrate, 30g fat, 3g fiber, 0mg cholesterol, 45mg sodium

Out-of-the-Ordinary ▶

Prep Time: 20 minutes

Cook Time: 1 hour

Average Rating: ★★★★★

7 Ratings ▲ 4 Reviews

What other cooks have done:

"I made this for dinner with a roasted chicken, and I really liked it. I didn't toast the walnuts, and it was still great."

Harvest Salad *(pictured on page 226)*

Submitted by: **Tiffany**

"Spinach salad with blue cheese, avocado, and dried cranberries is perfect with a holiday meal."

1   (7 ounce) package baby spinach
½   cup dried cranberries
½   cup crumbled blue cheese
2   tomatoes, chopped and seeded
1   avocado, peeled, pitted, and diced
½   red onion, thinly sliced
2   tablespoons red raspberry jam
2   tablespoons red wine vinegar
⅓   cup walnut oil or olive oil
   Salt and freshly ground black pepper to taste

1. In a large bowl, toss together the spinach, cranberries, blue cheese, tomatoes, avocado, and red onion. Set aside.

2. In a small bowl, whisk together jam, vinegar, walnut or olive oil, salt, and pepper. Taste and adjust amounts to suit your liking. Pour over the salad and toss to coat. **Yield:** 4 servings.

Per serving: About 338 calories, 7g protein, 21g carbohydrate, 27g fat, 5g fiber, 8mg cholesterol, 277mg sodium

Holiday Fare ▶

Prep Time: 15 minutes

Average Rating: ★★★★★

33 Ratings ▲ 31 Reviews

What other cooks have done:

"To save time, you could substitute bottled raspberry vinaigrette for the dressing listed here. It's certainly a time-saver for busy cooks."

Steak Salad

Submitted by: **Linda Miller**

"This is a quick and easy meal for those hot summer evenings."

1¾	pounds beef sirloin steak	¾	cup crumbled blue cheese	
⅓	cup olive oil	8	cups torn romaine lettuce	
3	tablespoons red wine vinegar	2	tomatoes, sliced	
2	tablespoons lemon juice	1	small green bell pepper, sliced	
1	clove garlic, minced	1	carrot, sliced	
½	teaspoon salt	½	cup sliced red onion	
⅛	teaspoon ground black pepper	¼	cup sliced pimento-stuffed green olives	
1	teaspoon Worcestershire sauce			

◄ From the Grill

Prep Time: 30 minutes
Cook Time: 10 minutes
Average Rating: ★★★★★
10 Ratings ▲ 7 Reviews
What other cooks have done:
"I used grilled chicken breast strips instead of steak, and I added sweet corn for color and taste. Delicious!"

1. Lightly oil cold grill rack and preheat grill for high heat.

2. Place steak on grill and cook for 3 to 5 minutes per side or to desired degree of doneness. Remove from heat and let stand 5 to 10 minutes. Slice steak into bite size pieces.

3. In a small bowl, whisk together olive oil, vinegar, lemon juice, garlic, salt, pepper, and Worcestershire sauce. Mix in the cheese. Cover and chill.

4. Arrange the lettuce, tomatoes, bell pepper, carrot, onion, and olives onto chilled plates. Top with steak and drizzle with dressing. Serve with crusty grilled French bread. **Yield:** 4 servings.

Per serving: About 616 calories, 41g protein, 12g carbohydrate, 45g fat, 4g fiber, 125mg cholesterol, 1057mg sodium

Salads That Are All Dressed Up for Winter ▼

While we do love the cool, refreshing crunch of summer salads, there are plenty of ways to outfit your salads for satisfying and cozy winter dining.

Get Your Greens Mixed Up

Greens that are in season during the winter months include arugula, spinach, endive, escarole, cabbage, sorrel, watercress, and mizuna. Some of these greens are easy to find in most supermarkets and most of them appear in the mixtures of baby salad greens (often called "mesclun") that are widely available in bulk and prepackaged. The exact mixture of greens will vary, depending on regional availability and the preference of the producer, but in general, the greens are chosen to complement each other and to create a lively and balanced flavor.

Wilt Without Guilt

Wilted greens are usually something that any savvy cook avoids at all costs, right? Well, it's a whole different story when you wilt them on purpose! A salad that's been gently warmed in a sauté pan or tossed with hot dressing can be a soothing, hearty dish. You don't want to cook those greens into obliteration; just warm them until they turn a little darker green and become a little bit limper and softer.

Other Ways to Winterize Your Salads

Cool and crunchy or warm and tender, any winter salad will welcome a few tasty toppings to add flavor and texture. Toasted nuts are a fabulous addition to any salad; they're great plain, or try sugaring them. Add a touch of chewy, tangy sweetness with some dried fruit. Try a handful of sweetened cranberries, sour cherries, or chopped apricots. Crumbles of flavorful cheese such as blue, Gorgonzola, or feta will mingle beautifully with the flavors of bold greens and sweet fruit. Turn that salad into a light but satisfying meal by topping it with sizzling strips of chicken or steak, and then complete the presentation by nestling a few hot and toasty crostini or breadsticks alongside each pile of dressed-up greens. Now that's a salad!

— Jennifer Anderson

For more information, visit **Allrecipes.com**

Cobb Salad

Submitted by: **Bill**

"Some of my favorite ingredients—chicken, egg, tomatoes, blue cheese, and avocado—are in this Cobb salad."

3 eggs	¾ cup crumbled blue cheese
8 slices bacon	1 avocado, peeled, pitted, and diced
1 head iceberg lettuce, rinsed, dried, and shredded	3 cups chopped green onions
3 cups chopped, cooked chicken	1 (8 ounce) bottle Ranch dressing
2 tomatoes, seeded and chopped	

1. Place eggs in a saucepan and cover completely with cold water. Bring water to a boil. Cover, remove from heat, and let eggs stand in hot water for 10 to 12 minutes. Remove from hot water, cool, peel, and chop.
2. Place bacon in a large, deep skillet. Cook over medium-high heat until evenly browned. Drain, crumble, and set aside.
3. Divide shredded lettuce among individual plates.
4. Evenly divide and arrange chicken, eggs, tomatoes, blue cheese, bacon, avocado, and green onions in a row on top of the lettuce.
5. Drizzle with dressing. **Yield:** 6 servings.

Per serving: About 700 calories, 32g protein, 12g carbohydrate, 58g fat, 5g fiber, 209mg cholesterol, 860mg sodium

BLT Salad

Submitted by: **D. L. Mooney**

"This recipe is reminiscent of the classic bacon, lettuce, and tomato sandwich. It's a great summertime salad."

1 pound bacon	Salt to taste
¾ cup mayonnaise	1 head romaine lettuce, rinsed, dried, and shredded
¼ cup milk	
1 teaspoon garlic powder	2 large tomatoes, chopped
⅛ teaspoon ground black pepper	2 cups seasoned croutons

1. Place bacon in a large, deep skillet. Cook over medium-high heat, turning frequently, until evenly browned. Drain, crumble, and set aside.
2. In a blender or food processor, combine mayonnaise, milk, garlic powder, and black pepper. Blend until smooth. Season with salt.
3. Combine lettuce, tomatoes, bacon, and croutons in a large salad bowl. Toss with dressing and serve immediately **Yield:** 6 servings.

Per serving: About 721 calories, 10g protein, 15g carbohydrate, 70g fat, 2g fiber, 66mg cholesterol, 865mg sodium

Chinese Chicken Salad III *(pictured on page 227)*

Submitted by: **Teri**

"Won ton wrappers (or skins) can be found in the deli or produce section of most supermarkets. Grill or broil the chicken breasts, or use leftovers from the night before."

3   tablespoons hoisin sauce
2   tablespoons peanut butter
2   teaspoons brown sugar
¾   teaspoon hot chile paste
1   teaspoon grated fresh
    ginger root
3   tablespoons rice wine
    vinegar
1   tablespoon sesame oil
16 (3.5 inch square) won ton
    wrappers, cut into thin
    strips

1   pound cooked boneless
    chicken breast, sliced
4   cups torn romaine lettuce
2   cups shredded carrots
1   bunch green onions,
    chopped
¼   cup chopped fresh
    cilantro

◄ One-Dish Meal

Prep Time: 20 minutes
Cook Time: 10 minutes
Average Rating: ★★★★★
39 Ratings ▲ 29 Reviews
What other cooks have done:
"I like to fry the won tons for a crispy touch. You can make the dressing ahead, take it to any potluck, and mix it at the event."

1. To prepare the dressing, whisk together the hoisin sauce, peanut butter, brown sugar, chile paste, ginger, vinegar, and sesame oil.
2. Preheat oven to 350°F (175°C). Spray a jellyroll pan with cooking spray, place won tons on prepared pan, and bake in the preheated oven for 10 minutes or until golden brown. Cool.
3. In a large bowl, combine the chicken, lettuce, carrots, green onions, and cilantro. Toss with dressing, sprinkle with won ton strips, and serve immediately. **Yield:** 4 servings.

Per serving: About 463 calories, 32g protein, 42g carbohydrate, 19g fat, 6g fiber, 76mg cholesterol, 752mg sodium

Grilled Chicken Salad with Seasonal Fruit

Submitted by: **Karena**

"Use fresh berries in summer and orange slices in winter. Any time of year this composed salad will bring rave reviews. It's beautiful in presentation and taste."

⅓ cup red wine vinegar
½ cup white sugar
1 cup vegetable oil
1 teaspoon salt
½ onion, minced
1 teaspoon powdered mustard
¼ teaspoon ground white pepper
½ cup pecans

2 heads Bibb lettuce, rinsed, dried, and torn into pieces
¾ pound grilled skinless, boneless chicken breast, sliced
2 large oranges, peeled and sectioned

1. Process red wine vinegar, sugar, vegetable oil, salt, onion, mustard, and white pepper in a blender or food processor.
2. Place nuts in a dry skillet. Toast over medium heat, turning frequently, until nuts are fragrant and lightly browned.
3. Arrange lettuce on plates, top with grilled chicken slices, orange segments, and pecans. Drizzle with dressing. Serve. **Yield:** 4 servings.

Per serving: About 916 calories, 28g protein, 46g carbohydrate, 72g fat, 7g fiber, 64mg cholesterol, 647mg sodium

Grilled Orange Vinaigrette Chicken Salad

Submitted by: **Jill**

"Try this tasty, cool salad for a perfect summer supper."

½ cup orange juice
½ cup white wine vinegar
¼ cup olive oil
¼ cup salt-free garlic and herb seasoning blend
1½ tablespoons white sugar
1 pound skinless, boneless chicken breast

1 head romaine lettuce, rinsed, dried, and chopped
1 (11 ounce) can mandarin oranges, drained
1 cup chopped fresh broccoli
1 cup chopped baby carrots

1. Preheat grill to medium-high heat.
2. Whisk together the orange juice, vinegar, olive oil, seasoning blend, and sugar. Cover and chill half of the dressing.
3. Brush chicken with remaining dressing and grill for 6 to 8 minutes on each side, basting frequently, until done. Set aside to cool; cut into strips.
4. Serve sliced chicken over lettuce, oranges, broccoli, and carrot. Drizzle reserved dressing over salad before serving. **Yield:** 6 servings.

Per serving: About 237 calories, 19g protein, 21g carbohydrate, 10g fat, 2g fiber, 44mg cholesterol, 71mg sodium

Hawaiian Chicken Salad

Submitted by: **Shirlie Burns**

"A delicious, fruity chicken salad that's a change from the standard. It's easy to double the recipe for a larger group."

2	(3 ounce) packages cream cheese, softened	3	(5 ounce) cans chunk chicken, drained
⅓	cup mayonnaise	1	cup blanched slivered almonds
1	(8 ounce) can pineapple tidbits, juice reserved	1½	cups seedless grapes, halved

1. In a medium bowl, beat cream cheese until fluffy. Mix in mayonnaise and 2 tablespoons reserved pineapple juice. Stir in the pineapple tidbits, chicken, almonds, and grapes until evenly coated. Chill until served. **Yield:** 6 servings.

Per serving: About 436 calories, 22g protein, 18g carbohydrate, 32g fat, 3g fiber, 80mg cholesterol, 531mg sodium

Winter Fruit Salad with Lemon Poppy Seed Dressing

Submitted by: **Nora LaCroix**

"This wonderful salad is great to serve for dinner at home or to take to a family gathering during the holidays."

½	cup white sugar	4	ounces shredded Swiss cheese
½	cup lemon juice	1	cup cashews
2	teaspoons diced onion	¼	cup dried cranberries
1	teaspoon Dijon-style prepared mustard	1	apple, peeled, cored, and cubed
½	teaspoon salt	1	pear, cubed
⅔	cup vegetable oil		
1	tablespoon poppy seeds		
1	head romaine lettuce, rinsed, dried, and torn into bite size pieces		

1. In a blender or food processor, combine sugar, lemon juice, onion, mustard, and salt. Process until well blended. With machine still running, add oil in a slow steady stream until mixture is thick and smooth. Stir in poppy seeds.

2. In a large serving bowl, combine the romaine lettuce, shredded Swiss cheese, cashews, dried cranberries, cubed apple, and cubed pear. Toss to mix, pour dressing over salad just before serving, and toss to coat. **Yield:** 12 servings.

Per serving: About 276 calories, 5g protein, 21g carbohydrate, 21g fat, 2g fiber, 9mg cholesterol, 208mg sodium

Artichoke Salad

Submitted by: **Christine Johnson**
"A flavorful Italian-style rice and artichoke salad."

1 (6.9 ounce) package chicken-flavored rice and pasta mix
2 (6.5 ounce) jars marinated artichoke hearts, diced
6 green onions, chopped
12 pimento-stuffed green olives, chopped
1 green bell pepper, chopped
½ cup mayonnaise
1 tablespoon Worcestershire sauce
1 tablespoon lemon juice
1 teaspoon curry powder
Dash hot sauce

1. Prepare rice as package directs, omitting butter. Chill.
2. In a mixing bowl, combine artichokes, green onions, green olives, and bell pepper. Add chilled rice mixture.
3. To prepare the dressing, whisk together the mayonnaise, Worcestershire sauce, lemon juice, curry powder, and hot sauce. Pour dressing over rice and vegetable mixture, stir well, and chill. **Yield:** 4 servings.

Per serving: About 634 calories, 8g protein, 64g carbohydrate, 41g fat, 3g fiber, 15mg cholesterol, 1856mg sodium

Sweet and Crunchy Salad

Submitted by: **Louise**
"What an easy and delicious summer salad! I usually double the recipe for parties. You can also use Oriental-flavored ramen noodles, if you like."

2 (3 ounce) packages chicken-flavored ramen noodles
½ cup vegetable oil
½ cup white sugar
⅓ cup white wine vinegar
1 (16 ounce) package shredded coleslaw mix
1 (8 ounce) can water chestnuts, drained
1 (11 ounce) can mandarin oranges, drained and chopped
1 bunch green onions, chopped
½ cup sunflower seeds
½ cup cashews

1. Place noodles in a bowl of warm water and soak for 15 minutes or until soft, reserving seasoning packs.
2. Whisk together the oil, sugar, vinegar, and reserved seasoning packs.
3. Drain the noodles and combine in a large bowl with the coleslaw, water chestnuts, oranges, green onions, and sunflower seeds.
4. Pour dressing over salad and toss to coat evenly. Refrigerate for 2 to 4 hours. Add cashews before serving. **Yield:** 6 servings.

Per serving: About 538 calories, 11g protein, 61g carbohydrate, 30g fat, 6g fiber, 0mg cholesterol, 404mg sodium

Creamy Coleslaw

Submitted by: **Kathy W.**
"Always a winner. Great for a barbecue or potluck dinner."

1 red onion, thinly sliced	¼ cup mayonnaise
1 red bell pepper, thinly sliced	½ cup sour cream
3 cups shredded cabbage	2 tablespoons Dijon-style prepared mustard
1 large carrot, shredded	1 teaspoon white wine vinegar
½ cup raisins	

1. In a large bowl, combine the onion, red bell pepper, cabbage, and carrot. Add raisins and toss well.
2. In a small bowl, whisk together the mayonnaise, sour cream, mustard, and vinegar.
3. Pour dressing over vegetable mixture and refrigerate for at least 2 hours before serving. **Yield:** 8 servings.

Per serving: About 136 calories, 2g protein, 13g carbohydrate, 9g fat, 2g fiber, 11mg cholesterol, 153mg sodium

◄ Covered-Dish Favorite

Prep Time: 15 minutes
Average Rating: ★★★★★
13 Ratings ▲ 10 Reviews
What other cooks have done:
"I get rave reviews every time I make this. I use only ¼ red onion so it's not overpowering and add an additional ½ cup of raisins. This is a great all-occasion coleslaw."

Cornbread Salad

Submitted by: **Rose**
"This is a great way to use up leftover cornbread!"

1 (16 ounce) package cornbread mix	3 tomatoes, chopped
10 slices bacon	1 cup chopped green bell pepper
1 (1 ounce) package Ranch dressing mix	1 cup chopped green onions
1½ cups sour cream	2 cups shredded Cheddar cheese
1½ cups mayonnaise	2 (11 ounce) cans whole kernel corn, drained
2 (15 ounce) cans pinto beans, drained	

1. Prepare cornbread according to package directions and set aside to cool.
2. Place bacon in a large, deep skillet. Cook over medium-high heat until evenly browned. Drain, crumble, and set aside. Whisk together the Ranch dressing mix, sour cream, and mayonnaise. Set aside.
3. Place half of the crumbled cornbread in a large serving dish. Top with half of beans.
4. Layer half each of the tomatoes, bell pepper, green onions, cheese, bacon, corn, and salad dressing. Repeat layering using remaining ingredients. Cover and chill 2 to 3 hours before serving. **Yield:** 12 servings.

Per serving: About 747 calories, 16g protein, 51g carbohydrate, 54g fat, 5g fiber, 64mg cholesterol, 1556mg sodium

◄ Crowd-Pleaser

Prep Time: 20 minutes
Cook Time: 10 minutes
Average Rating: ★★★★★
9 Ratings ▲ 6 Reviews
What other cooks have done:
"Use bacon bits to make the salad quicker, easier, and more kid-friendly. To make ahead, don't layer the salad. Just combine all the ingredients together except the dressing and toss with dressing just before serving."

Fabulous Hot Five-Bean Salad

Submitted by: **Jodi T.**

"Serve this dish hot. It's the best bean salad I've ever had. I make it with black beans, kidney beans, green beans, wax beans, and garbanzo beans. If you don't like one or more of the types of beans listed below, just substitute your favorites. This dish is especially good for taking to potluck suppers."

1	pound bacon	1	(15 ounce) can kidney beans, drained
⅔	cup white sugar		
2	tablespoons cornstarch	1	(15 ounce) can green beans, drained
1½	teaspoons salt		
	Pinch ground black pepper	1	(14.5 ounce) can wax beans, drained
¾	cup white vinegar		
½	cup water	1	(15 ounce) can garbanzo beans, drained
1	(15 ounce) can black beans, rinsed and drained		

1. Cut bacon into small pieces using kitchen shears and place in a large skillet. Cook, turning frequently, over medium–high heat until evenly browned. Drain, reserving ¼ cup drippings. Set bacon aside.

2. Return reserved drippings to skillet. Mix together sugar, cornstarch, salt, and pepper; blend into drippings. Stir in vinegar and water; cook and stir until boiling. Stir in beans. Cover, reduce heat, and simmer for 15 minutes, stirring occasionally.

3. Pour bean mixture into a serving dish. Crumble bacon over mixture. **Yield:** 12 servings.

Per serving: About 373 calories, 9g protein, 33g carbohydrate, 23g fat, 7g fiber, 26mg cholesterol, 1113mg sodium

Bountiful Beans ▼

Opening up a can of beans is perfect for quick-and-easy meals, but, if you have the time, try starting from "scratch" with dried beans. Dried beans are very nutritious and are rich in protein, fiber, folate, calcium, phosphorus, and iron.

Selection: Buy dried beans in a clear package so you can examine them for color/size and uniformity (so they'll cook evenly) and visible defects. Cracked seeds, pinholes, and foreign material are signs of low quality. Discard those with imperfections before soaking.

Soaking: Dried beans require soaking before cooking, but dried peas and lentils do not. For quick soaking, add 6 to 8 cups water to 1 pound dried beans and bring to a boil. Cover and cook 2 minutes; remove from heat, and let stand 1 hour. Then rinse and drain, and cook according to package directions. For overnight soaking, add 6 cups water to 1 pound dried beans. Let stand 8 hours at room temperature. Then cook

according to package directions. Beans soaked this way retain their shape better and cook faster.

Cooking: Cooking time varies depending on the age of the peas and beans. Most beans cook in 1 to 2½ hours. Split peas and lentils usually cook in 45 minutes to 1 hour. Check the package for more specifics. Simmer them gently to prevent skins from bursting, and stir occasionally to prevent sticking.

Storage: Store dried beans at room temperature in tightly covered containers up to 1 year or freeze for 2 years.

If you're in a rush, canned beans can be substituted for dried beans. When deciding how much, use this rule of thumb: 1 (15 ounce) can beans yields 1¾ cups drained, and 1 pound (about 2 cups) dried beans yields 5½ to 6½ cups cooked. For best results, drain the canned beans in a colander and rinse thoroughly with tap water before using.

Kerry's Beany Salad *(pictured on page 3)*

Submitted by: **Jessica**
"Yummy, yummy, yummy salad with black beans, rice, corn, and other good stuff. It's a good idea to prepare the rice and barley ahead—that way you can just throw the salad together."

½	cup pearl barley	¼	cup red wine vinegar
½	cup long-grain white rice	1	clove garlic, minced
1	(15 ounce) can black beans, rinsed and drained	1	teaspoon chili powder
		½	tablespoon salt
1	(15 ounce) can kidney beans, drained	¼	teaspoon crushed red pepper flakes
1	cup frozen whole corn kernels, cooked	¼	teaspoon ground black pepper
½	cup chopped green onions	½	cup olive oil
1	red bell pepper, chopped	8	leaves lettuce (optional)
¼	cup chopped fresh cilantro		

1. In a large saucepan, bring 2 cups of water to a boil. Stir in barley and reduce heat to medium-low. Cover and simmer for 30 minutes or until tender. Let cool.

2. In a saucepan, bring 1 cup water to a boil and add the rice. Reduce heat to low and simmer, covered, for about 20 minutes or until tender. Let cool.

3. In a large bowl, combine the cooled barley, rice, black beans, kidney beans, corn, onions, red bell pepper, and cilantro. Mix well.

4. In a small bowl, whisk together vinegar, garlic, chili powder, salt, red pepper flakes, and black pepper. Whisk in oil, pour over salad, and toss well. Line a bowl with lettuce leaves, if desired. Transfer salad to bowl to serve. **Yield:** 6 servings.

Per serving: About 371 calories, 8g protein, 47g carbohydrate, 19g fat, 9g fiber, 0mg cholesterol, 914mg sodium

◄ Family Favorite

Prep Time: 15 minutes
Cook Time: 50 minutes
Average Rating: ★★★★★
15 Ratings ▲ 8 Reviews
What other cooks have done:
"I double the vinegar, garlic, and red pepper flakes, and cut the oil in half. I use brown rice along with the barley and cook the grains together with some bouillon added to the water. And I use Italian parsley instead of cilantro."

Broccoli and Tortellini Salad

Submitted by: **Judy McNamara**

"Crisp, fresh broccoli and cheese tortellini with a creamy dressing are the basis of this salad. Raisins, sunflower seeds, and red onion dress it up."

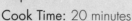

Family Favorite ▶

Prep Time: 10 minutes
Cook Time: 20 minutes
Average Rating: ★★★★★
87 Ratings ▲ 63 Reviews

What other cooks have done:
"I blanched the broccoli, soaked the raisins in hot water until they were plump, and toasted the sunflower seeds. I prepared the salad, without the dressing, the night before to let the flavors meld and added the dressing about an hour before serving."

6 slices bacon	3 heads fresh broccoli, cut into florets
20 ounces refrigerated cheese-filled tortellini	1 cup raisins
½ cup mayonnaise	1 cup sunflower seeds
½ cup white sugar	1 red onion, finely chopped
2 teaspoons cider vinegar	

1. Place bacon in a large, deep skillet. Cook over medium-high heat until evenly browned. Drain, crumble, and set aside.

2. Bring a large pot of lightly salted water to a boil. Cook tortellini in boiling water for 8 to 10 minutes or until al dente. Drain and rinse under cold water. In a small bowl, mix together mayonnaise, sugar, and vinegar to make the dressing.

3. In a large bowl, combine broccoli, tortellini, bacon, raisins, sunflower seeds, and red onion. Pour dressing over salad; toss. **Yield:** 12 servings.

Per serving: About 405 calories, 12g protein, 40g carbohydrate, 25g fat, 6g fiber, 22mg cholesterol, 327mg sodium

Antipasto Pasta Salad

Submitted by: **Dayna**

"This pasta, meat, and cheese combo serves a crowd and is great for a picnic."

Crowd-Pleaser ▶

Prep Time: 20 minutes
Cook Time: 15 minutes
Average Rating: ★★★★★
114 Ratings ▲ 78 Reviews

What other cooks have done:
"Instead of seashell pasta, I used a multi-colored rotini. This added a lot of color to the salad. I also used shredded mozzarella instead of Asiago, and used bottled Italian dressing instead of making my own."

1 pound seashell pasta	1 (.7 ounce) package Italian-style salad dressing mix
¼ pound Genoa salami, chopped	¾ cup extra virgin olive oil
¼ pound pepperoni, chopped	¼ cup balsamic vinegar
½ pound Asiago cheese, diced	2 tablespoons dried oregano
1 (6 ounce) can black olives, drained and chopped	1 tablespoon dried parsley
1 red bell pepper, diced	1 tablespoon grated Parmesan cheese
1 green bell pepper, chopped	Salt and ground black pepper to taste
3 tomatoes, chopped	

1. Cook the pasta in a large pot of salted boiling water until al dente. Rinse under cold water and drain.

2. In a large bowl, combine the pasta, salami, pepperoni, Asiago cheese, black olives, red bell pepper, green bell pepper, and tomatoes. Stir in the dressing mix. Cover and refrigerate for at least 1 hour.

3. To prepare the dressing, whisk together the olive oil, balsamic vinegar, oregano, parsley, Parmesan cheese, salt, and pepper. Just before serving, pour dressing over the salad and mix well. **Yield:** 12 servings.

Per serving: About 464 calories, 15g protein, 35g carbohydrate, 30g fat, 3g fiber, 32mg cholesterol, 989mg sodium

Patty's Pasta Salad

Submitted by: **Patty H.**

"I make this salad for almost every large family gathering I attend. It's always a great hit and there is seldom any left over. It's a great pasta salad that can easily be made the day before. You can vary the ingredients by using fresh broccoli, cauliflower, mushrooms, or cucumbers."

1½   pounds seashell pasta
1   (6 ounce) can pitted black olives, chopped
2   large tomatoes, chopped
4   ounces sliced pepperoni, each slice cut in half
½   cup chopped green olives
3   bunches green onions, chopped
2   cups chopped ham
2   cups shredded mozzarella cheese
1   (16 ounce) bottle zesty Italian salad dressing

1. In a large pot of salted boiling water, cook pasta until al dente, rinse under cold water, and drain.

2. In a large bowl, combine the pasta, black olives, tomatoes, pepperoni, green olives, green onions, and ham. Before serving, add shredded mozzarella and dressing. Toss well and serve. **Yield:** 12 servings.

Per serving: About 526 calories, 18g protein, 51g carbohydrate, 29g fat, 4g fiber, 32mg cholesterol, 1436mg sodium

◄ Make-Ahead

Prep Time: 15 minutes
Cook Time: 15 minutes
Average Rating: ★★★★★
12 Ratings ▲ 7 Reviews
What other cooks have done:
"Great party salad. Broccoli and cauliflower are a must. Also squeeze out the excess liquid from the tomatoes to keep from diluting the dressing."

Pea Salad

Submitted by: **Gerri Ewart**

"Pretty! The green salad features romaine lettuce topped with hard cooked eggs, peas, bacon, and cheese."

8   eggs
8   slices bacon
2   heads romaine lettuce, rinsed, dried, and torn into bite size pieces
1   (16 ounce) package frozen green peas, thawed
2   cups mayonnaise
3   tablespoons white sugar
2   tablespoons fat-free milk
3   cups shredded Cheddar cheese

1. Place eggs in a saucepan and cover completely with cold water. Bring water to a boil for 1 minute. Cover, remove from heat, and let eggs stand in hot water for 10 to 12 minutes. Remove from hot water and cool. Peel. Slice egg with an egg slicer or crumble.

2. Place bacon in a large skillet. Cook, turning frequently, over medium-high heat until evenly browned. Spread romaine lettuce in a 9x13 inch baking dish. Layer crumbled bacon, peas, and eggs over the lettuce.

3. In a small bowl, mix together mayonnaise, sugar, and milk until smooth. Pour over salad and top with cheese. Cover and chill in the refrigerator for 2 hours before serving. **Yield:** 10 servings.

Per serving: About 720 calories, 20g protein, 13g carbohydrate, 67g fat, 3g fiber, 245mg cholesterol, 753mg sodium

◄ Covered-Dish Favorite

Prep Time: 15 minutes
Cook Time: 30 minutes
Average Rating: ★★★★★
12 Ratings ▲ 7 Reviews
What other cooks have done:
"I served this at one of my barbecues and everyone loved it! You can make this lower in fat by using turkey bacon, light mayo, and skim milk."

Red Skinned Potato Salad

Submitted by: **Donna**

"Try this creamy salad that's chock-full of melt-in-your-mouth bacon, bits of hard boiled egg, crunchy celery, and spicy onion. Making this salad with red potatoes gives it a delectable, firm texture."

2 pounds new red potatoes, scrubbed clean	1 onion, finely chopped
6 eggs	1 stalk celery, finely chopped
1 pound bacon	1 cup mayonnaise
	Salt and pepper to taste

1. Bring a large pot of salted water to a boil. Add potatoes and cook until tender but still firm, about 15 minutes. Drain and place in the refrigerator to cool.

2. Place eggs in a saucepan and cover with cold water. Bring water to a boil and immediately remove from heat. Cover and let eggs stand in hot water for 10 to 12 minutes. Remove from hot water, cool, peel, and chop.

3. Place bacon in a large, deep skillet. Cook over medium-high heat until evenly browned. Drain, crumble, and set aside.

4. Chop the cooled potatoes, leaving the skin on. Add to a large bowl, along with the eggs, bacon, onion, and celery. Add mayonnaise and salt and pepper to taste. Chill for an hour before serving. **Yield:** 12 servings.

Per serving: About 425 calories, 8g protein, 15g carbohydrate, 37g fat, 2g fiber, 142mg cholesterol, 593mg sodium

---

Owen's Mozzarella and Tomato Salad

Submitted by: **Dell**

"A delicious salad for cheese lovers. It's also quick and easy to throw together."

4 large tomatoes, sliced	Ground black pepper to taste
Salt to taste	
10 ounces fresh mozzarella cheese, thickly sliced	8 leaves fresh basil, torn into strips
¼ cup olive oil	

1. Sprinkle tomatoes with salt. Alternate tomato and cheese slices on a platter; drizzle with olive oil. Sprinkle with freshly ground black pepper and basil strips. **Yield:** 4 servings.

Per serving: About 338 calories, 19g protein, 11g carbohydrate, 25g fat, 2g fiber, 41mg cholesterol, 347mg sodium

---

Mid-Summer Italian Bread Salad

Submitted by: **Tamara**

"Everything in this salad is fresh, except the bread! Prepare this salad by using a loaf of artisan bread or rosemary bread that's a touch stale. If your bread is too fresh, toast it until it's about half as dried and crunchy as a crouton."

1	clove garlic	1	clove garlic, minced
1	(1 pound) loaf Italian bread	2	cups chopped fresh basil
1	cup chopped tomatoes	⅛	cup chopped fresh thyme
1	cup cucumber, peeled, seeded, and chopped	¼	cup olive oil
1	cup chopped red onion	2	tablespoons balsamic vinegar

1. Rub a peeled clove of garlic around a wooden salad bowl.
2. Pull apart or chop the bread into bite-size pieces.
3. In the prepared salad bowl, combine the bread, tomatoes, cucumber, red onion, minced garlic, basil, and thyme. Add enough olive oil and vinegar to lightly coat, toss, and serve. **Yield:** 4 servings.

Per serving: About 470 calories, 12g protein, 66g carbohydrate, 18g fat, 6g fiber, 0mg cholesterol, 672mg sodium

---

◀ Healthy

Prep Time: 10 minutes
Average Rating: ★★★★★
8 Ratings ▲ 5 Reviews

What other cooks have done:
"I minced the garlic and added it to the dressing. Toast the bread in the oven first so it won't be soggy. I also left out the cucumbers and used all tomatoes."

Cherry Tomato Salad

Submitted by: **Keren**

"This recipe was passed on by a friend and has been passed on to many more friends. It's a colorful and delicious salad served in a homemade vinaigrette. Always an excellent choice when entertaining for dinner."

40	cherry tomatoes, halved	½	cup olive oil
1	cup pitted and sliced green olives	2	tablespoons red wine vinegar
1	(6 ounce) can black olives, drained and sliced	1	tablespoon white sugar
2	green onions, minced	1	teaspoon dried oregano
3	ounces pine nuts		Salt and pepper to taste

1. In a big bowl, combine cherry tomatoes, green olives, black olives, and green onions.
2. In a dry skillet, toast pine nuts over medium heat until golden brown, turning frequently. Stir into tomato mixture.
3. In a small bowl, mix together olive oil, red wine vinegar, sugar, and oregano. Season to taste with salt and pepper. Pour over salad and gently stir to coat. Chill for 1 hour. **Yield:** 6 servings.

Per serving: About 341 calories, 5g protein, 12g carbohydrate, 32g fat, 3g fiber, 0mg cholesterol, 940mg sodium

---

◀ Family Favorite

Prep Time: 15 minutes
Cook Time: 5 minutes
Average Rating: ★★★★★
19 Ratings ▲ 14 Reviews

What other cooks have done:
"I used kalamata olives instead of black olives and substituted some balsamic vinegar for part of the red wine vinegar. My husband and I couldn't stop eating it. I sprinkled a little feta on top at serving time—yum!"

Waldorf Salad II

Submitted by: **Penny**

"This traditional salad is delicious, and you can vary the ingredients to your preference. Try adding diced, roasted chicken to make this salad a meal."

½ cup mayonnaise	1 cup thinly sliced celery
1 tablespoon white sugar	½ cup chopped walnuts
1 teaspoon lemon juice	½ cup raisins (optional)
⅛ teaspoon salt	
3 apples, peeled, cored, and chopped	

1. In a medium bowl, whisk together the mayonnaise, sugar, lemon juice, and salt.
2. Stir in the apples, celery, walnuts, and raisins, if desired. Chill until ready to serve. **Yield:** 4 servings.

Per serving: About 345 calories, 4g protein, 44g carbohydrate, 20g fat, 5g fiber, 8mg cholesterol, 310mg sodium

Make-Ahead ▶

Prep Time: 20 minutes
Average Rating: ★★★★★
9 Ratings ▲ 9 Reviews
What other cooks have done:
"I added the chicken breast and also some red grapes. I served it over chopped romaine lettuce and made a meal of it."

Fruit Salad in Seconds

Submitted by: **Cathy Byron**

"Caught in a pinch for a salad when unexpected company showed up at mealtime, I improvised with this combination. Instantly it became one of my family's favorites. Best of all, it's quick and easy. You can use lemon yogurt instead of strawberry, if you wish."

1 pint fresh strawberries, sliced	3 bananas, peeled and sliced
1 pound seedless green grapes, halved	1 (8 ounce) container strawberry yogurt

1. In a large bowl, toss together strawberries, grapes, bananas, and strawberry yogurt. Serve immediately. **Yield:** 12 servings.

Per serving: About 81 calories, 2g protein, 19g carbohydrate, 1g fat, 2g fiber, 2mg cholesterol, 11mg sodium

Healthy ▶

Prep Time: 10 minutes
Average Rating: ★★★★★
17 Ratings ▲ 11 Reviews
What other cooks have done:
"I highly recommend trying this with lemon yogurt, and you can put in almost any fruit that's handy."

Sweet and Tart Strawberry Salad *(pictured on page 227)*

Submitted by: **Edie Moon**

"Delightful and unusual strawberry salad. Pepper and vinegar enhance the sweetness of fresh berries."

1½	pounds fresh strawberries, rinsed and halved	1	tablespoon balsamic vinegar
2½	tablespoons brown sugar	¼	teaspoon freshly ground black pepper

1. In a large bowl, toss berries with sugar and let stand at room temperature for 10 minutes.

2. In a small bowl, combine the vinegar and pepper. Pour over berries and toss to coat. Divide berries among 4 salad bowls and serve.

Yield: 4 servings.

Per serving: About 86 calories, 1g protein, 21g carbohydrate, 1g fat, 4g fiber, 0mg cholesterol, 6mg sodium

◄ Out-of-the-Ordinary

Prep Time: 10 minutes
Average Rating: ★★★★★
13 Ratings ▲ 8 Reviews
What other cooks have done:
"I would have never guessed this combo would be so good . . . it got rave reviews. It also went very well with chicken and a side of pasta with pesto sauce. A sophisticated meal without the sophisticated preparation."

Pistachio Fluff Fruit Salad

Submitted by: **Jane**

"Pistachio pudding is the basis for this light and fluffy dessert salad. The pudding is lightened with whipped topping. Add an extra can of mandarin oranges, if you like."

1	(3.4 ounce) package instant pistachio pudding mix	2	cups miniature marshmallows
1	(20 ounce) can crushed pineapple with juice	1	(15.25 ounce) can fruit cocktail, drained
1	(12 ounce) container frozen whipped topping, thawed	1	(11 ounce) can mandarin oranges, drained
2	large bananas, sliced		

1. Add instant pudding into a large bowl. Add pineapple and mix well. Mix in whipped topping. Stir in bananas, marshmallows, fruit cocktail, and oranges. Cover and refrigerate until thoroughly chilled.

Yield: 8 servings.

Per serving: About 334 calories, 2g protein, 60g carbohydrate, 11g fat, 2g fiber, 0mg cholesterol, 193mg sodium

◄ Make-Ahead

Prep Time: 10 minutes
Average Rating: ★★★★★
21 Ratings ▲ 15 Reviews
What other cooks have done:
"The best thing about this recipe was that there was no baking involved . . . it only took about 10 minutes to throw together! I would recommend adding crushed almonds or more pistachios for extra crunch."

Taffy Apple Salad

Submitted by: **Julie M.**

"Perfect salad for a summer picnic. This is a light dessert that everyone will enjoy. I recommend making this the day it will be served."

1. In a medium saucepan, combine the flour, sugar, egg yolk, vinegar, and reserved pineapple juice. Cook over medium heat until thick. Remove from heat and chill.

2. In a large bowl, combine the pineapple, apple, peanuts, and chilled cooked mixture. Fold in whipped topping and chill for at least 1 hour before serving. **Yield:** 12 servings.

Per serving: About 290 calories, 7g protein, 31g carbohydrate, 17g fat, 4g fiber, 18mg cholesterol, 10mg sodium

Orange Cream Fruit Salad

Submitted by: **Lori**

"A winner every time I make it. The orange flavor in the dressing is so refreshing."

1	(3.4 ounce) package instant vanilla pudding mix	1	(15 ounce) can sliced peaches, drained
1½	cups milk	1	(11 ounce) can mandarin oranges, drained
⅓	cup frozen orange juice concentrate, thawed		
¾	cup sour cream	2	bananas, sliced
1	(20 ounce) can pineapple tidbits, drained	1	apple, peeled, cored, and sliced

1. In a medium mixing bowl, combine pudding mix, milk, and orange juice concentrate. Beat with an electric mixer on medium speed for 2 minutes. Mix in sour cream.

2. In a large salad bowl, combine pineapple, peaches, oranges, bananas, and apple. Gently mix in orange dressing. Cover and refrigerate for 2 hours. **Yield:** 10 servings.

Per serving: About 215 calories, 3g protein, 43g carbohydrate, 5g fat, 2g fiber, 10mg cholesterol, 178mg sodium

Ambrosia Fruit Salad

Submitted by: **Kimberley Teal**
"Use a little juice from the maraschino cherries to color your salad a festive red."

1	(8 ounce) container frozen whipped topping, thawed	1	(11 ounce) can mandarin oranges, drained
2½	cups shredded coconut	3	cups miniature marshmallows
½	cup chopped walnuts	1	(10 ounce) jar maraschino cherries, drained (optional)
1	(8 ounce) can fruit cocktail, drained	1	teaspoon ground nutmeg
1	(8 ounce) can pineapple chunks, drained	1	teaspoon ground cinnamon

1. In a large bowl, combine the whipped topping, coconut, chopped walnuts, fruit cocktail, pineapple, mandarin oranges, marshmallows, cherries, if desired, nutmeg, and cinnamon. Mix together well and refrigerate for 30 to 45 minutes. **Yield:** 6 servings.

Per serving: About 561 calories, 4g protein, 84g carbohydrate, 26g fat, 3g fiber, 0mg cholesterol, 137mg sodium

Judy's Strawberry Pretzel Salad

Submitted by: **Tom Quinlin**
"This three-layer salad includes a pretzel crust, cream cheese center, and strawberry top."

1½	cups crushed pretzels	1	(6 ounce) package strawberry flavored gelatin
4½	tablespoons white sugar		
¾	cup butter, melted	2	cups boiling water
1	cup white sugar	1	(16 ounce) package frozen strawberries
2	(8 ounce) packages cream cheese		
1	(8 ounce) container frozen whipped topping, thawed		

1. Preheat oven to 350°F (175°C). Mix together the pretzels, 4½ tablespoons sugar, and melted butter. Press into a 9x13 inch pan. Bake in the preheated oven for 10 minutes or until lightly toasted. Set aside to cool completely.
2. In a medium bowl, beat 1 cup sugar and cream cheese until smooth. Fold in whipped topping. Spread evenly over the cooled crust. Refrigerate until set, about 30 minutes.
3. In a medium bowl, stir together the gelatin mix and boiling water. Stir in frozen strawberries until thawed. Pour over cream cheese mixture in pan. Refrigerate until completely chilled, at least 1 hour.
Yield: 8 servings.

Per serving: About 741 calories, 8g protein, 82g carbohydrate, 45g fat, 2g fiber, 108mg cholesterol, 669mg sodium

Champagne Salad

Submitted by: **Michele**
"You can store this great dessert in the freezer for weeks. It's a nice substitute for ice cream."

1 (8 ounce) package cream cheese, softened
1 cup white sugar
1 (15 ounce) can crushed pineapple, drained
1 (16 ounce) container frozen whipped topping, thawed
1 (10 ounce) package frozen strawberries, thawed
3 bananas, diced
¾ cup chopped walnuts

1. In a large bowl, beat the cream cheese and sugar. Fold in the pineapple, whipped topping, and strawberries and mix well. Stir in bananas and walnuts.
2. Freeze for 4 to 6 hours or overnight. Remove from freezer 1 hour before serving. **Yield:** 8 servings.

Per serving: About 525 calories, 6g protein, 60g carbohydrate, 32g fat, 3g fiber, 30mg cholesterol, 102mg sodium

Ruby Red Layered Salad

Submitted by: **Poni**
"This is an old family favorite recipe prepared every Christmas, and I wanna tell ya it's great! It's from the kitchen of my mother, Charlene Betty Stephenson. Thanks, Mom!"

1 (3 ounce) package raspberry flavored gelatin
2 cups boiling water, divided
1 (10 ounce) package frozen raspberries
1 (8 ounce) container sour cream
1 (3 ounce) package cherry flavored gelatin
1 (8 ounce) can crushed pineapple, drained
1 (16 ounce) can whole cranberry sauce

1. Dissolve raspberry gelatin in 1 cup hot water. Add frozen raspberries and stir until well mixed. Pour into a glass bowl. Refrigerate until almost firm, about 30 to 60 minutes.
2. Spread sour cream over firm gelatin. Refrigerate.
3. Dissolve cherry gelatin in 1 cup boiling water. Stir in pineapple and cranberry sauce. Chill until partially set, about 20 to 40 minutes.
4. Spoon cherry gelatin mixture over sour cream layer. Chill until firm, about 1 to 2 hours. **Yield:** 8 servings.

Per serving: About 333 calories, 4g protein, 55g carbohydrate, 12g fat, 3g fiber, 26mg cholesterol, 102mg sodium

Fried Onion Rings,
page 241

Harvest Salad, page 206

Sweet and Tart
Strawberry Salad,
page 221

Chinese Chicken Salad III,
page 209

Corn and Zucchini
Melody, page 238

Ranch Dressing II

Submitted by: **Dawnia**

"This homemade Ranch dressing is easy to make and convenient as commercial dressings. Use buttermilk in place of the sour cream, if you like."

1	cup mayonnaise	¼	teaspoon garlic powder
½	cup sour cream	¼	teaspoon onion powder
½	teaspoon dried chives	⅛	teaspoon salt
½	teaspoon dried parsley	⅛	teaspoon ground black
½	teaspoon dried dill weed		pepper

1. In a large bowl, whisk together the mayonnaise, sour cream, chives, parsley, dill, garlic powder, onion powder, salt, and pepper. Cover and refrigerate for 30 minutes before serving. **Yield:** 1½ cups.

Per 2 tablespoons: About 163 calories, 1g protein, 1g carbohydrate, 18g fat, 0g fiber, 14mg cholesterol, 143mg sodium

◄ Kid-Friendly

Prep Time: 5 minutes
Average Rating: ★★★★★
33 Ratings ▲ 28 Reviews
What other cooks have done:
"I used low-fat mayonnaise and fat-free sour cream. I also used fresh dill, dried minced onion, and fresh minced garlic, all for stronger flavor."

Bill's Blue Cheese Dressing

Submitted by: **William**

"For the best-tasting dressing, splurge on real blue cheese."

¾	cup sour cream	½	teaspoon powdered mustard
1⅓	cups mayonnaise	⅓	teaspoon garlic powder
4	ounces blue cheese, crumbled	½	teaspoon salt
1	teaspoon Worcestershire sauce	½	teaspoon ground black pepper

1. In a large bowl, whisk together the sour cream, mayonnaise, blue cheese, Worcestershire sauce, mustard, garlic powder, salt, and pepper. Cover and refrigerate for 24 hours before serving. **Yield:** 2½ cups.

Per 3 tablespoons: About 168 calories, 3g protein, 7g carbohydrate, 15g fat, 0g fiber, 20mg cholesterol, 432mg sodium

◄ Restaurant Fare

Prep Time: 15 minutes
Average Rating: ★★★★★
42 Ratings ▲ 36 Reviews
What other cooks have done:
"I served this with caramelized baked chicken wings and celery sticks, and my picky husband and son loved it. They couldn't believe that I made it!"

Honey Mustard Dressing II

Submitted by: **Mary Ann Benzon**

"You can use lime juice instead of lemon juice, if desired."

¼	cup mayonnaise	1	tablespoon honey
1	tablespoon prepared mustard	½	tablespoon lemon juice

1. Whisk together the mayonnaise, mustard, honey, and lemon juice. Pour over salad and toss evenly to coat. **Yield:** 6 tablespoons.

Per 2 tablespoons: About 102 calories, 0g protein, 11g carbohydrate, 7g fat, 0g fiber, 5mg cholesterol, 197mg sodium

◄ Family Favorite

Prep Time: 5 minutes
Average Rating: ★★★★★
19 Ratings ▲ 13 Reviews
What other cooks have done:
"I used low-cal, low-fat mayo, and the recipe held up like a champ."

Aunt Betty's French Dressing

Submitted by: **Maggie Lynch**

"A tasty red French dressing that has been a family favorite for years. For variations, I've used flavored vinegars, red wine vinegar, and balsamic vinegar."

⅔	cup ketchup	1	small onion, quartered
¾	cup white sugar	2	teaspoons paprika
½	cup white wine vinegar	2	teaspoons Worcestershire
½	cup vegetable oil		sauce

1. Combine the ketchup, sugar, vinegar, oil, onion, paprika, and Worcestershire sauce in a blender or food processor. Blend until the onion is well chopped. Chill before serving. **Yield:** 3 cups.

Per 2 tablespoons: About 73 calories, 0g protein, 9g carbohydrate, 5g fat, 0g fiber, 0mg cholesterol, 90mg sodium

Creamy Italian Dressing

Submitted by: **Cathy**

"Wonderful, thick dressing—my favorite."

1	cup mayonnaise	½	small onion
2	tablespoons red wine vinegar	1	tablespoon white sugar
		1	teaspoon salt
¾	teaspoon Italian seasoning	⅛	teaspoon ground black
½	teaspoon garlic salt		pepper

1. Combine the mayonnaise, vinegar, Italian seasoning, garlic salt, onion, sugar, salt, and pepper in a blender; blend on high until smooth. Cover and chill. **Yield:** 1½ cups.

Per 2 tablespoons: About 149 calories, 0g protein, 2g carbohydrate, 16g fat, 0g fiber, 10mg cholesterol, 162mg sodium

Vinaigrette

Submitted by: **Karen Castle**

"This recipe is simple to make and delicious, especially if you like garlic."

½	cup red wine vinegar	2	teaspoons salt
½	cup vegetable oil	1	clove crushed garlic
2	teaspoons white sugar		

1. Combine the vinegar, oil, sugar, salt, and garlic in a jar with a tight fitting lid. Shake well and refrigerate until ready to use. **Yield:** 1 cup.

Per 2 tablespoons: About 125 calories, 0g protein, 2g carbohydrate, 14g fat, 0g fiber, 0mg cholesterol, 581mg sodium

Side Dishes

Watch everyone go back for seconds with this amazing array of side dishes that round out any meal to perfection. Standouts such as Lemon-Horseradish New Potatoes, Butternut Squash Casserole, and Asparagus with Parmesan Crust will make anyone want to eat their veggies. A dish such as Risotto with Tomato, Corn, and Basil could stand in as the main dish when you're looking for a light meal. Any way you slice it, you've got the answer for a balanced dinner tonight.

Sautéed Apples

Submitted by: **Jenny**
"This is great served with any meal, especially breakfast. The syrup from the apples is delicious over homemade waffles. You can add raisins to the sauce, if you wish."

¼	cup butter	2	teaspoons cornstarch
4	large tart apples, peeled, cored, and sliced ¼ inch thick	½	cup cold water
		½	cup packed brown sugar
		½	teaspoon ground cinnamon

1. In a large skillet or saucepan, melt butter over medium heat; add apples. Cook, stirring constantly, until apples are almost tender, about 6 to 7 minutes.
2. Dissolve cornstarch in water; add to skillet. Stir in brown sugar and cinnamon. Boil for 2 minutes, stirring occasionally. Remove from heat and serve warm. **Yield:** 8 servings.

Per serving: About 150 calories, 0g protein, 26g carbohydrate, 6g fat, 3g fiber, 16mg cholesterol, 63mg sodium

Quick & Easy ▶

Prep Time: 5 minutes
Cook Time: 15 minutes
Average Rating: ★★★★★
14 Ratings ▲ 13 Reviews
What other cooks have done:
"I used these apples to top some waffles and had more than enough left over to reheat and put on top of vanilla ice cream the next day."

Asparagus with Parmesan Crust

Submitted by: **Kimber**
"Can be used as either a side dish or a warm appetizer. Indulge yourself with the finest balsamic vinegar you can find, and enjoy!"

1	pound thin asparagus spears		Freshly ground black pepper to taste
1	tablespoon extra virgin olive oil	¼	cup balsamic vinegar, or to taste
1	ounce shaved Parmesan cheese		

1. Preheat oven to 450°F (230°C).
2. Place asparagus on a baking sheet. Drizzle with olive oil and toss to coat. Arrange asparagus spears in a single layer. Spread Parmesan cheese over asparagus and season with freshly ground black pepper.
3. Bake in the preheated oven 12 minutes or until cheese is melted and asparagus is tender but crisp. Serve immediately on warm plates, sprinkling with balsamic vinegar to taste. **Yield:** 4 servings.

Per serving: About 102 calories, 6g protein, 8g carbohydrate, 6g fat, 2g fiber, 6mg cholesterol, 138mg sodium

Healthy ▶

Prep Time: 10 minutes
Cook Time: 12 minutes
Average Rating: ★★★★★
15 Ratings ▲ 9 Reviews
What other cooks have done:
"Use an olive oil-based cooking spray instead of the olive oil for a lighter taste. Also, try using bigger asparagus spears, or cut down on the cooking time for baby spears if you like a crispier texture."

Baked Beans

Submitted by: **Margie**

"You could almost say that these baked beans with a kick have been double-baked!"

1	(29 ounce) can baked beans with pork	½	cup ketchup
½	cup packed brown sugar	1	tablespoon Worcestershire sauce

1. Preheat oven to 350°F (175°C).

2. In a lightly greased 1½ quart baking dish, combine beans, brown sugar, ketchup, and Worcestershire sauce.

3. Bake, uncovered, in the preheated oven for 45 minutes or until bubbly. **Yield:** 6 servings.

Per serving: About 271 calories, 8g protein, 57g carbohydrate, 2g fat, 7g fiber, 3mg cholesterol, 732mg sodium

Grandma's Green Bean Casserole

Submitted by: **Amy**

"This recipe is much better than the standard mushroom soup and French fried onion version."

2	tablespoons butter	3	(15 ounce) cans green beans, drained
2	tablespoons all-purpose flour	12	buttery round crackers, crumbled
1	teaspoon salt		
1	teaspoon white sugar	1	tablespoon butter, melted
¼	cup onion, diced	2	cups shredded Cheddar cheese
1	(8 ounce) container sour cream		

1. Preheat oven to 350°F (175°C).

2. Combine 2 tablespoons butter and flour in a large skillet over medium heat and cook 5 minutes. Remove from heat. Stir in salt, sugar, onion, and sour cream; stir in beans.

3. Place bean mixture into a shallow lightly greased 2 quart baking dish. In a small bowl, toss together cracker crumbs and melted butter. Top beans with cheese and cracker crumbs.

4. Bake in the preheated oven for 30 minutes or until cheese is bubbling. **Yield:** 8 servings.

Per serving: About 278 calories, 10g protein, 13g carbohydrate, 21g fat, 3g fiber, 58mg cholesterol, 1009mg sodium

Green Bean and Mushroom Medley

Submitted by: **Michele**

"Fresh veggies tossed together make a perfect side dish for family gatherings."

½	pound fresh green beans, cut into 1 inch lengths	1	onion, sliced
2	carrots, cut into thick strips	1	teaspoon salt
¼	cup butter	½	teaspoon seasoned salt
1	(8 ounce) package sliced fresh mushrooms	¼	teaspoon garlic salt
		¼	teaspoon white pepper

1. Place green beans and carrots in 1 inch of boiling water. Cover and cook until tender but still firm. Drain.

2. Melt butter in a skillet over medium heat. Sauté mushrooms and onion until almost tender. Reduce heat, cover, and simmer 3 minutes. Stir in green beans, carrots, salt, seasoned salt, garlic salt, and white pepper. Cover and cook for 5 minutes over medium heat. **Yield:** 4 servings.

Per serving: About 152 calories, 2g protein, 10g carbohydrate, 12g fat, 4g fiber, 32mg cholesterol, 1133mg sodium

Broccoli-Rice Casserole

Submitted by: **Gina Williams**

"This is the best broccoli-rice casserole you'll ever eat!"

2	(10 ounce) packages frozen chopped broccoli	2½	cups water
3	cups instant rice	1	(16 ounce) package processed American cheese, cubed
1	(10.75 ounce) can condensed cream of mushroom soup	1	tablespoon butter
1	(10.75 ounce) can condensed cream of chicken soup	1	bunch celery, chopped
		1	large onion, chopped
			Salt and pepper to taste

1. Cook broccoli and rice according to package directions. Preheat oven to 350°F (175°C).

2. In a medium saucepan over low heat, mix cream of mushroom soup and cream of chicken soup with water. Gradually stir in cheese until melted. Be careful that the cheese doesn't burn.

3. Melt butter in a large skillet over medium-high heat and sauté celery and onion until soft.

4. In a large bowl, combine broccoli, rice, soup and cheese mixture, celery, onion, salt, and pepper. Pour into a greased 9x13 inch baking dish.

5. Bake in the preheated oven for 45 minutes or until bubbly and lightly brown. **Yield:** 10 servings.

Per serving: About 360 calories, 15g protein, 33g carbohydrate, 18g fat, 3g fiber, 48mg cholesterol, 1156mg sodium

Aunt Millie's Broccoli Casserole

Submitted by: **Kaylee**

"A family favorite for holidays and get-togethers, this recipe has been passed down in our family for years. It's so cheesy and delicious!"

4	heads fresh broccoli, chopped	1½	teaspoons salt
1½	cups shredded American cheese	2	teaspoons ground black pepper
1	(10.75 ounce) can condensed cream of mushroom soup	3	tablespoons butter
		2	cups crushed, seasoned croutons

1. Bring a pot of salted water to a boil. Add broccoli; cook until tender but still firm, about 5 minutes. Drain and cool under cold running water.

2. Preheat oven to 350°F (175°C).

3. In a saucepan over medium heat, combine the cheese, mushroom soup, salt, and pepper. Stir until melted; add broccoli, stir, and pour into a lightly greased 2 quart baking dish.

4. In a separate saucepan, melt the butter, add croutons, and stir to coat. Sprinkle over broccoli mixture.

5. Bake in the preheated oven for 30 minutes. **Yield:** 8 servings.

Per serving: About 249 calories, 11g protein, 19g carbohydrate, 16g fat, 5g fiber, 35mg cholesterol, 1210mg sodium

Beth's Scalloped Cabbage

Submitted by: **Beth Leslie**

"Serve this homespun casserole as a holiday side dish."

1	medium head cabbage, cut into small wedges	1	cup milk
2	tablespoons butter	⅔	cup cubed processed American cheese
2	tablespoons all-purpose flour	½	cup crushed buttery round crackers
½	teaspoon salt		

1. Preheat oven to 350°F (175°C). Grease a 2 quart baking dish.

2. Bring a large pot of salted water to a boil. Add cabbage and cook until barely tender, about 10 minutes; drain.

3. Meanwhile, in a small saucepan over low heat, melt butter. Blend in flour, salt, and milk. Cook, stirring, until slightly thickened. Stir in cheese until melted.

4. Transfer cabbage to prepared dish. Sprinkle cracker crumbs on top.

5. Bake in the preheated oven for 25 to 30 minutes. **Yield:** 6 servings.

Per serving: About: 237 calories, 7g protein, 21g carbohydrate, 14g fat, 4g fiber, 25mg cholesterol, 615mg sodium

Orange-Glazed Carrots

Submitted by: **Heidi**

"The whole family will enjoy this wonderfully easy, glazed carrot recipe. It's great for special occasions or an everyday meal."

1	pound baby carrots	2	tablespoons butter
¼	cup orange juice		Pinch salt
3	tablespoons brown sugar		

1. Place carrots in a shallow saucepan and cover with water. Boil until tender, about 10 minutes; drain. Pour orange juice over carrots and mix well. Simmer on medium heat for about 5 minutes.
2. Stir in brown sugar, butter, and salt; mix well. Heat until butter and sugar are melted. **Yield:** 4 servings.

Per serving: About 139 calories, 1g protein, 21g carbohydrate, 6g fat, 2g fiber, 16mg cholesterol, 199mg sodium

Carrot Soufflé

Submitted by: **Carol**

"A carrot soufflé as good as your favorite restaurant makes!"

1¾	pounds carrots, chopped	3	eggs, beaten
1	cup white sugar	¼	pound butter, softened
1½	teaspoons baking powder	2	teaspoons confectioners' sugar
1½	teaspoons vanilla extract		
2	tablespoons all-purpose flour		

1. Preheat oven to 350°F (175°C).
2. In a large pot of boiling water, steam or boil carrots until soft. Drain well and transfer to a large bowl.
3. While carrots are warm, add sugar, baking powder, and vanilla; beat at medium speed with an electric mixer until smooth.
4. Add flour, eggs, and butter and mix well.
5. Pour mixture into a 2 quart baking dish and bake in the preheated oven for 1 hour or until top is light golden brown. Sprinkle lightly with confectioners' sugar before serving. **Yield:** 8 servings.

Per serving: About 281 calories, 4g protein, 38g carbohydrate, 14g fat, 3g fiber, 111mg cholesterol, 267mg sodium

---

Quick & Easy ▶

Prep Time: 5 minutes
Cook Time: 15 minutes
Average Rating: ★★★★★
20 Ratings ▲ 14 Reviews

What other cooks have done:
"My daughter and I are not vegetable lovers. I am always in search of new dishes that we can try that will change our feelings about eating them. We gave this recipe a try and we really enjoyed it! It's easy, tasty, and quick."

Holiday Fare ▶

Prep Time: 15 minutes
Cook Time: 1 hour
Average Rating: ★★★★★
23 Ratings ▲ 20 Reviews

What other cooks have done:
"I replaced the eggs with an egg substitute to cut out some of the fat, and it was still delicious!"

Cauliflower Casserole

Submitted by: **Betty Houston**

"A quick, delightful dish that's easy to make and sure to please! Those who say they hate cauliflower always enjoy this dish."

1	large head cauliflower, broken into small florets		Pinch salt
½	cup butter, melted	1	teaspoon crushed red pepper flakes
¼	cup grated Parmesan cheese	1	cup shredded Cheddar cheese
⅔	cup Italian-seasoned breadcrumbs		

1. Preheat oven to 350°F (175°C).

2. Bring a pot of water to a boil. Add cauliflower and cook for about 10 minutes. Drain and place in a lightly greased 2 quart baking dish.

3. In a small bowl, combine butter, Parmesan cheese, breadcrumbs, salt, and red pepper flakes. Sprinkle mixture over casserole and top with Cheddar cheese.

4. Bake in the preheated oven for 20 minutes or until cheese is melted and bubbly. **Yield:** 6 servings.

Per serving: About 308 calories, 11g protein, 15g carbohydrate, 24g fat, 4g fiber, 64mg cholesterol, 624mg sodium

◀ **Make-Ahead**

Prep Time: 15 minutes

Cook Time: 20 minutes

Average Rating: ★★★★★

25 Ratings ▲ 21 Reviews

What other cooks have done:

"To make a moister casserole, I break up the cauliflower into smaller pieces and use less breadcrumbs. This is one of my favorite side dishes for company."

Awesome and Easy Creamy Corn Casserole

Submitted by: **Ruthie Crickmer**

"This truly is the most delicious recipe—like a cross between corn soufflé and a slightly sweet corn pudding! I know you'll love the ease of preparation and especially the taste. The ingredients can be doubled and baked in a 9x13 inch baking dish in almost the same amount of cooking time."

½	cup butter, melted	1	(14.75 ounce) can creamed corn
2	eggs, beaten		
1	(8.5 ounce) package dry cornbread mix	1	(8 ounce) container sour cream
1	(15 ounce) can whole kernel corn, drained		

1. Preheat oven to 350°F (175°C). Lightly grease a 9x9 inch baking dish.

2. In a medium bowl, combine butter, eggs, cornbread mix, whole kernel and creamed corn, and sour cream. Spoon mixture into the prepared dish.

3. Bake in the preheated oven for 45 minutes or until the top is golden brown. **Yield:** 8 servings.

Per serving: About 377 calories, 7g protein, 40g carbohydrate, 22g fat, 2g fiber, 98mg cholesterol, 887mg sodium

◀ **Family Favorite**

Prep Time: 5 minutes

Cook Time: 45 minutes

Average Rating: ★★★★★

255 Ratings ▲ 182 Reviews

What other cooks have done:

"We tried this with 2 pounds of sage sausage cooked and crumbled into the batter before baking. Awesome is definitely the word for it."

Corn and Zucchini Melody *(pictured on page 228)*

Submitted by: **Gail**

"Zucchini, corn, and onions sautéed and combined with crumbled bacon and cheese make a quick and easy way to use some fresh veggies from your garden."

4	slices bacon	1	small red onion, chopped
2	cups cubed zucchini (about 2 medium zucchini)	¼	teaspoon pepper
1½	cups fresh corn kernels	¼	cup finely shredded Monterey Jack cheese

1. Place bacon in a large, deep skillet. Cook over medium-high heat until evenly browned. Drain, reserving 1 tablespoon of drippings, crumble, and set aside.

2. In the skillet with the bacon drippings, sauté the zucchini, corn, and onion over medium heat until crisp tender, about 10 to 13 minutes. Season with pepper.

3. Spoon vegetables into a bowl and sprinkle with cheese and crumbled bacon. **Yield:** 5 servings.

Per serving: About 208 calories, 6g protein, 14g carbohydrate, 15g fat, 2g fiber, 20mg cholesterol, 204mg sodium

Corn Fritters

Submitted by: **Joan Zaffary**

"Nothing warms up a cool night like a plateful of old-time corn fritters! Dig in—these are delicious!"

1	cup sifted all-purpose flour	1	egg
1	teaspoon baking powder	1	tablespoon shortening, melted
½	teaspoon salt		
¼	teaspoon white sugar	½	cup milk
2	cups whole kernel corn	3	cups vegetable oil

1. In a bowl, combine flour, baking powder, salt, and sugar. Stir the corn into the dry mixture.

2. In a separate bowl, beat egg, melted shortening, and milk. Pour the wet mixture into the dry and stir until blended.

3. Heat oil in a heavy pot or deep fryer to 365°F (185°C).

4. Drop spoonfuls of the fritter batter into the hot oil and fry until golden; drain on paper towels. **Yield:** 12 servings.

Per serving: About 84 calories, 3g protein, 14g carbohydrate, 2g fat, 1g fiber, 20mg cholesterol, 198mg sodium

Pat's Mushroom Sauté

Submitted by: **Lanni**

"My son-in-law makes the best sautéed mushrooms, and now, so do I! Eat them hot out of the pan."

2	tablespoons butter	⅛	teaspoon dried oregano
½	tablespoon olive oil	1	pound button mushrooms, sliced
½	tablespoon balsamic vinegar		
1	clove garlic, minced		

1. Melt butter with oil in a large skillet over medium heat. Stir in balsamic vinegar, garlic, oregano, and mushrooms. Sauté for 20 minutes or until tender. **Yield:** 4 servings.

Per serving: About 94 calories, 2g protein, 5g carbohydrate, 8g fat, 1g fiber, 16mg cholesterol, 63mg sodium

Baked Mushrooms

Submitted by: **Gail**

"These are easy to make and taste great."

1	pound fresh mushrooms, quartered	¼	teaspoon seasoning salt
1	onion, diced		Dash of pepper
1	clove garlic, chopped	2	tablespoons chopped fresh parsley
1	green bell pepper, diced	2	tablespoons water
½	teaspoon Italian seasoning	¼	cup melted butter

1. Preheat oven to 350°F (175°C).
2. In a lightly greased 1 quart baking dish, combine mushrooms, onion, garlic, bell pepper, Italian seasoning, seasoning salt, pepper, and parsley. Pour water and butter over mixture and cover.
3. Bake in the preheated oven for 40 to 45 minutes. **Yield:** 6 servings.

Per serving: About 99 calories, 2g protein, 7g carbohydrate, 8g fat, 2g fiber, 21mg cholesterol, 121mg sodium

Fried Okra

Submitted by: **Linda Martin**

"A simple Southern classic! Okra is dredged in seasoned cornmeal, then fried until golden."

10	pods okra, sliced in ¼ inch pieces	¼	teaspoon salt
1	egg, lightly beaten	¼	teaspoon ground black pepper
1	cup cornmeal	½	cup vegetable oil

1. In a small bowl, soak okra in egg for 5 to 10 minutes. In a medium bowl, combine cornmeal, salt, and pepper.

2. Heat oil in a large skillet over medium-high heat. Dredge okra in the cornmeal mixture, coating evenly. Carefully place okra in hot oil, stirring continuously. Reduce heat to medium when okra first starts to brown and cook until golden. Drain on paper towels. **Yield:** 4 servings.

Per serving: About 397 calories, 5g protein, 29g carbohydrate, 29g fat, 3g fiber, 53mg cholesterol, 164mg sodium

Classic Comfort Food ▶

Prep Time: 15 minutes

Cook Time: 15 minutes

Average Rating: ★★★★★

13 Ratings ▲ 12 Reviews

What other cooks have done:

"This recipe is definitely simple Southern cooking at its best. My grandma always cooked summer squashes (yellow or zucchini) and mushrooms this way, and they're good, too."

Grilled Onions

Submitted by: **Linda Smith**

"If you like onions, you'll love this grilled treat! When I grill, I like to try and make the whole meal on the grill. This dish can be prepared as an appetizer or as a side dish."

4	large onions	½	cup butter
4	cubes chicken bouillon		

1. Prepare grill for indirect heat.

2. Peel off outer layer of onions. Slice off (and reserve) a small section of 1 end of each onion and make a small hole in the center of onion. Fill the center of each onion with a bouillon cube and 2 tablespoons butter. Replace top of onion and wrap in aluminum foil.

3. Place onions on grill and close grill. Cook for 1 hour or until tender. Cut into bite size chunks and place in a serving dish with all the juices in the foil. **Yield:** 8 servings.

Per serving: About 135 calories, 1g protein, 7g carbohydrate, 12g fat, 1g fiber, 32mg cholesterol, 696mg sodium

Family Favorite ▶

Prep Time: 5 minutes

Cook Time: 1 hour

Average Rating: ★★★★★

16 Ratings ▲ 11 Reviews

What other cooks have done:

"I made an herbed butter with some fresh rosemary and just a pinch of garlic powder the second time I made this. If you like onions, this is bliss! Especially when Vidalias are in season."

Fried Onion Rings *(pictured on page 225)*

Submitted by: **Jill**

"These are very delicate and the best I've had. Have also made other veggies with this batter. Can be refrigerated or frozen, then reheated in oven or microwave. Carbonated water can be substituted for beer in this recipe."

1 quart vegetable oil	Pinch ground black pepper
1 cup all-purpose flour	4 large onions, peeled and
1 cup beer	sliced into rings
Pinch salt	

1. In a large, deep skillet, heat oil to 375°F (190°C).
2. In a medium bowl, combine flour, beer, salt, and pepper. Mix until smooth. Dredge onion slices in the batter until evenly coated. Deep-fry in the hot oil until golden brown. Drain on paper towels. **Yield:** 12 servings.

Per serving: About 225 calories, 2g protein, 13g carbohydrate, 18g fat, 1g fiber, 0mg cholesterol, 31mg sodium

◄ Kid-Friendly

Prep Time: 15 minutes
Cook Time: 20 minutes
Average Rating: ★★★★★
37 Ratings ▲ 27 Reviews
What other cooks have done:
"I thinly sliced the onions and salted them as soon as they came out of the oil with very fine salt."

Baked Pineapple Casserole

Submitted by: **Cheryl**

"A bread and pineapple casserole that goes great with a ham dinner."

½ cup butter or margarine, softened	Pinch ground nutmeg (optional)
1 cup white sugar	5 slices white bread, torn
4 eggs	1 (20 ounce) can crushed
Pinch ground cinnamon (optional)	pineapple with juice

1. Preheat oven to 350°F (175°C). Grease a 2 quart baking dish.
2. In a mixing bowl, beat butter and sugar. Beat in eggs, one at a time. Stir in cinnamon and nutmeg, if desired. Stir bread and crushed pineapple into the mixture. Transfer mixture to the prepared baking dish.
3. Bake in the preheated oven for 1 hour or until bubbly and lightly browned. **Yield:** 6 servings.

Per serving: About 425 calories, 6g protein, 59g carbohydrate, 19g fat, 1g fiber, 142mg cholesterol, 224mg sodium

◄ Holiday Fare

Prep Time: 10 minutes
Cook Time: 1 hour
Average Rating: ★★★★★
47 Ratings ▲ 36 Reviews
What other cooks have done:
"This is great as a side dish or as dessert with ice cream. It's also wonderful reheated in the morning for breakfast."

Honey-Roasted Red Potatoes

Submitted by: **Stephanie Moon**

"These slightly sweet potatoes are perfect with most entrées."

1	pound red potatoes, quartered	1	tablespoon honey
2	tablespoons diced onion	1	teaspoon powdered mustard
2	tablespoons butter, melted		Pinch salt
			Pinch ground black pepper

1. Preheat oven to 375°F (190°C). Lightly coat a 7x11 inch baking dish with cooking spray.

2. Place potato in a single layer in prepared dish and top with onion. In a small bowl, combine melted butter, honey, mustard, salt, and pepper; drizzle over potato and onion.

3. Bake in the preheated oven for 35 minutes or until tender, stirring halfway through the cooking time. **Yield:** 4 servings.

Per serving: About 173 calories, 3g protein, 28g carbohydrate, 6g fat, 3g fiber, 16mg cholesterol, 163mg sodium

Lemon-Horseradish New Potatoes *(pictured on page 152)*

Submitted by: **Teresa**

"These new potatoes served with a zesty sauce have been a long-standing favorite at our house. If you're in a hurry, just boil the potatoes and serve with the sauce."

¼	cup butter	2	tablespoons fresh lemon juice
½	teaspoon salt		
¼	teaspoon pepper	1½	pounds unpeeled new potatoes, halved
2	tablespoons prepared horseradish		

1. Preheat oven to 350°F (175°C).

2. Melt butter in a 7x11 inch baking dish in the oven. Stir in salt, pepper, horseradish, and lemon juice. Place potatoes in dish and toss to coat with butter mixture.

3. Cover and bake in the preheated oven for 1 hour or until potatoes are tender. **Yield:** 4 servings.

Per serving: About 241 calories, 3g protein, 32g carbohydrate, 12g fat, 3g fiber, 31mg cholesterol, 799mg sodium

Cowboy Mashed Potatoes

Submitted by: **Bruticus**

"Quick, easy, and delicious mashed potatoes with corn and carrots."

1 pound red potatoes	1 (10 ounce) package frozen white corn, thawed
1 pound Yukon gold (yellow) potatoes	¼ cup butter
1 fresh jalapeño pepper, sliced	½ cup shredded Cheddar cheese
12 ounces baby carrots	Salt and pepper to taste
4 cloves garlic	

1. Place red potatoes, yellow potatoes, jalapeño pepper, carrots, and garlic cloves in a large pot. Cover with water and bring to a boil over high heat. Cook 15 to 20 minutes or until potatoes are tender. Drain water from pot.

2. Stir in corn and butter. Mash the mixture with a potato masher until butter is melted and potatoes have reached desired consistency. Mix in cheese, salt, and pepper. Serve hot. **Yield:** 10 servings.

Per serving: About 154 calories, 5g protein, 20g carbohydrate, 7g fat, 3g fiber, 20mg cholesterol, 175mg sodium

◀ Hot & Spicy

Prep Time: 20 minutes
Cook Time: 20 minutes
Average Rating: ★★★★★
64 Ratings ▲ 44 Reviews
What other cooks have done:
"The vegetables were great in this. I left the potatoes fairly chunky. I also added green beans and a little sour cream to the mix. After being refrigerated, it was delicious as a cold potato salad dish."

Baja Stuffed Potatoes

Submitted by: **Dominique**

"My brother, Paul, invented these double stuffed potatoes for a barbecue we had in Mexico."

6 large baking potatoes	2 (11 ounce) cans Mexican-style corn, drained
3 tablespoons olive oil	2 (4.5 ounce) cans chopped green chiles, drained
¾ cup sour cream	
1½ cups shredded Monterey Jack cheese with peppers, divided	

1. Preheat oven to 400°F (200°C).

2. Pierce each potato several times and rub generously with oil. Bake in the preheated oven until softened, about 45 to 55 minutes.

3. Meanwhile, in a medium bowl combine sour cream, 1 cup cheese, corn, and chiles.

4. When the potatoes are cooked, cut a slit in the top of each one and squeeze or scoop out the flesh, leaving a ½ inch thick shell. Combine the potato flesh with the cheese mixture; mix well. Spoon the potato mixture back into the shells and top with remaining ½ cup cheese. Place them on a baking sheet.

5. Bake in the preheated oven for 15 minutes or until cheese is melted and golden brown. **Yield:** 6 servings.

Per serving: About 468 calories, 13g protein, 56g carbohydrate, 23g fat, 4g fiber, 42mg cholesterol, 1358mg sodium

◀ Meatless Main Dish

Prep Time: 20 minutes
Cook Time: 1 hour 10 minutes
Average Rating: ★★★★★
10 Ratings ▲ 7 Reviews
What other cooks have done:
"These potatoes were really good and pretty easy to make. My wife and I like spicy foods, so the next time I make them I might add a chopped jalapeño to boost the pepper Jack cheese."

Greek-Style Potatoes

Submitted by: **Cathie**

"Greek-Style Potatoes is a simple recipe that can be adjusted to your taste. I sometimes add a little more lemon. The potatoes are moist and perfect served with green beans and baked chicken with a little tomato and feta on top."

⅓	cup olive oil	2	cubes chicken bouillon
1½	cups water		Ground black pepper to
2	cloves garlic, finely chopped		taste
¼	cup fresh lemon juice	6	potatoes, peeled and
1	teaspoon dried thyme		quartered
1	teaspoon dried rosemary		

1. Preheat oven to 350°F (175°C).

2. In a small bowl, mix olive oil, water, garlic, lemon juice, thyme, rosemary, bouillon, and pepper.

3. Arrange potatoes evenly in a 2 quart baking dish. Pour the olive oil mixture over the potatoes. Cover and bake 1½ to 2 hours in the preheated oven, turning occasionally, until tender but firm. **Yield:** 4 servings.

Per serving: About 316 calories, 4g protein, 36g carbohydrate, 18g fat, 3g fiber, 1mg cholesterol, 590mg sodium

Cheesy Potato Casserole

Submitted by: **Annette Byrdy**

"I have tried many potato casseroles and this one always gets rave reviews and recipe requests. It's the easiest to make, too!"

1	(16 ounce) package processed American cheese, cubed	2	cups mayonnaise
		1	white onion, chopped
		1	(3 ounce) jar bacon bits
1	(2 pound) package frozen hash brown potatoes, thawed		

1. Preheat oven to 350°F (175°C).

2. In the microwave, melt cheese in a large microwave-safe bowl. Stir in potatoes, mayonnaise, and onion. Spread in a lightly greased 9x13 inch baking dish and top with bacon bits.

3. Bake in the preheated oven for 1 hour or until hot and bubbly. **Yield:** 12 servings.

Per serving: About 361 calories, 11g protein, 28g carbohydrate, 27g fat, 1g fiber, 49mg cholesterol, 1067mg sodium

Butternut Squash Casserole

Submitted by: **Valerie Moore**

"This recipe is in great demand from my friends and family. It tastes similar to sweet potato soufflé with a custardlike texture. Serve with ham or pork."

1	butternut squash	¼	cup butter or margarine, melted
1	cup white sugar		
1½	cups milk	½	(16 ounce) package vanilla wafers, crushed
1	teaspoon vanilla extract		
	Pinch salt	½	cup butter or margarine, melted
2	tablespoons all-purpose flour		
		1	cup brown sugar
3	eggs		

1. Preheat oven to 425°F (220°C).

2. Pierce butternut squash with a fork and cook in the microwave on high until soft, 2 to 3 minutes. Cut in half, scoop out seeds, and cube squash. Bring a large pot of water to a boil. Add squash and cook until tender, about 15 minutes. Drain and mash.

3. In a bowl, combine 3 cups mashed butternut squash, white sugar, milk, vanilla, salt, flour, eggs, and ¼ cup melted butter. Pour into a lightly greased 9x13 inch baking dish.

4. Bake in the preheated oven for 45 minutes or until set.

5. In a medium bowl, combine crushed vanilla wafers, ½ cup melted butter, and brown sugar. Crumble over top of cooked casserole and return to oven to brown. **Yield:** 15 servings.

Per serving: About 320 calories, 4g protein, 49g carbohydrate, 14g fat, 0g fiber, 44mg cholesterol, 210mg sodium

◄ Holiday Fare

Prep Time: 15 minutes

Cook Time: 1 hour

Average Rating: ★★★★★

17 Ratings ▲ 15 Reviews

What other cooks have done:

"I used two small bags of frozen butternut squash. It was so easy, and even my mother loved it! She brought the leftovers home."

Summer Squash Casserole

Submitted by: **Jen**

"You can use zucchini or yellow squash, or a combination of the two! To make it lower in fat, use low-fat sour cream, low-fat soup, and cut the butter in half."

4	zucchini, chopped	3	medium carrots, grated
2	onions, chopped	1	(6 ounce) package croutons
1	(10.75 ounce) can condensed cream of mushroom soup	½	cup butter, melted
		8	ounces shredded mozzarella cheese
½	cup sour cream		

1. Preheat oven to 350°F (175°C).

2. Boil squash and onions in water for 5 minutes. Drain and place squash and onions in bowl. Mix in soup, sour cream, carrot, croutons, and butter. Pour into a greased 9x13 inch baking dish. Top with cheese.

3. Cover and bake in the preheated oven for 1 hour. **Yield:** 5 servings.

Per serving: About 599 calories, 17g protein, 46g carbohydrate, 40g fat, 6g fiber, 96mg cholesterol, 1518mg sodium

◄ Family Favorite

Prep Time: 20 minutes

Cook Time: 1 hour

Average Rating: ★★★★★

16 Ratings ▲ 10 Reviews

What other cooks have done:

"I suggest crushing the croutons and adding a dash or two of seasoning salt for extra kick."

Sweet Potato Soufflé

Submitted by: **Ricki Heronemus**

"Sweet potato side dish—so good it's almost dessert. Even if you don't like sweet potatoes, you'll like this."

3	cups mashed cooked sweet potatoes	½	cup milk
¾	cup white sugar	1	cup flaked coconut
¼	cup butter, softened	⅓	cup all-purpose flour
2	eggs	1	cup packed brown sugar
1	teaspoon vanilla extract	1	cup chopped walnuts
		⅓	cup melted butter

1. Preheat oven to 350°F (175°C).
2. Combine the mashed sweet potatoes with the white sugar, ¼ cup butter, eggs, vanilla, and milk. Spoon into a lightly greased 2 quart baking dish.
3. Combine the coconut, flour, brown sugar, chopped nuts, and melted butter. Sprinkle over the sweet potatoes.
4. Bake in the preheated oven for 30 to 35 minutes. **Yield:** 9 servings.

Per serving: About 531 calories, 7g protein, 70g carbohydrate, 27g fat, 3g fiber, 85mg cholesterol, 254mg sodium

Scalloped Tomatoes

Submitted by: **Linda**

"This is a variation of my mother's recipe."

¼	cup butter	½	teaspoon dried basil
1	onion, chopped	4	teaspoons brown sugar
1	teaspoon salt	5	tomatoes, sliced
	Ground black pepper to taste	2	cups white bread cubes

1. Preheat oven to 375°F (190°C).
2. Sauté butter and onion in a medium saucepan until onion is transparent. Add salt, pepper, basil, brown sugar, and tomato to the saucepan and stir. Stir in bread until all of the ingredients are well blended.
3. Pour the tomato-bread mixture into a greased 9x13 inch baking dish. Bake for 30 to 35 minutes. **Yield:** 6 servings.

Per serving: About 131 calories, 2g protein, 13g carbohydrate, 8g fat, 1g fiber, 21mg cholesterol, 503mg sodium

Roasted Vegetables

Submitted by: **Saundra**

"This casserole dish of seasonal vegetables can be made a day ahead—just reheat before serving. Lemon juice can be substituted for balsamic vinegar."

1	small butternut squash, cubed	1	tablespoon chopped fresh thyme
2	red bell peppers, seeded and diced	2	tablespoons chopped fresh rosemary
1	sweet potato, peeled and cubed	¼	cup olive oil
3	Yukon Gold potatoes, cubed	2	tablespoons balsamic vinegar
1	red onion, quartered		Salt and pepper to taste

1. Preheat oven to 475°F (245°C).
2. In a large bowl, combine the squash, red bell pepper, and potatoes. Separate the red onion quarters into pieces and add them to the bowl.
3. In a separate bowl, stir together thyme, rosemary, olive oil, vinegar, salt, and pepper. Toss with vegetables until coated. Place on 2 (10x15 inch) jellyroll pans.
4. Roast in the preheated oven for 35 to 40 minutes, stirring every 10 minutes, or until vegetables are cooked through and browned. **Yield:** 12 servings.

Per serving: About 124 calories, 2g protein, 20g carbohydrate, 5g fat, 1g fiber, 0mg cholesterol, 8mg sodium

◄ Company is Coming

Prep Time: 20 minutes
Cook Time: 40 minutes
Average Rating: ★★★★★
35 Ratings ▲ 21 Reviews
What other cooks have done:
"I used potatoes and zucchini (yellow and green), red peppers, and portobello mushrooms. These roasted veggies complement any meal."

Foil-Wrapped Veggies

Submitted by: **Marni Rachmiel**

"Open the finished packets carefully—the veggies are hot!"

2½	pounds new potatoes, cut into ¼ inch thick pieces	1	sprig fresh rosemary
1	large sweet potato, cubed	1	sprig fresh thyme
2	onions, sliced ¼ inch thick	2	tablespoons olive oil
½	pound green beans, trimmed and cut into 1 inch pieces		Salt and pepper to taste
		⅓	cup olive oil

1. Preheat a grill for high heat.
2. In a large bowl, combine new potatoes, sweet potato, onion, green beans, rosemary, and thyme. Toss with 2 tablespoons oil, salt, and pepper.
3. Using 2 to 3 layers of foil, create desired number of foil packets. Brush inside surfaces of packets liberally with ⅓ cup oil. Distribute vegetable mixture evenly in the packets. Seal tightly. Place packets on the prepared grill. Cook 30 minutes or to desired doneness. **Yield:** 10 servings.

Per serving: About 212 calories, 3g protein, 28g carbohydrate, 10g fat, 4g fiber, 0mg cholesterol, 83mg sodium

◄ From the Grill

Prep Time: 15 minutes
Cook Time: 30 minutes
Average Rating: ★★★★★
14 Ratings ▲ 9 Reviews
What other cooks have done:
"We did this and put them in the oven instead of on the grill, and they turned out great. Kids really like these because they can put in what they like and say they made it."

Company Couscous

Submitted by: **Nancy Trempe**

"Couscous is the best! It's fast and tastes great. This recipe is savory and is perfect with chicken."

1	cup uncooked couscous	1	cup cherry tomatoes
1	cup boiling water	1	cup fresh basil leaves
3	tablespoons olive oil		Pinch salt
1	clove garlic, minced		Pinch ground black pepper
4	green onions, sliced		Dash balsamic vinegar
¼	cup diced red bell pepper	¼	cup grated Parmesan cheese

1. Preheat oven to 350°F (175°C).
2. Stir couscous into boiling water and return water to a boil. Cover and remove from heat. Let stand 5 minutes, then fluff with a fork.
3. While the couscous is cooking, heat oil in a large skillet over medium heat. Stir in garlic, green onions, and bell pepper, and sauté briefly. Stir in tomatoes, basil, cooked couscous, salt, and pepper. Transfer to a lightly greased 1½ quart baking dish. Splash with some balsamic vinegar.
4. Bake in the preheated oven for 20 minutes. Sprinkle with Parmesan cheese while still warm. **Yield:** 4 servings.

Per serving: About 377 calories, 15g protein, 50g carbohydrate, 13g fat, 13g fiber, 5mg cholesterol, 325mg sodium

Meatless Main Dish ▶

Prep Time: 15 minutes

Cook Time: 20 minutes

Average Rating: ★★★★★

17 Ratings ▲ 14 Reviews

What other cooks have done:

"I used chicken stock instead of water to cook the couscous and added a little extra balsamic."

Maria's Rice

Submitted by: **Melissa Davidson**

"This is the easiest and best-tasting side dish ever. It goes really well with roast, pork chops, or a rotisserie chicken. I have taken this recipe to tons of parties and everyone loves it."

1	cup uncooked white rice	1	(10.5 ounce) can beef broth
1	(10.5 ounce) can condensed French onion soup	½	cup butter, sliced

1. Preheat oven to 425°F (220°C).
2. In a 9x9 inch baking dish, combine rice, soup, and broth. Place butter slices on top of the mixture.
3. Cover with foil and bake in the preheated oven for 30 minutes. Remove cover and bake 30 more minutes until rice is tender and liquid is absorbed. **Yield:** 6 servings.

Per serving: About 290 calories, 5g protein, 30g carbohydrate, 17g fat, 1g fiber, 43mg cholesterol, 857mg sodium

Kid-Friendly ▶

Prep Time: 5 minutes

Cook Time: 1 hour

Average Rating: ★★★★★

27 Ratings ▲ 19 Reviews

What other cooks have done:

"This was so easy, but to make it even easier, I used quick-cooking rice to cut down on the cooking time. I didn't have a can of soup so I used dry onion soup mix with a 14 ounce can of broth and added mushrooms. It was tasty!"

Home-Style Brown Rice Pilaf

Submitted by: **Jen**

"Comfort food at its best with mild flavors, and it's simple to make. You can use almonds in place of the cashews, and cilantro in place of the parsley."

1½	cups water	1	cup chickpeas
½	teaspoon salt	2	eggs, beaten
¾	cup uncooked brown rice		Freshly ground black
3	tablespoons butter		pepper
1½	cups chopped onion	¼	cup chopped fresh parsley
1	clove garlic, minced	¼	cup chopped cashews
2	carrots, sliced		Soy Sauce
2	cups sliced fresh mushrooms		

1. Bring 1½ cups water and salt to boil; add rice. Return to a boil, cover the pot, and simmer for 45 to 50 minutes or until rice is tender and water is absorbed.

2. Approximately 20 minutes before rice is finished cooking, heat the butter in a large skillet over medium heat. Stir in onion and sauté until softened. Add the garlic and carrot and continue stirring for 5 minutes.

3. Place mushrooms in skillet and cook until mushrooms begin to brown, about 10 minutes. Add the chickpeas and cook 1 more minute.

4. When the rice is finished cooking, pour the eggs into the skillet and cook the mixture, stirring constantly, until the eggs are cooked. Remove the skillet from the heat; stir in pepper, parsley, and nuts.

5. Spoon the cooked rice into the skillet and stir well. Serve the pilaf hot with soy sauce on the side for added flavor. **Yield:** 4 servings.

Per serving: About 413 calories, 12g protein, 55g carbohydrate, 17g fat, 7g fiber, 130mg cholesterol, 666mg sodium

◄ **Family Favorite**

Prep Time: 10 minutes
Cook Time: 1 hour 15 minutes
Average Rating: ★★★★★
16 Ratings ▲ 14 Reviews
What other cooks have done:
"I added a little bit of soy sauce and hot sauce to the water for the rice. I also added a bit more salt, some crushed red pepper flakes, and a lot of fresh ground black pepper to the vegetables as they were cooking so that the spicy taste combined with the veggies during cooking."

Mexican Rice II

Submitted by: **Sylvia Eccles**

"This is a wonderful side dish for any Mexican dinner."

3	tablespoons vegetable oil	½	teaspoon ground cumin
1	cup uncooked long-grain rice	¼	cup chopped onion
1	teaspoon garlic salt	½	cup tomato sauce
		2	cups chicken broth

1. Heat oil in a large saucepan over medium heat and add rice. Cook, stirring constantly, until golden. Sprinkle with garlic salt and cumin.

2. Stir in onion and cook until tender. Stir in tomato sauce and chicken broth; bring to a boil. Reduce heat to low, cover, and simmer for 20 to 25 minutes. Fluff with a fork. **Yield:** 4 servings.

Per serving: About 300 calories, 5g protein, 42g carbohydrate, 12g fat, 1g fiber, 0mg cholesterol, 1140mg sodium

◄ **Restaurant Fare**

Prep Time: 5 minutes
Cook Time: 25 minutes
Average Rating: ★★★★★
15 Ratings ▲ 12 Reviews
What other cooks have done:
"I used dried minced onions and 2 ounces of tomato paste for the tomato sauce, and it turned out great."

Risotto with Tomato, Corn, and Basil

Submitted by: **Jessica**

"This dish is best suited for the end of summer when the tomatoes and corn are at their best. Using milk in the risotto gives it a lovely richness and creaminess."

2½	cups water	1	medium tomato, peeled, seeded, and chopped
2	cups milk	½	cup grated Parmesan cheese
2	tablespoons butter	½	cup fresh basil leaves, cut into thin strips, divided
1	cup minced onion		
1	clove garlic, minced	½	teaspoon salt
¾	cup uncooked Arborio rice		Ground black pepper to taste
3	tablespoons white wine		
1⅓	cups fresh corn kernels		

1. Combine the water and milk in a medium saucepan; simmer over low heat.

2. Melt the butter in a large skillet over medium-high heat. Add the onion and cook for 3 to 4 minutes, stirring occasionally. Add the garlic and the rice; stir constantly for 1 minute. Add the white wine and stir until completely absorbed.

3. Begin to add the heated milk-water mixture ½ cup at a time, stirring rice constantly. Wait until each addition is almost completely absorbed before adding the next. When the rice has cooked for 15 minutes and most of the liquid has been incorporated, add the corn and tomato along with the remaining milk-water mixture. Cook, stirring constantly, until the rice is tender but still slightly chewy.

4. Stir in the Parmesan cheese, most of the basil, salt, and pepper. Spoon the risotto immediately onto plates, top with the remaining basil strips, and serve. **Yield:** 4 servings.

Per serving: About 402 calories, 15g protein, 55g carbohydrate, 13g fat, 3g fiber, 35mg cholesterol, 660mg sodium

Risotto Demystified! ▼

A humble wooden spoon becomes a magic wand when it stirs a few simple ingredients—rice, butter, broth, and cheese—into the miraculously creamy dish full of complex textures and flavors that we call risotto. Once you master the basic technique of risotto-making, there are infinite possibilities at your fingertips.

First, the Rice

You can't use just any old rice to make risotto. Risotto rice is short and plump, high in starch, and is able to absorb liquid while the grains remain separate from each other and a little bit firm to the bite. Arborio rice is grown in North America and can be found in most well-stocked grocery stores and makes wonderful risotto. Never wash the rice you're going to use for risotto, or you will rinse away all the starch. The starch is vital for that unique, creamy texture that makes risotto so special.

Next, the Liquid

Making risotto requires more liquid than your average pot of rice. Risotto rice is very absorbent, and some of the liquid evaporates while it's cooking since you don't cover the pot. You can use water to make risotto, but the flavor will be richer if you use stock. If you suspect the broth you have may wind up being a bit on the salty side, use half broth and half water as your cooking liquid.

The Technique

Risotto requires constant attention while it's cooking. It must be stirred perpetually in order to ensure even liquid absorption and a creamy texture, and to keep the rice from sticking to the pan. The liquid must also be added a little at a time as the rice absorbs it. Other than the attentive stirring, risotto is really quite easy to make, and the results are delightfully worth the effort. *- Jennifer Anderson*

For more information, visit **Allrecipes.com**

Four-Cheese Macaroni

Submitted by: **Kimberly**

"A very rich and creamy version of macaroni and cheese that's great any time of the year. My whole family loves it."

1 (16 ounce) package elbow macaroni	1½ cups half-and-half
½ cup butter	8 ounces cubed pasteurized prepared cheese product
½ cup shredded Muenster cheese	2 eggs, beaten
½ cup shredded mild Cheddar cheese	¼ teaspoon salt
½ cup shredded sharp Cheddar cheese	⅛ teaspoon ground black pepper
½ cup shredded Monterey Jack cheese	1 tablespoon butter

1. Bring a large pot of lightly salted water to a boil. Add pasta and cook for 8 to 10 minutes or until al dente; drain well and return to cooking pot.

2. In a small saucepan over medium heat, melt ½ cup butter; stir into the macaroni.

3. In a large bowl, combine the Muenster cheese, Cheddar cheeses, and Monterey Jack cheese; mix well.

4. Preheat oven to 350°F (175°C).

5. Add the half-and-half, 1½ cups of cheese mixture, cubed cheese, and eggs to macaroni; mix together and season with salt and pepper. Transfer to a lightly greased deep 2½ quart baking dish. Sprinkle with the remaining ½ cup of cheese mixture and 1 tablespoon of butter.

6. Bake in the preheated oven for 35 minutes or until hot and bubbling around the edges. **Yield:** 6 servings.

Per serving: About 816 calories, 31g protein, 62g carbohydrate, 49g fat, 2g fiber, 197mg cholesterol, 922mg sodium

---

◄ Classic Comfort Food

Prep Time: 25 minutes
Cook Time: 35 minutes
Average Rating: ★★★★★
11 Ratings ▲ 8 Reviews
What other cooks have done:
"I made this dish looking for an alternative to the store-bought boxed stuff. I was so happy with it! If you have a food processor, it will help with all the shredding. It goes by like a breeze."

Peanut Butter Noodles

Submitted by: **Amy Barthelemy**
"This is an easy side dish with an Asian twist. Omit the chile paste for a more kid-friendly dish."

8	ounces Udon noodles or spaghetti	1½	tablespoons honey
½	cup chicken broth	1	to 2 teaspoons hot chili paste (optional)
1½	tablespoons minced fresh ginger root	3	cloves garlic, minced
3	tablespoons soy sauce	¼	cup chopped green onions
3	tablespoons peanut butter	¼	cup chopped peanuts

1. Cook noodles in a large pot of boiling water 8 to 10 minutes until done. Drain.
2. Meanwhile, combine chicken broth, ginger, soy sauce, peanut butter, honey, chili paste, and garlic in a small saucepan. Cook over medium heat until peanut butter melts and is heated through. Add noodles and toss to coat. Garnish with green onions and peanuts.
Yield: 4 servings.

Per serving: About 329 calories, 11g protein, 46g carbohydrate, 12g fat, 2g fiber, 0mg cholesterol, 1167mg sodium

Lemon Pepper Pasta

Submitted by: **Jane Streich**
"A fast and easy side dish that you can throw together in a flash helps make dinner a breeze."

1	pound spaghetti	1	tablespoon minced fresh basil
2	tablespoons olive oil		Ground black pepper to taste
3	tablespoons lemon juice, to taste		

1. Bring a large pot of lightly salted water to a boil. Add pasta and cook for 8 to 10 minutes or until al dente; drain.
2. In a small bowl, combine olive oil, lemon juice, basil, and black pepper. Mix well and toss with the pasta. Serve hot or cold. **Yield:** 4 servings.

Per serving: About 484 calories, 15g protein, 86g carbohydrate, 9g fat, 3g fiber, 0mg cholesterol, 8mg sodium

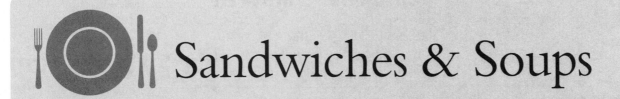

Sandwiches & Soups

When a multicourse meal doesn't fit into your busy game plan, reach for these satisfying recipes that elevate soups and sandwiches into world-class fare. Look for kid-friendly favorites such as Awesome Grilled Cheese Sandwiches and classic comfort food mainstays such as Grandma's Chicken Noodle Soup. Solve your lunchtime dilemmas with a Cucumber Sandwich packed full of fresh veggies, and for an elegant evening, try creamy Butternut Squash Soup.

Cucumber Sandwich *(pictured on page 262)*

Submitted by: **Jennifer**

"I worked at a sandwich shop that made these vegetable sandwiches stuffed with cucumbers, sprouts, tomatoes, and avocados. They were a veggie dream!"

2	thick slices whole wheat bread	1	teaspoon red wine vinegar
2	tablespoons cream cheese, softened	1	tomato, sliced
		1	lettuce leaf
6	slices cucumber	2	tablespoons sliced pepperoncini
2	tablespoons alfalfa sprouts	½	avocado
1	teaspoon olive oil		

1. Spread each slice of bread with 1 tablespoon cream cheese. On 1 slice of bread, arrange cucumber slices in a single layer. Cover with sprouts, then sprinkle with oil and vinegar. Layer tomato slices, lettuce, and pepperoncini.

2. Cut avocado in half and remove seed, reserving half of avocado for another use. Mash avocado and spread on other slice of bread. Close sandwich and serve immediately. **Yield:** 1 serving.

Per serving: About 502 calories, 11g protein, 46g carbohydrate, 33g fat, 11g fiber, 32mg cholesterol, 1029mg sodium

---

Quick & Easy ▶

Prep Time: 10 minutes

Average Rating: ★★★★★

44 Ratings ▲ 25 Reviews

What other cooks have done:

"I used a soft tortilla and made this into a wrap. I also used feta cheese instead of cream cheese because I happened to have it on hand. Delicious!"

Almost Eggless Egg Salad

Submitted by: **Jill**

"The only egg in this sandwich is in the mayonnaise; use soy mayonnaise for a vegan variation. Serve on wheat toast with crisp lettuce and fresh tomato slices."

2	tablespoons mayonnaise	1	tablespoon dried parsley
1	tablespoon sweet pickle relish	1	pound firm tofu, sliced and well drained
1	teaspoon white vinegar	1	tablespoon minced onion
1	teaspoon prepared mustard	2	tablespoons minced celery
1	teaspoon white sugar		Salt to taste
½	teaspoon ground turmeric		Ground black pepper to taste
¼	teaspoon dried dill weed		

1. In a small bowl, combine mayonnaise, sweet pickle relish, vinegar, mustard, sugar, turmeric, dill, and parsley. Mix well and set aside.

2. Place drained tofu in a large bowl and crumble with a fork. Stir in onion and celery. Mix in reserved mayonnaise mixture. Season to taste with salt and pepper. Chill for several hours to allow flavors to blend. **Yield:** 4 servings.

Per serving: About 153 calories, 10g protein, 5g carbohydrate, 12g fat, 1g fiber, 4mg cholesterol, 100mg sodium

---

Make-Ahead ▶

Prep Time: 10 minutes

Average Rating: ★★★★☆

25 Ratings ▲ 20 Reviews

What other cooks have done:

"I freeze the tofu and then 'quick-thaw' it in a colander by pouring hot water over it. Squeeze out moisture with hands, crumble, and proceed with the recipe. The tofu has a texture similar to chicken or tuna flakes."

Awesome Grilled Cheese Sandwiches

Submitted by: **Michelle**

"My husband and I were sick of frying grilled cheeses on the stove because you have so many pieces of bread to use, and you have to stand there for a long time if you feed up to six people like we do. So we came up with this idea. For a variation, place a slice of ham in the sandwiches."

18	slices bread	4	tablespoons butter, softened
9	slices Cheddar cheese		

1. Preheat oven to 450°F (230°C).
2. Butter 1 side of 9 pieces of bread and place butter side down on a nonstick baking sheet. Arrange cheese on each piece of bread. Spread butter on 9 remaining slices of bread and place them buttered side up on top of the cheese.
3. Bake in the preheated oven for 6 to 8 minutes. Turn the sandwiches and bake 6 to 8 more minutes or until golden brown. **Yield:** 9 servings.

Per serving: About 226 calories, 9g protein, 13g carbohydrate, 15g fat, 1g fiber, 44mg cholesterol, 363mg sodium

◄ **Kid-Friendly**

Prep Time: 10 minutes
Cook Time: 16 minutes
Average Rating: ★★★★★
18 Ratings ▲ 15 Reviews
What other cooks have done:
"We do a lot of grilled cheese on the weekends for a quick lunch. Sometimes I use American, Cheddar, and even Swiss. For a little change, we also add ham, deli turkey breast, or crisp bacon."

Portobello Mushroom Burgers

Submitted by: **Bob Cody**

"The 'steak' of veggie burgers. Serve on a bun with lettuce, tomato, and aïoli sauce."

4	large portobello mushroom caps	1	tablespoon minced garlic
¼	cup balsamic vinegar		Salt and pepper to taste
2	tablespoons olive oil	4	ounces thinly sliced provolone cheese (optional)
1	teaspoon dried basil		
1	teaspoon dried oregano		

1. Cut stems off mushrooms; place smooth side up in a shallow dish.
2. In a small bowl, whisk together vinegar, oil, basil, oregano, garlic, and salt and pepper. Pour over mushrooms. Let stand at room temperature for about 15 minutes, turning twice.
3. Brush cold grill rack with oil and preheat the grill for medium-high heat.
4. Place mushrooms on the preheated grill, reserving marinade for basting. Grill for 5 to 8 minutes on each side or until tender. Brush with marinade frequently. Top with cheese, if desired, during the last 2 minutes of grilling. **Yield:** 4 servings.

Per serving: About 204 calories, 10g protein, 10g carbohydrate, 15g fat, 2g fiber, 20mg cholesterol, 260mg sodium

◄ **From the Grill**

Prep Time: 15 minutes
Cook Time: 16 minutes
Average Rating: ★★★★☆
24 Ratings ▲ 16 Reviews
What other cooks have done:
"We made these for our July 4th cookout and everyone loved them. We put a little Caesar dressing on these burgers to make them perfect."

Cheesy Tuna Melts

Submitted by: **Sal**

"Crisp muffins, creamy tuna salad, and bubbly melted cheese on top make a great quick snack for hungry people in a hurry."

1	(6 ounce) can tuna, drained	4	English muffins, split and
⅓	cup chopped celery		toasted
2	tablespoons mayonnaise	8	slices ripe tomato
	Pinch salt	8	slices Cheddar cheese

1. Preheat oven to broil.

2. In a bowl, mix together tuna, celery, mayonnaise, and salt. Spread tuna mixture onto the toasted muffin halves and place them on a baking sheet. Top each half with a slice of tomato and a slice of cheese.

3. Broil until cheese is melted, about 3 to 5 minutes. **Yield:** 8 servings.

Per serving: About 225 calories, 15g protein, 16g carbohydrate, 11g fat, 0g fiber, 37mg cholesterol, 444mg sodium

Tasty Tuna Burgers

Submitted by: **Holly**

"These tasty tuna burgers are so delicious. My husband is a very fussy eater, and he loves these tasty tuna burgers."

1	(6 ounce) can tuna, drained	½	teaspoon dried dill weed
1	egg	¼	teaspoon salt
½	cup Italian seasoned breadcrumbs	⅛	teaspoon ground black pepper
⅓	cup minced onion		Dash hot sauce
¼	cup minced celery		Dash Worcestershire sauce
¼	cup minced red bell pepper	4	hamburger buns, split
¼	cup mayonnaise	1	tomato, sliced
2	tablespoons chili sauce	4	lettuce leaves (optional)

1. Combine tuna, egg, breadcrumbs, onion, celery, red bell pepper, mayonnaise, chili sauce, dill weed, salt, pepper, hot sauce, and Worcestershire sauce. Mix well. Shape into 4 patties (mixture will be very soft and delicate).

2. Coat a nonstick skillet with cooking spray; fry tuna patties for about 3 to 4 minutes per side or until cooked through. These are fragile, so be careful when turning them.

3. Serve on buns with tomato slices and lettuce leaves, if desired. **Yield:** 4 servings.

Per serving: About 309 calories, 19g protein, 42g carbohydrate, 9g fat, 3g fiber, 70mg cholesterol, 874mg sodium

Grilled Chicken Cordon Bleu Sandwiches

Submitted by: **Deirdre Dee**

"Serve with a salad for lunch, or with soup and salad for a meal."

2 tablespoons butter, softened	1 thick slice deli cooked
2 slices whole wheat bread	chicken breast
1 tablespoon sour cream	1 slice deli ham
2 slices Swiss cheese	

1. Spread butter on 1 side of the bread slices. Spread sour cream on the other side of the bread slices. On 1 slice of bread, buttered side down, layer 1 cheese slice, chicken, ham, and remaining cheese slice. Top with remaining bread slice, buttered side up.

2. In a small skillet over medium heat, grill sandwich until meat is heated through and cheese is melted. **Yield:** 1 serving.

Per serving: About 697 calories, 35g protein, 29g carbohydrate, 50g fat, 4g fiber, 161mg cholesterol, 1040mg sodium

◄ **Quick & Easy**

Prep Time: 5 minutes
Cook Time: 10 minutes
Average Rating: ★★★★☆
78 Ratings ▲ 38 Reviews
What other cooks have done:
"I used sliced French bread for these sandwiches, and they were great. It was a hit for the whole family. My daughter asked me to cook an extra one for her to take in her lunch. We used Dijon mustard instead of sour cream."

Savory Crescent Chicken

Submitted by: **Sandy Rowe**

"A quick and easy warm chicken sandwich. Two 5-ounce cans of chunk chicken, drained and flaked, can be substituted for cubed cooked chicken."

1 (3 ounce) package cream cheese, softened	2 tablespoons milk
1 tablespoon butter, softened	1 tablespoon chopped pimento (optional)
2 cups cubed, cooked chicken	1 (8 ounce) can refrigerated crescent rolls
1 tablespoon minced onion	1 tablespoon butter, melted
¼ teaspoon salt	¾ cup croutons, crushed
⅛ teaspoon ground black pepper	

1. Preheat oven to 350°F (175°C).

2. In a medium bowl, beat cream cheese and 1 tablespoon softened butter until smooth. Add the chicken, onion, salt, pepper, milk, and pimento, if desired. Mix well.

3. Separate crescent dough into 4 rectangles. Firmly press perforations to seal. Spoon ½ cup of the chicken mixture onto the center of each rectangle. Pull 4 corners of dough to center of chicken mixture and twist firmly. Pinch edges to seal.

4. Place sandwiches on an ungreased baking sheet. Brush tops of sandwiches with 1 tablespoon of melted butter; sprinkle with crushed croutons. Bake in the preheated oven for 25 to 30 minutes or until golden brown. **Yield:** 4 servings.

Per serving: About 492 calories, 26g protein, 29g carbohydrate, 30g fat, 0g fiber, 92mg cholesterol, 818mg sodium

◄ **Family Favorite**

Prep Time: 10 minutes
Cook Time: 30 minutes
Average Rating: ★★★★★
43 Ratings ▲ 32 Reviews
What other cooks have done:
"These were awesome! A small tip though: Instead of putting them on a baking sheet, I used a muffin tin. This made them extra kid-friendly and fun."

Monte Cristo Sandwich

Submitted by: **Carolyn**

"A quick and easy sandwich with ham, turkey, and Swiss slices, dipped in an egg/milk mixture and fried to a golden brown. A hot alternative to the usual lunch or snack. Try it with berry jam on the side."

2	slices bread	2	slices Swiss cheese
1	teaspoon mayonnaise	2	slices cooked turkey
1	teaspoon prepared mustard	1	egg
2	slices cooked ham	½	cup milk

1. Spread bread with mayonnaise and mustard. Alternate ham, Swiss, and turkey slices on bread.

2. Beat egg and milk in a small bowl. Coat the sandwich with the egg and milk mixture. Heat a greased skillet over medium heat and brown the sandwich on both sides. Serve hot. **Yield:** 1 serving.

Per serving: About 581 calories, 52g protein, 21g carbohydrate, 31g fat, 1g fiber, 345mg cholesterol, 496mg sodium

Drip Beef Sandwiches

Submitted by: **Tammy Christie**

"I serve this tender, wonderfully flavored meat with flour tortillas, cheese, and refried beans for people to build their own burritos."

5	pounds chuck roast	2	tablespoons whole black
2	cubes beef bouillon		peppercorns
2	tablespoons salt	2	teaspoons dried oregano
2	teaspoons garlic salt	1½	teaspoons dried rosemary
2	bay leaves		

1. Place roast in a large pot with water to cover. Mix in bouillon, salt, and garlic salt. Add the bay leaves, peppercorns, oregano, and rosemary in a coffee filter and secure tightly with a rubber band. Add to the pot.

2. Bring to a boil over high heat, then reduce heat to low, cover with a lid, and simmer for 6 to 8 hours. Remove coffee filter and discard. Remove roast from the pot and shred with two forks. Reserve broth for dipping, if desired. **Yield:** 8 servings.

Per serving: About 585 calories, 55g protein, 2g carbohydrate, 38g fat, 1g fiber, 184mg cholesterol, 2569mg sodium

Slow-Cooker Barbecue

Submitted by: **Brandy**

"My mom used to make this for us when we were kids. It's so good it almost melts in your mouth! Serve on sub rolls."

3	pounds chuck roast		Salt and pepper to taste
1	teaspoon garlic powder	1	(18 ounce) bottle barbecue
1	teaspoon onion powder		sauce

1. Place roast in a slow cooker. Sprinkle with garlic powder and onion powder and season with salt and pepper. Pour barbecue sauce over meat. Cook on High for 1 hour, reduce heat to Low, and cook 5 to 7 more hours.

2. Remove meat from slow cooker, shred, and return to slow cooker. Cook for 1 more hour. Serve hot. **Yield:** 8 servings.

Per serving: About 449 calories, 31g protein, 9g carbohydrate, 32g fat, 1g fiber, 121mg cholesterol, 629mg sodium

◄ Kid-Friendly

Prep Time: 15 minutes
Cook Time: 9 hours
Average Rating: ★★★★★
71 Ratings ▲ 47 Reviews
What other cooks have done:
"I took this dish to our church fellowship dinner, and by the time I went through the line, it had vanished. I'm glad I tasted it at home because it was delicious. I used celery salt, garlic powder, and salt and pepper as my seasonings."

Easy Slow-Cooker French Dip

Submitted by: **Robyn Bloomquist**

"This makes a delicious French dip sandwich, perfect for the working mom! Nobody will be able to detect the presence of beer in this recipe, but it adds a wonderful flavor. French fries make a great side dish, and they're good for dipping, too."

4	pounds rump roast	1	(12 ounce) can or bottle
1	(10.5 ounce) can beef broth		beer
1	(10.5 ounce) can	6	French rolls
	condensed French	2	tablespoons butter, softened
	onion soup		

1. Trim excess fat from the rump roast and place roast in a slow cooker. Add the beef broth, onion soup, and beer. Cook on High for 1 hour, reduce heat to Low and cook 7 more hours.

2. Preheat oven to 350°F (175°C).

3. Split French rolls and spread with butter. Bake in the preheated oven for 10 minutes or until heated through.

4. Slice the meat on the diagonal and place on the rolls. Serve with sauce for dipping. **Yield:** 6 servings.

Per serving: About 849 calories, 66g protein, 30g carbohydrate, 49g fat, 2g fiber, 195mg cholesterol, 1039mg sodium

◄ Family Favorite

Prep Time: 10 minutes
Cook Time: 8 hours
Average Rating: ★★★★★
298 Ratings ▲ 212 Reviews
What other cooks have done:
"I made this for a very casual dinner party and served it on crusty rolls with melted provolone cheese."

Pepperoncini Beef *(pictured on page 263)*

Submitted by: **Joyce**
"Roast beef cooked in a slow cooker with garlic and pepperoncini makes a delicious and simple filling for sandwiches. Serve on hoagie rolls with provolone or mozzarella cheese and your choice of condiments. When making the sandwiches, place meat in rolls, cover with cheese, and zap in a microwave for a few seconds. Don't forget to use the pepperoncini in the sandwiches."

3 pounds chuck roast	1 (16 ounce) jar sliced pepperoncini
4 cloves garlic, sliced	

1. Make small cuts in roast and insert garlic slices in cuts. Place roast in a slow cooker and pour the entire contents of the jar of pepperoncini, including liquid, over meat. Cook on High 1 hour, reduce heat to Low, and cook 7 more hours or until meat is tender and shreds easily with a fork. **Yield:** 12 servings.

Per serving: About 276 calories, 20g protein, 2g carbohydrate, 21g fat, 0g fiber, 81mg cholesterol, 865mg sodium

Sloppy Joes II

Submitted by: **Tamara**
"This is the recipe my mother used for sloppy joes, and it always gets compliments."

1 pound lean ground beef	¾ cup ketchup
¼ cup chopped onion	1 tablespoon brown sugar
¼ cup chopped green bell pepper	Salt to taste
½ teaspoon garlic powder	Ground black pepper to taste
1 teaspoon prepared mustard	

1. In a skillet over medium heat, brown the ground beef, onion, and green pepper; drain off liquids.
2. Stir in the garlic powder, mustard, ketchup, and brown sugar; mix thoroughly. Reduce heat and simmer for 30 minutes. Season with salt and pepper to taste. **Yield:** 6 servings.

Per serving: About 246 calories, 14g protein, 12g carbohydrate, 16g fat, 1g fiber, 57mg cholesterol, 483mg sodium

Real Italian Calzones,
page 266

Cucumber Sandwich,
page 254

Pepperoncini Beef,
page 260

Chicken Tortilla Soup,
page 276

Gyroll, facing page

Gyroll *(pictured on facing page)*

Submitted by: **Adam Pack**

"Well-seasoned lamb, along with feta cheese, zucchini, and black olives, gets sealed into pizza dough and baked until golden. This simple version of a gyro sandwich substitutes pizza dough for the much harder-to-make pita bread."

1	tablespoon olive oil		Dash hot sauce
1	pound ground lamb or ground chuck	⅔	cup chopped fresh parsley
6	cloves garlic, crushed	2	(10 ounce) cans refrigerated pizza crusts
1	large onion, sliced	6	ounces feta cheese
1	tablespoon dried oregano	½	zucchini, diced
1	teaspoon ground cumin	1	(4¼ ounce) can chopped ripe olives
1	teaspoon salt	½	teaspoon garlic powder
2	teaspoons freshly ground black pepper		

1. Preheat oven to 400°F (205°C).

2. Heat oil in a large skillet over medium–high heat. Brown meat with garlic and onion; drain fat. Add oregano, cumin, salt, pepper, and hot sauce to the meat mixture and cook 3 minutes. Add parsley and cook until the parsley wilts, about 1 minute. Remove mixture from heat and allow to cool.

3. Roll 1 pizza crust on a floured surface to an 11x17 inch rectangle. Sprinkle half each of feta, zucchini, and olives to within 1 inch of all sides. Spoon half of meat mixture over olives. Roll up, starting at long side, jellyroll fashion, sealing edges as you roll. Seal seam and tuck ends under. Repeat procedure using the other pizza crust and remaining cheese, zucchini, and meat mixture.

4. Place gyrolls on a lightly greased large baking sheet. Sprinkle each with garlic powder. Bake in the preheated oven for 5 minutes. Reduce heat to 325°F (165°C) and bake 35 more minutes or until golden brown. **Yield:** 4 servings.

Per serving: About 693 calories, 32g protein, 67g carbohydrate, 33g fat, 5g fiber, 95mg cholesterol, 2950mg sodium

◄ Crowd-Pleaser

Prep Time: 25 minutes
Cook Time: 40 minutes
Average Rating: ★★★★★
29 Ratings ▲ 23 Reviews
What other cooks have done:
"I used a half-and-half combination of ground lamb and turkey to cut some of the fat, and used a basil and sun-dried tomato flavored feta."

Real Italian Calzones (pictured on page 261)

Submitted by: **Jenny**

"This is a real calzone, because there's no tomato sauce inside of it. We eat it at least once a week. Have a bowl of tomato or spaghetti sauce on the table for people to top their calzone with, if desired."

1	(.25 ounce) package active dry yeast	1	teaspoon olive oil
1	cup warm water	½	cup ricotta cheese
1	tablespoon olive oil	1½	cups shredded Cheddar cheese
1	teaspoon white sugar	½	cup sliced pepperoni
1	teaspoon salt	½	cup sliced fresh mushrooms
2½	cups all-purpose flour, divided	1	tablespoon dried basil
		1	egg, beaten

1. In a small bowl, dissolve yeast in water. Add the oil, sugar, and salt; mix in 1 cup of the flour until smooth. Gradually stir in the rest of the flour until dough is smooth and workable. Knead dough on a lightly floured surface for about 5 minutes or until elastic. Place dough in a bowl containing 1 teaspoon olive oil, then flip the dough, cover, and let rise in a warm place, 85F° (29°C), for 40 minutes or until almost doubled.

2. While dough is rising, combine the ricotta cheese, Cheddar cheese, pepperoni, mushrooms, and basil in a large bowl. Mix well, cover, and refrigerate.

3. Preheat oven to 375°F (190°C).

4. When dough is ready, punch it down and separate it into 2 equal parts. Roll out into thin circles on a lightly floured surface. Fill each circle with half of the cheese filling and fold over, securing edges by folding in and pressing with a fork. Brush the top of each calzone with egg and place on a lightly greased baking sheet.

5. Bake in the preheated oven for 30 minutes. Slice each calzone into wedges and serve hot. **Yield:** 4 servings.

Per serving: About 712 calories, 30g protein, 66g carbohydrate, 36g fat, 4g fiber, 130mg cholesterol, 1482mg sodium

Strawberry Soup

Submitted by: **Michelle**

"Using plain yogurt instead of heavy cream lowers the fat and calories in this soup, and it's still just as good. It's a very simple and refreshing soup."

2 pints strawberries	½ cup water
2 cups plain yogurt	⅛ teaspoon ground
½ cup orange juice	cardamom
½ cup white sugar	or cinnamon

1. Puree the strawberries, yogurt, orange juice, sugar, water, and ground cardamom in batches in a food processor or blender until smooth. Chill and serve. **Yield:** 5 servings.

Per serving: About 194 calories, 6g protein, 40g carbohydrate, 2g fat, 3g fiber, 6mg cholesterol, 71mg sodium

◄ Healthy

Prep Time: 5 minutes

Average Rating: ★★★★★

30 Ratings ▲ 23 Reviews

What other cooks have done:

"I have made it with less sugar and topped with sour cream for a cool, refreshing appetizer and have also served it with angel food cake and low-fat vanilla ice cream for a low-cal dessert."

Cooking Basics: Cold Summer Soups ▼

You may be in the habit of thinking of soups purely as hot and hearty winter fare, but cool, refreshing summer soups are a real lifesaver when you can't bear the thought of cooking. Cold soups fall into two very basic categories: savory and sweet. The savory ones are generally based on vegetables (or at least fruits that masquerade as vegetables, such as tomatoes and avocados), and the sweet ones are centered around ripe summer fruit.

Savory Soups

The king of the cold soup universe has to be gazpacho. Invented in Spain, this soup has been around in various incarnations for hundreds of years. The most well-known version has a base of fresh chopped tomatoes with finely diced bell peppers, onion, garlic, and cucumbers mixed in. It's often thickened with breadcrumbs and can be garnished with fresh chopped parsley, tarragon, or cilantro, along with extra virgin olive oil, sliced olives, avocado chunks, croutons, or even hard-cooked eggs. Hearty bowls of gazpacho accompanied by a platter of garnishes and some fresh bread make an ideal light meal.

Another cold savory soup that has enjoyed decades of popularity is vichyssoise. Despite the very French-sounding name, it was actually invented in the United States. It was first served in the Ritz-Carlton in New York almost 100 years ago. It has a base of pureed potatoes and leeks, enriched with a swirl of cream and sprinkled with bright, crunchy chives just before serving.

The list of delicious, cold savory soups doesn't end with gazpacho and vichyssoise, though! Try cucumber, avocado, beet, zucchini, or carrot. Just about any soup based on pureed vegetables is delightful served cold. Just try out whatever is in season in your area and have fun!

Sweet Soups

Chilled fruit soups are a refreshing way to begin or end any summer meal. Berry and stone fruit soups at their best have a perfect combination of sweet and tart flavors, featuring raspberries, blueberries, blackberries, strawberries, cherries, apricots, or plums. Berry soups are often accented with a touch of wine and a splash of cream or sour cream; sometimes they're even pureed with yogurt—like a fruit smoothie in a bowl. Melon soups are also increasingly popular. The vivid sherbet colors of honeydew, cantaloupe, and watermelon are invigorating, and it's impossible not to feel refreshed while slurping down spoonful after icy-cold spoonful of a sweet melon soup.

All you really need to whip up a refreshing, cool soup is some ripe fruit, a blender, and a yen for experimentation. If the fruit's a little on the sour side, mix in honey, sugar, maple syrup, fruit syrup, or fruit-flavored yogurt. Add a touch of spice with cinnamon, cardamom, nutmeg, or mint. Don't underestimate the power of a squeeze of lemon juice for waking up flavors, either. A splash of wine, champagne, or kirsch will add a rich smoothness—just make sure to simmer the soup a little before cooling and serving, if you want to cook off that alcohol. Drizzle a bit of cream, crème fraîche, or sour cream over the top just before serving to present a marvelous contrast in color, flavor, and texture. If you want to take it a step further, play around with some fun garnishes, too. Top each bowl with a few morsels of the fruit that was pureed into the soup, or use a different fruit that will create a striking color contrast with the soup itself. For the pièce de résistance, toast some cubes of angel food or pound cake to make sweet, crispy dessert croutons.

- Jennifer Anderson

For more information, visit **Allrecipes.com**

Broccoli-Cheese Soup

Submitted by: **Karin Christian**

"Here's a very flavorful soup that's good for serving with quiche at luncheons or special gatherings. To make this soup a little fancier, add 1 cup sliced mushrooms and 1 cup white wine and sauté along with the onions."

½	cup butter	2	cups milk
1	onion, chopped	1	tablespoon garlic powder
1	(16 ounce) package frozen chopped broccoli	⅔	cup cornstarch
4	(14 ounce) cans chicken broth	1	cup water
1	(16 ounce) loaf pasteurized prepared cheese product, cubed		

1. In a stockpot, melt butter over medium heat. Cook onion in butter until softened. Stir in frozen broccoli and chicken broth. Simmer until broccoli is tender, about 10 to 15 minutes.

2. Reduce heat and stir in cheese cubes until melted. Mix in milk and garlic powder.

3. In a small bowl, stir cornstarch into water until dissolved. Mix into soup; cook and stir until thick. **Yield:** 12 servings.

Per serving: About 270 calories, 10g protein, 16g carbohydrate, 18g fat, 1g fiber, 57mg cholesterol, 1229mg sodium

Rich and Creamy Tomato Basil Soup

Submitted by: **Holly**

"The secret to the richness of this soup is to use butter, fresh basil leaves, and heavy cream. Please do not substitute, or you will not have the same quality result."

4	tomatoes, peeled, seeded, and diced	½	cup butter
4	cups tomato juice		Salt to taste
14	fresh basil leaves		Ground black pepper to taste
1	cup heavy whipping cream		

1. Combine tomatoes and juice in a stockpot. Simmer 30 minutes.

2. Puree tomatoes and juice with basil leaves in a blender or food processor in batches.

3. Return mixture to stockpot; add heavy cream and butter and heat through. Add salt and pepper to taste. Adjust seasonings to personal taste preference. **Yield:** 5 servings.

Per serving: About 485 calories, 4g protein, 19g carbohydrate, 46g fat, 3g fiber, 144mg cholesterol, 383mg sodium

Cream of Spinach Soup

Submitted by: **Joyce Marciszewski**

"This is a fast, easy way to make creamed soups. You can also use most any frozen vegetable. Cream of broccoli is also delicious."

1½	cups water	¼	cup all-purpose flour
3	chicken bouillon cubes	3	cups milk
1	(10 ounce) package frozen chopped spinach	1	tablespoon grated onion
3	tablespoons butter or margarine		Salt to taste
			Ground black pepper to taste

1. Combine water, bouillon cubes, and spinach in a medium saucepan. Bring to a boil and cook until tender.
2. In a large saucepan, melt the butter over medium heat. Stir in flour until smooth. Whisk in milk and heat through. Season with grated onion, salt, and pepper. Stir in spinach mixture. **Yield:** 4 servings.

Per serving: About 223 calories, 10g protein, 19g carbohydrate, 13g fat, 2g fiber, 38mg cholesterol, 1099mg sodium

◀ **Quick & Easy**

Prep Time: 5 minutes
Cook Time: 20 minutes
Average Rating: ★★★★★
22 Ratings ▲ 18 Reviews

What other cooks have done:
"I used half-and-half in place of milk and fresh spinach for frozen. I also threw in some broccoli. I put half the mixture in the blender for variation of texture. I was able to get my kids to eat their spinach and broccoli!"

Butternut Squash Soup

Submitted by: **Mary**

"Delicious and very easy to make. You can use 3 to 4 cups of chicken broth instead of the water and bouillon cubes. It also works well with half as much cream cheese if you don't want it too rich."

½	onion, chopped	¼	teaspoon ground black pepper
¼	cup butter or margarine	⅛	teaspoon ground cayenne pepper
6	cups peeled and cubed butternut squash	2	(8 ounce) packages cream cheese
3	cups water		
4	cubes chicken bouillon		
½	teaspoon dried marjoram		

1. In a large saucepan, sauté onion in butter until tender. Add squash, water, bouillon, marjoram, black pepper, and cayenne pepper. Bring to a boil; cook 20 minutes or until squash is tender.
2. Puree squash mixture and cream cheese in a blender or food processor in batches until smooth. Return to saucepan and heat through. Do not allow to boil. **Yield:** 6 servings.

Per serving: About 397 calories, 8g protein, 20g carbohydrate, 33g fat, 0g fiber, 82mg cholesterol, 1081mg sodium

◀ **Holiday Fare**

Prep Time: 25 minutes
Cook Time: 35 minutes
Average Rating: ★★★★★
77 Ratings ▲ 62 Reviews

What other cooks have done:
"To cut down on the cook time, skip a step and microwave your squash. Just cut a half inch hole in the squash (to avoid explosions) and microwave it whole until tender when poked with a fork, about 15 minutes. Turn a few times during cooking. Then just cut it in half, scoop out the seeds, and scoop out the cooked squash from the peel."

Jamie's Minestrone

Submitted by: **Jamie**

"I created this soup after becoming tired of the excess salt and lack of veggies in canned minestrone. It's great with a hearty bread, romaine salad, and a nice Merlot."

Healthy ▶

Prep Time: 20 minutes
Cook Time: 1 hour
Average Rating: ★★★★★
85 Ratings ▲ 71 Reviews

What other cooks have done:
"Fabulous recipe! I did some substitutions though: I used potatoes instead of zucchini, and I added white wine instead of red. I also used Italian-crushed tomatoes and only one small can of tomato sauce. This is a great recipe that can easily be modified to suit both your tastes and whatever you have in the cupboard."

3	tablespoons olive oil	3	zucchini, quartered and sliced
3	cloves garlic, chopped		
2	onions, chopped	1	tablespoon chopped fresh oregano
2	cups chopped celery		
5	carrots, sliced	2	tablespoons chopped fresh basil
2	cups chicken broth		
2	cups water		Salt and pepper to taste
4	cups tomato sauce	2	cups baby spinach, rinsed
1	tablespoon red wine (optional)	½	cup seashell pasta, uncooked
1	cup canned kidney beans, drained	2	tablespoons grated Parmesan cheese
1	(15 ounce) can green beans, undrained	1	tablespoon olive oil

1. In a large stockpot, heat olive oil over medium–low heat and sauté garlic for 2 to 3 minutes. Add onion and sauté for 4 to 5 minutes. Add celery and carrot and sauté for 1 to 2 minutes.

2. Add chicken broth, water, and tomato sauce; bring to a boil, stirring frequently. If desired, add red wine. Reduce heat to low and add kidney beans, green beans, zucchini, oregano, basil, salt, and pepper. Simmer for 30 minutes. Stir in spinach and simmer 5 more minutes.

3. Fill a medium saucepan with water and bring to a boil. Add pasta and cook until tender. Drain and set aside.

4. Once pasta is cooked and soup is heated through, place 2 tablespoons cooked pasta into individual serving bowls. Ladle soup on top of pasta and sprinkle Parmesan cheese on top. Sprinkle with olive oil and serve. **Yield:** 8 servings.

Per serving: About 223 calories, 9g protein, 32g carbohydrate, 8g fat, 8g fiber, 1mg cholesterol, 1266mg sodium

Moroccan Lentil Soup

Submitted by: **Grace and Mae**
"Thick, delicious, and nutritious, especially in the winter!"

2	onions, chopped	1	(14.5 ounce) can diced tomatoes, undrained
2	cloves garlic, minced	½	cup diced carrots
1	teaspoon grated fresh ginger	½	cup chopped celery
1	tablespoon olive oil	1	teaspoon garam masala ★
6	cups water	1½	teaspoons ground cardamom
1	cup red lentils		
1	(15 ounce) can garbanzo beans, drained	½	teaspoon ground cayenne pepper
1	(19 ounce) can cannellini beans, drained	½	teaspoon ground cumin

1. In a large pot, sauté the onions, garlic, and ginger in olive oil for about 5 minutes.
2. Add the water, lentils, garbanzo beans, cannellini beans, diced tomatoes, carrot, celery, garam masala, cardamom, cayenne pepper, and cumin. Bring to a boil for a few minutes, then reduce heat and simmer for 1 to 1½ hours, until the lentils are soft.
3. Puree half the soup in a food processor or blender. Return the pureed soup to the pot and stir. **Yield:** 6 servings.

★ Garam masala is a blend of dry-roasted, ground spices such as black pepper, cinnamon, cloves, coriander, cumin, cardamom, dried chiles, fennel, mace, and nutmeg. Find it in Indian markets or in the gourmet section of the supermarket.

Per serving: About 355 calories, 20g protein, 62g carbohydrate, 4g fat, 19g fiber, 0mg cholesterol, 432mg sodium

◄ Meatless Main Dish

Prep Time: 20 minutes
Cook Time: 1 hour 45 minutes
Average Rating: ★★★★★
15 Ratings ▲ 8 Reviews
What other cooks have done:
"This is a very flavorful and filling soup! I served this with homemade bread bowls (probably not very Moroccan, but very tasty) and my family went crazy over it. I loved the spices and flavor and have made it two times so far this month ... it's that good! If you like the flavor and aroma of cardamom, then I recommend trying this soup."

Wisconsin Cheese Soup II

Submitted by: **Rachel**

"I got this recipe from a friend. It's wonderful! Try serving it with a loaf of crusty French bread."

1	cup sliced carrot	¼	cup all-purpose flour
2	cups chopped broccoli	¼	teaspoon ground black pepper
1	cup water		
1	teaspoon chicken bouillon granules	2	cups milk
¼	cup chopped onion	2	cups shredded sharp Cheddar cheese
¼	cup butter		

1. In a small saucepan over medium-high heat, combine carrot, broccoli, water, and bouillon. Bring to a boil. Cover, reduce heat, and simmer for 5 minutes. Remove from heat and set aside.
2. In a large saucepan, cook onion in butter over medium heat until onion is translucent. Stir in flour and pepper; cook 1 minute. Stir in milk. Bring to a boil, then stir in cheese until melted. Stir in reserved vegetables and cooking liquid. Heat through and serve. **Yield:** 4 servings.

Per serving: About 449 calories, 21g protein, 19g carbohydrate, 33g fat, 3g fiber, 99mg cholesterol, 571mg sodium

Rich and Simple French Onion Soup

Submitted by: **Lori Levin**

"We have been trying French onion soup in restaurants for years, and my family and friends agree none can compare to my recipe for taste and simplicity."

¼	cup butter	1	teaspoon dried thyme
2	tablespoons olive oil		Pepper to taste
4	cups sliced onions (2 large onions)	6	slices French bread
		6	slices provolone cheese
4	(10.5 ounce) cans beef broth	6	slices Swiss cheese
2	tablespoons dry sherry (optional)	¼	cup shredded Parmesan cheese

1. Melt butter in an 8 quart stockpot on medium heat. Add olive oil and stir. Add onion and stir occasionally until tender and translucent, about 10 minutes. Do not brown the onions.
2. Add beef broth, sherry, and thyme. Season with pepper and simmer, uncovered, for 30 minutes. Preheat the oven to Broil.
3. Ladle soup into individual, oven safe serving bowls and place 1 slice of bread on top (it can also be broken into pieces, whichever you prefer). Layer provolone, Swiss, and Parmesan cheese on top of bread. Place bowls on a baking sheet and broil until cheese bubbles and browns slightly. **Yield:** 6 servings.

Per serving: About 731 calories, 28g protein, 56g carbohydrate, 43g fat, 5g fiber, 95mg cholesterol, 1807mg sodium

Beef, Barley, Vegetable Soup

Submitted by: **Margo Collins**
"Serve with a hearty bread and enjoy."

3 pounds chuck roast
½ cup barley
1 bay leaf
2 tablespoons vegetable oil
3 carrots, chopped
3 stalks celery, chopped
1 onion, chopped
1 (16 ounce) package frozen mixed vegetables

4 cups water
4 beef bouillon cubes
1 tablespoon white sugar
¼ teaspoon ground black pepper
2 (14½ ounce) cans diced stewed tomatoes
Salt and ground black pepper to taste

1. In a slow cooker, cook chuck roast on High for 1 hour, reduce heat to Low and cook 5 more hours or until meat is tender. Add barley and bay leaf during the last hour of cooking. Remove meat and chop into bite-size pieces. Discard bay leaf. Set beef, broth, and barley aside.
2. Heat oil in a large stockpot over medium-high heat. Sauté carrot, celery, onion, and frozen mixed vegetables until tender. Add water, beef bouillon cubes, sugar, ¼ teaspoon pepper, stewed tomatoes, and beef/barley mixture. Bring to boil, reduce heat, and simmer 10 to 20 minutes. Season with salt and additional pepper to taste. **Yield:** 8 servings.

Per serving: About 561 calories, 34g protein, 29g carbohydrate, 35g fat, 7g fiber, 121mg cholesterol, 817mg sodium

Basic Soup Stocks ▼

In this modern age of food science, grocery stores are crammed with canned, cubed, and powdered soup stock. Pre-packaged stocks have made it quick and easy to whip up a big, flavorful pot of soup. But if time isn't an issue, why not do it the old-fashioned way and make your own stock from scratch? We think you'll find the flavorful rewards are far greater than the extra effort involved.

A homemade stock adds depth and body to any soup. Your choices for flavor are limited only by the contents of your vegetable crisper, your leftovers, and your imagination. Stock provides a background to soup, so the ingredients you choose should be supportive, not overwhelming. There are several keys to good, basic stocks.

• Stocks are not compost heaps. If you wouldn't eat that moldy old mushroom or aging chicken as is, then don't subject your stock to them! Yesterday's, or even last week's, vegetables are fine, as long as they're still good. The beauty of stock ingredients is that the ideal ingredients are usually the trimmings from the soup you're about to make (leek roots and leaves, tiny, end-of-the-head garlic cloves, potato parings, etc.)

• Use a stockpot that's tall and narrow to help slow water loss from evaporation.

• To extract the most flavor from your stock ingredients, start with cold water.

• Meat stocks benefit from long, slow cooking. Vegetable stocks do not. Quick vegetable stocks should take 25 to 30 minutes; basic vegetable stocks, 45 minutes to one hour. Chicken or beef stocks can take anywhere from one hour to five; longer if you're using a slow cooker.

• Certain herbs and vegetables will turn bitter as they steep. Strain as soon as the stock is finished. Also, some vegetables should be avoided altogether in stocks. The cabbage family (turnips, rutabagas, Brussels sprouts, broccoli, cauliflower, etc.) does not do well in stock. Nor do most powdered herbs, ground black pepper, onion skins, artichoke trimmings, or too many greens. When in doubt, simmer the ingredient separately first, and taste the water.

- Ursula Dalzell

For more information, visit **Allrecipes.com**

Baked Potato Soup

Submitted by: **Sherry Haupt**

"Use leftover baked potatoes to make this thick and creamy soup."

12 slices bacon	1¼ cups shredded Cheddar cheese
⅔ cup butter or margarine	1 (8 ounce) container sour cream
⅔ cup all-purpose flour	
7 cups milk	1 teaspoon salt
4 potatoes, baked, cooled, peeled, and cubed	1 teaspoon ground black pepper
4 green onions, chopped	

1. Place bacon in a large, deep skillet. Cook over medium heat until browned. Drain, crumble, and set aside.

2. In a stockpot or Dutch oven, melt the butter over medium heat. Whisk in flour until smooth. Gradually stir in milk, whisking constantly until thickened. Stir in potato and onion. Bring to a boil, stirring frequently. Reduce heat and simmer 10 minutes. Mix in bacon, cheese, sour cream, salt, and pepper. Continue cooking, stirring frequently, until cheese is melted. **Yield:** 6 servings.

Per serving: About 959 calories, 25g protein, 50g carbohydrate, 74g fat, 2g fiber, 101mg cholesterol, 1346mg sodium

Grandma's Chicken Noodle Soup

Submitted by: **Corwynn Darkholme**

"My grandmother gave me this recipe. It's very tasty, and I believe that everyone will like it. If you would like to add even more flavor, try using smoked chicken."

2½ cups wide egg noodles	1 cup chopped celery
1 teaspoon vegetable oil	1 cup chopped onion
12 cups chicken broth	⅓ cup cornstarch
1½ teaspoons salt	¼ cup water
1 teaspoon poultry seasoning	3 cups diced, cooked chicken

1. Bring a large pot of lightly salted water to a boil. Add egg noodles and oil and boil for 8 minutes or until tender. Drain.

2. In a large saucepan or Dutch oven, combine broth, salt, and poultry seasoning. Bring to a boil. Stir in celery and onion. Reduce heat, cover, and simmer 15 minutes.

3. In a small bowl, mix cornstarch and water together until cornstarch is completely dissolved. Gradually add to soup, stirring constantly. Stir in noodles and chicken and heat through. **Yield:** 8 servings.

Per serving: About 146 calories, 16g protein, 11g carbohydrate, 4g fat, 1g fiber, 34mg cholesterol, 1664mg sodium

Cream of Chicken with Wild Rice Soup

Submitted by: **Thomas**

"This makes a lovely chicken and wild rice soup."

1⅓ cups wild rice, uncooked
1 (3 pound) whole chicken,
 cut into pieces
7 cups water
1 cup chopped celery
1 cup chopped onion
2 tablespoons vegetable oil
1 cup sliced fresh mushrooms
2 tablespoons chicken
 bouillon granules

¾ teaspoon ground white
 pepper
½ teaspoon salt
½ cup butter or margarine
¾ cup all-purpose flour
4 cups milk
¾ cup white wine

1. Cook the wild rice according to package directions, but remove from heat about 15 minutes before it's done. Drain the excess liquid and set aside.

2. In a stockpot over high heat, combine the chicken and the water. Bring to a boil and then reduce heat to low. Simmer for 40 minutes or until chicken is cooked and tender. Remove chicken from the pot and allow to cool. Strain the broth from the pot and reserve for later. When chicken is cool, remove the meat from the bones, cut into bite size pieces, and reserve. Discard the fat and the bones.

3. In the same stockpot over medium heat, sauté the celery and onion in the oil for 5 minutes. Add the mushrooms and cover. Cook for 5 to 10 minutes, stirring occasionally, until everything is tender. Return the broth to the stockpot and add the partially cooked wild rice. Stir in the bouillon, white pepper, and salt; simmer, uncovered, for 15 minutes.

4. Meanwhile, melt butter in a medium saucepan over medium heat. Stir in the flour until smooth. Whisk in the milk and continue cooking until mixture is bubbly and thick. Add some of the broth mixture to the milk mixture, continuing to stir, then stir all of the milk mixture into the broth mixture.

5. Mix in the reserved chicken and the white wine. Allow this to heat through for about 15 minutes. **Yield:** 8 servings.

Per serving: About 567 calories, 34g protein, 38g carbohydrate, 30g fat, 3g fiber, 84mg cholesterol, 450mg sodium

Chicken Tortilla Soup *(pictured on page 263)*

Submitted by: **Star Pooley**

"Here's a soup that's quick to make, flavorful, and filling! Serve with warm cornbread or tortillas. This also freezes well."

1 tablespoon olive oil	1 (4.5 ounce) can chopped green chiles
1 onion, chopped	1 (15 ounce) can black beans, rinsed and drained
3 cloves garlic, minced	2 boneless chicken breast halves, cooked and cut into bite-size pieces
2 teaspoons chili powder	
1 teaspoon dried oregano	
1 (28 ounce) can crushed tomatoes	¼ cup chopped fresh cilantro
1 (10.5 ounce) can chicken broth	Crushed tortilla chips
1¼ cups water	Cubed avocado
1 cup frozen whole corn kernels	Shredded Monterey Jack cheese
1 cup white hominy	Sliced green onion

1. In a medium stockpot, heat oil over medium heat. Sauté onion and garlic in oil until soft. Stir in chili powder, oregano, tomatoes, broth, and water. Bring to a boil; simmer for 5 to 10 minutes, stirring occasionally.
2. Stir in corn, hominy, chiles, beans, and chicken. Simmer for 10 minutes. Add cilantro just before serving.
3. Ladle soup into individual serving bowls and top with crushed tortilla chips, avocado, cheese, and sliced green onion. **Yield:** 4 servings.

Per serving: About 378 calories, 23g protein, 30g carbohydrate, 20g fat, 8g fiber, 46mg cholesterol, 951mg sodium

Exotic and Flavorful Soups ▼

You've eaten them at Thai restaurants, you've read about them in books—it's time to take the plunge and start experimenting with international soups. International soups are no more difficult to make than the old American standbys! In fact, many of them are simpler and quicker. All it takes are the correct ingredients and a few good recipes.

The Basics

All right, so now you're ready to take the plunge. You want to make soup unlike any other that has ever passed your lips. First off, to help you decide where to start, here are some of the basic names and ingredients that characterize some international soups:
Bisque: a cream soup with a shellfish base (French)
Gazpacho: clear tomato soup made with fresh vegetables and herbs, served chilled (Spanish)
Bouillabaisse: fresh seafood soup with a vegetable base (French)
Borscht: soup made with fresh beets, served hot or cold (Russian)
Minestrone: vegetable and pasta based soup, sometimes made with sausage (Italian)

Posole: made of pork or chicken and broth, and hominy (Mexican)
Won Ton: clear broth with dumplings (bite-size packages filled with vegetables, and meat) (Chinese)

What Does That Recipe Call for?

Some ingredients, particularly those in Asian soups, may be unfamiliar to you. That doesn't mean you can't use them! Make a list of the ingredients that you don't recognize and take a trip to your neighborhood's international grocery store. Look over the vegetables and spices and ask the grocer about them. They'll be able to explain which type of flavor these vegetables and spices yield as well as the best techniques for cutting, chopping, or sprinkling these delicacies. We can't tell you how many times we've come across international ingredients, been a little skeptical about them, and ended up adding them as permanent (and highly useful) additions to our spice rack! Get adventurous and use those international ingredients! - Tammy Weisberger
For more information, visit **Allrecipes.com**

Adrienne's Tom Ka Gai

Submitted by: **Adrienne Barnett**
"Fragrant, spicy, and absolutely delicious Thai chicken soup. Add noodles at the end with the cilantro, if you like."

2 teaspoons peanut oil	1 skinless, boneless chicken breast, thinly sliced
2 cloves garlic, thinly sliced	1 onion, thinly sliced
2 tablespoons grated fresh ginger root	2 cups bok choy, shredded
¼ cup chopped lemongrass	4 cups water
2 teaspoons crushed red pepper flakes	1 (10 ounce) can coconut milk
1 teaspoon ground coriander	¼ cup fish sauce
1 teaspoon ground cumin	¼ cup chopped fresh cilantro

1. In a large saucepan over medium heat, heat peanut oil. Stir in garlic, ginger, lemongrass, red pepper, coriander, and cumin and cook until fragrant, 2 minutes. Stir in chicken and onion and cook, stirring, until chicken is white and onion is translucent, 5 minutes. Stir in bok choy and cook until it begins to wilt, 5 to 10 minutes. Stir in water, coconut milk, fish sauce, and cilantro. Simmer until chicken is cooked and flavors are well blended, about 30 minutes. **Yield:** 4 servings.

Per serving: About 255 calories, 17g protein, 9g carbohydrate, 18g fat, 2g fiber, 34mg cholesterol, 1165mg sodium

◄ Around-the-World Cuisine

Prep Time: 15 minutes
Cook Time: 45 minutes
Average Rating: ★★★★★
12 Ratings ▲ 11 Reviews
What other cooks have done:
"Amazing! My friends told me that it was better than the Tom Ka Gai that we get at our favorite Asian restaurant. I added dried oyster mushrooms and egg noodles. I couldn't find lemongrass and had to use dried lemon zest, but it turned out wonderful."

Restaurant-Style Zuppa Toscana

Submitted by: **Nancy**
"This creamy soup is very similar to the one served at our favorite restaurant."

1 (16 ounce) package smoked sausage	1 quart water
¾ cup chopped onion	2 potatoes, cut into ¼ inch slices
6 slices bacon	2 cups kale, washed, dried, and shredded
1½ teaspoons minced garlic	⅓ cup heavy whipping cream
2 tablespoons chicken soup base	

1. Preheat oven to 300°F (150°C). Place sausage in a baking pan and bake in the preheated oven for 25 minutes or until done. Cut links in half lengthwise, then cut at an angle into ½ inch slices.
2. Place onion and bacon in a large saucepan and cook over medium heat until onion is almost translucent. Remove bacon and crumble. Set aside.
3. Add garlic to the onion and cook 1 more minute. Add chicken soup base, water, and potato; simmer 15 minutes. Add crumbled bacon, sausage, kale, and cream. Simmer 4 minutes and serve. **Yield:** 6 servings.

Per serving: About 464 calories, 16g protein, 16g carbohydrate, 38g fat, 2g fiber, 103mg cholesterol, 1758mg sodium

◄ One-Dish Meal

Prep Time: 15 minutes
Cook Time: 55 minutes
Average Rating: ★★★★★
15 Ratings ▲ 9 Reviews
What other cooks have done:
"I find I like the texture better after the soup is cooled and then reheated. Also, I always add an entire bunch of kale and mild Italian sausage. For family or entertaining, this is fabulous!"

Italian Sausage Soup

Submitted by: **Karen Marshall**

"This hearty winter favorite is brimming with sausage, beans, and vegetables."

1	pound Italian sausage	¼	teaspoon ground black pepper
1	clove garlic, minced		
2	(14 ounce) cans beef broth	1	(15 ounce) can great Northern beans, undrained
1	(14.5 ounce) can Italian-style stewed tomatoes, undrained		
		2	small zucchini, cubed
1	cup sliced carrot	2	cups spinach, rinsed, torn, and packed
¼	teaspoon salt		

1. In a stockpot or Dutch oven, brown sausage with garlic. Stir in broth, tomatoes, and carrot; season with salt and pepper. Reduce heat, cover, and simmer 15 minutes.

2. Stir in beans with liquid and zucchini. Cover and simmer 15 minutes or until zucchini is tender.

3. Remove from heat and add spinach. Replace lid, allowing the heat from the soup to cook the spinach leaves. Soup is ready to serve after 5 minutes. **Yield:** 6 servings.

Per serving: About 385 calories, 19g protein, 22g carbohydrate, 24g fat, 6g fiber, 58mg cholesterol, 1249mg sodium

Split Pea and Ham Soup

Submitted by: **Sue**

"A good way to use leftover ham; quite inexpensive, and very tasty, too. I hope that you enjoy it. Some people like to add carrots or other types of vegetables. Don't forget to serve with buttered bread toasted in the oven."

1	cup chopped onion	1	pound ham bone or chopped ham
1	teaspoon vegetable oil		
1	pound dried split peas		Salt and pepper to taste

1. In a medium pot, sauté onion in oil. Remove from heat and add split peas and ham bone or chopped ham. Add enough water to cover ingredients and season with salt and pepper.

2. Cover and cook until peas dissolve, about 2 hours, adding water as needed to reach desired consistency.

3. Remove soup from heat and let stand to thicken. Once thickened, you may need to heat through to serve. **Yield:** 4 servings.

Per serving: About 412 calories, 28g protein, 72g carbohydrate, 3g fat, 30g fiber, 0mg cholesterol, 18mg sodium

Italian Wedding Soup

Submitted by: **Star Pooley**
"Coming from Rhode Island, a very ethnic state, this soup was traditionally served at Italian weddings. Serve with grated Parmesan cheese."

½	pound extra-lean ground beef	½	teaspoon dried basil
1	egg, lightly beaten	½	teaspoon onion powder
2	tablespoons dry breadcrumbs	6	cups chicken broth
		2	cups thinly sliced escarole
1	tablespoon grated Parmesan cheese	1	cup uncooked orzo pasta
		⅓	cup finely chopped carrot

1. In a medium bowl, combine the beef, egg, breadcrumbs, cheese, basil, and onion powder; shape into ¾ inch balls.
2. In large saucepan, heat broth to boiling; stir in escarole, orzo pasta, chopped carrot, and meatballs. Return to a boil, then reduce heat to medium. Cook at a slow boil for 10 minutes or until pasta is al dente. Stir frequently to prevent sticking. **Yield:** 4 servings.

Per serving: About 443 calories, 28g protein, 48g carbohydrate, 14g fat, 3g fiber, 93mg cholesterol, 1216mg sodium

◄ One-Dish Meal

Prep Time: 20 minutes
Cook Time: 30 minutes
Average Rating: ★★★★★
130 Ratings ▲ 103 Reviews
What other cooks have done:
"This recipe was loved by all and I even got requests for the recipe from others! If you make a large batch, I would recommend cooking the orzo separately and putting how much you want into each bowl just before serving so that you can save the leftover soup for another meal. Store the cooked orzo separately from the leftover soup."

Slow-Cooker Taco Soup

Submitted by: **Janeen**
"Enjoy this quick, throw together slow-cooker soup with a Mexican accent. Teenagers love it. Serve topped with corn chips, shredded Cheddar cheese, and a dollop of sour cream. Make sure you adjust the amount of green chiles if you're sensitive to peppers."

1	pound ground beef	1	(8 ounce) can tomato sauce
1	onion, chopped	2	cups water
1	(16 ounce) can chili beans, undrained	2	(14.5 ounce) cans peeled and diced tomatoes
1	(15 ounce) can kidney beans, undrained	1	(4.5 ounce) can diced green chiles
1	(15 ounce) can whole kernel corn, undrained	1	(1.25 ounce) package taco seasoning mix

1. In a medium skillet, cook the ground beef over medium heat until browned. Drain.
2. Place the ground beef, onion, chili beans, kidney beans, corn, tomato sauce, water, diced tomatoes, green chiles, and taco seasoning mix in a slow cooker. Mix to blend and cook on Low setting for 8 hours. **Yield:** 8 servings.

Per serving: About 362 calories, 19g protein, 38g carbohydrate, 17g fat, 9g fiber, 48mg cholesterol, 1267mg sodium

◄ Hot & Spicy

Prep Time: 10 minutes
Cook Time: 8 hours
Average Rating: ★★★★★
152 Ratings ▲ 118 Reviews
What other cooks have done:
"The best soup recipe I've found yet. I added some extras such as sliced black olives and leftover turkey, and I used frozen corn instead of canned. My husband and I are contractors, so we eat out of coolers every day, and this has to be by far the highlight of our day."

Chicken Andouille Gumbo

Submitted by: **Christine L.**

"Sausage makes this soup very spicy. It can be prepared two days ahead."

Prep Time: 10 minutes

Cook Time: 3 hours 10 minutes

Average Rating: ★★★★★

40 Ratings ▲ 27 Reviews

What other cooks have done:

"I followed this recipe fairly closely but substituted frozen okra for the fresh, added an onion, and an extra chile pepper because we like things spicy. I also made it a day in advance, thinking it would be better the day after. It was thick and flavorful. I served it over rice along with cheesy corn spoonbread."

12 cups water	2 stalks celery, chopped
1 (3 pound) whole chicken, cut into pieces	2 cloves garlic, minced
2 tablespoons vegetable oil	1 bay leaf
1½ pounds okra, sliced	2 teaspoons salt
½ cup all-purpose flour	1 teaspoon dried thyme
½ cup vegetable oil	1 teaspoon dried basil
1 pound andouille sausage	1 teaspoon cayenne pepper
1 (28 ounce) can Italian-style whole peeled tomatoes, undrained	1 teaspoon ground black pepper
1 green bell pepper, chopped	1 teaspoon filé powder ★
	Hot cooked rice (optional)

1. Combine water and chicken in a large pot. Bring to boil. Reduce heat and simmer until chicken is tender, about 1 hour. Using tongs, transfer chicken to strainer and cool, saving cooking liquid. Remove meat from bones in pieces.

2. Heat 2 tablespoons oil in a heavy skillet over medium heat. Add okra and cook until no longer sticky, stirring frequently, about 20 minutes.

3. Stir flour and ½ cup oil in a large heavy Dutch oven. Cook over medium heat until deep golden brown, stirring frequently, about 6 minutes. Add 4 cups reserved chicken cooking broth, okra, sausage, tomatoes with their juices, bell pepper, celery, garlic, bay leaf, salt, thyme, basil, cayenne pepper, and black pepper. Cover partially and simmer until thickened, about 1½ hours.

4. Spoon off any fat from surface of gumbo. Add chicken pieces and filé powder to gumbo and simmer 15 minutes. (If preparing ahead, cover and refrigerate. Bring to a simmer before serving.) Discard bay leaf. Mound rice in shallow bowls, if desired. Ladle gumbo over rice and serve. **Yield:** 8 servings.

★ Filé powder is a Creole seasoning made from ground, dried leaves of the sassafras tree. Find it in the spice or gourmet section of the supermarket.

Per serving: About 732 calories, 41g protein, 18g carbohydrate, 55g fat, 5g fiber, 166mg cholesterol, 1190mg sodium

Chicken and Dumplings III

Submitted by: **Melissa**

"My mom used to make this recipe for us growing up. Now I make it for my family and they all love it! It's simple yet delicious."

7	boneless chicken thighs	1	(12 ounce) can refrigerated
2	(10.75 ounce) cans		buttermilk biscuits
	condensed cream of		Salt and pepper to taste
	celery soup		

1. In a large pot over high heat, combine the chicken and enough water to cover and boil for 15 to 20 minutes. Drain some of the water, reserving 3 cups in the pot. Remove chicken and allow it to cool, then pull it apart into bite size pieces; return to pot.
2. Reduce heat to medium and add the soup. Roll the biscuit dough into tiny balls and add to the soup. Continue simmering over medium heat for 7 to 8 minutes or until the dough balls are cooked through. (Note: Do not allow dough to cook too long or the balls will start to harden.) Add salt and pepper to taste. **Yield:** 6 servings.

Per serving: About 374 calories, 21g protein, 32g carbohydrate, 18g fat, 2g fiber, 68mg cholesterol, 1437mg sodium

Cheesy Potato and Corn Chowder

Submitted by: **Jackay**

"Comfort food . . . hot and tasty for those cold winter days."

2	tablespoons butter or	1	(4.5 ounce) can chopped
	margarine		green chiles
1	cup chopped celery	1	(2 ounce) package country
1	cup chopped onion		style gravy mix
2	(14 ounce) cans chicken	2	cups milk
	broth	1	cup shredded Mexican-
3	cups peeled and cubed		style processed cheese
	potatoes		food
1	(15 ounce) can whole		
	kernel corn, undrained		

1. In a large saucepan, melt butter over medium-high heat. Add celery and onion; cook and stir until tender, about 5 minutes.
2. Add chicken broth; bring to a boil. Add potato; cook over low heat for 20 to 25 minutes or until potato is soft, stirring occasionally.
3. Stir in corn and chiles; return to boiling. Dissolve gravy mix in milk; stir into boiling mixture. Add cheese; cook and stir over low heat until cheese is melted. **Yield:** 7 servings.

Per serving: About 306 calories, 13g protein, 39g carbohydrate, 12g fat, 3g fiber, 22mg cholesterol, 1743mg sodium

My Best Clam Chowder

Submitted by: **Sharon Johnson**
"Add a little red wine vinegar before serving for extra flavor."

3	(6.5 ounce) cans minced clams, undrained	¾	cup all-purpose flour
1	cup minced onion	1	quart half-and-half
1	cup diced celery	2	tablespoons red wine vinegar
2	cups cubed potato	1½	teaspoons salt
1	cup diced carrot		Ground black pepper to taste
¾	cup butter		

1. Drain juice from clams into a large skillet. Add onion, celery, potato, and carrot. Add water to cover; cook over medium heat until tender.
2. Meanwhile, in a large heavy saucepan, melt the butter over medium heat. Whisk in flour until smooth. Whisk in half-and-half and stir constantly until thick and smooth. Stir in vegetables and clam juice. Heat through, but do not boil.
3. Stir in clams just before serving. If they cook too much they get tough. When clams are heated through, stir in vinegar and season with salt and pepper. **Yield:** 8 servings.

Per serving: About 502 calories, 24g protein, 29g carbohydrate, 33g fat, 2g fiber, 137mg cholesterol, 761mg sodium

Salmon Chowder

Submitted by: **Kenulia**
"I'm not a big fan of fish, but I love this soup!"

3	tablespoons butter	1	teaspoon dried dill weed
¾	cup chopped onion	2	(16 ounce) cans salmon, drained
½	cup chopped celery	1	(12 ounce) can evaporated milk
1	teaspoon garlic powder		
2	cups diced potato	1	(15 ounce) can creamed corn
2	cups diced carrot		
2	cups chicken broth	1	(8 ounce) block Cheddar cheese, shredded
1	teaspoon salt		
1	teaspoon ground black pepper		

1. In a large pot over medium heat, melt butter. Cook onion, celery, and garlic powder in butter until onion is translucent. Stir in potato, carrot, broth, salt, pepper, and dill weed. Bring to a boil, cover, reduce heat, and simmer 20 minutes.
2. Stir in salmon, evaporated milk, corn, and Cheddar until cheese is melted and soup is heated through. **Yield:** 8 servings.

Per serving: About 478 calories, 36g protein, 27g carbohydrate, 26g fat, 2g fiber, 103mg cholesterol, 1598mg sodium

Greek Potato Stew

Submitted by: **Diane**

"A delicious stew ripe with the flavors of Greece will impress your family every time."

⅓ cup olive oil
2½ pounds potatoes, peeled and cubed
2 cloves garlic, minced
¾ cup whole, pitted kalamata olives

1⅓ cups chopped tomato
1 teaspoon dried oregano
Salt and pepper to taste

1. In a large sauté pan, heat the oil over medium heat. Add the potato and stir. Stir in the garlic. Add the olives and cook and stir for several minutes. Stir in the tomato and oregano.
2. Reduce heat, cover, and simmer for 30 minutes or until potato is tender. Season to taste with salt and pepper. **Yield:** 6 servings.

Per serving: About 346 calories, 5g protein, 39g carbohydrate, 20g fat, 4g fiber, 0mg cholesterol, 469mg sodium

French Beef Stew

Submitted by: **Corwynn Darkholme**

"Quick and easy, this is a very hearty stew, in truth, a meal in itself. Serve with warm, crusty French bread, if desired."

1½ pounds beef stew meat, cubed
¼ cup all-purpose flour
2 tablespoons vegetable oil
Salt and pepper to taste
2 (14.5 ounce) cans Italian-style diced tomatoes, undrained

1 (14 ounce) can beef broth
4 carrots, chopped
2 potatoes, peeled and chopped
¾ teaspoon dried thyme
2 tablespoons Dijon-style prepared mustard

1. Combine meat and flour in a heavy-duty, zip-top plastic bag and toss to coat evenly.
2. In a 6 quart saucepan, brown meat in hot vegetable oil. Season with salt and pepper.
3. Add diced tomatoes, beef broth, carrot, potato, and thyme. Bring to a boil; reduce heat to medium low, cover, and simmer for 1 hour or until beef is tender.
4. Blend in mustard and serve. **Yield:** 8 servings.

Per serving: About 327 calories, 19g protein, 16g carbohydrate, 20g fat, 3g fiber, 57mg cholesterol, 477mg sodium

Beef Stew IV

Submitted by: **Joanne**
"Revive an old-time favorite with this heartwarming stew."

1	pound beef stew meat, cubed	¼	teaspoon paprika
3	tablespoons all-purpose flour	1	clove garlic, minced
3	tablespoons shortening	1	teaspoon Worcestershire sauce
1	teaspoon salt	1	bay leaf
⅛	teaspoon ground black pepper	3	carrots, quartered
4	cups water	3	potatoes, peeled and quartered
1	onion, diced	1	tablespoon cornstarch
		½	cup frozen corn kernels

1. Dredge beef in flour. In a medium stockpot, brown beef on all sides in shortening. Add salt, pepper, water, onion, paprika, garlic, Worcestershire sauce, and bay leaf. Bring to a boil, cover, and simmer for 2 hours or until meat is tender.

2. Add carrot and potato and simmer for 45 minutes or until tender.

3. Remove meat from stew. Discard bay leaf. Add 1 tablespoon cornstarch and mix to thicken stew. After mixing, let sit for a few minutes to thicken. Add additional cornstarch to thicken as needed.

4. Once thickened, add meat and corn to stew; heat through and serve. **Yield:** 6 servings.

Per serving: About 361 calories, 17g protein, 25g carbohydrate, 21g fat, 3g fiber, 51mg cholesterol, 471mg sodium

Veal Stew

Submitted by: **Marie Kenney**
"My aunt gave me this delicious recipe years ago, and it's still my favorite veal dish. The tomato and white wine sauce keeps the meat tender and moist during cooking. Serve over buttered noodles."

¼	cup olive oil	1	(8 ounce) can tomato sauce
1	onion, chopped	½	cup white wine
2	cloves garlic, minced		Salt and pepper to taste
2	pounds veal, trimmed and cubed		

1. In a large pot, heat oil over medium heat. Add onion and garlic; cook and stir until onion is tender.

2. Add meat to the pot and brown evenly. Stir in tomato sauce and white wine. Season with salt and pepper to taste. Bring to a boil, reduce heat to low, cover, and simmer for 1½ hours. **Yield:** 4 servings.

Per serving: About 463 calories, 45g protein, 7g carbohydrate, 25g fat, 1g fiber, 204mg cholesterol, 557mg sodium

Irish Lamb Stew

Submitted by: **Danny O'Flaugherty**
"This hearty and traditional Irish lamb stew is best when refrigerated overnight and reheated the next day."

1½	pounds thickly sliced bacon, diced	½	cup water
6	pounds boneless lamb shoulder, cut into 2 inch pieces	4	cups beef stock
		2	teaspoons white sugar
½	teaspoon salt	4	cups diced carrot
½	teaspoon ground black pepper	2	large onions, cut into bite-size pieces
½	cup all-purpose flour	3	potatoes
3	cloves garlic, minced	1	teaspoon dried thyme
1	large onion, chopped	2	bay leaves
		1	cup white wine

1. Sauté bacon in a large frying pan; remove bacon, reserving drippings in pan.
2. Put lamb, salt, pepper, and flour in a large bowl; toss to coat meat evenly. Brown meat in drippings in pan. Remove meat and set aside.
3. Add the garlic and onion to the frying pan and sauté until the onion becomes golden. Deglaze pan with ½ cup water.
4. Place cooked meat in a large stockpot. Add garlic and onion, bacon, beef stock, and sugar. Cover and simmer for 1½ hours or until tender. Add carrot and remaining ingredients to pot and simmer covered for 20 minutes until vegetables are tender. Discard bay leaves before serving. **Yield:** 10 servings.

Per serving: About 965 calories, 56g protein, 21g carbohydrate, 70g fat, 3g fiber, 215mg cholesterol, 1106mg sodium

◄ Make-Ahead

Prep Time: 20 minutes
Cook Time: 1 hour 50 minutes
Average Rating: ★★★★★
21 Ratings ▲ 17 Reviews
What other cooks have done:
"I wanted an authentic Irish stew, and this was it. I used beer instead of wine, and I would make sure the potatoes are cubed. It's absolutely better after a few days, if your family doesn't eat it all at once!"

Insanely Easy Vegetarian Chili

Submitted by: **Tianne**

"You can pretty much throw whatever you have into the pot and it'll be great. I added some leftover salsa once. It's very colorful, not to mention delicious."

1	tablespoon vegetable oil	1	(28 ounce) can chopped tomatoes, with juice
1	cup chopped onion		
¾	cup chopped carrot	1	(19 ounce) can kidney beans with liquid
3	cloves garlic, minced		
1	cup chopped green bell pepper	1	(11 ounce) can whole kernel corn, undrained
1	cup chopped red bell pepper	1	tablespoon ground cumin
¾	cup chopped celery	1½	teaspoons oregano
1	tablespoon chili powder	1½	teaspoons crushed basil leaves
1½	cups chopped fresh mushrooms		

1. Heat oil in a large saucepan and add onion, carrot, and garlic; sauté until tender. Stir in green bell pepper, red bell pepper, celery, and chili powder. Cook, stirring often, until vegetables are tender, about 6 minutes.
2. Add mushrooms to the vegetables; cook 4 minutes. Stir in tomatoes, kidney beans, corn, cumin, oregano, and basil. Bring to a boil and reduce heat to medium. Cover and simmer for 20 minutes, stirring occasionally. **Yield:** 8 servings.

Per serving: About 157 calories, 7g protein, 30g carbohydrate, 3g fat, 8g fiber, 0mg cholesterol, 479mg sodium

Fantastic Black Bean Chili

Submitted by: **Rebecca Slone**

"This freezes well and doubles easily for a crowd. Top with shredded cheese."

1	onion, diced	1½	tablespoons chili powder
2	cloves garlic, minced	1	tablespoon dried oregano
1	pound ground turkey	1	tablespoon dried basil
3	(15 ounce) cans black beans, undrained	1	tablespoon red wine vinegar
1	(14.5 ounce) can crushed tomatoes, undrained		

1. In a large, heavy pot over medium heat, cook onion and garlic until onion is translucent. Add turkey and cook, stirring, until meat is browned. Stir in beans, tomatoes, chili powder, oregano, basil, and vinegar. Reduce heat to low, cover, and simmer 1 hour or until flavors are well blended. **Yield:** 6 servings.

Per serving: About 345 calories, 28g protein, 44g carbohydrate, 8g fat, 17g fiber, 60mg cholesterol, 988mg sodium

Debdoozie's Blue Ribbon Chili

Submitted by: **Deb**

"This is the tastiest, easiest chili recipe you'll ever find. I recommend serving it with sliced jalapeño peppers and crackers or cornbread."

2	pounds ground beef	1	(8 ounce) jar salsa
½	onion, chopped	¼	cup chili seasoning mix
1	teaspoon ground black pepper	1	(15 ounce) can light red kidney beans, undrained
½	teaspoon garlic salt	1	(15 ounce) can dark red kidney beans, undrained
2½	cups tomato sauce		

1. In a large saucepan over medium heat, combine the ground beef and the onion and sauté for 10 minutes, or until meat is browned and onion is tender. Drain, if desired.

2. Add the black pepper, garlic salt, tomato sauce, salsa, chili seasoning mix, and light and dark kidney beans. Mix well, reduce heat to low, and simmer for at least an hour. **Yield:** 8 servings.

Per serving: About 504 calories, 27g protein, 27g carbohydrate, 32g fat, 9g fiber, 96mg cholesterol, 1277mg sodium

◀ One-Dish Meal

Prep Time: 10 minutes
Cook Time: 1 hour 10 minutes
Average Rating: ★★★★★
31 Ratings ▲ 21 Reviews
What other cooks have done:
"I used picante sauce instead of salsa. I also used chili powder and cumin in place of the packaged chili seasoning. I will definitely make this again."

Cha Cha's White Chicken Chili

Submitted by: **Cathy**

"Cha Cha says: 'It's kinda spicy, so watch out!' Substitute more green chiles for the jalapeños, if you're timid!"

1	tablespoon vegetable oil	1	teaspoon ground cayenne pepper
1	onion, chopped	2	(10.5 ounce) cans chicken broth
3	cloves garlic, crushed	3	cups chopped cooked chicken breast
1	(4.5 ounce) can diced jalapeño peppers	3	(15 ounce) cans white beans
1	(4.5 ounce) can chopped green chiles	1	cup shredded Monterey Jack cheese
2	teaspoons ground cumin		
1	teaspoon dried oregano		

1. Heat the oil in a large saucepan over medium-low heat. Slowly cook and stir the onion until tender. Mix in the garlic, jalapeño peppers, green chiles, cumin, oregano, and cayenne. Continue to cook and stir the mixture until tender, about 3 minutes. Mix in the chicken broth, chicken, and white beans. Simmer 15 minutes, stirring occasionally.

2. Remove the mixture from heat. Slowly stir in the cheese until melted. Serve warm. **Yield:** 4 servings.

Per serving: About 757 calories, 62g protein, 77g carbohydrate, 23g fat, 17g fiber, 104mg cholesterol, 1908mg sodium

◀ Hot & Spicy

Prep Time: 10 minutes
Cook Time: 20 minutes
Average Rating: ★★★★★
49 Ratings ▲ 42 Reviews
What other cooks have done:
"I cooked the chicken in the broth. I also toasted whole cumin seeds and then ground and added them. You may also want to adjust the amounts of broth, beans, and chicken to yield the consistency you like best (thick or thin). Careful on the jalapeños if the folks you're making it for are sensitive to fiery flavors."

Cincinnati Chili

Submitted by: **Holly**

"An unusual chili, with cinnamon, cloves, and even chocolate! It's best to make this a day ahead and refrigerate it overnight."

1	tablespoon vegetable oil	½	(1 ounce) square unsweetened chocolate
½	cup chopped onion		
2	pounds ground beef	2	(10.5 ounce) cans beef broth
¼	cup chili powder		
1	teaspoon ground cinnamon	1	(15 ounce) can tomato sauce
1	teaspoon ground cumin		
¼	teaspoon ground allspice	2	tablespoons cider vinegar
¼	teaspoon ground cloves		Hot cooked spaghetti
¼	teaspoon ground cayenne pepper	½	cup shredded Cheddar cheese
1	bay leaf		

1. Heat oil in a large saucepan over medium heat. Add onion and cook, stirring frequently, until tender, about 6 minutes.

2. Add beef and cook until browned. Drain, if desired.

3. Add chili powder, cinnamon, cumin, allspice, cloves, cayenne pepper, bay leaf, chocolate, beef broth, tomato sauce, and cider vinegar. Stir to mix well. Bring to a boil. Reduce heat to low; cover and simmer 1½ hours, stirring occasionally.

4. Discard the bay leaf. Serve over hot, drained spaghetti. Top with shredded Cheddar cheese. **Yield:** 8 servings.

Per serving: About 430 calories, 22g protein, 8g carbohydrate, 35g fat, 3g fiber, 100mg cholesterol, 701mg sodium

Desserts

Dive into decadent desserts with this all-star collection of sweet confections that will put the final dazzling touch on your next meal. Stately layer cakes and blue-ribbon pies make perfect fare for entertaining, and simple snack cakes and puddings come together quickly for everyday cooking. And keep that cookie jar overflowing with homemade goodies perfect for the holidays or any time of the year.

Incredibly Delicious Italian Cream Cake

Submitted by: **Rory**

"This is an old recipe from my aunt. It's both famous and infamous in our family, and absolutely irresistible."

1	teaspoon baking soda	8	ounces cream cheese, softened
1	cup buttermilk		
½	cup butter, softened	½	cup butter, softened
½	cup shortening	1	teaspoon vanilla extract
2	cups white sugar	4	cups confectioners' sugar
5	eggs	2	tablespoons half-and-half or whipping cream
1	teaspoon vanilla extract		
1	cup flaked coconut	½	cup chopped walnuts
1	teaspoon baking powder	1	cup flaked coconut
2	cups all-purpose flour		

1. Preheat oven to 350°F (175°C). Grease 3 (9 inch) round pans. In a small bowl, dissolve the baking soda in the buttermilk; set aside.

2. In a large bowl, cream together ½ cup butter, shortening, and white sugar until light and fluffy. Mix in the eggs, buttermilk mixture, 1 teaspoon vanilla, 1 cup coconut, baking powder, and flour. Stir until just combined. Pour batter into the prepared pans.

3. Bake in the preheated oven for 30 to 35 minutes or until a toothpick inserted in the center of the cake comes out clean. Allow cake to cool.

4. In a medium bowl, combine cream cheese, ½ cup butter, 1 teaspoon vanilla, and confectioners' sugar. Beat until light and fluffy. Mix in a small amount of half-and-half to attain the desired consistency. Stir in chopped nuts and 1 cup coconut. Spread between layers and on top and sides of cooled cake. **Yield:** 12 servings.

Per serving: About 778 calories, 8g protein, 98g carbohydrate, 41g fat, 1g fiber, 154mg cholesterol, 439mg sodium

Tiramisu Layer Cake *(pictured on page 298)*

Submitted by: **Bettina Bryant**

"Fancy taste without all the work. This cake is wonderful for a get-together or just a special occasion at home. Using a box cake mix as a base is a real time-saver!"

1 (18.25 ounce) package moist white cake mix	2 tablespoons coffee liqueur
1 teaspoon instant coffee powder	2 cups heavy whipping cream
¼ cup brewed coffee, cooled	¼ cup confectioners' sugar
1 tablespoon coffee liqueur	2 tablespoons coffee liqueur
1 (8 ounce) container mascarpone cheese	2 tablespoons unsweetened cocoa powder
½ cup confectioners' sugar	1 (1.55 ounce) milk chocolate bar

1. Preheat oven to 350°F (175°C). Grease and flour 3 (9 inch) round pans.

2. Prepare the cake mix according to package directions. Divide ⅔ of batter between 2 pans. Stir instant coffee into remaining batter; pour into remaining pan.

3. Bake in the preheated oven for 20 to 25 minutes or until a toothpick inserted in the center of the cake comes out clean. Let cool in pan for 10 minutes, then turn out onto a wire rack to cool completely. In a measuring cup, combine brewed coffee and 1 tablespoon coffee liqueur; set aside.

4. To make filling: In a small bowl, using an electric mixer set on low speed, combine mascarpone, ½ cup confectioners' sugar, and 2 tablespoons coffee liqueur; beat just until smooth. Cover filling with plastic wrap and refrigerate.

5. To make frosting: In a medium bowl, using an electric mixer set on medium-high speed, beat the cream, ¼ cup confectioners' sugar, and 2 tablespoons coffee liqueur until stiff. Fold ½ cup of frosting into filling mixture.

6. To assemble the cake: Place 1 plain cake layer on a serving plate. Using a thin skewer, poke holes in cake, about 1 inch apart. Pour one third of reserved coffee mixture over cake, then spread with half of the filling mixture. Top with coffee-flavored cake layer; poke holes in cake. Pour another third of the coffee mixture over the second layer and spread with the remaining filling. Top with remaining cake layer; poke holes in cake. Pour remaining coffee mixture on top. Spread sides and top of cake with frosting. Place cocoa in a sieve and lightly dust top of cake.

7. Use a vegetable peeler and run it down the edge of the chocolate bar. Garnish cake with chocolate curls. Chill at least 30 minutes before serving. **Yield:** 12 servings.

Per serving: About 476 calories, 5g protein, 47g carbohydrate, 30g fat, 1g fiber, 82mg cholesterol, 310mg sodium

◄ Company is Coming

Prep Time: 30 minutes
Cook Time: 25 minutes
Average Rating: ★★★★★
1 Rating ▲ 1 Review
What other cooks have done:
"I substituted regular cream cheese for the mascarpone and it worked fine. The cake was delicious and a real crowd-pleaser."

Better Than Sex Cake II

Submitted by: **Elaine**

"Rich chocolate cake, caramel, toffee, and whipped topping—need I say more?!"

1	(18.25 ounce) package devil's food cake mix	3	(1.4 ounce) chocolate covered toffee bars, chopped
½	(14 ounce) can sweetened condensed milk	1	(8 ounce) container frozen whipped topping, thawed
6	ounces caramel ice cream topping		

1. Bake cake according to package directions in a 9x13 inch pan; cool on a wire rack for 5 minutes. Make slits across the top of the cake, making sure not to go through to the bottom.

2. In a saucepan over low heat, combine sweetened condensed milk and caramel topping, stirring until smooth and blended. Slowly pour the warm topping mixture over the top of the warm cake, letting it sink into the slits; then sprinkle the chopped chocolate toffee bars liberally across the entire cake while still warm.

3. Let cake cool completely and top with whipped topping. If desired, decorate the top of the cake with some more chocolate toffee bar chunks and swirls of caramel topping. Refrigerate and serve right from the pan. **Yield:** 15 servings.

Per serving: About 310 calories, 5g protein, 47g carbohydrate, 12g fat, 0g fiber, 16mg cholesterol, 334mg sodium

Make-Ahead ▶

Prep Time: 30 minutes

Cook Time: 35 minutes

Average Rating: ★★★★★

181 Ratings ▲ 132 Reviews

What other cooks have done:

"I used two 8 inch round pans to create a layer cake. Since I made the cake the night before the party, I thought it'd be better not to put on the whipped topping for fear that it would make the cake soggy. The cake looked so pretty with the caramel and toffee glaze that I decided that I'd rather serve the whipped topping on the side, and let people help themselves."

Honey Bun Cake

Submitted by: **Jennifer Walker**

"This cake tastes just like the name suggests—like a honey bun. It tastes wonderful served with vanilla ice cream."

1	(18.25 ounce) package yellow cake mix	1	cup brown sugar
¾	cup vegetable oil	1	tablespoon ground cinnamon
4	eggs	2	cups confectioners' sugar
1	(8 ounce) container sour cream	¼	cup milk
		1	tablespoon vanilla extract

1. Preheat oven to 325°F (165°C).

2. In a large mixing bowl, combine cake mix, oil, eggs, and sour cream. Stir by hand approximately 50 strokes, or until most large lumps are gone. Pour half of the batter into an ungreased 9x13 inch glass baking dish. Combine the brown sugar and cinnamon, and sprinkle over the batter in the cake pan. Spoon the other half of the batter into the cake pan, covering the brown sugar and cinnamon. Swirl the cake with a knife until it looks like a honey bun.

Kid-Friendly ▶

Prep Time: 30 minutes

Cook Time: 40 minutes

Average Rating: ★★★★★

181 Ratings ▲ 138 Reviews

What other cooks have done:

"I made this for my husband's office for a breakfast meeting and everyone loved it. Instead of vanilla in the icing, I added rum and they really enjoyed it. It was very easy to make and turned out perfect."

3. Bake in the preheated oven for 40 minutes or until a toothpick inserted into the center of the cake comes out clean.

4. In a small bowl, whisk together the confectioners' sugar, milk, and vanilla until smooth. Spread frosting on cake while it's still warm. Serve warm. **Yield:** 24 servings.

Per serving: About 251 calories, 2g protein, 34g carbohydrate, 12g fat, 0g fiber, 40mg cholesterol, 161mg sodium

Banana Cake VI *(pictured on page 300)*

Submitted by: **Cindy Carnes**
"Do it the old-fashioned way and bake this cake from scratch—you won't be disappointed."

1½	cups mashed bananas (about 4 medium)	2	teaspoons vanilla extract
2	teaspoons lemon juice	1½	cups buttermilk
3	cups all-purpose flour	½	cup butter, softened
1½	teaspoons baking soda	1	(8 ounce) package cream cheese, softened
¼	teaspoon salt	1	teaspoon vanilla extract
¾	cup butter, softened	3½	cups confectioners' sugar
2	cups white sugar	½	cup chopped toasted walnuts
3	eggs		

1. Preheat oven to 350°F (175°C). Grease and flour a 9x13 inch pan. In a small bowl, mix mashed bananas with lemon juice. Set aside. In a medium bowl, mix flour, baking soda, and salt. Set aside.

2. In a large bowl, cream ¾ cup butter and 2 cups sugar until light and fluffy. Beat in the eggs, one at a time, then stir in 2 teaspoons vanilla. Beat in the flour mixture alternately with the buttermilk. Stir in banana mixture. Pour batter into prepared pan.

3. Bake in the preheated oven for 1 hour 5 minutes or until a toothpick inserted into the center of the cake comes out clean. Cool in pan on a wire rack.

4. In a large bowl, cream ½ cup butter and cream cheese until smooth. Beat in 1 teaspoon vanilla. Add confectioners' sugar and beat on low speed until combined, then on high until frosting is smooth. Spread on cooled cake. Sprinkle with chopped nuts. **Yield:** 12 servings.

Per serving: About 682 calories, 8g protein, 103g carbohydrate, 28g fat, 2g fiber, 126mg cholesterol, 506mg sodium

◀ Family Favorite

Prep Time: 30 minutes
Cook Time: 1 hour 5 minutes
Average Rating: ★★★★★
64 Ratings ▲ 52 Reviews
What other cooks have done:
"The cake was so tender and moist. Also, instead of the cream cheese frosting, I made a chocolate fudge frosting topped with toasted chopped pecans. Incredible!"

Sour Cream Coffee Cake III

Submitted by: **Jan Taylor**

"Enjoy this cake with a delicious cup of tea or coffee in the morning."

1	cup butter, softened	1	teaspoon baking powder
2	cups white sugar	⅛	teaspoon salt
2	eggs	⅓	cup all-purpose flour
1	cup sour cream	½	cup packed brown sugar
½	teaspoon vanilla extract	2	tablespoons melted butter
2	cups all-purpose flour	1	teaspoon ground cinnamon

1. Preheat oven to 350°F (175°C). Grease a 9x13 inch pan.

2. Cream 1 cup butter and white sugar. Add eggs, sour cream, and vanilla. Add 2 cups flour, baking powder, and salt. Spread half of batter in pan.

3. Mix together ⅓ cup flour, brown sugar, 2 tablespoons melted butter, and cinnamon. Sprinkle cake batter with half of filling. Spread second half of batter over filling, then sprinkle remaining filling on top.

4. Bake in the preheated oven 35 to 40 minutes. **Yield:** 18 servings.

Per serving: About 306 calories, 3g protein, 41g carbohydrate, 15g fat, 1g fiber, 60mg cholesterol, 177mg sodium

Chocolate Angel Food Cake II

Submitted by: **Karla**

"For best flavor and texture, serve the cake on the day it's made."

¾	cup cake flour	12	egg whites
¼	cup unsweetened cocoa powder	1	teaspoon cream of tartar
1½	cups white sugar, divided	¼	teaspoon salt
3	(1 ounce) squares semisweet chocolate, grated	¼	teaspoon vanilla extract
		1½	teaspoons lemon juice Confectioners' sugar

1. Preheat oven to 325°F (165°C). If your 9 inch tube pan does not have a removable bottom, line with parchment paper. Sift together the flour, cocoa, and ¾ cup of the sugar. Set aside. Measure 3 tablespoons of the flour mixture and toss with the grated chocolate.

2. In a large bowl, using an electric mixer set at low speed, beat egg whites until foamy. Increase speed to medium and stir in cream of tartar and salt; continue to beat until egg whites form soft peaks. Mix in remaining ¾ cup sugar; beat until stiff peaks form. Stir in vanilla and lemon juice.

3. Gently fold the flour mixture into the beaten egg whites. Fold in the grated chocolate, stirring just until no white streaks remain.

4. Pour the batter into the prepared pan. Smooth the surface of the batter and tap the pan lightly to remove air bubbles. Bake in the preheated oven for 1 hour or until the surface springs back when touched. Cool completely and sprinkle with confectioners' sugar. **Yield:** 10 servings.

Per serving: About 220 calories, 6g protein, 45g carbohydrate, 3g fat, 2g fiber, 0mg cholesterol, 125mg sodium

---

Crowd-Pleaser ▶

Prep Time: 20 minutes

Cook Time: 40 minutes

Average Rating: ★★★★★

48 Ratings ▲ 37 Reviews

What other cooks have done:

"I added powdered sugar icing to the top and it was great. My family loved it. The cake is so moist it melts in your mouth."

Healthy ▶

Prep Time: 30 minutes

Cook Time: 1 hour

Average Rating: ★★★★★

8 Ratings ▲ 8 Reviews

What other cooks have done:

"I thought I was going to pass out from smelling it baking. It's awesome! I added bittersweet chocolate in addition to the semisweet. I also ground up some of the chocolate in my processor and sprinkled it over the cake once it was cooled. I'll never make or eat regular angel food cake again!"

Southern Praline Pecan Cake

Submitted by: **Debbie Halford**

"This is an easy and wonderful recipe. All my friends love it."

1	(18.25 ounce) package butter pecan cake mix	¾	cup vegetable oil
1	(16 ounce) container coconut pecan frosting	1	cup water
4	eggs	1	cup chopped pecans, divided

1. Preheat oven to 350°F (175°C). Spray a 9 or 10 inch Bundt pan with nonstick cooking spray.
2. Combine the cake mix with the frosting, eggs, oil, water, and ½ cup of the chopped pecans. Mix until combined.
3. Sprinkle the remaining ½ cup pecans in the prepared Bundt pan, then pour in the cake batter.
4. Bake in the preheated oven for 50 minutes or until a toothpick inserted into center of cake comes out clean. **Yield:** 16 servings.

Per serving: About 415 calories, 3g protein, 41g carbohydrate, 27g fat, 2g fiber, 53mg cholesterol, 257mg sodium

Pumpkin Cake

Submitted by: **D Adams**

"This recipe is good anytime of the year, but it's perfect for the holidays."

1	cup vegetable oil	1	teaspoon ground allspice
3	eggs, lightly beaten	1	teaspoon ground cinnamon
1	(15 ounce) can pumpkin puree	1	teaspoon ground cloves
2½	cups white sugar	¼	teaspoon salt
1	teaspoon vanilla extract	½	cup chopped walnuts (optional)
2½	cups all-purpose flour		Confectioners' sugar for dusting
1	teaspoon baking soda		
1	teaspoon ground nutmeg		

1. Preheat oven to 350°F (175°C). Grease a 10 inch Bundt pan or tube pan.
2. Cream oil, beaten eggs, pumpkin, sugar, and vanilla together.
3. Sift the flour, baking soda, nutmeg, allspice, cinnamon, cloves, and salt together. Add the flour mixture to the pumpkin mixture and mix until just combined. If desired, stir in chopped nuts. Pour batter into the prepared pan.
4. Bake in the preheated oven for 1 hour or until a toothpick inserted into the center of cake comes out clean. Let cake cool in pan for 5 minutes, then turn out onto a plate and dust with confectioners' sugar. **Yield:** 12 servings.

Per serving: About 484 calories, 5g protein, 66g carbohydrate, 23g fat, 2g fiber, 53mg cholesterol, 256mg sodium

Chocolate Lovers' Favorite Cake

Submitted by: **Susan Feiler**
"This easy recipe is a chocoholic's dream come true!"

1	(18.25 ounce) package devil's food cake mix	1	cup butter, melted
1	(3.4 ounce) package instant chocolate pudding mix	5	eggs
1	(16 ounce) container sour cream	1	teaspoon almond extract
		1	(12 ounce) package semisweet chocolate chips

1. Preheat oven to 350°F (175°C). Grease a 10 inch Bundt pan.
2. In a large bowl, stir together cake mix and pudding mix. Make a well in the center and pour in sour cream, melted butter, eggs, and almond extract. Beat on low speed until blended. Scrape bowl and beat 4 minutes on medium speed. Stir in chocolate chips. Pour batter into prepared pan.
3. Bake in the preheated oven for 55 to 60 minutes. Let cool in pan for 10 minutes, then turn out onto a wire rack and cool completely.
Yield: 12 servings.

Per serving: About 601 calories, 9g protein, 57g carbohydrate, 40g fat, 2g fiber, 155mg cholesterol, 640mg sodium

Kentucky Butter Cake

Submitted by: **Suzanne Stull**
"Don't pass up this moist and buttery cake made from readily available ingredients with a luscious butter sauce."

3	cups all-purpose flour	2	teaspoons vanilla extract
2	cups white sugar	4	eggs
1	teaspoon salt	¾	cup white sugar
1	teaspoon baking powder	⅓	cup butter
½	teaspoon baking soda	2	teaspoons vanilla extract
1	cup buttermilk	3	tablespoons water
1	cup butter, softened		

1. Preheat oven to 325°F (165°C). Grease and flour a 10 inch Bundt pan.
2. In a large bowl, mix the flour, 2 cups sugar, salt, baking powder, and baking soda. Blend in buttermilk, 1 cup butter, 2 teaspoons vanilla, and eggs. Beat for 3 minutes at medium speed. Pour batter into prepared pan.
3. Bake in the preheated oven for 1 hour or until a toothpick inserted into center of cake comes out clean. Prick holes in the warm cake. Slowly pour butter sauce over cake. Cool before removing from pan.
4. To make butter sauce: In a saucepan, combine ¾ cup sugar, ⅓ cup butter, 2 teaspoons vanilla, and water. Cook over medium heat, until fully melted and combined, but do not boil. **Yield:** 12 servings.

Per serving: About 509 calories, 6g protein, 71g carbohydrate, 23g fat, 1g fiber, 127mg cholesterol, 529mg sodium

Old-Fashioned Coconut
Cream Pie, page 322

Tiramisu Layer Cake,
page 291

Irish Cream Truffle
Fudge, page 343

Creamy Caramel Flan,
page 23

Caramel Shortbread
Squares, page 336

Banana Cake VI,
page 293

Black Bottom Cupcakes,
page 308

Chocolate Trifle, page 331

Chocolate Chip Cookie
Ice Cream Cake, page 312

Pecan-Sour Cream Pound Cake,
facing page

Pecan-Sour Cream Pound Cake *(pictured on facing page)*

Submitted by: **Carole Resnick**

"I won first place with this cake at the Cuyahoga County Fair in Cleveland, Ohio, in 1993. For a nuttier variation, you can substitute 1 cup of the flour with 1 cup of ground pecans."

¼	cup chopped pecans	6	eggs
3	cups cake flour	1	teaspoon vanilla extract
¼	teaspoon salt	1	(8 ounce) container sour cream
¼	teaspoon baking soda		
1	cup unsalted butter, softened	2	cups confectioners' sugar
		3	tablespoons orange juice
3	cups white sugar	1	teaspoon vanilla extract

1. Preheat oven to 300°F (150°C). Grease and flour a 10 inch tube pan. Sprinkle pecans in pan; set aside. Mix together flour, salt, and baking soda into a medium bowl; set aside.
2. In a large bowl, cream butter and white sugar until light and fluffy. Beat in eggs, one at a time, then stir in vanilla. Add flour mixture alternately with sour cream. Pour batter over pecans in the prepared pan.
3. Bake in the preheated oven for 80 to 90 minutes or until a toothpick inserted into the center of the cake comes out clean. Let cool in pan for 20 minutes, then turn out onto a wire rack.
4. In a small bowl, combine confectioners' sugar, orange juice, and 1 teaspoon vanilla. Drizzle over warm cake. **Yield:** 12 servings.

Per serving: About 597 calories, 7g protein, 90g carbohydrate, 24g fat, 1g fiber, 156mg cholesterol, 168mg sodium

◄ Blue Ribbon Winner

Prep Time: 30 minutes
Cook Time: 1 hour 30 minutes
Average Rating: ★★★★★
59 Ratings ▲ 49 Reviews
What other cooks have done:
"Add the same amount of lemon extract as vanilla extract for just a touch of lemon and it's excellent. This is definitely the best cake I've ever made. I could have eaten the whole cake myself—it came out so nicely."

Aunt Johnnie's Pound Cake

Submitted by: **Jean Higginbotham**
"Absolutely wonderful plain or served with strawberries and whipped cream."

½	cup shortening	2	teaspoons almond extract
1	cup butter, softened	½	teaspoon baking powder
2½	cups white sugar	3	cups cake flour
5	eggs	1	cup milk

1. Preheat oven to 300°F (150°C). Lightly grease and flour a 10 inch Bundt pan.
2. Cream shortening, butter, and sugar until light and fluffy. Beat in eggs, one at a time, beating well after each addition. Mix in almond extract. Combine baking powder and flour. Stir into creamed mixture alternately with the milk, beginning and ending with flour. Pour batter into prepared pan.
3. Bake in the preheated oven for 1 to 1½ hours or until a toothpick inserted into center of cake comes out clean. Let cool in pan for 10 minutes; turn out onto a wire rack and cool completely. **Yield:** 12 servings.

Per serving: About 547 calories, 6g protein, 71g carbohydrate, 27g fat, 1g fiber, 131mg cholesterol, 214mg sodium

Apple Bundt Cake

Submitted by: **Carol**
"This is a good wholesome cake, especially nice for the fall."

2	cups apples, peeled, cored, and diced	2	cups white sugar
		1	cup vegetable oil
1	tablespoon white sugar	¼	cup orange juice
1	teaspoon ground cinnamon	2½	teaspoons vanilla extract
3	cups all-purpose flour	4	eggs
1	tablespoon baking powder	1	cup chopped walnuts
½	teaspoon salt	¼	cup confectioners' sugar

1. Preheat oven to 350°F (175°C). Grease and flour a 10 inch Bundt or tube pan. In a medium bowl, combine the diced apples, 1 tablespoon white sugar, and 1 teaspoon cinnamon; set aside. Sift together the flour, baking powder, and salt; set aside.
2. In a large bowl, combine 2 cups white sugar, oil, orange juice, vanilla, and eggs. Beat at high speed until smooth. Stir in flour mixture. Fold in nuts.
3. Pour ⅓ of the batter into prepared pan. Sprinkle with ½ of the apple mixture. Alternate layers of batter and filling, ending with batter.
4. Bake in the preheated oven for 55 to 60 minutes or until the top springs back when lightly touched. Let cool in pan for 10 minutes, then turn out onto a wire rack and cool completely. Sprinkle with confectioners' sugar. **Yield:** 12 servings.

Per serving: About 526 calories, 7g protein, 67g carbohydrate, 27g fat, 2g fiber, 71mg cholesterol, 241mg sodium

Irish Cream Bundt Cake

Submitted by: **Sue Haser**

"Great tasting glazed Bundt cake flavored with Irish cream. Excellent for any time or any occasion."

1	cup chopped pecans	½	cup vegetable oil
1	(18.25 ounce) package yellow cake mix	¾	cup Irish cream liqueur
		½	cup butter
1	(3.4 ounce) package instant vanilla pudding mix	¼	cup water
		1	cup white sugar
4	eggs	¼	cup Irish cream liqueur
¼	cup water		

1. Preheat oven to 325°F (165°C). Grease and flour a 10 inch Bundt pan. Sprinkle chopped nuts evenly in pan.

2. In a large bowl, combine cake mix and pudding mix. Mix in eggs, ¼ cup water, ½ cup oil, and ¾ cup liqueur. Beat for 5 minutes at high speed. Pour batter over nuts in pan.

3. Bake in the preheated oven for 1 hour or until a toothpick inserted in the cake comes out clean. Cool for 10 minutes in the pan, then invert onto the serving dish. Prick top and sides of cake. Spoon glaze over top and brush onto sides of cake. Allow to absorb glaze and repeat until all glaze is used up.

4. To make the glaze: In a saucepan, combine butter, ¼ cup water, and 1 cup sugar. Bring to a boil and continue boiling for 5 minutes, stirring constantly. Remove from heat and stir in ¼ cup liqueur. **Yield:** 12 servings.

Per serving: About 596 calories, 5g protein, 69g carbohydrate, 31g fat, 1g fiber, 92mg cholesterol, 498mg sodium

◄ Out-of-the-Ordinary

Prep Time: 15 minutes
Cook Time: 1 hour
Average Rating: ★★★★★
53 Ratings ▲ 44 Reviews
What other cooks have done:
"I made this for a Fourth of July picnic and it went over really well! I had only chocolate cake mix and pudding available, so that's what I used and it was absolutely blissful."

Black Bottom Cupcakes *(pictured on page 301)*

Submitted by: **Laura Duncan Allen**
"Serve these little gems with a tall glass of ice cold milk."

Kid-Friendly ▶

Prep Time: 30 minutes

Cook Time: 30 minutes

Average Rating: ★★★★★

50 Ratings ▲ 34 Reviews

What other cooks have done:

"I made these to send to my son's kindergarten class for his 6th birthday. The kids loved them and I liked how easy they were to send to school without the big frosting mess! We saved a few for ourselves and my husband's comment was, 'Why don't you ever make things like this for us?'"

1	(8 ounce) package cream cheese, softened	¼	cup unsweetened cocoa powder
1	egg	1	teaspoon baking soda
⅓	cup white sugar	½	teaspoon salt
⅛	teaspoon salt	1	cup water
1	cup miniature semisweet chocolate chips	⅓	cup vegetable oil
1½	cups all-purpose flour	1	tablespoon cider vinegar
1	cup white sugar	1	teaspoon vanilla extract

1. Preheat oven to 350°F (175°C). Line muffin tins with paper cups or lightly spray with cooking spray.
2. In a medium bowl, beat the cream cheese, egg, ⅓ cup sugar, and ⅛ teaspoon salt until light and fluffy. Stir in the chocolate chips; set aside.
3. In a large bowl, mix together the flour, 1 cup sugar, cocoa, baking soda, and ½ teaspoon salt. Make a well in the center and add the water, oil, vinegar, and vanilla. Stir until well blended. Fill muffin tins ⅓ full with the batter and top with a dollop of the cream cheese mixture.
4. Bake in the preheated oven for 25 to 30 minutes. **Yield:** 2 dozen.

Per serving: About 178 calories, 2g protein, 23g carbohydrate, 9g fat, 1g fiber, 19mg cholesterol, 144mg sodium

Cream Puff Cake

Submitted by: **Nancy**
"This is like a giant éclair filled with cream cheese and drizzled with chocolate."

Crowd-Pleaser ▶

Prep Time: 20 minutes

Cook Time: 35 minutes

Average Rating: ★★★★★

72 Ratings ▲ 59 Reviews

What other cooks have done:

"I made this for a church social, and it was the first to go! Kids and grown-ups liked it. I can't wait to try variations like strawberries and bananas, chocolate pudding, or coconut cream. Everyone who tried it asked for the recipe."

½	cup butter	4	cups milk
1	cup water	3	(3.4 ounce) packages instant vanilla pudding mix
1	cup all-purpose flour		
4	eggs	1	(12 ounce) container frozen whipped topping, thawed
1	(8 ounce) package cream cheese	¼	cup chocolate syrup

1. Preheat oven to 400°F (200°C).
2. In a large heavy saucepan, heat butter and water to boiling over medium-high heat. Add flour and reduce heat to low. Cook and stir until it forms a ball and pulls away from the pan. Remove from heat; transfer to a large bowl. Beat in eggs, one at a time, beating well after each egg. Spread mixture in bottom and up sides of an ungreased 9x13 inch pan. Bake in the preheated oven for 35 minutes. Cool shell completely.
3. In a large bowl, combine cream cheese and milk; beat until smooth. Add pudding mix and beat until thickened. Spread over cooled shell. Top with whipped topping; drizzle with chocolate syrup. **Yield:** 24 servings.

Per serving: About 216 calories, 4g protein, 23g carbohydrate, 12g fat, 0g fiber, 59mg cholesterol, 280mg sodium

Strawberry Shortcake *(pictured on page 1)*

Submitted by: **Denyse**
"An old fashioned, tender shortcake with two layers of strawberries topped with whipped cream."

3	pints fresh strawberries	⅓	cup shortening
½	cup white sugar	1	egg, lightly beaten
2¼	cups all-purpose flour	⅔	cup milk
4	teaspoons baking powder	1	(12 ounce) container frozen
2	tablespoons white sugar		whipped topping
¼	teaspoon salt		

1. Slice the strawberries and toss them with ½ cup of sugar. Set aside.
2. Preheat oven to 425°F (220°C). Grease and flour an 8 inch round pan.
3. In a medium bowl, combine the flour, baking powder, 2 tablespoons sugar, and salt. With a pastry blender, cut in the shortening until the mixture resembles coarse crumbs. Make a well in the center and add the beaten egg and milk. Stir until just combined.
4. Spread the batter into the prepared pan. Bake in the preheated oven for 15 to 20 minutes or until golden brown. Let cool partially in pan on a wire rack.
5. Slice partially cooled cake in half horizontally, making 2 layers. Place half of the strawberries on 1 layer and top with the other layer. Top with remaining strawberries and cover with the whipped topping.
Yield: 9 servings.

Per serving: About 380 calories, 6g protein, 48g carbohydrate, 19g fat, 4g fiber, 61mg cholesterol, 309mg sodium

◄ Family Favorite

Prep Time: 30 minutes
Cook Time: 20 minutes
Average Rating: ★★★★☆
14 Ratings ▲ 10 Reviews
What other cooks have done:
"I added a little bit more sugar to the shortcake batter and then topped it with melted margarine and sprinkled with sugar before baking."

The Strawberry Story ▼

When springtime gently settles across the land, we kick off one of the most anxiously anticipated events of the year: strawberry season! We find it impossible to resist these plump, glistening, ruby-red gems winking at us from the grocery store displays, farmers' markets, and roadside stands everywhere. The tart sweetness of these berries is the height of perfection whether they are drizzled with cream, dipped in chocolate, sliced over ice cream, or simply scarfed out of the basket on the way home from the market. Packed with vitamins A, C, and B6, and boasting a meager 48 calories per cup, strawberries are an indulgence that you won't regret in the morning!

Your Nose Knows

When you're buying strawberries, you should let your nose be your guide. The aroma of your strawberries should make your mouth water. If it doesn't, either you don't like strawberries (highly unlikely!) or the strawberries are not really ripe (entirely possible). When strawberries are farmed on a large, commercial scale, they're often picked while still green in order to help them stand up to shipping. Unfortunately, even though strawberries will continue to get redder and softer once they have been picked, they will not get any sweeter. So, a basket of strawberries may look tantalizingly red, but if you cannot catch a whiff of their ripe, sweet fragrance, you'll probably be disappointed with their flavor.

If you do manage to get your strawberries home without eating them all, make room for them in the refrigerator. If they did not come in a ventilated container with a plastic lid, place them in a bowl, cover with plastic wrap, and poke several holes in the plastic. This storage method is intended to allow the berries to breathe, but also to prevent them from losing too much moisture. Strawberries will decay much more quickly after they've been washed, so hold off until you are ready to use them.

-*Jennifer Anderson*

For more information, visit **Allrecipes.com**

Cannoli Cake Roll

Submitted by: **Shirley**
"A decadent and rich jellyroll style cake makes a wonderful presentation and is well worth the effort!"

Company is Coming ▶

Prep Time: 1 hour 15 minutes
Cook Time: 10 minutes
Average Rating: ★★★★★
17 Ratings ▲ 14 Reviews

What other cooks have done:
"I made this the night before my mom's 60th birthday party. It looked so good we called my mom over that night and ate it. Shhh, don't tell the rest of the family. I did have to make something else to replace it. It really isn't hard at all, and it's well worth it."

5	eggs, separated	½	teaspoon vanilla extract
1	teaspoon vanilla extract	¼	teaspoon ground cinnamon
¼	cup white sugar		
¼	teaspoon cream of tartar	¼	cup mini semisweet chocolate chips
¼	teaspoon salt		
¼	cup white sugar	¾	cup heavy whipping cream
¾	cup cake flour, sifted		
2	tablespoons orange liqueur	3	tablespoons confectioners' sugar
1	tablespoon water	2	tablespoons orange liqueur
1	tablespoon white sugar	½	teaspoon vanilla extract
	Confectioners' sugar for dusting	¼	cup chopped pistachio nuts
1¼	cups ricotta cheese	1	tablespoon mini semisweet chocolate chips
4	ounces cream cheese		
½	cup confectioners' sugar		

1. Preheat oven to 375°F (190°C). Grease a 10x15 inch jellyroll pan and line with parchment paper.

2. In small bowl, with mixer at high speed, beat egg yolks, vanilla, and ¼ cup sugar until very thick and lemon colored, about 5 minutes. Set beaten yolk mixture aside.

3. In large bowl, with clean beaters and with mixer at high speed, beat egg whites, cream of tartar, and salt until soft peaks form. Beating at high speed, gradually sprinkle in ¼ cup sugar until sugar dissolves and whites stand in stiff peaks.

4. Transfer egg yolk mixture to another large bowl. With rubber spatula, gently fold beaten egg whites into egg yolk mixture, one-third at a time. Fold flour, one-third at a time, into egg mixture.

5. With spatula, spread batter evenly in pan. Bake in the preheated oven for 10 minutes or until top of cake springs back when lightly touched with finger.

6. Meanwhile, mix 2 tablespoons orange liqueur with 1 tablespoon water and 1 tablespoon sugar until sugar dissolves.

7. Sprinkle a clean cloth towel with confectioners' sugar. When cake is done, immediately invert hot cake onto towel. Carefully peel off parchment paper and discard. Brush cake with orange liqueur mixture. Starting from a long side, roll up cake with towel jellyroll fashion. Place cake roll, seam side down, on a wire rack to completely cool, about 1 hour.

8. In food processor, with knife blade attached, blend the ricotta cheese, cream cheese, ½ cup confectioners' sugar, ½ teaspoon vanilla, and cinnamon until smooth. Transfer filling to bowl and stir in ¼ cup chocolate chips. Cover and refrigerate filling while cake cools.

9. Gently unroll cooled cake. With spatula, spread ricotta filling over cake almost to edges. Starting from same long side, roll cake without towel. Place rolled cake, seam side down, on a platter.

10. In small bowl, with mixer at medium speed, beat whipping cream and 3 tablespoons confectioners' sugar until soft peaks form. Fold in 2 tablespoons orange liqueur and ½ teaspoon vanilla. Spread frosting over cake. Refrigerate cake at least 2 hours before serving. Sprinkle top of cake with chopped pistachios and chocolate chips just before serving. **Yield:** 15 servings.

Per serving: About 230 calories, 5g protein, 26g carbohydrate, 11g fat, 0g fiber, 31mg cholesterol, 119mg sodium

Funnel Cakes II

Submitted by: **Sally**
"These are Pennsylvania Dutch cakes. The batter is poured through a funnel into cooking oil and fried."

1	egg	½	teaspoon cream of tartar
1	cup milk	2	tablespoons white sugar
1⅔	cups all-purpose flour		Vegetable oil
¼	teaspoon salt	¼	cup confectioners' sugar for
¾	teaspoon baking soda		dusting

1. In a mixing bowl, beat together egg and milk. Beat in flour, salt, baking soda, cream of tartar, and white sugar until smooth.

2. Heat about 1 inch of vegetable oil in a frying pan to 375°F (190°C).

3. Pour ½ cup batter through funnel into oil in a circular motion to form a spiral. Fry 30 seconds or until lightly browned; turn over to brown the other side, about 30 seconds more. Cook until golden brown and remove to drain on paper towels. Sprinkle with confectioners' sugar while still warm. **Yield:** 10 servings.

Per serving: About 118 calories, 4g protein, 23g carbohydrate, 1g fat, 1g fiber, 23mg cholesterol, 172mg sodium

◄ Blue Ribbon Winner

Prep Time: 10 minutes
Cook Time: 10 minutes
Average Rating: ★★★★★
26 Ratings ▲ 17 Reviews
What other cooks have done:
"I think these are better than the ones you get at the fair, and they don't take very long to make. I'm going to make them for Valentine's Day by using my heart insert for my springform pan. I'm going to try them with whipping cream and fruit on top."

Chocolate Chip Cookie Ice Cream Cake *(pictured on page 303)*

Submitted by: **Arvilla**

"Vary this dessert by using different flavors of ice cream."

1	(18 ounce) package small chocolate chip cookies	2	quarts vanilla ice cream
¼	cup butter or margarine, melted	1	cup whipped cream or frozen whipped topping
1	cup hot fudge topping	12	cherries (optional)

1. Crush half the cookies (about 20) to make crumbs. Combine crumbs with melted butter and press into the bottom of a 9 inch springform pan. Stand remaining cookies around edge of pan. Spread ¾ cup fudge topping over crust. Freeze 15 minutes.

2. Meanwhile, soften 1 quart of ice cream in microwave or on countertop. After crust has chilled, spread softened ice cream over fudge layer. Freeze 30 minutes.

3. Scoop remaining quart of ice cream into balls and arrange over spread ice cream layer. Freeze until firm, 4 hours or overnight. To serve, garnish with remainder of fudge topping, whipped cream, and cherries, if desired. **Yield:** 12 servings.

Per serving: About 529 calories, 6g protein, 68g carbohydrate, 27g fat, 2g fiber, 43mg cholesterol, 324mg sodium

Chantal's New York Cheesecake

Submitted by: **Chantal Rogers**

"This cake is easy to make, and it's so delicious. Everyone that's tried it has said it tasted just like the ones in a deli. You'll love it!"

15	graham crackers, crushed	¾	cup milk
2	tablespoons butter, melted	4	eggs
4	(8 ounce) packages cream cheese	1	cup sour cream
1½	cups white sugar	1	tablespoon vanilla extract
		¼	cup all-purpose flour

1. Preheat oven to 350°F (175°C). Grease a 9 inch springform pan.

2. In a medium bowl, mix graham cracker crumbs with melted butter. Press into bottom of springform pan.

3. In a large bowl, mix cream cheese with sugar until smooth. Blend in milk, and add the eggs, one at a time, mixing just enough to incorporate. Mix in sour cream, vanilla, and flour until smooth. Pour filling into prepared crust.

4. Bake in the preheated oven for 1 hour. Turn the oven off and let cake cool in oven with the door closed for 1 hour (this prevents cracking). Chill in refrigerator until serving. **Yield:** 12 servings.

Per serving: About 534 calories, 10g protein, 44g carbohydrate, 36g fat, 1g fiber, 168mg cholesterol, 385mg sodium

Irish Cream Chocolate Cheesecake

Submitted by: **Elaine**

"If you like Irish cream and chocolate, you'll love this recipe. After numerous attempts with the ingredients, this is the recipe I now use."

1½ cups chocolate cookie crumbs
⅓ cup confectioners' sugar
⅓ cup unsweetened cocoa powder
¼ cup butter, melted
3 (8 ounce) packages cream cheese, softened
1¼ cups white sugar
¼ cup unsweetened cocoa powder
3 tablespoons all-purpose flour
3 eggs
½ cup sour cream
¼ cup Irish cream liqueur

1. Preheat oven to 350°F (175°C). In a large bowl, mix together the cookie crumbs, confectioners' sugar, and ⅓ cup cocoa. Add melted butter and stir until well mixed. Pat into the bottom of a 9 inch springform pan. Bake in the preheated oven for 10 minutes; set aside. Increase oven temperature to 450°F (230°C).

2. In a large bowl, combine cream cheese, white sugar, ¼ cup cocoa, and flour. Beat at medium speed until well blended and smooth. Add eggs, one at a time, mixing well after each addition. Blend in the sour cream and Irish cream liqueur; mix on low speed. Pour filling over baked crust.

3. Bake in the preheated oven for 10 minutes. Reduce oven temperature to 250°F (120°C) and continue baking for 1 hour.

4. With a knife, loosen cake from rim of pan. Let cool, then remove the rim of pan. Chill before serving. If your cake cracks, a helpful tip is to dampen a spatula and smooth the top, then sprinkle with some chocolate wafer crumbs. **Yield:** 12 servings.

Per serving: About 458 calories, 8g protein, 42g carbohydrate, 29g fat, 2g fiber, 129mg cholesterol, 308mg sodium

◄ Holiday Fare

Prep Time: 20 minutes
Cook Time: 1 hour 20 minutes
Average Rating: ★★★★★
117 Ratings ▲ 86 Reviews
What other cooks have done:
"This was the second cheesecake I ever made, and it turned out perfect. I love this recipe. I used Kahlúa instead of Irish cream and got the most wonderful flavor combination. What a wonderful cheesecake and a great holiday party dessert!"

Chocolate Turtle Cheesecake *(pictured on page 4)*

Submitted by: **Stephanie**

"A cheesecake reminiscent of the turtle shaped chocolate and caramel nut candy. Garnish with whipped cream, chopped nuts, and maraschino cherries, if desired."

2	cups vanilla wafer crumbs	1	cup chopped pecans
2	tablespoons unsalted butter, melted	2	(8 ounce) packages cream cheese, softened
1	(14 ounce) package individually wrapped caramels	½	cup white sugar
		1	teaspoon vanilla extract
1	(5 ounce) can evaporated milk	2	eggs
		½	cup semisweet chocolate chips, melted

1. Preheat oven to 350°F (175°C). In a large bowl, mix together the cookie crumbs and melted butter. Press into the bottom of a 9 inch springform pan.

2. In a heavy saucepan over low heat, melt the caramels with the evaporated milk. Heat and stir frequently until smooth, about 15 minutes. Pour caramel sauce into crust and top with pecans.

3. In a large bowl, combine cream cheese, sugar, and vanilla; beat well until smooth. Add eggs, one at a time, mixing well after each addition. Blend melted chocolate chips into cream cheese mixture. Pour chocolate batter over pecans.

4. Bake in the preheated oven for 40 to 50 minutes or until filling is almost set. Turn oven off, partially open door, and let cheesecake cool in oven 1 hour. Remove from oven and loosen cake from the edges of pan. Chill for 4 hours or overnight. **Yield:** 16 servings.

Per serving: About 433 calories, 7g protein, 47g carbohydrate, 26g fat, 2g fiber, 65mg cholesterol, 230mg sodium

Chocolate Frosting

Submitted by: **Tianne**

"This classic frosting has great texture and color as well as taste. Smooth and easily spread, it turns any cake, cookie, or cupcake into something deliciously special."

¼	cup butter or margarine, softened	⅓	cup milk
		1	teaspoon vanilla extract
½	cup unsweetened cocoa powder	3½	cups confectioners' sugar

1. In a large bowl, beat butter and cocoa together until combined. Add milk and vanilla; beat until smooth. Gradually beat in confectioners' sugar to desired consistency. Adjust with more milk or confectioners' sugar, if necessary. **Yield:** 2 cups (12 servings).

Per serving: About 188 calories, 1g protein, 39g carbohydrate, 4g fat, 1g fiber, 1mg cholesterol, 48mg sodium

Special Buttercream Frosting

Submitted by: **Rick Mazzuca**
"Ideal buttercream for frosting and borders."

2	cups shortening	2	teaspoons vanilla extract
8	cups confectioners' sugar	⅔	cup whipping cream
½	teaspoon salt		

1. Cream shortening until fluffy. Add confectioners' sugar and continue creaming until well blended.
2. Add salt, vanilla, and whipping cream and blend on low speed until moistened. Add additional whipping cream if necessary. Beat at high speed until frosting is fluffy. **Yield:** 7½ cups (36 servings).

Per serving: About 222 calories, 0g protein, 27g carbohydrate, 13g fat, 0g fiber, 7mg cholesterol, 34mg sodium

Cream Cheese Frosting II

Submitted by: **JJ**
"Your basic cream cheese frosting will crown any cake to perfection."

½	cup butter, softened	4	cups confectioners' sugar
8	ounces cream cheese, softened	2	teaspoons vanilla extract

1. Beat softened butter and cream cheese until well blended.
2. Add confectioners' sugar and vanilla. Beat until creamy. **Yield:** 2 cups (12 servings).

Per serving: About 291 calories, 2g protein, 40g carbohydrate, 14g fat, 0g fiber, 41mg cholesterol, 134mg sodium

Grandma's Secret Pie Crust

Submitted by: **Felicia Bass**
"The secret's out! A great basic pie crust recipe."

3	cups all–purpose flour	1	tablespoon white
1	teaspoon salt		vinegar
1¼	cups shortening	¼	cup water
1	egg, beaten		

1. Preheat oven to 425°F (220°C). In a large bowl, mix together flour and salt. Cut in shortening with 2 butter knives or a pastry blender.
2. In a separate bowl, mix together egg, vinegar, and water. Drizzle wet mixture into dry mixture, cutting it in.
3. Roll out dough and fit into 2 (9 inch) pie dishes.
4. Bake in the preheated oven for 12 minutes. **Yield:** 2 pie crusts (16 servings).

Per serving: About 232 calories, 3g protein, 18g carbohydrate, 17g fat, 1g fiber, 13mg cholesterol, 150mg sodium

Apple Selection Chart ▼

The apple variety you choose should depend on what you'll use it for. This chart features the most popular varieties of apples available to shoppers. Look on page 61 for more information about selecting the right apple for your cooking and baking needs.

Type	Appearance	Flavor	Uses
Braeburn	Red with yellow-green overtone	Tart-sweet	All-purpose
Cortland	Large, red with greenish-yellow highlights	Pleasing tartness	All-purpose
Empire	Red	Tart-sweet	All-purpose
Fuji	Yellowish-green	Sweet-slightly spicy	All-purpose
Gala	Red with golden overtone	Sweet	Eating
Golden Delicious	Yellow with a faint pink blush	Sweet	All-purpose
Granny Smith	Bright green	Tart	All-purpose
Jonathan	Bright red	Slightly tart	All-purpose
McIntosh	Red with green overtone	Tart-sweet	All-purpose
Pippin	Pale yellowish-green	Slightly tart	All-purpose
Red Delicious	Red; elongated body	Sweet	Eating
Rome	Deep red	Tart-sweet	Cooking
Stayman	Dull red	Tart	All-purpose
Winesap	Dark red	Tangy-winy	All-purpose
York	Red with yellowish overtone	Slightly tart	Cooking

Apple Pie by Grandma Ople *(pictured on cover)*

Submitted by: **Rebecca Clyma**

"This was my grandmother's apple pie recipe. I have never seen another one quite like it. It will always be my favorite. I've won several first place prizes in local competitions. I hope it becomes one of your favorites as well!"

½ cup unsalted butter	½ cup packed brown sugar
3 tablespoons all-purpose flour	6 Granny Smith apples, peeled, cored, and thinly sliced
¼ cup water	Pastry for a 9 inch double crust pie
½ cup white sugar	

1. Preheat oven to 425°F (220°C). Melt the butter in a saucepan. Stir in flour to form a paste. Add water, white sugar, and brown sugar; bring to a boil. Reduce temperature and let simmer about 2 minutes. Add apple to sugar mixture and mix well.

2. Line pie dish with 1 pie crust. Fill crust with apples, mounded slightly. Cut remaining crust into ½ inch strips. Arrange strips in a lattice design over apples.

3. Bake in the preheated oven for 15 minutes. Reduce temperature to 350°F (175°C). Continue baking for 50 to 55 minutes, shielding pie after 10 to 15 minutes, until apples are soft. **Yield:** 8 servings.

Per serving: About 521 calories, 3g protein, 70g carbohydrate, 27g fat, 6g fiber, 31mg cholesterol, 241mg sodium

Apple Crumble Pie

Submitted by: **Penny Lehoux**

"Yummy variety of apple pie that's quick and easy. It was a hit with my boyfriend's pals at college whenever I made this favorite!"

5 cups apples, peeled, cored, and thinly sliced	¾ teaspoon ground cinnamon
Pastry for a 9 inch deep dish single crust pie	⅓ cup white sugar
	¾ cup all-purpose flour
½ cup white sugar	6 tablespoons butter

1. Preheat oven to 400°F (200°C). Arrange apple slices in unbaked pie crust. Mix ½ cup sugar and cinnamon; sprinkle over apples.

2. Mix ⅓ cup sugar with flour; cut in butter until crumbly. Spoon mixture over apples.

3. Bake in the preheated oven for 35 to 40 minutes or until apples are soft and top is lightly browned. **Yield:** 8 servings.

Per serving: About 344 calories, 3g protein, 54g carbohydrate, 15g fat, 3g fiber, 23mg cholesterol, 175mg sodium

Blackberry Pie

Submitted by: **Michelle Verdiere**

"I've been using this recipe for years, and it's always a success. Frozen or fresh blackberries can be used. Serve with vanilla ice cream."

4 cups fresh blackberries, divided	Pastry for a 9 inch double crust pie
½ cup white sugar	2 tablespoons milk
½ cup all-purpose flour	¼ cup white sugar

1. Preheat oven to 425°F (220°C). Combine 3½ cups berries with ½ cup sugar and flour. Line pie dish with 1 pie crust. Spoon the berry mixture into the crust. Spread the remaining ½ cup berries over the sweetened berries and cover with the top crust. Seal and crimp the edges. Brush the top crust with milk and sprinkle with ¼ cup sugar.
2. Bake in the preheated oven for 15 minutes. Reduce the temperature to 375°F (190°C) and bake 20 to 25 more minutes. **Yield:** 8 servings.

Per serving: About 254 calories, 3g protein, 44g carbohydrate, 8g fat, 5g fiber, 1mg cholesterol, 119mg sodium

Sweet Potato Pie

Submitted by: **Joyce Waits**

"A special friend in Atlanta, Georgia, gave me this recipe. It has long been a favorite, and everyone who tastes it says it's the best they've ever had."

1 (1 pound) sweet potato	½ teaspoon ground nutmeg
½ cup butter, softened	½ teaspoon ground cinnamon
1 cup white sugar	1 teaspoon vanilla extract
½ cup milk	Pastry for a 9 inch single crust pie
2 eggs	

1. Boil sweet potato whole in skin for 40 to 50 minutes or until done. Run cold water over the sweet potato and remove the skin.
2. Preheat oven to 350°F (175°C). Break apart sweet potato in a bowl. Add butter and beat on medium speed with a mixer until creamy. Stir in sugar, milk, eggs, nutmeg, cinnamon, and vanilla. Beat on medium speed until mixture is smooth. Pour filling into unbaked pie crust.
3. Bake in the preheated oven for 55 to 60 minutes or until knife inserted in center comes out clean. Pie will puff up like a soufflé and will sink down as it cools. **Yield:** 8 servings.

Per serving: About 401 calories, 5g protein, 50g carbohydrate, 21g fat, 3g fiber, 85mg cholesterol, 265mg sodium

Blueberry Pie

Submitted by: **Beth**

"Best when made with fresh picked blueberries! It's a beautiful sight with a lattice top."

¾	cup white sugar	4	cups fresh blueberries
3	tablespoons cornstarch		Pastry for a 9 inch double
¼	teaspoon salt		crust pie
½	teaspoon ground cinnamon	1	tablespoon butter

1. Preheat oven to 425°F (220°C).

2. In a large bowl, mix sugar, cornstarch, salt, and cinnamon, and sprinkle over blueberries.

3. Line pie dish with 1 pie crust. Pour berry mixture into the crust and dot with butter. Cut remaining crust into ½ to ¾ inch wide strips and make lattice top. Crimp and flute edges.

4. Bake pie in the preheated oven on lower shelf of oven for about 50 minutes or until crust is golden brown. **Yield:** 8 servings.

Per serving: About 365 calories, 3g protein, 52g carbohydrate, 17g fat, 4g fiber, 4mg cholesterol, 326mg sodium

◄ Family Favorite

Prep Time: 30 minutes

Cook Time: 50 minutes

Average Rating: ★★★★★

66 Ratings ▲ 52 Reviews

What other cooks have done:

"I made this over the summer with fresh blueberries. I added a little extra cornstarch, and it turned out great. I used a homemade crust and added a bit more cinnamon, just because I like cinnamon."

Award-Winning Peaches and Cream Pie

Submitted by: **Debbi Borsick**

"I won five blue ribbons and 'Best Pie of Show' with this pie."

¾	cup all-purpose flour	1	(29 ounce) can sliced
½	teaspoon salt		peaches, drained and
1	teaspoon baking powder		syrup reserved
1	(3.4 ounce) package instant	1	(8 ounce) package cream
	vanilla pudding mix		cheese, softened
3	tablespoons butter, softened	½	cup white sugar
1	egg	1	tablespoon white sugar
½	cup milk	1	teaspoon ground cinnamon

1. Preheat oven to 350°F (175°C). Grease sides and bottom of a 10 inch deep dish pie dish.

2. In a medium bowl, mix together flour, salt, baking powder, and pudding mix. Add butter, egg, and milk. Beat for 2 minutes. Pour mixture into prepared pan. Arrange peach slices on top of the pudding mixture.

3. In a small mixing bowl, beat cream cheese until fluffy. Add ½ cup sugar and 3 tablespoons reserved peach syrup. Beat for 2 minutes. Spoon mixture over peaches to within 1 inch of pan edge. Mix together 1 tablespoon sugar and 1 teaspoon cinnamon and sprinkle over top.

4. Bake in the preheated oven for 30 to 35 minutes, until golden brown. Chill before serving. **Yield:** 8 servings.

Per serving: About 371 calories, 6g protein, 54g carbohydrate, 15g fat, 1g fiber, 70mg cholesterol, 440mg sodium

◄ Blue Ribbon Winner

Prep Time: 30 minutes

Cook Time: 35 minutes

Average Rating: ★★★★★

224 Ratings ▲ 178 Reviews

What other cooks have done:

"What a wonderful dessert! The second time I used chocolate pudding mix, frozen raspberries, and raspberry cream cheese (leaving out the cinnamon/sugar topping). That adaptation was also a hit. I'm looking forward to trying different combinations of fruit and pudding flavors."

Brown Family's Favorite Pumpkin Pie

Submitted by: **Cindy B.**
"Serve with whipped topping or ice cream."

2 eggs	Pastry for a 9 inch single
1 (15 ounce) can pumpkin	crust pie
puree	¼ cup packed brown sugar
1 teaspoon ground cinnamon	2 tablespoons all-purpose
½ teaspoon ground ginger	flour
½ teaspoon ground nutmeg	1 teaspoon ground cinnamon
½ teaspoon salt	2 tablespoons butter, chilled
1 (14 ounce) can sweetened	1 cup chopped walnuts
condensed milk	

1. Preheat oven to 425°F (220°C). Separate the eggs and beat the whites until fluffy.
2. In a large bowl, mix the pumpkin, egg yolks, 1 teaspoon cinnamon, ginger, nutmeg, and salt. Mix in condensed milk until smooth. Gently fold in the beaten egg whites. Pour filling into unbaked crust.
3. Bake in the preheated oven for 15 minutes. Remove the pie from the oven and reduce the heat to 350°F (175°C).
4. While the pie is baking, prepare the streusel topping. Combine the brown sugar, flour, and 1 teaspoon cinnamon. With 2 knives or a pastry blender, cut in the cold butter until the mixture is crumbly. Mix in the chopped nuts. Sprinkle the topping over the pie. Return the pie to the oven and bake 40 more minutes or until set. **Yield:** 8 servings.

Per serving: About 467 calories, 10g protein, 52g carbohydrate, 26g fat, 4g fiber, 78mg cholesterol, 501mg sodium

---

Rhubarb and Strawberry Pie

Submitted by: **Terri**
"Nothing tastes better with vanilla ice cream. Use fresh or frozen rhubarb."

1 cup white sugar	Pastry for a 9 inch double
½ cup all-purpose flour	crust pie
2 pints fresh strawberries	2 tablespoons butter
1 pound fresh rhubarb,	1 egg yolk, lightly beaten
chopped	2 tablespoons white sugar

1. Preheat oven to 400°F (200°C). Mix 1 cup sugar and flour. Add strawberries and rhubarb. Toss gently to coat. Let stand for 30 minutes.
2. Line pie dish with 1 pie crust. Pour filling into crust. Dot with butter; cover with top crust. Seal edges of crusts with water. Brush top of pie with beaten egg yolk. Sprinkle with 2 tablespoons sugar. Cut small holes in top of crust to let steam escape.
3. Bake in the preheated oven for 35 to 40 minutes or until bubbly and brown. Cool on rack. **Yield:** 8 servings.

Per serving: About 436 calories, 5g protein, 64g carbohydrate, 19g fat, 5g fiber, 34mg cholesterol, 268mg sodium

The Old Boy's Strawberry Pie

Submitted by: **Gaye**

"This is a summertime tradition in my family. 'The Old Boy' is my dad, but my mom remembers her grandmother making a pie like this when she was young."

4 cups fresh strawberries, hulled	¾ cup white sugar
½ cup white sugar	¾ cup all-purpose flour
½ cup all-purpose flour	6 tablespoons butter, softened
1 tablespoon cornstarch	Pinch ground nutmeg
Pastry for a 9 inch single crust pie	2 tablespoons butter
	1 tablespoon white sugar

1. Preheat oven to 400°F (200°C). Place a drip pan on lowest shelf to catch pie juices.

2. Place strawberries in a deep bowl. In a separate bowl, mix together ½ cup sugar, ½ cup flour, and cornstarch. Gently coat berries with sugar mixture; be careful not to crush berries. Pour berries into unbaked pie crust, mounding them in the middle. (Mounding is necessary because the berries will sink as they bake.)

3. In a mixing bowl, beat ¾ cup sugar, ¾ cup flour, butter, and nutmeg. Cover berries with crumb topping; dot with butter. Wrap edges of pie crust with foil to prevent excessive browning.

4. Bake in the preheated oven for 20 minutes, then reduce heat to 375°F (190°C) and bake for 40 more minutes. When there are 10 minutes left of baking, sprinkle 1 tablespoon sugar over crumb topping and finish baking. **Yield:** 8 servings.

Per serving: About 408 calories, 4g protein, 62g carbohydrate, 17g fat, 3g fiber, 23mg cholesterol, 206mg sodium

◄ Family Favorite

Prep Time: 15 minutes

Cook Time: 1 hour

Average Rating: ★★★★★

27 Ratings ▲ 22 Reviews

What other cooks have done:
"I added more strawberries. We like it served with some vanilla ice cream."

Relish That Rhubarb ▼

With the right dish, you can turn even the most adamant objector into a rhubarb fan.

What's It Good for?

Rhubarb is considered a vegetable, but it's most often treated as a fruit—though it's rarely eaten raw. Just like fresh cranberries, rhubarb is almost unbearably tart on its own and needs the sweetness of sugar, honey, or fruit juice added to it to balance out the acidity.

Apart from pies, crisps, crumbles, and cobblers, rhubarb is wonderful in quick breads, cakes, ice cream, or sorbet. Rhubarb sauces or chutneys taste marvelous on desserts of all kinds, as well as on breakfast breads like pancakes or waffles, not to mention main dishes like fish, pork chops, ham, and chicken. Rhubarb pairs up delightfully with other fruits to create a complex sweet-tart flavor. Some rhubarb matches made in heaven are strawberries, raspberries, blueberries, apples, cherries, oranges, peaches, apricots, pears, or raisins. If you've got some favorite fruit dessert recipes already, try substituting up to half of the fruit with chopped rhubarb (you'll probably want to add some extra sugar).

Picking and Preparing

Different varieties of rhubarb will be deep crimson, rosy pink, or even pink-streaked green when fully ripe. If you're selecting rhubarb in the grocery store, choose medium-size stalks that are firm and blemish-free. Avoid anything that's limp, shriveled, or spotted brown. The stalks are the only edible part of the rhubarb plant; the leaves and roots are poisonous. If there are any bits of leaf or root still remaining, trim them off completely and throw them away. Rhubarb stalks are stringy like celery, and some people prefer to peel off the strings. However, most of the color is in the strings, and the texture will break down during cooking anyway, so de-stringing is not necessary, especially if you like that distinctive bright pink color in your rhubarb concoctions. *- Jennifer Anderson*

For more information, visit **Allrecipes.com**

Banana Cream Pie III

Submitted by: **Angie**
"Very easy banana cream pie."

3	bananas, divided	2	cups frozen whipped topping, thawed and divided
1	(9 inch) pie crust, baked		
2½	cups cold milk		
2	(3.4 ounce) packages instant vanilla pudding mix		

1. Slice 2 bananas and arrange in a baked and cooled pie crust.
2. Pour cold milk into a medium bowl. Add pudding mix and whisk until thoroughly combined. Fold in ½ cup of the whipped topping. Pour into crust.
3. Chill at least 3 hours before serving. Garnish with remaining whipped topping and slices of the remaining banana. **Yield:** 8 servings.

Per serving: About 309 calories, 4g protein, 49g carbohydrate, 12g fat, 1g fiber, 6mg cholesterol, 498mg sodium

Old-Fashioned Coconut Cream Pie *(pictured on page 297)*

Submitted by: **Carol H.**
"A tried and true, old-fashioned coconut cream pie. Took many years of searching and baking to find the right one, and this is it!"

½	cup all-purpose flour	1	cup flaked coconut, toasted
¾	cup white sugar	1	teaspoon vanilla extract
¼	teaspoon salt	1	(9 inch) pie crust, baked
3	cups half-and-half	3	cups frozen whipped topping, thawed
2	egg yolks, beaten		

1. In a heavy medium saucepan, combine flour, sugar, and salt. Gradually stir in half-and-half. Bring to a boil over medium heat, stirring constantly, 5 minutes. Remove pan from heat. Place egg yolks in a bowl and gradually whisk in 1 cup of hot mixture. Whisk egg yolk mixture back into remaining half-and-half mixture. Cook over low heat 3 minutes. Stir in ½ cup coconut and vanilla. Cover and cool. Spoon cooled filling into baked crust. Cover with plastic wrap and chill thoroughly.
2. Before serving, top with whipped topping and remaining ½ cup toasted coconut. **Yield:** 8 servings.

Note: To toast coconut, spread it in an ungreased pan and bake in a 350°F (175°C) oven for 5 to 7 minutes or until golden brown, stirring occasionally.

Per serving: About 428 calories, 7g protein, 46g carbohydrate, 24g fat, 1g fiber, 87mg cholesterol, 271mg sodium

Grandma's Lemon Meringue Pie

Submitted by: **Emilie S.**
"What a very fun recipe because Grandma makes it sweet and simple. This pie is thickened with cornstarch, flour, and egg yolks, and it contains no milk."

1	cup white sugar	2	lemons, zested and juiced
2	tablespoons all-purpose flour	2	tablespoons butter
3	tablespoons cornstarch	4	egg yolks, beaten
¼	teaspoon salt	1	(9 inch) pie crust, baked
1½	cups water	4	egg whites
		6	tablespoons white sugar

1. Preheat oven to 350°F (175°C).
2. In a medium saucepan, whisk together 1 cup sugar, flour, cornstarch, and salt. Stir in water, lemon zest, and juice. Cook over medium-high heat, stirring frequently, until mixture comes to a boil. Stir in butter. Place egg yolks in a small bowl and gradually whisk in ½ cup of hot sugar mixture. Whisk egg yolk mixture back into remaining sugar mixture. Bring to a boil; continue to cook while stirring constantly until thick. Remove from heat. Pour filling into baked pie crust.
3. In a large glass or metal bowl, whip egg whites until foamy. Add 6 tablespoons sugar gradually and continue to whip until stiff peaks form. Spread meringue over pie, sealing the edges at the crust.
4. Bake in the preheated oven for 10 minutes or until meringue is golden brown. **Yield:** 8 servings.

Per serving: About 301 calories, 4g protein, 50g carbohydrate, 11g fat, 2g fiber, 114mg cholesterol, 238mg sodium

◄ Covered-Dish Favorite

Prep Time: 30 minutes
Cook Time: 10 minutes
Average Rating: ★★★★★
71 Ratings ▲ 50 Reviews
What other cooks have done:
"I used milk instead of water for a creamier filling. Also, when filling was cooking, I tasted it and added more sugar or lemon juice depending on the taste I was looking for. Some people like it more tart. Also, I added 1 teaspoon of lemon juice to the meringue mix, just for a little extra zing."

Easy Key Lime Pie

Submitted by: **Pat Legler**
"This is the 1999 American Pie Council's National Pie Championship's first place winner in the Quick and Easy category."

5	egg yolks, beaten	2	cups frozen whipped topping, thawed
1	(14 ounce) can sweetened condensed milk		Lime slices for garnish
½	cup Key lime juice		
1	(9 inch) prepared graham cracker crust		

1. Preheat oven to 375°F (190°C).
2. Combine the egg yolks, sweetened condensed milk, and lime juice. Mix well. Pour into unbaked graham cracker crust.
3. Bake in the preheated oven for 15 minutes. Allow to cool. Top with whipped topping and garnish with lime slices. **Yield:** 8 servings.

Per serving: About 324 calories, 7g protein, 44g carbohydrate, 14g fat, 0g fiber, 150mg cholesterol, 231mg sodium

◄ Blue Ribbon Winner

Prep Time: 20 minutes
Cook Time: 15 minutes
Average Rating: ★★★★★
210 Ratings ▲ 146 Reviews
What other cooks have done:
"I put ground graham crackers on the top of the pie after it cooled and that gave it added taste."

Honey-Crunch Pecan Pie

Submitted by: **Sarah Spaugh**

"A double winner! It won First Place in the nut category and the Best of Show Award for the American Pie Council's 2000 National Pie Championship."

Prep Time: 30 minutes

Cook Time: 1 hour 5 minutes

Average Rating: ★★★★★

64 Ratings ▲ 52 Reviews

What other cooks have done:

"I tripled the pecans in this pie recipe (to 3 cups) and used a frozen, pre-made pie crust. I also dressed up the pie by drizzling melted chocolate over the top."

2	cups all-purpose flour	2	tablespoons butter, melted
1	teaspoon salt	1	teaspoon vanilla extract
¾	cup shortening	1	cup chopped pecans
6	tablespoons cold water	1	tablespoon bourbon (optional)
1	teaspoon white vinegar		
4	eggs, lightly beaten	⅓	cup packed brown sugar
¼	cup packed brown sugar	3	tablespoons butter
¼	cup white sugar	3	tablespoons honey
½	teaspoon salt	1½	cups pecan halves
1	cup light corn syrup		

1. Preheat oven to 350°F (175°C).

2. In a medium bowl, mix together flour and 1 teaspoon salt. Cut in shortening until mixture is crumbly. Gradually add cold water and vinegar. Cut together until mixture will hold together. Press dough into a ball and flour each side lightly. Wrap in plastic and chill for 20 minutes. Roll out between 2 sheets of wax paper into a circle ⅛ inch thick. Remove wax paper and press dough into a 9 inch pie dish.

3. In a large bowl, combine eggs, ¼ cup brown sugar, white sugar, ½ teaspoon salt, corn syrup, melted butter, vanilla, and chopped pecans. Add bourbon, if desired. Mix well. Spoon mixture into un-baked pie crust.

4. Bake in the preheated oven for 25 to 30 minutes or until almost set. Remove and cover edges of crust with aluminum foil. Return to oven for 20 minutes.

5. Combine ⅓ cup brown sugar, butter, and honey in a medium saucepan. Cook over low heat, stirring occasionally, until sugar dissolves, about 2 minutes. Add pecan halves. Stir just until coated. Spoon topping evenly over pie.

6. Keep foil on edges of crust and return pie to oven for 10 to 15 more minutes, until topping is bubbly and golden brown. Cool to room temperature before serving. **Yield:** 8 servings.

Per serving: About 857 calories, 10g protein, 89g carbohydrate, 55g fat, 4g fiber, 126mg cholesterol, 598mg sodium

No-Bake Peanut Butter Pie

Submitted by: **Megan Rogers**

"Creamy and delicious—melts in your mouth. This pie is a real crowd-pleaser."

1	(8 ounce) package cream cheese, softened	1	(16 ounce) container frozen whipped topping, thawed
1½	cups confectioners' sugar	2	(9 inch) prepared graham cracker crusts
1	cup peanut butter		
1	cup milk		

1. Beat together cream cheese and confectioners' sugar. Mix in peanut butter and milk. Beat until smooth. Fold in whipped topping.

2. Spoon into 2 (9 inch) graham cracker pie crusts, cover, and freeze. **Yield:** 16 servings (2 [9 inch] pies).

Per serving: About 433 calories, 7g protein, 41g carbohydrate, 28g fat, 1g fiber, 17mg cholesterol, 302mg sodium

Milk Tart

Submitted by: **Rene Conradie**

"This custard pie with a sweet pastry crust is a South African favorite, especially at tea time. I got this wonderful recipe from a friend."

½	cup butter, softened	1	tablespoon butter
1	cup white sugar	2½	tablespoons all-purpose flour
1	egg		
2	cups all-purpose flour	2½	tablespoons cornstarch
2	teaspoons baking powder	½	cup white sugar
	Pinch salt	2	eggs, beaten
4	cups milk	½	teaspoon ground cinnamon
1	teaspoon vanilla extract		

1. Preheat oven to 350°F (175°C).

2. In a medium mixing bowl, cream together ½ cup butter and 1 cup sugar. Add 1 egg and beat until mixture is smooth. In a separate bowl, mix together 2 cups flour, baking powder, and salt. Stir flour mixture into sugar mixture just until ingredients are combined. Press mixture into bottom and up sides of 2 (9 inch) pie dishes.

3. Bake in the preheated oven for 10 to 15 minutes, until golden brown.

4. In a large saucepan, combine milk, vanilla, and 1 tablespoon butter. Bring to a boil over medium heat, then remove from heat.

5. In a separate bowl, mix together 2½ tablespoons flour, cornstarch, and ½ cup sugar. Add beaten eggs to sugar mixture and whisk until smooth. Slowly whisk mixture into milk. Return pan to heat and bring to a boil, stirring constantly. Boil 5 minutes, stirring constantly. Pour half of mixture into each pastry shell. Sprinkle with cinnamon. Chill before serving. **Yield:** 16 servings (2 [9 inch] tarts).

Per serving: About 241 calories, 5g protein, 36g carbohydrate, 9g fat, 1g fiber, 62mg cholesterol, 194mg sodium

Apple, Cranberry, and Pear Crisp

Submitted by: **Barb Y**

"Here's a variation of traditional apple crisp that I dreamed up one day when I didn't have enough apples but did have pears in the fruit bowl and leftover toasted hazelnuts. We love it. Raisins or dried cherries can be substituted for cranberries."

2	Rome apples	½	cup all-purpose flour
2	pears	½	cup packed brown sugar
½	cup dried cranberries	½	cup quick cooking oats
1	tablespoon all-purpose flour	¼	cup ground walnuts
2	tablespoons honey	½	cup butter
1½	tablespoons lemon juice		

1. Preheat oven to 375°F (190°C). Peel apples and pears and cut into ½ inch cubes. Combine with dried cranberries, 1 tablespoon flour, honey, and lemon juice. Place mixture in a greased 8x8 inch square baking dish.
2. Blend together ½ cup flour, brown sugar, oats, nuts, and butter until crumbly. Do not overmix. Sprinkle flour mixture over fruit.
3. Bake in the preheated oven for 45 minutes or until brown and crisp on top. **Yield:** 6 servings.

Per serving: About 432 calories, 4g protein, 64g carbohydrate, 19g fat, 5g fiber, 41mg cholesterol, 164mg sodium

Apple-Pecan Cobbler

Submitted by: **Lori Smith**

"An excellent cobbler to make in the fall when the weather starts to turn cooler."

4	cups thinly sliced apples	1	teaspoon baking powder
½	cup white sugar	¼	teaspoon salt
½	teaspoon ground cinnamon	1	egg, beaten
½	cup chopped pecans	½	cup evaporated milk
1	cup all-purpose flour	⅓	cup butter, melted
1	cup white sugar	¼	cup chopped pecans

1. Preheat oven to 325°F (165°C). Generously grease a 2 quart baking dish.
2. Arrange apple slices in an even layer in baking dish. In a small bowl, mix together ½ cup sugar, cinnamon, and ½ cup pecans. Sprinkle mixture over apples.
3. In a medium bowl, mix together flour, 1 cup sugar, baking powder, and salt. In a separate bowl, whisk together egg, evaporated milk, and melted butter. Add milk mixture to flour mixture and stir until smooth. Pour mixture over apples and sprinkle top with ¼ cup pecans.
4. Bake in the preheated oven for 55 minutes. **Yield:** 8 servings.

Per serving: About 416 calories, 5g protein, 63g carbohydrate, 18g fat, 3g fiber, 52mg cholesterol, 238mg sodium

Cherry Crunch

Submitted by: **Timothy S. Lindabury**

"Cherry pie filling is lovingly sandwiched between two layers of oats. Substitute apple pie filling and sprinkle a little extra cinnamon over the top, if you like."

1	cup rolled oats	½	cup butter
1	cup all-purpose flour	1	(21 ounce) can cherry pie filling
¾	cup packed brown sugar		
½	teaspoon ground cinnamon		

1. Preheat oven to 375°F (190°C).

2. In a medium bowl, combine the oats, flour, brown sugar, and cinnamon. Cut in butter until mixture resembles coarse crumbs.

3. Sprinkle half of crumb mixture in a 9x9 inch square baking dish. Cover with cherry pie filling. Sprinkle remaining crumb mixture over pie filling.

4. Bake in the preheated oven for 40 minutes or until topping is golden brown. Serve warm. **Yield:** 9 servings.

Per serving: About 354 calories, 5g protein, 59g carbohydrate, 12g fat, 3g fiber, 28mg cholesterol, 124mg sodium

◄ Kid-Friendly

Prep Time: 15 minutes

Cook Time: 40 minutes

Average Rating: ★★★★★

17 Ratings ▲ 14 Reviews

What other cooks have done:

"I served it warm with ice cream and it was a huge hit! It was easy and inexpensive to make. You can change it up by adding different pie fillings or even a cream cheese mixture."

Rhubarb Crunch

Submitted by: **Carolyn**

"A childhood favorite. We ate it with milk or vanilla ice cream!"

3	cups diced rhubarb	1	cup quick cooking oats
1	cup white sugar	1½	cups all-purpose flour
3	tablespoons all-purpose flour	1	cup butter
1	cup packed light brown sugar		

1. Preheat oven to 375°F (190°C). Lightly grease a 9x13 inch baking dish.

2. In a large bowl, combine rhubarb, white sugar, and 3 tablespoons flour. Stir well and spread evenly in baking dish. Set aside.

3. In a large bowl, combine brown sugar, oats, and 1½ cups flour. Stir well, then cut in butter until mixture is crumbly. Sprinkle mixture over rhubarb layer.

4. Bake in the preheated oven for 40 minutes. Serve hot or cold. **Yield:** 12 servings.

Per serving: About 390 calories, 4g protein, 58g carbohydrate, 17g fat, 2g fiber, 41mg cholesterol, 165mg sodium

◄ Crowd-Pleaser

Prep Time: 15 minutes

Cook Time: 40 minutes

Average Rating: ★★★★☆

55 Ratings ▲ 42 Reviews

What other cooks have done:

"I made this recipe with frozen rhubarb and used the whole bag (about 5 cups). I also used only ½ cup of butter and 1 cup flour. The recipe came out great, and I will definitely make it again."

Virginia Apple Pudding

Submitted by: **Dorothy and Kathy Keizer**

"Try this wonderful old family recipe served warm, topped with vanilla ice cream."

½ cup butter, melted	¼ teaspoon salt
1 cup white sugar	1 cup milk
1 cup all-purpose flour	2 cups chopped, peeled apple
2 teaspoons baking powder	1 teaspoon ground cinnamon

1. Preheat oven to 375°F (190°C).

2. In a 2 quart baking dish, combine butter, sugar, flour, baking powder, salt, and milk until smooth. Set aside.

3. In a microwave-safe bowl, combine chopped apple and cinnamon. Microwave until apples are soft, 2 to 5 minutes. Pour apples into center of batter.

4. Bake in the preheated oven 30 minutes, until golden. **Yield:** 4 servings.

Per serving: About 581 calories, 6g protein, 87g carbohydrate, 25g fat, 3g fiber, 67mg cholesterol, 535mg sodium

---

Bread Pudding

Submitted by: **Missi**

"The sauce makes the dessert! I don't use raisins, but a lot of people like to add them."

3 cups bread cubes	1 teaspoon vanilla extract
4 cups hot milk	1 cup white sugar
¾ cup white sugar	½ cup butter
1 tablespoon butter	½ cup heavy whipping cream
½ teaspoon salt	1 teaspoon vanilla extract
4 eggs, lightly beaten	

1. Preheat oven to 350°F (175°C). Butter an 8x8 inch glass baking dish.

2. Soak bread in hot milk for 5 minutes. Add ¾ cup sugar, 1 tablespoon butter, salt, eggs, and 1 teaspoon vanilla to bread mixture and stir well. Pour into the prepared baking dish.

3. Place baking dish inside a large roasting pan and place roasting pan on oven rack. Fill roasting pan with boiling water to reach halfway up the sides of the baking dish. Bake in the preheated oven for 1 hour. Cool on a wire rack.

4. While pudding cools, in a large saucepan over medium heat, combine 1 cup sugar, ½ cup butter, whipping cream, and 1 teaspoon vanilla. While stirring, bring to a boil, then reduce heat to low and stir 3 more minutes. Spoon over bread pudding while warm. **Yield:** 9 servings.

Per serving: About 450 calories, 8g protein, 48g carbohydrate, 26g fat, 0g fiber, 342mg cholesterol, 347mg sodium

Gramma's Apple Bread Pudding

Submitted by: **Meshel**

"Gramma's bread pudding is the ultimate in comfort food. It's great for using up bread and apples."

4	cups soft French bread cubes	½	teaspoon vanilla extract
¼	cup raisins	2	eggs, beaten
2	cups peeled and sliced Gala apples	¼	cup white sugar
		¼	cup packed brown sugar
1	cup packed brown sugar	½	cup milk
1¾	cups milk	½	cup butter or margarine
¼	cup butter or margarine	1	teaspoon vanilla extract
1	teaspoon ground cinnamon		

1. Preheat oven to 350°F (175°C). Grease a 7x11 inch baking dish.

2. In a large bowl, combine bread, raisins, and apples. In a small saucepan over medium heat, combine 1 cup brown sugar, 1¾ cups milk, and ¼ cup butter. Cook and stir until butter melts. Pour over bread mixture in bowl.

3. In a small bowl, combine cinnamon, ½ teaspoon vanilla, and eggs. Pour bread mixture into prepared dish and drizzle egg mixture on top.

4. Bake in the preheated oven 40 to 50 minutes, until center is set and apples are tender. Serve with warm vanilla sauce.

5. Combine sugar, ¼ cup brown sugar, ½ cup milk, and ½ cup butter in a saucepan over medium heat and bring to a boil. Boil 3 to 4 minutes until slightly thickened. Remove from heat and stir in 1 teaspoon vanilla. **Yield:** 6 servings.

Per serving: About 545 calories, 7g protein, 73g carbohydrate, 26g fat, 1g fiber, 78mg cholesterol, 411mg sodium

◀ Crowd-Pleaser

Prep Time: 15 minutes
Cook Time: 50 minutes
Average Rating: ★★★★★
26 Ratings ▲ 22 Reviews
What other cooks have done:
"I omitted the raisins and added 1 tablespoon of bourbon and ¼ cup of chopped, toasted pecans. I did not make the vanilla sauce, but served it with vanilla ice cream instead. Also, I used mostly whole wheat bread with a little cinnamon bread thrown in. It came out great!"

Creamy Rice Pudding

Submitted by: **Erica G.**

"My mom gets credit for this recipe for rice pudding. It's the best I've ever tasted, and it gets rave reviews from everyone I serve it to. Sprinkle with nutmeg or cinnamon, if desired. For creamier pudding, use short or medium grain rice."

1½	cups water	1	egg, beaten
¾	cup uncooked white rice	⅔	cup golden raisins
2	cups milk, divided	1	tablespoon butter
⅓	cup white sugar	½	teaspoon vanilla extract
¼	teaspoon salt		

1. In a medium saucepan, bring 1½ cups water to a boil. Add rice and stir. Reduce heat, cover, and simmer for 20 minutes.

2. In another saucepan, combine cooked rice, 1½ cups milk, sugar, and salt. Cook over medium heat until thick and creamy, 15 to 20 minutes. Stir in remaining ½ cup milk, beaten egg, and raisins. Cook 2 more minutes, stirring constantly. Remove from heat and stir in butter and vanilla. Serve warm. **Yield:** 4 servings.

Per serving: About 365 calories, 9g protein, 68g carbohydrate, 7g fat, 1g fiber, 70mg cholesterol, 255mg sodium

The Best Banana Pudding

Submitted by: **Kenneth Strother**

"The best no-bake banana pudding you'll ever find (or so I've been told by many)."

1	(5.1 ounce) package instant vanilla pudding mix	1	(12 ounce) container frozen whipped topping, thawed
2	cups cold milk	1	(16 ounce) package vanilla wafers
1	(14 ounce) can sweetened condensed milk	14	bananas, sliced
1	tablespoon vanilla extract		

1. In a large mixing bowl, beat pudding mix and milk for 2 minutes. Blend in condensed milk until smooth. Stir in vanilla and fold in whipped topping.

2. Layer wafers, bananas, and pudding mixture in a glass serving bowl. Chill until served. **Yield:** 20 servings.

Per serving: About 337 calories, 4g protein, 58g carbohydrate, 10g fat, 2g fiber, 8mg cholesterol, 207mg sodium

Chocolate Trifle *(pictured on page 302)*

Submitted by: **Wayne**
"At church functions, folks line up for this trifle. And it's so easy to make!"

1	(19.8 ounce) package brownie mix	1	(8 ounce) container frozen whipped topping, thawed
1	(3.4 ounce) package instant chocolate pudding mix	1	(12 ounce) container frozen whipped topping, thawed
½	cup water	1	(1.4 ounce) chocolate candy bar
1	(14 ounce) can sweetened condensed milk		

1. Prepare brownie mix according to package directions and cool completely. Cut into 1 inch squares.
2. In a large bowl, combine pudding mix, water, and condensed milk. Mix until smooth, then fold in 8 ounces whipped topping.
3. In a trifle bowl or glass serving dish, place half of the brownies, half of the pudding mixture, and half of the 12 ounce container of whipped topping. Repeat layers. Shave chocolate onto top layer for garnish. Refrigerate 8 hours before serving. **Yield:** 12 servings.

Per serving: About 498 calories, 5g protein, 74g carbohydrate, 20g fat, 0g fiber, 12mg cholesterol, 298mg sodium

◄ Family Favorite

Prep Time: 30 minutes
Cook Time: 25 minutes
Average Rating: ★★★★
97 Ratings ▲ 69 Reviews
What other cooks have done:
"I made this in individual servings in my ice cream fountain glasses. My guests loved it!"

Joy's Prizewinning Trifle

Submitted by: **Joy**
"A fantastic recipe that's beautiful to look at and even better to eat."

1	(8 ounce) container sour cream	3	kiwis, peeled and sliced
1	(3.4 ounce) package instant vanilla pudding mix	1	pint fresh strawberries, sliced
1	(12 ounce) container frozen whipped topping, thawed	3	bananas, peeled and sliced
1	(9 inch) angel food cake	1	(15 ounce) can crushed pineapple, drained
			Fresh mint sprig

1. In a medium bowl, fold sour cream and pudding mix into the whipped topping.
2. Cut the cake into thirds, horizontally. Line a large trifle or other glass serving bowl with kiwi and strawberry slices, reserving two whole strawberries and two kiwi slices. Place 1 layer of cake in bowl, top with ⅓ each of bananas, pineapple, and whipped topping mixture. Repeat layering until all ingredients are used.
3. Make fan garnishes of reserved strawberries by slicing just below the stem. Garnish assembled trifle with fanned strawberries, reserved kiwi slices, and a sprig of mint. Refrigerate until serving. **Yield:** 15 servings.

Per serving: About 240 calories, 3g protein, 39g carbohydrate, 8g fat, 2g fiber, 7mg cholesterol, 270mg sodium

◄ Make-Ahead

Prep Time: 30 minutes
Average Rating: ★★★★★
17 Ratings ▲ 13 Reviews
What other cooks have done:
"I've made this recipe a handful of times; everyone loves it and asks for the recipe. It's very easy and fun to prepare. I vary the fruit by using what's fresh and in season. You can use any fruit you want. I sometimes use light sour cream, and no one can tell the difference. I also use banana pudding for extra flavor."

Chocolate Éclair

Submitted by: **Bailey**

"Creamy vanilla pudding, hearty graham crackers, and rich chocolate frosting make this the most awesome dessert. The most important part of this dessert is waiting about 24 hours to serve it ... the crackers need time to absorb the pudding mixture, and it truly makes a difference in the taste if you don't wait."

1. In a large bowl, combine pudding mix and confectioners' sugar. Whisk in milk until mixture is smooth, then gradually fold in whipped topping.

2. Place a layer of graham crackers in a 9x13 inch pan. Spread ⅓ of pudding mixture over crackers. Cover pudding with another layer of graham crackers. Continue layering until pudding mixture is gone. Cover last pudding layer with another layer of graham crackers.

3. Remove lid and seal from frosting and microwave at 20 second intervals, stirring between intervals, until frosting is pourable, about 1 minute. Spread frosting evenly over top layer of graham crackers. Refrigerate 24 hours before serving. **Yield:** 16 servings.

Per serving: About 370 calories, 4g protein, 63g carbohydrate, 12g fat, 1g fiber, 3mg cholesterol, 419mg sodium

Bananas Foster II

Submitted by: **Buttermebread**

"On Father's Day, we all tried this delicious dessert, which everyone loved. Bananas warmed in buttery rum sauce over vanilla ice cream."

¼	cup butter	3	bananas, peeled and sliced diagonally
⅔	cup packed dark brown sugar	¼	cup coarsely chopped walnuts
3½	tablespoons rum	1	pint vanilla ice cream
1½	teaspoons vanilla extract		
½	teaspoon ground cinnamon		

1. In a large, deep skillet over medium heat, melt butter. Stir in sugar, rum, vanilla, and cinnamon. When mixture begins to bubble, place bananas and walnuts in pan. Cook until bananas are hot, 1 to 2 minutes. Serve at once over vanilla ice cream. **Yield:** 4 servings.

Per serving: About 537 calories, 5g protein, 73g carbohydrate, 24g fat, 3g fiber, 60mg cholesterol, 186mg sodium

Chewy Chocolate Cookies

Submitted by: **Linda Whittaker**
"Friends and family always request these cookies at Christmas."

1¼	cups butter, softened	1	teaspoon baking soda
2	cups white sugar	½	teaspoon salt
2	eggs	2	cups semisweet chocolate
2	teaspoons vanilla extract		chips
2	cups all-purpose flour		
¾	cup unsweetened cocoa powder		

1. Preheat oven to 350°F (175°C).
2. In a large bowl, cream together the butter and sugar until light and fluffy. Beat in the eggs, one at a time; stir in vanilla. Sift together the flour, cocoa, baking soda, and salt; stir into the creamed mixture. Mix in chocolate chips. Drop dough by teaspoonfuls onto ungreased baking sheets.
3. Bake in the preheated oven for 8 to 9 minutes. Cookies will be soft. Cool slightly on baking sheets; remove from sheets onto wire racks to cool completely. **Yield:** 4 dozen.

Per cookie: About 134 calories, 1g protein, 18g carbohydrate, 7g fat, 1g fiber, 22mg cholesterol, 103mg sodium

◄ Kid-Friendly

Prep Time: 15 minutes
Cook Time: 9 minutes per batch
Average Rating: ★★★★★
59 Ratings ▲ 46 Reviews
What other cooks have done:
"I love chocolate, and these are so easy, kid-friendly, and delicious! All my friends want the recipe. Try using milk chocolate chips—very yummy."

Chewy Chocolate Chip-Oatmeal Cookies

Submitted by: **Dr. Amy**
"I came up with something that my boyfriend went crazy over! He said I blew his mother's recipe away."

1	cup butter, softened	½	teaspoon baking soda
1	cup packed light brown sugar	1	teaspoon salt
½	cup white sugar	3	cups quick cooking oats
2	eggs	1	cup chopped walnuts
2	teaspoons vanilla extract	1	cup semisweet chocolate
1¼	cups all-purpose flour		chips

1. Preheat the oven to 325°F (165°C).
2. In a large bowl, cream together the butter, brown sugar, and white sugar until smooth. Beat in eggs, one at a time, then stir in vanilla. Combine the flour, baking soda, and salt; stir into the creamed mixture until just blended. Mix in the oats, walnuts, and chocolate chips. Drop by heaping spoonfuls onto ungreased baking sheets.
3. Bake in the preheated oven for 12 minutes. Allow cookies to cool on baking sheets for 5 minutes before transferring to wire racks to cool completely. **Yield:** 3½ dozen.

Per cookie: About 145 calories, 2g protein, 17g carbohydrate, 8g fat, 1g fiber, 22mg cholesterol, 121mg sodium

◄ Classic Comfort Food

Prep Time: 15 minutes
Cook Time: 12 minutes per batch
Average Rating: ★★★★★
101 Ratings ▲ 77 Reviews
What other cooks have done:
"I made them into a bar cookie, and they were great, too. I used old-fashioned rolled oats and they turned out great."

Oatmeal-Peanut Butter Cookies

Submitted by: **Michele**

"A nice change of pace from the usual peanut butter cookie. My husband never liked peanut butter cookies until I made this recipe."

½	cup shortening	2	eggs
½	cup butter or margarine, softened	1½	cups all-purpose flour
1	cup packed brown sugar	2	teaspoons baking soda
¾	cup white sugar	1	teaspoon salt
1	cup peanut butter	1	cup quick cooking oats

1. Preheat oven to 350°F (175°C).

2. In a large bowl, cream together shortening, butter, brown sugar, white sugar, and peanut butter until smooth. Beat in the eggs, one at a time, until well blended. Combine the flour, baking soda, and salt; stir into the creamed mixture. Mix in the oats until just combined. Drop by teaspoonfuls onto ungreased baking sheets.

3. Bake in the preheated oven for 10 to 15 minutes or until just light brown. Don't overbake. Transfer to wire racks to cool completely and store in an airtight container. **Yield:** 4 dozen.

Per cookie: About 121 calories, 2g protein, 13g carbohydrate, 7g fat, 1g fiber, 9mg cholesterol, 152mg sodium

White Chocolate Macadamia Nut Cookies III

Submitted by: **Mary**

"This recipe is always a hit ... better than the ones I've had at restaurants."

1	cup butter, softened	2½	cups all-purpose flour
¾	cup packed light brown sugar	1	teaspoon baking soda
½	cup white sugar	½	teaspoon salt
2	eggs	1	cup coarsely chopped macadamia nuts
½	teaspoon vanilla extract	1	cup coarsely chopped white chocolate
½	teaspoon almond extract		

1. Preheat oven to 350°F (175°C).

2. In a large bowl, cream together the butter, brown sugar, and white sugar until smooth. Beat in the eggs, one at a time; stir in vanilla and almond extracts. Combine the flour, baking soda, and salt; gradually stir into the creamed mixture. Mix in the macadamia nuts and white chocolate. Drop dough by teaspoonfuls onto ungreased baking sheets.

3. Bake in the preheated oven for 10 minutes or until golden brown. Transfer to wire racks to cool completely. **Yield:** 4 dozen.

Per cookie: About 122 calories, 1g protein, 13g carbohydrate, 7g fat, 0g fiber, 20mg cholesterol, 97mg sodium

Iced Pumpkin Cookies

Submitted by: **Gina**

"Wonderful spicy iced pumpkin cookies that both kids and adults love!"

2½	cups all-purpose flour		1½	cups white sugar
1	teaspoon baking powder		1	cup canned pumpkin
1	teaspoon baking soda		1	egg
2	teaspoons ground cinnamon		1	teaspoon vanilla extract
½	teaspoon ground nutmeg		2	cups confectioners' sugar
½	teaspoon ground cloves		3	tablespoons milk
½	teaspoon salt		1	tablespoon butter, melted
½	cup butter, softened		1	teaspoon vanilla extract

1. Preheat oven to 350°F (175°C). Combine flour, baking powder, baking soda, cinnamon, nutmeg, ground cloves, and salt; set aside.
2. In a medium bowl, cream together the ½ cup of butter and white sugar. Add pumpkin, egg, and 1 teaspoon vanilla to butter mixture, and beat until creamy. Mix in dry ingredients. Drop on baking sheets by tablespoonfuls; flatten slightly.
3. Bake in the preheated oven for 15 to 20 minutes. Cool cookies on wire racks.
4. Combine confectioners' sugar, milk, 1 tablespoon melted butter, and 1 teaspoon vanilla. Add milk as needed to achieve drizzling consistency. Drizzle glaze over cookies with a fork. **Yield:** 3 dozen.

Per cookie: About 122 calories, 1g protein, 22g carbohydrate, 3g fat, 1g fiber, 14mg cholesterol, 129mg sodium

◄ Holiday Fare

Prep Time: 20 minutes
Cook Time: 20 minutes per batch
Average Rating: ★★★★★
120 Ratings ▲ 92 Reviews
What other cooks have done:
"I added ½ cup more sugar than the recipe calls for and ½ teaspoon ginger as well. I also added 1 cup chopped walnuts and 1 cup raisins. I skipped the icing, and they turned out well. They're the best pumpkin cookies I've ever had."

No-Bake Cookies III

Submitted by: **Robin**

"You'll have easy peanut butter-cocoa flavored cookies without turning on the oven."

2	cups white sugar			Pinch salt
3	tablespoons unsweetened cocoa powder		3	cups quick cooking oats
½	cup butter		½	cup peanut butter
½	cup milk		1	teaspoon vanilla extract

1. In a saucepan, bring sugar, cocoa, butter, milk, and salt to a rapid boil for 1 minute.
2. Add oats, peanut butter, and vanilla; mix well.
3. Working quickly, drop by teaspoonfuls onto wax paper and let cool.
Yield: 4 dozen.

Per cookie: About 106 calories, 3g protein, 16g carbohydrate, 4g fat, 1g fiber, 6mg cholesterol, 42mg sodium

◄ Quick & Easy

Prep Time: 15 minutes
Cook Time: 1 minute
Average Rating: ★★★★★
153 Ratings ▲ 100 Reviews
What other cooks have done:
"I used 1 cup of vanilla flavored soy milk and no butter. If you make them this way, be sure to let them sit uncovered for longer than usual ...mine took an extra hour or two to become firm."

Caramel Shortbread Squares *(pictured on page 300)*

Submitted by: **Julia**

"These cookies consist of a shortbread crust, firm caramel center, and a milk chocolate top."

⅔	cup butter, softened	2	tablespoons light corn syrup
¼	cup white sugar		
1¼	cups all-purpose flour	½	cup sweetened condensed milk
½	cup butter		
½	cup packed light brown sugar	1¼	cups milk chocolate chips

1. Preheat oven to 350°F (175°C).

2. In a medium bowl, mix together ⅔ cup butter, ¼ cup white sugar, and 1¼ cups flour until evenly crumbly. Press into an ungreased 9x9 inch square pan. Bake in the preheated oven for 20 minutes.

3. In a 2 quart heavy saucepan, combine ½ cup butter, brown sugar, corn syrup, and sweetened condensed milk. Bring to a boil over medium-high heat, about 8 minutes. Reduce heat to medium and continue to boil 22 minutes or until caramel-colored. Remove from heat and beat vigorously with a wooden spoon for about 3 minutes. Pour over baked crust. Cool until it begins to firm, about 20 to 25 minutes.

4. Melt chocolate chips and pour over caramel layer. Cover the layer completely. Chill. Cut into squares. **Yield:** 16 servings.

Per square: About 297 calories, 2g protein, 33g carbohydrate, 19g fat, 0g fiber, 42mg cholesterol, 155mg sodium

Deep-Dish Brownies

Submitted by: **Biz McMahon**

"My all-time favorite, make-from-scratch brownie recipe!"

¾	cup butter, melted	½	cup unsweetened cocoa powder
1½	cups white sugar		
1½	teaspoons vanilla extract	½	teaspoon baking powder
3	eggs	½	teaspoon salt
¾	cup all-purpose flour		

1. Preheat oven to 350°F (175°C). Grease an 8x8 inch square pan.

2. In a large bowl, blend melted butter, sugar, and vanilla. Beat in eggs, one at a time. Combine the flour, cocoa, baking powder, and salt. Gradually blend into the egg mixture. Spread the batter into the prepared pan.

3. Bake in the preheated oven for 40 to 45 minutes or until brownies begin to pull away from the sides of the pan. Let brownies cool, then cut into squares. **Yield:** 18 servings.

Per brownie: About 170 calories, 2g protein, 22g carbohydrate, 9g fat, 1g fiber, 56mg cholesterol, 168mg sodium

Paul's Pumpkin Bars

Submitted by: **Deb Martin**

"These are very moist, and so far I haven't found anyone who doesn't love them!"

4	eggs	2	teaspoons ground cinnamon
1⅔	cups white sugar	1	teaspoon salt
1	cup vegetable oil	1	(3 ounce) package cream
1	(15 ounce) can pumpkin		cheese, softened
	puree	½	cup butter, softened
2	cups all-purpose flour	1	teaspoon vanilla extract
2	teaspoons baking powder	2	cups sifted confectioners'
1	teaspoon baking soda		sugar

1. Preheat oven to 350°F (175°C).

2. In a medium bowl, mix the eggs, sugar, oil, and pumpkin with an electric mixer until light and fluffy. Sift together the flour, baking powder, baking soda, cinnamon, and salt. Stir into the pumpkin mixture until thoroughly combined.

3. Spread the batter evenly into an ungreased 10x15 inch jellyroll pan. Bake in the preheated oven for 25 to 30 minutes. Cool before frosting.

4. To make the frosting: Cream together the cream cheese and butter. Stir in vanilla. Add confectioners' sugar a little at a time, beating until mixture is smooth. Spread evenly on top of the cooled bars. Cut into bars. **Yield:** 2 dozen.

Per bar: About 279 calories, 3g protein, 34g carbohydrate, 15g fat, 1g fiber, 50mg cholesterol, 293mg sodium

◄ Holiday Fare

Prep Time: 15 minutes
Cook Time: 30 minutes
Average Rating: ★★★★★
60 Ratings ▲ 49 Reviews
What other cooks have done:
"This came out of the oven like a beautiful cake! I hated to slice this into bars because the cake presentation was so pretty. I iced with the cream cheese frosting, let the frosting harden, cut into bars, then wrapped them up individually in plastic wrap, and tied off the ends with pretty orange ribbon. I brought these to my friend's home in a cute Halloween bowl and everyone raved over these treats."

Freezing Cookies and Cookie Dough ▼

Too many cookies on your hands? Want to have a large variety of cookies ready-made at your fingertips? Like to have cookie dough around for those last-minute needs? Move those frozen chicken pot pies and cartons of ice cream aside. It's cookie-freezing time!

Freezing Unbaked Cookie Dough

Most cookie doughs freeze extremely well and can be kept frozen for up to 4 to 6 weeks. The most important thing to keep in mind is that the dough will absorb any odd odors present in your freezer if it's not properly wrapped and sealed. To prevent this smell-sponge effect, as well as freezer burn, wrap the dough securely twice. It's also a very good idea to write the type of cookie dough and the date it was frozen on the package. When you're ready to bake, simply let the dough defrost in the refrigerator. This will take several hours, so plan ahead. The cookie doughs that freeze best are shortbreads, chocolate chip, peanut butter, refrigerator, sugar, and brownies, just to name a few. The types of cookie doughs that do not freeze well are cake-like cookies and cookies that have a very liquidy batter, such as madeleines and tuiles.

Freezing Already Baked Cookies

Freezing baked cookies is a great way to preserve their freshness. Baked cookies will keep in the freezer for up to 3 to 4 weeks. As with freezing cookie dough, the most important thing to keep in mind is that you don't want your cookies to absorb any odors. Double-wrap the cookies securely and write the date and the type of cookie on the package. When you're ready to eat the frozen cookies, just let them come to room temperature, or, for you impatient types, pop them in the microwave on high for about 30 seconds. (Times will differ depending on the size of cookie you're defrosting.) We still haven't come across a baked cookie that doesn't freeze well. So feel free to freeze loads of assorted cookies to keep yourself supplied with yummy goodies, any time.

- Ursula Dalzell

For more information, visit **Allrecipes.com**

Cream Cheese Sugar Cookies

Submitted by: **Karin Christian**

"A soft, chewy, and flavorful sugar cookie. It's very important to chill the dough—it's too sticky to roll unless well chilled."

1	cup white sugar	½	teaspoon almond extract
1	cup butter, softened	½	teaspoon vanilla extract
1	(3 ounce) package cream cheese, softened	1	egg yolk
½	teaspoon salt	2¼	cups all-purpose flour

1. In a large bowl, combine the sugar, butter, cream cheese, salt, almond and vanilla extracts, and egg yolk. Beat until smooth. Stir in flour until well blended. Chill the dough for 8 hours or overnight.
2. Preheat oven to 375°F (190°C).
3. On a lightly floured surface, roll out the dough ⅓ at a time to ⅛ inch thickness, refrigerating remaining dough until ready to use. Cut into desired shapes with lightly floured cookie cutters. Place 1 inch apart on ungreased baking sheets. Leave cookies plain for frosting, or brush with beaten egg white and decorate with candy sprinkles or colored sugar.
4. Bake in the preheated oven for 7 to 10 minutes or until light and golden brown. Cool cookies completely on wire racks before frosting. **Yield:** 6 dozen.

Per cookie: About 53 calories, 1g protein, 6g carbohydrate, 3g fat, 0g fiber, 11mg cholesterol, 46mg sodium

Soft Gingerbread Cookies

Submitted by: **Sara**

"These cookies are warm and delicious on a cold winter's day. Cut them into any shape to fit your holiday celebrations."

¾	cup molasses	1	teaspoon baking soda
⅓	cup packed brown sugar	1	teaspoon ground ginger
⅓	cup water	½	teaspoon ground allspice
2	tablespoons butter, softened	½	teaspoon ground cloves
3¼	cups all-purpose flour	½	teaspoon ground cinnamon

1. In a medium bowl, mix together the molasses, brown sugar, water, and butter until smooth. Combine the flour, baking soda, ginger, allspice, cloves, and cinnamon; stir into the wet mixture until all of the dry ingredients are absorbed. Cover the dough and chill for at least 3 hours.
2. Preheat oven to 350°F (175°C). On a lightly floured surface, roll the dough out to ¼ inch thickness. Cut out into desired shapes. Place cookies 1 inch apart onto ungreased baking sheets.
3. Bake in the preheated oven for 8 to 10 minutes. Remove from the baking sheets to cool on wire racks. **Yield:** 3 dozen.

Per cookie: About 73 calories, 1g protein, 15g carbohydrate, 1g fat, 0g fiber, 2mg cholesterol, 45mg sodium

Joey's Peanut Butter Cookies

Submitted by: **P.L. Weiss**

"My boyfriend's special recipe makes the best peanut buttery tasting cookies."

1	cup peanut butter	3	tablespoons milk
½	cup butter, softened	1	teaspoon vanilla extract
½	cup white sugar	1¼	cups all-purpose flour
½	cup packed brown sugar	¾	teaspoon baking powder
1	egg	¼	teaspoon salt

1. Preheat oven to 375°F (190°C).
2. In a large bowl, cream together the peanut butter, butter, white sugar, and brown sugar until well blended. Beat in the egg, milk, and vanilla. Combine the flour, baking powder, and salt; stir into creamed mixture. Roll tablespoonfuls of dough into balls. Place cookies 2 inches apart onto ungreased baking sheets. Press each ball once with fork tines.
3. Bake in the preheated oven for 8 to 10 minutes or until edges are lightly browned. **Yield:** 3 dozen.

Per cookie: About 106 calories, 3g protein, 11g carbohydrate, 6g fat, 1g fiber, 13mg cholesterol, 90mg sodium

Caramel-Filled Chocolate Cookies

Submitted by: **Lisa**

"Chocolate cookie dough is wrapped around caramel-filled chocolate candies."

1	cup butter, softened	¾	cup unsweetened cocoa powder
1	cup white sugar		
1	cup packed brown sugar	1	cup chopped walnuts, divided
2	eggs		
2	teaspoons vanilla extract	1	tablespoon white sugar
2¼	cups all-purpose flour	48	chocolate covered caramel candies
1	teaspoon baking soda		

1. Beat butter until creamy. Gradually beat in 1 cup white sugar and brown sugar. Beat in eggs and vanilla. Combine flour, baking soda, and cocoa. Gradually add to butter mixture, beating well. Stir in ½ cup nuts. Cover and chill at least 2 hours.
2. Preheat oven to 375°F (190°C).
3. Combine remaining ½ cup nuts with the 1 tablespoon sugar. Divide the dough into 4 parts. Work with 1 part at a time, leaving the remainder in the refrigerator until needed. Divide each part into 12 pieces. Quickly press each piece of dough around a chocolate covered caramel. Roll into a ball. Dip the tops into the sugar mixture. Place sugar side up 2 inches apart on greased baking sheets.
4. Bake in the preheated oven for 8 minutes. Cool 3 to 4 minutes on baking sheets; remove to wire racks to cool completely. **Yield:** 4 dozen.

Per cookie: About 125 calories, 2g protein, 16g carbohydrate, 7g fat, 1g fiber, 20mg cholesterol, 76mg sodium

Ultimate Double Chocolate Cookies

Submitted by: **Carol P.**

"A chocolate cookie with the intensity of hot fudge sauce."

2	(8 ounce) packages semisweet chocolate baking squares, chopped
2	cups all-purpose flour
½	cup Dutch process cocoa powder
2	teaspoons baking powder
1	teaspoon salt
10	tablespoons butter, softened
1½	cups packed brown sugar
½	cup white sugar
4	eggs
2	teaspoons instant coffee granules
2	teaspoons vanilla extract

1. Melt chocolate over a double boiler or in the microwave, stirring occasionally, until smooth. Sift together flour, cocoa, baking powder, and salt; set aside.

2. In a medium bowl, cream butter with brown sugar and white sugar until smooth. Beat in eggs, one at a time, then stir in coffee granules and vanilla until well blended. Stir in melted chocolate. Using a wooden spoon, stir in the dry ingredients just until everything comes together. Cover and let stand for 35 minutes so the chocolate can set up.

3. Preheat the oven to 350°F (175°C). Line 2 baking sheets with parchment paper. Roll dough into 1 inch balls and place onto the prepared baking sheets, leaving 2 inches between cookies.

4. Bake in the preheated oven for 8 to 10 minutes. Cookies will be set, but the centers will still be very soft because of the chocolate. Allow cookies to cool on the baking sheets for 10 minutes before transferring to wire racks to cool completely. **Yield:** 3½ dozen.

Per cookie: About 144 calories, 2g protein, 22g carbohydrate, 7g fat, 1g fiber, 28mg cholesterol, 88mg sodium

---

Crowd-Pleaser ▶

Prep Time: 25 minutes

Cook Time: 10 minutes per batch

Average Rating: ★★★★★

21 Ratings ▲ 15 Reviews

What other cooks have done:

"This is the best chocolate cookie I think I will ever eat. The chocolate flavor opens in the mouth to a size much grander than you would expect. And then the chewy center, that fudgy brownie effect. Man, I'm ready to go spend some serious money on some serious chocolate and find out how far off the chart I can launch this cookie."

Chocolate Rum Balls

Submitted by: **Donna**

"The holidays will sparkle when you whip up a batch of these favorites!"

3¼	cups crushed vanilla wafers
¾	cup confectioners' sugar
¼	cup unsweetened cocoa powder
1½	cups chopped walnuts
3	tablespoons light corn syrup
½	cup rum
	Confectioners' sugar

1. In a large bowl, stir together the crushed vanilla wafers, ¾ cup confectioners' sugar, cocoa, and nuts. Blend in corn syrup and rum.

2. Shape into 1 inch balls and roll in additional confectioners' sugar. Store in an airtight container for several days to develop the flavor. Roll again in confectioners' sugar before serving. **Yield:** 4 dozen.

Per cookie: About 100 calories, 1g protein, 12g carbohydrate, 5g fat, 1g fiber, 0mg cholesterol, 39mg sodium

---

Party Food ▶

Prep Time: 45 minutes

Average Rating: ★★★★★

40 Ratings ▲ 28 Reviews

What other cooks have done:

"At first this was messy, but then I started dusting my hands with confectioners' sugar before making the rum balls, and it worked out great."

Chocolate Crinkles II

Submitted by: **Ingrid**

"Chocolate cookies coated in confectioners' sugar . . . very good!"

1	cup unsweetened cocoa powder	2	teaspoons vanilla extract
2	cups white sugar	2	cups all–purpose flour
½	cup vegetable oil	2	teaspoons baking powder
4	eggs	½	teaspoon salt
		½	cup confectioners' sugar

1. In a medium bowl, mix together cocoa, white sugar, and vegetable oil. Beat in eggs, one at a time, then stir in the vanilla. Combine the flour, baking powder, and salt; stir into the cocoa mixture. Cover dough and chill for at least 4 hours.

2. Preheat oven to 350°F (175°C). Line baking sheets with parchment paper. Roll dough into 1 inch balls. Coat each ball in confectioners' sugar before placing onto prepared baking sheets.

3. Bake in the preheated oven for 10 to 12 minutes. Let stand on the baking sheets for a minute before transferring to wire racks to cool. **Yield:** 6 dozen.

Per cookie: About 58 calories, 1g protein, 10g carbohydrate, 2g fat, 1g fiber, 12mg cholesterol, 34mg sodium

◀ Kid-Friendly

Prep Time: 20 minutes
Cook Time: 12 minutes per batch
Average Rating: ★★★★★
35 Ratings ▲ 28 Reviews
What other cooks have done:
"My 3½-year-old daughter loved helping me roll the balls in powdered sugar. We also rolled some in coconut and some in ground almonds."

Buckeyes

Submitted by: **Tammy Winters**

"This recipe is so good that I double it whenever I make it."

1½	cups peanut butter	½	teaspoon vanilla extract
6	cups confectioners' sugar	4	cups semisweet chocolate chips, melted
1	cup butter, softened		

1. Blend peanut butter, confectioners' sugar, butter, and vanilla.

2. Roll into 1 inch balls and place on baking sheets lined with wax paper.

3. Insert a toothpick into the top of each ball (to be used later as the handle for dipping) and chill in freezer until hard, about 30 minutes.

4. Dip frozen peanut butter balls in melted chocolate, holding onto the toothpick. Leave a small portion of peanut butter showing at the top.

5. Place chocolate-covered balls on the wax paper lined baking sheet and refrigerate 2 hours. **Yield:** 5 dozen.

Per candy: About 166 calories, 2g protein, 21g carbohydrate, 10g fat, 1g fiber, 9mg cholesterol, 63mg sodium

◀ Holiday Fare

Prep Time: 30 minutes
Average Rating: ★★★★★
42 Ratings ▲ 34 Reviews
What other cooks have done:
"These were wonderful! My guests were very unhappy when they were gone. I froze them (without the chocolate) for three weeks and then dipped them two days before I served them, and it worked out very well."

Chocolate-Covered Orange Balls

Submitted by: **Vickie**

"I won second place in a cooking contest with this recipe. It's a great holiday treat!"

1 (16 ounce) package confectioners' sugar
1 (12 ounce) package vanilla wafers, crushed
1 cup chopped walnuts
½ cup butter, softened
1 (6 ounce) can frozen orange juice concentrate, thawed
1½ pounds milk chocolate, melted

1. In a large bowl, combine the confectioners' sugar, vanilla wafers, walnuts, butter, and orange juice. Mix well and shape into 1 inch round balls; chill for 1 hour.
2. Dip balls into melted chocolate and place in decorative paper cups. **Yield:** 3 dozen.

Per candy: About 244 calories, 2g protein, 33g carbohydrate, 12g fat, 1g fiber, 11mg cholesterol, 71mg sodium

Snowballs

Submitted by: **Earla Taylor**

"These nut and butter cookies with a sugar coating are great for the holidays when sampling lots of cookies. Just pop one in your mouth and enjoy!"

1 cup butter, softened
½ cup white sugar
1 tablespoon vanilla extract
2 cups sifted all-purpose flour
¾ teaspoon salt
1 cup chopped pecans
¾ cup sifted confectioners' sugar

1. Preheat oven to 325°F (165°C). Lightly grease 2 baking sheets.
2. Cream the butter, sugar, and vanilla until light and fluffy.
3. Sift together the flour and salt; stir into the butter mixture and add the pecans. Dust your hands with a little of the confectioners' sugar and roll the dough into 1 inch balls.
4. Place 2 inches apart on the baking sheets and bake in the preheated oven for 25 minutes or just until brown. Remove to racks to cool for 15 minutes, then roll in the confectioners' sugar. **Yield:** 4 dozen.

Per candy: About 87 calories, 1g protein, 8g carbohydrate, 6g fat, 0g fiber, 11mg cholesterol, 81mg sodium

Microwave Oven Peanut Brittle

Submitted by: **Linda C.**
"I have used this for years and it's very good, much easier than the traditional method and tastes just as good."

1½	cups peanuts	1	tablespoon butter
1	cup white sugar	1	teaspoon vanilla extract
½	cup light corn syrup	1	teaspoon baking soda
	Pinch salt (optional)		

1. Grease a baking sheet and set aside. In a glass bowl, combine peanuts, sugar, corn syrup, and salt. Cook in microwave for 6 to 7 minutes on high; mixture should be bubbly and peanuts browned. Stir in butter and vanilla; cook 2 to 3 minutes longer.
2. Quickly stir in baking soda, just until mixture is foamy. Pour immediately onto prepared baking sheet. Let cool 15 minutes or until set. Break into pieces and store in an airtight container. **Yield:** 16 servings.

Per serving: About 162 calories, 4g protein, 23g carbohydrate, 8g fat, 1g fiber, 2mg cholesterol, 125mg sodium

◄ Classic Comfort Food

Prep Time: 10 minutes
Cook Time: 10 minutes
Average Rating: ★★★★★
87 Ratings ▲ 72 Reviews
What other cooks have done:
"This recipe works perfectly with the microwave. It comes out identical to the traditional version and is so much faster. My only advice is to be very careful pouring the boiling candy onto a baking sheet, and allow the empty bowl to cool, then soak for a while."

Irish Cream Truffle Fudge *(pictured on page 299)*

Submitted by: **Ruth Crickmer**
"Wicked, good stuff! The creamy sweet confection will disappear as fast as a wink."

3	cups semisweet chocolate chips	1½	cups chopped pecans
1	cup white chocolate chips	1	cup semisweet chocolate chips
¼	cup butter	½	cup white chocolate chips
3	cups sifted confectioners' sugar	2	tablespoons butter
1	cup Irish cream liqueur	¼	cup Irish cream liqueur

1. Butter a 9x9 inch pan.
2. In the top half of a double boiler, heat the 3 cups semisweet chocolate chips, 1 cup white chocolate chips, and ¼ cup butter until melted.
3. Stir in the confectioners' sugar and 1 cup Irish cream until mixture is smooth. Stir in nuts. Spoon mixture in the prepared pan and press and smooth top with a spatula.
4. In the top half of a double boiler, melt 1 cup semisweet chocolate chips, ½ cup white chocolate chips, and 2 tablespoons butter until melted. Remove from heat and stir in ¼ cup Irish cream until smooth. With a knife, spread topping over cooled fudge. Refrigerate until firm, 1 to 2 hours at least. This fudge can be frozen. **Yield:** 2 dozen.

Per candy: About 380 calories, 3g protein, 47g carbohydrate, 20g fat, 3g fiber, 10mg cholesterol, 44mg sodium

◄ Make-Ahead

Prep Time: 30 minutes
Cook Time: 30 minutes
Average Rating: ★★★★★
23 Ratings ▲ 21 Reviews
What other cooks have done:
"I cut into squares first, then dipped each in chocolate so the top chocolate layer wouldn't shatter when cut."

Metric Equivalents

The recipes that appear in this cookbook use the standard United States method for measuring liquid and dry or solid ingredients (teaspoons, tablespoons, and cups). The information on this chart is provided to help cooks outside the U.S. successfully use these recipes. All equivalents are approximate.

METRIC EQUIVALENTS FOR DIFFERENT TYPES OF INGREDIENTS

A standard cup measure of a dry or solid ingredient will vary in weight depending on the type of ingredient. A standard cup of liquid is the same volume for any type of liquid. Use the following chart when converting standard cup measures to grams (weight) or milliliters (volume).

Standard Cup	Fine Powder	Grain	Granular	Liquid Solids	Liquid
	(ex. flour)	(ex. rice)	(ex. sugar)	(ex. butter)	(ex. milk)
1	140 g	150 g	190 g	200 g	240 ml
¾	105 g	113 g	143 g	150 g	180 ml
⅔	93 g	100 g	125 g	133 g	160 ml
½	70 g	75 g	95 g	100 g	120 ml
⅓	47 g	50 g	63 g	67 g	80 ml
¼	35 g	38 g	48 g	50 g	60 ml
⅛	18 g	19 g	24 g	25 g	30 ml

USEFUL EQUIVALENTS FOR DRY INGREDIENTS BY WEIGHT

(To convert ounces to grams, multiply the number of ounces by 30.)

1 oz	=	¹⁄₁₆ lb	=	30 g
4 oz	=	¼ lb	=	120 g
8 oz	=	½ lb	=	240 g
12 oz	=	¾ lb	=	360 g
16 oz	=	1 lb	=	480 g

USEFUL EQUIVALENTS FOR LENGTH

(To convert inches to centimeters, multiply the number of inches by 2.5.)

1 in					=	2.5 cm		
6 in	=	½ ft			=	15 cm		
12 in	=	1 ft			=	30 cm		
36 in	=	3 ft	=	1 yd	=	90 cm		
40 in					=	100 cm	=	1 m

USEFUL EQUIVALENTS FOR LIQUID INGREDIENTS BY VOLUME

¼ tsp							=	1 ml			
½ tsp							=	2 ml			
1 tsp							=	5 ml			
3 tsp	=	1 tbls			=	½ fl oz	=	15 ml			
		2 tbls	=	⅛ cup	=	1 fl oz	=	30 ml			
		4 tbls	=	¼ cup	=	2 fl oz	=	60 ml			
		5⅓ tbls	=	⅓ cup	=	3 fl oz	=	80 ml			
		8 tbls	=	½ cup	=	4 fl oz	=	120 ml			
		10⅔ tbls	=	⅔ cup	=	5 fl oz	=	160 ml			
		12 tbls	=	¾ cup	=	6 fl oz	=	180 ml			
		16 tbls	=	1 cup	=	8 fl oz	=	240 ml			
1	pt	=	2 cups	=	16 fl oz	=	480 ml				
1	qt	=	4 cups	=	32 fl oz	=	960 ml				
					33 fl oz	=	1000 ml	= 1 liter			

USEFUL EQUIVALENTS FOR COOKING/OVEN TEMPERATURES

	Fahrenheit	Celsius	Gas Mark
Freeze Water	32° F	0° C	
Room Temperature	68° F	20° C	
Boil Water	212° F	100° C	
Bake	325° F	165° C	3
	350° F	175° C	4
	375° F	190° C	5
	400° F	200° C	6
	425° F	220° C	7
	450° F	230° C	8
Broil			Grill

Common Substitutions

Ingredient	Amount	Substitution
Allspice	1 teaspoon	• ½ teaspoon ground cinnamon, ¼ teaspoon ground ginger, and ¼ teaspoon ground cloves
Arrowroot starch	1 teaspoon	• 1 tablespoon flour OR 1 teaspoon cornstarch
Baking powder	1 teaspoon	• ¼ teaspoon baking soda plus ½ teaspoon cream of tartar OR ¼ teaspoon baking soda plus ½ cup buttermilk (decrease liquid in recipe by ½ cup)
Beer	1 cup	• 1 cup nonalcoholic beer OR 1 cup chicken broth
Brandy	¼ cup	• 1 teaspoon imitation brandy extract plus enough water to make ¼ cup
Breadcrumbs	1 cup	• 1 cup cracker crumbs OR 1 cup matzo meal OR 1 cup ground oats
Broth – beef or chicken	1 cup	• 1 bouillon cube plus 1 cup boiling water OR 1 tablespoon soy sauce plus enough water to make 1 cup OR 1 cup vegetable broth
Brown sugar	1 cup, packed	• 1 cup white sugar plus ¼ cup molasses and decrease the liquid in recipe by ¼ cup OR 1 cup white sugar OR 1¼ cups confectioners' sugar
Butter (salted)	1 cup	• 1 cup margarine OR 1 cup shortening plus ½ teaspoon salt OR ⅞ cup vegetable oil plus ½ teaspoon salt OR ⅞ cup lard plus ½ teaspoon salt
Butter (unsalted)	1 cup	• 1 cup shortening OR ⅞ cup vegetable oil OR ⅞ cup lard
Buttermilk	1 cup	• 1 cup yogurt OR 1 tablespoon lemon juice or vinegar plus enough milk to make 1 cup
Cheddar cheese	1 cup shredded	• 1 cup shredded Colby Cheddar OR 1 cup shredded Monterey Jack cheese
Chervil	1 tablespoon fresh	• 1 tablespoon fresh parsley
Chicken base	1 tablespoon	• 1 cup canned or homemade chicken broth or stock. Reduce liquid in recipe by 1 cup
Chocolate (semisweet)	1 ounce	• 1 (1 ounce) square of unsweetened chocolate plus 4 teaspoons sugar OR 1 ounce semisweet chocolate chips plus 1 teaspoon shortening
Chocolate (unsweetened)	1 ounce	• 3 tablespoons unsweetened cocoa plus 1 tablespoon shortening or vegetable oil
Cocoa	¼ cup	• 1 (1 ounce) square unsweetened chocolate
Corn syrup	1 cup	• 1¼ cup white sugar plus ⅓ cup water OR 1 cup honey OR 1 cup light treacle syrup
Cottage cheese	1 cup	• 1 cup farmers cheese OR 1 cup ricotta cheese
Cracker crumbs	1 cup	• 1 cup breadcrumbs OR 1 cup matzo meal OR 1 cup ground oats
Cream (half-and-half)	1 cup	• ⅞ cup milk plus 1 tablespoon butter
Cream (heavy)	1 cup	• 1 cup evaporated milk OR ¾ cup milk plus ⅓ cup butter

Ingredient	Amount	Substitution
Cream (light)	1 cup	•1 cup evaporated milk OR ¾ cup milk plus 3 tablespoons butter
Cream (whipped)	1 cup	•1 cup frozen whipped topping, thawed
Cream cheese	1 cup	•1 cup pureed cottage cheese OR 1 cup plain yogurt, strained overnight in cheesecloth
Cream of tartar	1 teaspoon	•2 teaspoons lemon juice or vinegar
Crème fraîche	1 cup	•Combine 1 cup heavy cream and 1 tablespoon plain yogurt. Let stand for 6 hours at room temperature.
Egg	1 whole (3 tablespoons)	•2½ tablespoons powdered egg substitute plus 2½ tablespoons water OR ¼ cup liquid egg substitute OR ¼ cup silken tofu pureed OR 3 tablespoons mayonnaise OR ½ banana mashed with ½ teaspoon baking powder OR 1 tablespoon powdered flax seed soaked in 3 tablespoons water
Evaporated milk	1 cup	•1 cup light cream
Farmers cheese	8 ounces	•8 ounces dry cottage cheese OR 8 ounces creamed cottage cheese, drained
Fats for baking	1 cup	•1 cup applesauce OR 1 cup fruit puree
Flour – bread	1 cup	•1 cup all-purpose flour plus 1 teaspoon wheat gluten
Flour – cake	1 cup	•1 cup all-purpose flour minus 2 tablespoons
Flour – self-rising	1 cup	•⅞ cup all-purpose flour plus 1½ teaspoons baking powder and ½ teaspoon salt
Garlic	1 clove	•⅛ teaspoon garlic powder OR ½ teaspoon granulated garlic OR ½ teaspoon garlic salt (reduce salt in recipe)
Ginger – dry	1 teaspoon, ground	•2 teaspoons chopped fresh ginger
Ginger – fresh	1 teaspoon, minced	•½ teaspoon ground dried ginger
Green onion	½ cup, chopped	•½ cup chopped onion OR ½ cup chopped leek OR ½ cup chopped shallots
Hazelnuts	1 cup whole	•1 cup macadamia nuts OR 1 cup almonds
Herbs – fresh	1 tablespoon, chopped	•1 teaspoon chopped dried herbs
Honey	1 cup	•1¼ cups white sugar plus ⅓ cup water OR 1 cup corn syrup OR 1 cup light treacle syrup
Hot sauce	1 teaspoon	•¾ teaspoon cayenne pepper plus 1 teaspoon vinegar
Ketchup	1 cup	•1 cup tomato sauce plus 1 teaspoon vinegar plus 1 tablespoon sugar
Lemon grass	2 fresh stalks	•1 tablespoon lemon zest
Lemon juice	1 teaspoon	•½ teaspoon vinegar OR 1 teaspoon white wine OR 1 teaspoon lime juice
Lemon zest	1 teaspoon, grated	•½ teaspoon lemon extract OR 2 tablespoons lemon juice
Lime juice	1 teaspoon	•1 teaspoon vinegar OR 1 teaspoon white wine OR 1 teaspoon lemon juice
Lime zest	1 teaspoon, grated	•1 teaspoon grated lemon zest
Macadamia nuts	1 cup	•1 cup almonds OR 1 cup hazelnuts
Mace	1 teaspoon	•1 teaspoon ground nutmeg
Margarine	1 cup	•1 cup shortening plus ½ teaspoon salt OR 1 cup butter OR ⅞ cup vegetable oil plus ½ teaspoon salt OR ⅞ cup lard plus ½ teaspoon salt
Mayonnaise	1 cup	•1 cup sour cream OR 1 cup plain yogurt

Ingredient	Amount	Substitution
Milk – whole	1 cup	•1 cup soy milk OR 1 cup rice milk OR 1 cup water or juice OR ¼ cup dry milk powder plus 1 cup water OR ⅔ cup evaporated milk plus ⅓ cup water
Mint – fresh	¼ cup chopped	•1 tablespoon dried mint leaves
Mustard – prepared	1 tablespoon	•Mix together 1 tablespoon dried mustard, 1 teaspoon water, •1 teaspoon vinegar, and 1 teaspoon sugar
Onion	1 cup, chopped	•1 cup chopped green onions OR 1 cup chopped shallots OR 1 cup chopped leek OR ¼ cup dried minced onion
Orange zest	1 tablespoon, grated	•½ teaspoon orange extract OR 1 teaspoon lemon juice
Parmesan cheese	½ cup, grated	•½ cup grated Asiago cheese OR ½ cup grated Romano cheese
Parsley – fresh	1 tablespoon, chopped	•1 tablespoon chopped fresh chervil OR 1 teaspoon dried parsley
Pepperoni	1 ounce	•1 ounce salami
Raisins	1 cup	•1 cup dried currants OR 1 cup dried cranberries OR 1 cup chopped pitted prunes
Rice – white	1 cup, cooked	•1 cup cooked barley OR 1 cup cooked bulgur OR 1 cup cooked brown or wild rice
Ricotta	1 cup	•1 cup dry cottage cheese OR 1 cup silken tofu
Rum	1 tablespoon	•½ teaspoon rum extract, plus enough water to make 1 tablespoon
Saffron	¼ teaspoon	•¼ teaspoon turmeric
Semisweet chocolate chips	1 cup	•1 cup chocolate candies OR 1 cup peanut butter or other flavored chips OR 1 cup chopped nuts OR 1 cup chopped dried fruit
Shallots – fresh	½ cup, chopped	•½ cup chopped onion OR ½ cup chopped leek OR ½ cup chopped green onions
Shortening	1 cup	•1 cup butter OR 1 cup margarine minus ½ teaspoon salt from recipe
Sour cream	1 cup	•1 cup plain yogurt OR 1 tablespoon lemon juice or vinegar plus enough cream to make 1 cup OR ¾ cup buttermilk mixed with ⅓ cup butter
Soy sauce	½ cup	•¼ cup Worcestershire sauce mixed with ¼ cup water
Stock – beef or chicken	1 cup	•1 beef or chicken bouillon cube dissolved in 1 cup water
Sweetened condensed milk	1 (14 ounce) can	•¾ cup white sugar mixed with ½ cup water and 1⅛ cups dry powdered milk (Bring to a boil, and cook, stirring frequently, until thickened, about 20 minutes.)
Vegetable oil – for baking	1 cup	•1 cup applesauce OR 1 cup fruit puree
Vegetable oil – for frying	1 cup	•1 cup lard OR 1 cup vegetable shortening
Vinegar	1 teaspoon	•1 teaspoon lemon or lime juice OR 2 teaspoons white wine
White sugar	1 cup	•1 cup brown sugar OR 1¼ cups confectioners' sugar OR ¾ cup honey OR ¾ cup corn syrup
Wine	1 cup	•1 cup chicken or beef broth OR 1 cup fruit juice mixed with 2 teaspoons vinegar OR 1 cup water
Yeast – active dry	1 (.25 ounce) package	•1 cake compressed yeast OR 2½ teaspoons active dry yeast OR 2½ teaspoons rapid rise yeast
Yogurt	1 cup	•1 cup sour cream OR 1 cup buttermilk OR 1 cup sour milk

Recommended Storage Guide

IN THE PANTRY

Baking powder and soda	1 year
Flour, all-purpose	10 to 15 months
Milk, evaporated and sweetened condensed	1 year
Mixes	
cake	1 year
pancake	6 months
Peanut butter	6 months
Salt and pepper	18 months
Shortening	8 months
Spices (discard if aroma fades)	
ground	6 months
whole	1 year
Sugar	18 months

IN THE REFRIGERATOR

Butter and margarine	1 month
Buttermilk	1 to 2 weeks
Eggs (fresh in shell)	3 to 5 weeks
Half-and-half	7 to 10 days

Meat	
casseroles, cooked	3 to 4 days
steaks, chops, roasts, uncooked	3 to 5 days
Milk, whole or fat-free	1 week
Poultry, uncooked	1 to 2 days
Sour cream	3 to 4 weeks
Whipping cream	10 days

IN THE FREEZER

Breads	
quick	2 to 3 months
yeast	3 to 6 months
Butter	6 months
Cakes	
cheesecakes and pound cakes	2 to 3 months
unfrosted	2 to 5 months
with cooked frosting	not recommended
with creamy-type frosting	3 months
Candy and fudge	6 months
Casseroles	1 to 2 months
Cheese	4 months

Cookies	
baked, unfrosted	8 to 12 months
dough	1 month
Eggs (not in shell)	
whites	1 year
yolks	8 months
Ice cream	1 to 3 months
Meat	
cooked	2 to 3 months
ground, uncooked	3 to 4 months
roasts, uncooked	9 months
steaks or chops, uncooked	4 to 6 months
Nuts	8 months
Pies	
pastry shell	2 to 3 months
fruit	1 to 2 months
pumpkin	2 to 4 months
custard, cream, meringue	not recommended
Poultry	
cooked	3 to 4 months
parts, uncooked	9 months
whole, uncooked	12 months
Soups and stews	2 to 3 months

Nutritional Analysis

Nutrition Analyses Based on Premier Databases

   Allrecipes.com is proud to provide ESHA Research's nutrient databases for recipe nutrition analysis. ESHA Research is the premier nutrition analysis provider for the world's nutrition and health industries, having provided nutrient information to health care providers and the world's top food manufacturing firms for more than 15 years. Its nutrient databases total more than 22,000 foods, track 165 nutrient factors, and combine nutrient data from over 1,200 scientific sources of information. For more information about ESHA Research, visit their website at **http://www.esha.com.**

Using Allrecipes.com Information with Care

   Allrecipes.com is committed to providing recipe-based nutritional information so that individuals may, by choice or under a doctor's advice, adhere to specific dietary requirements and make healthful recipe choices. The nutrition values that appear in this book and on **Allrecipes.com** nutrition pages are based on individual recipe ingredients. While we have taken the utmost care in providing you with the most accurate nutritional values possible, please note that this information is not intended for medical nutrition therapy. If you are following a strict diet for medical or dietary reasons, it's important that you, first, consult your physician or registered dietitian before planning your meals based on recipes at **Allrecipes.com,** and, second, remain under appropriate medical supervision while using the nutrition information at **Allrecipes.com.**

Recipe Title Index

This index alphabetically lists every recipe by exact title.

General Recipe Index

This index lists every recipe by food category and/or major ingredient.

Favorite Recipes Journal

Jot down your family's and your favorite recipes for quick and handy reference. Remember to include the dishes that drew rave reviews when company came for dinner.

Recipe	Source/Page	Remarks